Detail from *A Compleat Map of North-Carolina*, Collet 1770.

"Poor Carolina"

A. Roger Ekirch

"Poor Carolina"

Politics and Society in
Colonial North Carolina,
1729–1776

The University of North Carolina Press   Chapel Hill

© 1981 The University of North Carolina Press

All rights reserved

Manufactured in the United States of America

Library of Congress Cataloging in Publication Data

Ekirch, A   Roger, 1950–
  "Poor Carolina": politics and society in colonial
North Carolina, 1729–1776.

  Bibliography: p.
  Includes index.
  1. North Carolina—Economic conditions. 2. North
Carolina—Social conditions. 3. North Carolina—Politics
and government—Colonial period, ca. 1600–1775.
I. Title.
HC107.N8E37   330.9756'02   80–39889
ISBN 0–8078–1475-X

For my father

ARTHUR A. EKIRCH, JR.

and my mother

DOROTHY G. EKIRCH

Contents

Part III. ❧ Conclusion

Figures and Tables

Acknowledgments

It is a pleasure to acknowledge the many people who assisted in the book's preparation. I am grateful to the staffs of the Southern Historical Collection at the University of North Carolina at Chapel Hill, the Duke University Library, the Massachusetts Historical Society, the William L. Clements Library at the University of Michigan, the Library of Congress, the British Library, and the Public Record Office of Northern Ireland. Special thanks are expressed to Thornton Mitchell, George Stevenson, Joseph Mobley, and William S. Price of the North Carolina Division of Archives and History in Raleigh.

My largest debt is to Jack Greene. Whenever my own interest in this project waned, his was constant. Working closely with him was an invaluable experience. A. J. R. Russell-Wood, who read an early version of the manuscript, furnished intellectual adrenalin and provocative conversation. Robert Brugger, Philip D. Morgan, Sung Bok Kim, Robert Weir, and James Whittenburg generously offered their time and criticism at various stages. I also benefited from the advice of Crandall Shifflett, Rachel Klein, and Jere Daniell. Portions of chapter 6 were published earlier in *Perspectives in American History*, and they appear here with the permission of the editor, Donald Fleming. I am also grateful to him for his helpful comments.

Contemporaries from Johns Hopkins University deserve much of my gratitude. Daniel Wilson, André-Philippe Katz, and Paul Paskoff were all patient listeners and incisive critics of my thoughts. The book profited immensely as a result.

The Humanities Summer Stipend Program at Virginia Polytechnic Institute and State University supplied the resources for the study's completion. I am very grateful to Carolyn Alls, Diane Cannaday, and Lisa Donis for assistance with the typing. I also wish to thank Charles McAllister, John David Bishop, Jay Peacock, Patrick Sharpe, and Clyde H. Perdue for their help at various stages. My family was a rich source of inspiration. My sisters and brothers-in-law were available whenever I needed fresh scenery and relaxation. My mother and father were simply tremendous. Whether it was an encouraging word or a careful reading of some early chapters, the depth of their love was always certain.

A. Roger Ekirch
Blacksburg, Virginia
August 1980

Introduction

The public life of provincial America was reasonably harmonious during the mid-eighteenth century. In contrast to earlier decades, when economic, religious, ethnic, and regional controversies had frequently plunged the British colonies into internal strife, provincial politics exhibited a notable degree of stability. That government institutions less often fell victim to the self-interested priorities of competing factions derived partly from the growing integration of early American society. Previously antagonistic interests, such as merchants and planters, Anglicans and dissenters, and rival cliques of land speculators, became increasingly interlocked by the early eighteenth century. At the same time, nearly every colony produced a governing elite, distinguished not only by its cohesion and shared interests but also by its wealth, education, ancestry, and nativity.

The authority of political leaders was consequently well established and widely acknowledged. Moreover, these elites, unlike prior generations of political leaders, did not need to view politics in essentially opportunistic terms. Just as stability was now a distinctive feature of politics for most colonies, so too was the sense of responsibility that many leaders brought to their public duties. Even in New York, famous for the factious character of its politics in the later colonial period, competing interests were reasonably restrained in their multifarious battles and were often willing to compromise in the face of civil breakdown.[1] Political life in mid-eighteenth-century North Carolina, the subject of this work, was an exception to this dominant pattern of provincial politics. Carolina politics normally revolved around conflicting private, group, and regional interests, and resulted at times in social discord and the collapse of civil institutions. This study is not a comprehensive political narrative but represents an attempt to analyze the most salient episodes in the colony's public life within the context of economic, demographic, social, and cultural developments. It begins in 1729, when North Carolina became a royal colony. After nearly seventy years of weak and spiritless rule, marked by provincial factionalism and periodic civil disorder, seven of the eight Lords Proprietors agreed to sell their interest in both Carolinas to the crown. Whether the resulting change in government authority affected the texture of politics, as hoped by imperial officials, is one question raised by this book. By focusing on the royal period, this study also tries to build a firmer foundation for comparing North Carolina politics with that of other royal colonies, notably neighboring Virginia and South Carolina. Further, the late 1720s marked the beginning of an important era of demographic growth and territorial expansion that, however, failed to bring substantial economic progress. The impact of these factors on the political process is a major concern of the present work. It ends on the eve of the American Revolution with the Regulator riots, an ideologically charged crusade that erupted in response to long-standing propensities within the colony's political system. Although the Revolutionary era in North Carolina still needs systematic analysis, such study is not necessary to an understanding of mid-eighteenth-century politics and lies largely outside the boundaries of this work.

An examination of North Carolina politics is necessary for three reasons. First, it will deepen understanding of an early American colony that historians long have neglected. Chiefly because North Carolina neither played a major role in the American Revolution nor produced a society of religious divines or luminous aristocrats, it has commanded little attention among scholars—even among those who have written syntheses of the colonial South. Except for a few specialized articles, most of the treatment accorded colonial North Carolina has consisted of detailed political narratives lacking in interpretive analysis; nor has a serious attempt been made to explain the social context of politics. In fact, the only major occurrence in the colony's history to arouse much interest is the Regulator movement. Ever since the nineteenth century, when Whig historians first tried to explain this chain of backcountry disturbances, scholars have offered a spate of conflicting interpretations. But neither the origins of the Regulators nor the response they prompted among the colony's political leaders can be appreciated without a better understanding of the provincial setting in which the riots arose.

Because North Carolina was one of the few provinces to experience serious civil strife during the mid-eighteenth century, this study offers a prime opportunity to determine the origins of political instability, when it did arise, in the late colonial period. Recent short-range studies of North Carolina have occasionally pointed to external conflicts between the colony and Great Britain over imperial policy, or to the destabilizing effects of class conflict. North Carolina's scant historiography reflects, in large measure, two well-established, if dated, approaches to early American politics: the Imperial and the Progressive schools. Notably, however, none of the historians associated with these viewpoints has ever attempted to explain why the factors they locate in the experience of North Carolina did not exert a comparable influence in other colonies.

Slightly less common is the scholarly view that North Carolinians had acquired a peculiar habit of antiauthoritarianism by the eighteenth century. If not from the mysterious properties of the air, this ingrained hostility to government allegedly resulted from prior decades of political unrest. But this hardly explains why the unrest occurred in the first place. Moreover, the potential for antiauthoritarianism becoming some sort of provincial character trait was just as strong elsewhere, when practically every other British colony, especially Virginia and South Carolina, experienced an early history of political turbulence. The question inevitably remains why public affairs became increasingly stable in many other provinces but stayed factious in North Carolina.[2]

A final reason to examine colonial North Carolina is that it provides an occasion to analyze the political life of a relatively new and underdeveloped society. Although in the 1580s it had been the site of the first English attempt at colonization in the New World, North Carolina was still undergoing many of the same processes of settlement, economic growth, and social articulation that had been experienced much earlier by most other colonies, including its southern neighbors. "There is a fine field for improvement of all kinds in this Country," noted a resident in the 1750s. Governor Gabriel Johnston (1734–52) wrote that his duties consisted of "civilizing a wild Barbarous people and Endeavouring at least to bring them on a par with our Neighboring Colonies." His successor Arthur Dobbs (1754–65) lamented, "We are one of the latest Colonies, and scarcely arrived at the state of Manhood our neighbouring Colonies have attained."[3]

"Poor" was the term commentators most commonly employed to describe the colony and its inhabitants. This adjective was normally used in discussing North Carolina's troubled economy and the small profits it afforded planters. A former governor, for instance, made several proposals in 1736 for "the improvement of Trade in that poor Country." Ten years later, a resident complained that importing finished goods through South Carolina and Virginia was "at the Expence of the poor *North-Carolina* Planters." Similarly, a printer in 1769 told a prospective associate, "The country here is poor and of course little is to be expected."[4] "Poor Carolina" was also more broadly applied as an expression of inadequacy and inferiority. Thus, an Anglican missionary in 1760 thought that "no other part of this continent . . . calls louder" for "schools" to encourage "Religion and virtue" than "this poor and illiterate Province," and a visitor from Massachusetts contrasted "poor North Carolina" with the presumed social "superiority" of South Carolina. A resident bemoaned in 1762 that "this poor Country appears still doomed a Sacrifice to the intestine Divisions of her children."[5]

The first chronicler of North Carolina, Hugh Williamson, wrote in 1812 that its early political life was "a history of disasters, misrule, and oppression; a more constant succession of grievances, than fell to the lot of any other colony." His melodramatic prose notwithstanding, he correctly discerned the principal features of early Carolina politics. North Carolina lagged behind most of its sister colonies not only economically and socially but politically as well. Although considerable amounts of harmony and responsibility characterized the public realm of late provincial America, North Carolina experienced political turmoil that culminated in 1771 in the Battle of Alamance, the only real pitched battle between colonists in early American history. North Carolinians, according to

James Murray, were ever "broiling and squabbling about public affairs." A "prey" to "internal dissensions" is how another commentator put it.[6]

In his two-volume history, Williamson also noted, "If I had been disposed to record disputes that originated in pride, resentment, the spirit of party, avarice or a dishonest temper, I might have swelled this work to a considerable bulk. Such details of follies and vices cannot be interesting." Because most later historians have shared Williamson's lack of interest, this book attempts to describe North Carolina's embroiled politics and, in doing so, to analyze the social determinants of political instability in "such a poor country as this."[7]

Part I
Backdrop to Politics

1   The Limits of Growth

North Carolina is a striking Exception to the general
Rule . . . that the Riches of a Country are in Proportion
to the Number of Inhabitants.
—William Hooper, 1776

During the eighteenth century, North Carolina registered rapid gains in population and settled territory. On the eve of the American Revolution, its inhabitants extended westward three hundred miles from the Atlantic Ocean to the Appalachians. Principally because of immigration from the north, it was the fourth most populous colony in British North America. Economic growth, however, was substantially less impressive. Shortages of capital, labor, and a marketable cash crop all combined to render the economy less productive than the plantation systems of Virginia and South Carolina. An even more serious handicap was North Carolina's jagged coastline. Atlantic traders were forced to contend with hazardous sandbars and indeterminable delays—usually at the expense of Carolina planters. By the end of the colonial period, planters reaped larger profits than they had in earlier years, but their gains still did not come easily.

The Contours of Expansion

When it became a royal possession in 1729, North Carolina was a small, fledgling colony. In comparing it to neighboring Virginia, Hugh Jones wrote in 1724, "it is vastly inferior, its trade is smaller, and its inhabitants thinner, and for the most part poorer." Proposals were even submitted to the crown in the 1720s to annex North Carolina to either Virginia or South Carolina. The colony's population numbered at most thirty-five thousand inhabitants, who resided chiefly around the banks and inlets of Albemarle Sound. Within this northeastern corner of the province were only six counties: Currituck, Pasquotank, Perquimans, Chowan, Bertie, and Tyrrell. To the south lay the more sparsely populated counties of Hyde, Beaufort, Craven, and Carteret, which all bordered mammoth Pamlico Sound. New Hanover County, encompassing the still undeveloped Cape Fear valley, contained only scattered settlers.[1]

The colony's urban life was confined to a few small towns, all of fairly recent origin. Established in 1706 on Pamlico Sound, Bath was the oldest. Others included Edenton, in Chowan County; New Bern, at the confluence of the Neuse and Trent rivers in Craven County; Beaufort, just south of Pamlico Sound; and Brunswick, at the mouth of the Cape Fear River. Of Edenton, the largest town and the proprietary capital, William Byrd II noted in 1728, "There may be forty or fifty houses, most of them small and built without expense."[2]

North Carolina's rural orientation stemmed from its overwhelmingly agricultural economy. Livelihood was rooted almost entirely in the soil. In contrast to neighboring provinces, however, plantation agriculture, characterized by the full-scale utilization of slave labor in the intensive cultivation of a few high-return staple crops, such as tobacco or rice, had not yet developed by 1729. Instead, planters produced only a small amount of tobacco in addition to a variety of less profitable commodities, ranging from Indian corn, peas, and pork in the Albemarle Sound region to naval stores farther south. Slaves, who constituted at most a sixth of the total population, were little relied on. The trade of the colony was such, Governor Gabriel Johnston warned in 1735, that Carolina would ever "remain in a poor and Low Condition." According to a 1736

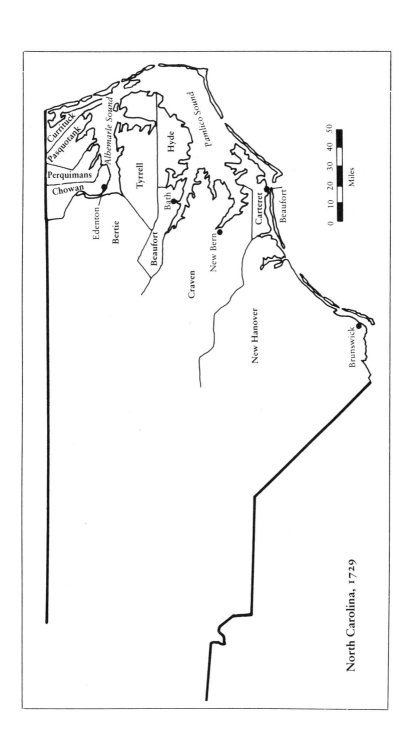

North Carolina, 1729

estimate, provincial exports amounted to less than a tenth of the value of South Carolina's trade.[3]

During the decades following its purchase by the crown, North Carolina grew tremendously. Both in population and settled territory, it ceased to be what one observer contemptuously called "an inconsiderable Colony." "The Country," Councillor Nathaniel Rice testified in 1752, "is in a flourishing condition, the western parts settling very fast." Between 1730 and 1750, the population had risen to almost 70,000; by 1770, it had more than doubled, to around 175,000.[4]

Some of this growth was the result of natural increase. Governor Arthur Dobbs thought in 1761 that the rise in population following his arrival in 1754 resulted "considerably" from a high birthrate. Shortly thereafter, an Anglican missionary wrote, "The Necessaries of Life are so cheap, and so easily acquired, and propagation being unrestricted, that the Encrease of People . . . is inconceivable."[5] But eastern North Carolina's unhealthy environment suggests that death rates from disease were also quite high. Much of the coastal plain consisted of swamps and poorly drained marshland, prime breeding areas for malaria-carrying mosquitoes. Throughout the eighteenth century, reports were frequent of the dangerous living conditions along the coast. "This is a dismal climate," noted a resident of Brunswick in 1763, "and when one gets sickly here, I have hardly ever known an instance of his recovering." A South Carolinian, who was no doubt familiar with the maladies of his own province, pronounced Edenton "a most extreme unhealthy spot." A Cape Fear resident wrote, "Oh! that Heaven had cast the common lot of three or four families with mine . . . somewhere where health is not so dreadfully capricious as it is along the sea coast. . . . We literally die daily."[6]

A more important cause of the colony's population rise was immigration. Besides migrants from such diverse parts of the Atlantic world as New England, the West Indies, and England, a number of South Carolinians plus some Welshmen from Pennsylvania and Delaware started to arrive in the province in the late 1720s, followed by Scottish Highlanders during the next decade. After 1750 thousands of new settlers came overland from the north, most of them dissenting Protestants—Presbyterians, Baptists, Quakers, and

Moravians—from Pennsylvania. In 1755 the provincial council of that colony noted the probable loss of "thousands" to Carolina. Eight years later, Benjamin Franklin calculated that forty thousand people had recently emigrated there from his colony.[7]

Although each migrant had his own purpose for moving, economic reasons were very common. South Carolina, for instance, experienced in the mid-1720s a massive depression that persuaded a number of people to leave, and emigrating Scottish Highlanders had suffered from high taxes and land rents. Later migrants from colonies to the north had faced rising land prices in addition to Indian attacks during the 1750s.

Local circumstances that lured immigrants to North Carolina ranged from its temperate climate to the absence of a strong Anglican church. But by far the most compelling attraction was the vast reaches of uninhabited, cheap, fertile land. "Land is not wanting for men in Carolina," wrote Governor George Burrington (1731–1734), "but men for land." Because of its small population and immense geographic proportions—more than forty thousand square miles— North Carolina offered more good land to prospective settlers than most of its sister colonies during the mid-eighteenth century. A Pennsylvanian reported in 1731 that many Welsh were settling in North Carolina, "where land is cheap." A Scottish immigrant in 1735 expected to obtain a thousand acres for as little as "1s or 18ps" per acre. In 1755 an agent for a Maryland land company enthusiastically described the Carolina piedmont as having "pleasant air, good water, fertile land, and beyond expectation according to its appearance." As late as 1773, a company of Scottish farmers sent two agents to North Carolina to look for "16,000 or 20,000 acres, all contiguous, and conveniently situated and not yet occupied," because they could not "be got in the middle provinces."[8]

Corresponding to the colony's demographic growth was a significant expansion in settled territory. By 1740 North Carolina contained thirteen counties, and a Cape Fear clergyman estimated that "in some Places" people "have settled upwards of one hundred and fifty Miles back from ye Sea." Ten years later, the counties numbered nineteen, and by 1776 thirty-five, stretching as far west as Rowan and Tryon, near the mountains. At the beginning of the Revolution, practically three-fourths of the present state was inhabited.[9]

Earlier migrants had kept to the eastern coastal plain, particu-

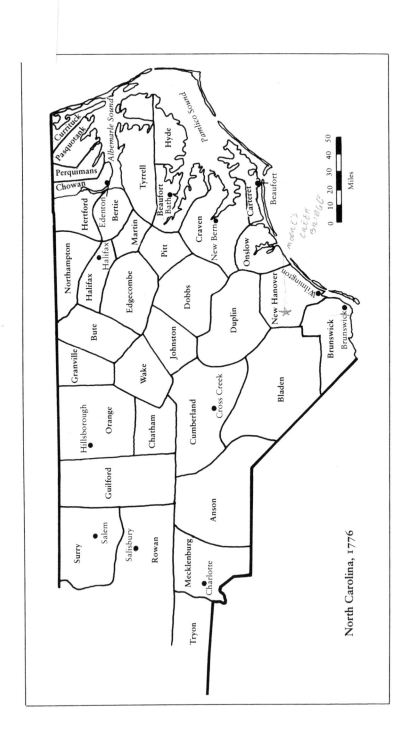

North Carolina, 1776

larly the Cape Fear and bordering areas, but those after 1750 flocked to the backcountry. "People from all parts are Crowding in Here Daily," Governor Gabriel Johnston reported in 1750, "and they all Choose to go Backwards." Less than twenty years later, a newspaper account proclaimed: "There is scarce any history, either antient or modern, which affords an account of such a rapid and sudden increase of inhabitants in a back frontier country, as that of North Carolina. . . . Twenty years ago there were not twenty taxable persons within the limits of the . . . County of Orange; in which there are now four thousand taxables. The increase of inhabitants, and flourishing state of the other adjoining back counties, are no less surprising and astonishing."[10] Entering North Carolina by means of the Great Wagon Road, northern migrants dispersed across the piedmont, which in 1776 encompassed as many as thirteen counties. In population, backcountry settlers totaled roughly half of the colony's inhabitants.

A Checkered Economy

By the traditional standards of population and territorial settlement, North Carolina was well on its way to becoming a major colony in British North America during the middle decades of the eighteenth century. But its economic progress was significantly less impressive. "We still continue vastly behind the rest of the British settlements," Governor Johnston lamented in 1748, "in making a proper use of a good soil and an excellent climate." A Moravian bishop observed six years later, "Trade and business are poor in North Carolina." Near the end of the colonial period, William Hooper, a leading Cape Fear politican, noted, "North Carolina is a striking Exception to the general Rule . . . that the Riches of a Country are in Proportion to the Number of Inhabitants."[11]

The colony's economic problems were varied. Some of them—those generated by droughts, disease, floods, and wild animals—were common to nearly any agricultural area. Hurricanes were also damaging, as in 1769 when a severe storm ravaged New Bern and left "her streets full of the tops of houses, timber, shingles, dry goods, barrels and hogsheads."[12] Further difficulties arose from the effects of European warfare from the 1740s to 1763. High taxes, low export values, the rising price of imports, and vessels captured by the enemy were among the problems encountered by North Carolinians. Although massive British military spending during the French and Indian War contributed to unprecedented prosperity in many colonies, the conflict seriously disrupted Carolina's economy. James Murray, a Cape Fear planter, wrote his brother: "I told you of the small progress I had made for some years as a planter in which I shared only the fate Common to our River and province[,] for it has been singularly unlucky in feeling all the disadvantages without tasting the Wealth that the War has poured on almost every other English Colony on the Continent."[13]

A more fundamental problem afflicting the colony's economy was a chronic shortage of currency. Despite sizable issues of paper money in 1729, 1735, 1748, 1754, 1760, and 1761, totaling more than £135,000, all forms of currency were constantly in short supply. The high taxes of the French and Indian War and British passage of the Currency Act of 1764 caused the situation to worsen. In 1765 only about £70,000 in paper currency circulated among a citizenry of more than a hundred thousand, and by 1768 the amount was only £60,000. "The great Scarcity of Currency makes people cautious of purchasing," wrote Edenton's Samuel Johnston, Jr., in 1765, "and even those who are possessed of the most considerable property are little to be depended on." Later, Johnston again noted the difficulties of "those who are even in good Circumstances to procure sufficient [money] to answer their common Occasions." The shortage was more severe in the Cape Fear, where Scottish merchants who enjoyed new sources of credit had not established trading stores, as they had in the Albemarle region beginning in the late 1750s. James Murray, who hoped to leave the Cape Fear for Boston, wrote his sister, "You talk of selling my House and Negroes: no such thing is to be done here, there are no monyed men to purchase. I may give them away if I will, at less than half the value or keep them for better Times, or carry such as can be transported to a better market."[14]

A second major handicap facing Carolina's economy was a relative scarcity of agricultural labor. Not only were indentured servants few in number, but only toward the end of the colonial period did black slaves become at all numerous, though planters fully recognized the value of their labor. "When I shall turn planter God knows," wrote Murray in 1736. "It will not be till I can turn some Money out of the country to buy some negroes." A writer from the same locale in 1743 bemoaned the "want" of slaves to "cultivate the Lands," a scarcity that he feared would encourage the colony's "old Distemper" of "*Poverty*." As late as 1787, one North Carolinian stated that the "immediate addition of One hundred Thousand Slaves to the State" would contribute to its "present ease and affluence."[15]

Even by 1755, according to tax lists for nineteen out of twenty-two counties, blacks constituted about 36 percent of the taxable population, or less than 20 percent of North Carolina's total population, as shown in table 1.1. Ten years later, a writer thought that blacks constituted slightly more than a fifth of the colony's inhabitants.[16]

Tax returns for twenty-two of twenty-nine counties in 1767 yield a slightly higher figure of 26 percent. Blacks were least numerous in the backcountry, but, even in sixteen coastal plain counties for which figures are available, they made up only 33 percent of the inhabitants in 1767. Just in two counties, New Hanover (56 percent) and Brunswick (68 percent), both located in the lower Cape Fear, did they constitute more than 50 percent. "The white men," it was noted in a 1769 description of North Carolina's population, "are

T A B L E 1.1 *Percentage of Blacks in North Carolina's Population, 1755 and 1767*[17]

		Black Percentage of Taxable Population	Black Percentage of Total Population
1755	(19 of 22 counties)	36.2	19.9
1767	(22 of 29 counties)	44.1	25.7
	(6 piedmont counties)	29.9	15.7
	(16 coastal plain counties)	52.5	32.6

vastly superior to the number of Slaves."[18] By contrast, blacks in Virginia and South Carolina made up about 42 percent and 61 percent of their respective populations during the late colonial period.[19]

Yet another persistent difficulty was that North Carolina lacked a valuable staple commodity for its export trade. Throughout the mid-1700s, it continued to export a diverse number of commodities. Nearly every planter produced some Indian corn; the colony exported about 62,000 bushels in 1753, and fifteen years later nearly twice that amount. Much of another grain, wheat, was produced in the rapidly growing backcountry. Tobacco was confined chiefly to the northeast. Although the amount shipped through Carolina ports increased from perhaps as few as 100,000 pounds in 1753 to 1,605,000 pounds by 1772, probably no more than five thousand to seven thousand acres were devoted to cultivation of the crop at the time. Other exports included dairy products, beeswax, deerskins, peas, cattle hides, and large quantities of beef and pork.[20]

More important were the colony's various forest products. As early as the 1730s, the Cape Fear began to export sawed lumber, and by 1766 about fifty sawmills were in operation. By the eve of the Revolution, North Carolina annually exported between 3,000,000 and 4,000,000 feet of lumber, most of it to the West Indies. Within the Albemarle region, shingles and staves provided key exports.[21] Naval stores, however, were eastern North Carolina's foremost commodity for overseas trade. Other than marshland, much of the outer coastal plain consisted of broad sandy hills and plains covered by vast forests of long-leaf pine trees. These proved suitable for lumber products but were even better for making tar, pitch, and turpentine, especially in the Cape Fear valley. In 1753 colonists exported 84,012 barrels of naval stores through their ports. By 1768 the amount had risen to 127,697 barrels, roughly 60 percent of all naval stores exported from British North America. Most went to Great Britain and other North American colonies.[22]

Yet neither naval stores nor wood products provided the sufficiently profitable staple that North Carolina planters sought. Governor William Tryon (1765–71) wrote the Board of Trade in 1767 that, despite the English bounty for "Plank and Ton Timber into Great Britain," lumber producers shouldered excessive expenses.

Similarly, though England paid bounties of £2 4s. per ton of tar, £1 per ton of pitch, and £1 10s. per ton of turpentine, the industry's heyday had been during the first quarter of the eighteenth century, when producers in South Carolina reaped bounties of £4 for tar and pitch and £3 for turpentine. When England in 1726 first discontinued and then three years later started paying smaller bounties, South Carolinians increasingly abandoned the production of naval stores. North Carolina planters, according to Governor Johnston, were also "generally resolved to make no more" of these commodities because they brought "so low a price in London," but tar, pitch, and turpentine remained what James Murray derisively called "the Grand Export of the Province." "It is long since every thinking Man," he wrote in 1768, "was sensible that the Province would never thrive till you make a better export." Another Carolinian railed that "we grapple with lightwood knots, and spend our time and labour on a commodity of little or no value" in contrast to the "pitch of opulence our neighbours of South Carolina are arrived" by "leaving the making of naval-stores to their more sharpsighted neighbours."[23]

Further difficulties surfaced in 1770 when several English importers of naval stores insisted that Parliament discontinue the trade bounties, which were due to expire in four years, until North Carolinians agreed to regulations improving the quality of their products. "The Naval Stores that have been Imported . . . has been so adulterated and bad," the importers complained, "that scarcely one Barrel in Twenty has been Intitled to receive the Bounty."[24]

Because of their persistent "want of a proper staple commodity," as a New Bern resident put it in 1765, some planters had already begun to explore the possibilities of cultivating rice and indigo, South Carolina's high-profit staples that required a considerably larger ratio of labor to land than other crops. Within the Cape Fear, where climatic and soil conditions were the most favorable and where the largest slaveholdings existed, rice was planted as early as 1731. Forty years later, exports shipped through North Carolina ports totaled 629 barrels.[25] Indigo production, which began in the mid-1740s, also showed promise. "We are likely to have many Competitors with us in this branch," wrote South Carolina merchant Henry Laurens in 1755. "The Virginians this Year are buying up amongst us large quantity of Seed, the People of North Carolina a good deal." That same year, one Cape Fear planter deemed indigo to be one of "the greatest Blessings this Province has seen of a long time." In 1772 about 1,300 pounds were shipped out of the region.[26]

Despite the increase in production, both crops failed to assume a significant place in North Carolina's economy. In the early 1770s the total amount of land devoted to rice and indigo probably amounted to no more than five hundred acres and eighty acres respectively. One planter's lament in 1758 that "Indico proves a very precarious crop" held true up to the Revolution. A later visitor, Johann Schoepf, thought North Carolinians "either not rich enough or too slothful" for the demands of rice culture.[27]

The varied problems facing North Carolinians were characteristic of a pioneer economy. Scarcities of capital and labor as well as the need for marketable commodities had plagued nearly every British colony in its early history. These problems were also mutually reinforcing. Lack of currency and capital inhibited planters from buying slaves at reasonable rates and local merchants from engaging directly in the Atlantic slave trade. "It would not be easy to enter into any Contract for them [slaves] as there are few men of Substance among us," James Murray wrote in 1752 to a leading English merchant who was interested in establishing just such a trade. "This [Richard?] Quince," he continued, "is one of our top merchants. You see how little his draughts are to be depended on."[28] The shortage of labor, which persisted through the colonial period, contributed to the dependence on less profitable staple commodities, which in turn hindered North Carolina's economic growth by keeping cash and credit in short supply. "Our exports being bad," complained a Wilmington resident in 1768, "we receive very little specie."[29]

"The badness of our Navigation"

Currency and labor shortages, the absence of a valuable staple, as well as more particular problems all dampened North Carolina's economy, but a more fundamental handicap overshadowed and, in some cases, caused these difficulties in the first place. Stretching for 320 miles, the colony's coastline consisted of narrow islands and sandbanks broken by shallow channels leading to Albemarle and Pamlico sounds and numerous interior inlets. The only North Carolina port directly open to the Atlantic was Brunswick, at the mouth of the Cape Fear River, but a treacherous sandbar offshore limited incoming traffic to small vessels. "Within the whole province," wrote J. F. D. Smyth, "there is not one good harbour, being all obstructed with bars, and fluctuating sand-banks." Because of such obstructions, navigating the waters of Carolina often proved to be a dangerous and time-consuming enterprise that resulted in "great expense and delay" and frequent shipwrecks.[30]

Navigation dangers and the lack of deep-water ports produced several negative effects on provincial commerce and capital formation. For one thing, high freight and insurance costs significantly lessened the value of local exports. Cullen Pollock, a wealthy Bertie County planter who owned more than fifty slaves, wrote a friend in 1741:

> Altho you have certainly as good Land as any in this province, and very Good Slaves, Yet the badness of our Navigation makes our Land and Slaves of very little profit to us. . . . And as our Navigation is bad so we have very few Vessells except those that are very small, which makes freight excessive dear and very often not to be had at any rate, So that it is almost as well to sell our grain at a very low price here, as to give the excessive high freight and run the risque of it being halfe spoiled by the Weavle before we get freight. I dont know of any one in this part of the Country that has made it worth their while in making Tobaco. Our Stocks of Hogs and Catle faile very much. This is realy our case; and I dont see any prospect of things turning out Better 'till Navigation can be made more easie.

Because he "Suffered very much for want of Freight," Pollock considered building his own "Vessell if it will not cost to[o] dear."[31]

But, if he did so, few possessed the capital to follow in his tracks. Toward the end of the colonial period, the largest vessel constructed in the province did not exceed two hundred tons burden, and North Carolina ranked only eleventh among its sister provinces in ship construction.[32] Meanwhile, planters continued to suffer from high shipping costs. "There are so many delays, demurs, and disappointments in that Country," wrote Charleston's Henry Laurens in 1764, "that no Ship will remove from here under 7/6 or 10/ per Ton Extra, and then not without a Bondsman here which few People for those very reason[s] chuse to be."[33]

Besides lessening the return from exports, high shipping rates also raised the cost of imported goods. Carolinians complained incessantly about the "exorbitantly dear" price of finished products. A 1731 visitor to the Cape Fear found "the cheapest Goods imported are 50 per cent dearer than at Philadelphia, and most things 100 per cent dearer." As late as 1760, a resident of Brunswick found "every thing here is 3 or 4 times dearer than in Europe," and a contemporary thought "a nominal Hundred pounds Sterling scarcely equal to £40 Sterling in S. Carolina: Virginia or any other of the Northern Provinces." From New Bern a person wrote, "All sorts of wares and merchandize are . . . much dearer . . . in this province, than in any other on this continent."[34]

Because of the economic burdens imposed by their poor port facilities, North Carolinians conducted a considerable trade through neighboring Virginia and South Carolina. Backcountry planters, even more disadvantaged in their transportation facilities than easterners, funneled much of their wheat, corn, and livestock products north to Petersburg or south down the Great Pedee River. In 1767, upon the urgings of Governor Tryon, Moravian settlers in the backcountry explored the possibilities of carrying their produce overland to the Cape Fear River and down to Brunswick. But they continued to trade mostly with Charleston merchants after discovering, among other problems, that Brunswick traders were selling goods "at a cost practically as high as the selling price" back home.[35]

All told, only about a half of the colony's trade went through its own ports. One consequence was that coastal towns remained small through the mid-eighteenth century. Although the more important towns of Edenton, New Bern, and Wilmington, founded in the mid-1730s on the Cape Fear, all increased in population, none had more than fifteen hundred inhabitants by the start of the American Revolution.[36] Reliance upon trading outlets in Virginia and South Carolina also led to high overland freight costs, severe markups on imported goods, trade duties, and currency restrictions. Governor Burrington estimated in 1735 that planters lost "the value of half their Goods" to merchants from Virginia and other colonies. "We

... send our peddling to some or other of the neighbouring colonies," wrote Murray, "for which we have European or other goods at their price, and the necessity of our country obliges them to give almost what advance the importer pleases on the goods he thus buys at second hand." Citing "Trade" as "the vital principal part" of a country's "Constitution," Governor Josiah Martin (1771–75) declared in 1773: "Every Circumstance that places us on a more unfavorable footing than our neighbors is to enrich them at our expence, and build the increase of their trade upon the ruin of our own. . . . We need but look to the Colonies next adjoining us, to discover the invidious distinction."[37]

"Very little Advances"

By the close of the colonial period, North Carolina's economy was more expansive and prosperous than it had been in earlier years. No longer did the province represent a tiny outpost removed from the main trading patterns of the Atlantic world. Between 1740 and 1770 the number of ships entering coastal ports annually had risen from 153 to 473.[38] Slaves were more numerous than they had been in the 1730s. Moreover, it was estimated that the annual value of goods exported through North Carolina ports averaged £76,000 sterling by 1768–1772, as opposed to only £8,000 in 1736.[39] Understandably, then, Governor Martin in 1772 detected "a spirit of industry and improvement dawning in this Province." Josiah Quincy, Jr., visiting in 1773, remarked that "Husbandmen and agriculture increase in number and improvement."[40]

Yet the economy was still underdeveloped during the last decades of British rule. Progress had been achieved during the mid-eighteenth century, but economic prospects remained checkered. "It is well known that this province," wrote the author of *American Husbandry*, "is now making a great progress in its cultivation and exports," but "her want of ports . . . must ever keep her comparatively low." North Carolina, the chronicler Alexander Cluny pointed out in 1769, had lain under "almost total Neglect . . . till very lately" and "very little Advances made even yet, in the Improvement of it." "It is far behind the neighbouring Provinces in Industry and application," echoed a visitor.[41] These and similar

TABLE 1.2 *Average Annual Value of Southern Exports,*
1768–1772[42] *(in pounds sterling)*

	Total Estimated Value	White Population	Value per White Resident
North Carolina	£152,000	130,025	£1.17
Virginia	£731,000	259,272	£2.82
South Carolina	£447,800	49,047	£9.13

lamentations are confirmed by trade figures. Assuming that half of the colony's goods were sent through Virginia and South Carolina, if one then doubles the average annual value of North Carolina exports sent through its own ports from 1768 to 1772 (£76,000 sterling) in order to account for total exports, the per capita value of North Carolina exports based upon the colony's total white population amounted to only £1.17 sterling, as shown in table 1.2.

By contrast, the annual per capita export values for Virginia and South Carolina were £2.82 and £9.13 sterling respectively! Not surprisingly, planter Cullen Pollock could write as late as 1773, "Providence has wisely ordained that [no] Situation in this world shall be without its Alloy, much less a poor Carolina Planter." James Murray, after migrating to Boston, counseled a former Cape Fear neighbor, "I fear you'll be like many whom I have known— stick [stuck] by the unprofitable Cares of a Carolina Planter."[43] On the eve of the Revolution, the Carolina economy still did not commonly yield quick riches; rather, it continued to offer frequent doses of disappointment, frustration, and discontent.

2   Carolina Society and Culture

*You must by no means suffer your imagination to dress
up fairy scenes of ease, elegance, and pleasure where
you are going. In a young country you must not expect
the appearance of luxury or riches.*
—Henry Eustace McCulloh to James Iredell,
    September 5, 1768

Eighteenth-century North Carolina bore the badges of a
new society. Half-formed social and cultural configurations sharply
distinguished it from more settled areas in the colonial South. The
colony, in many respects, recalled the early years of neighboring
Virginia and South Carolina. This chapter seeks to explore several
fundamental questions. What was the structure of North Carolina
society? How, if at all, did that structure vary from region to region
and time to time over the years from 1729 to 1776? What were the
life-styles, cultural traits, and values of the inhabitants? Finally, to
what extent did a fully articulated elite emerge in North Carolina?

"Very few if any rich people"

One year before North Carolina became a royal colony,
William Byrd II undertook a grueling tour of the Albemarle region
as a boundary commissioner for Virginia. In the spring and autumn
of 1728, he and others in the surveying expedition trampled

through swampland and pine forests more than two hundred miles into the interior. The trip formed the basis of Byrd's celebrated work in colonial satire, *The History of the Dividing Line*, and its more blunt, secret counterpart. For him, North Carolina was at best an isolated, undifferentiated wilderness inhabited by uncivilized rustics, who paid "no tribute, either to God or Caesar." He found few gentlemen, except for an occasional "homebred squire," or those who "stuck by us as long as our good liquor lasted."[1]

Surviving records, though scanty, confirm Byrd's view of North Carolina's social structure. Quitrent lists, compiled in 1735, exist for seven northeastern counties, where the colony's population was concentrated at the time. According to these lists, which give the amount of acreage that landholders possessed, each county contained a preponderance of small to middling landowners. Except in Bertie County, on the western fringes of settlement where holdings were more substantial, a majority of planters owned less than 250 acres. Equally noteworthy was the relative absence of men who possessed large estates. Few owned more than 1,000 acres, and only four in excess of 5,000. Moreover, fewer than ten men held title to land in more than one county.[2]

Unfortunately, these lists provide no clues to the extent of landholding among adult white males in the colony, but it is likely that most men did, in fact, own land. "A very little Money will purchase a vast Quantity of Land in North Carolina," Governor George Burrington noted in 1732. He estimated that improved plantations, equipped with houses, barns, and orchards, only cost "about thirty or forty pistoles." A 1720 Perquimans County tax list, itemizing both landholders and nonlandholders, reveals that nearly three-quarters, or 72 percent, of all household heads owned land. A recent study of slightly earlier tax lists has arrived at a similar figure for neighboring Pasquotank County as well as for Perquimans.[3]

Additional material in the form of later tax lists also points to the scarcity of wealthy men and to the undifferentiated structure of Albemarle society. Based upon returns from four out of a probable six tax districts, table 2.1 gives a rough profile of slaveholding in Pasquotank in 1739. It should, however, be noted that this listing records only holdings of taxable slaves (twelve years and older). Nonetheless, more than 63 percent of all households did not own any taxable slaves at all. Of those that did, the overwhelming number possessed from one to five. Not one household contained more than ten.

A complete 1740 tax list for Perquimans also exists. It is not directly comparable to the Pasquotank list because black and white taxables were not differentiated. Despite this shortcoming, this list, as shown in table 2.2, also suggests the narrow spectrum of slave-holdings in the Albemarle. About 1 percent of all household heads maintained more than ten taxables, black and white, and only one man, James Henby, Jr., had as many as twenty-one.

Less is known about the degree of stratification in the less-populated regions to the south of the Albemarle counties around this time. Nevertheless, according to a 1719 Craven County tax list, not a single household contained more than ten total taxables, and only two had more than five taxables. The distribution of land in Craven was similarly truncated. As much as 79 percent of all household heads owned land, but only 6 percent held more than a thousand acres. None owned in excess of ten thousand.[4]

Some men in the newly settled Cape Fear valley did possess larger concentrations of wealth than was common elsewhere in North Carolina. By the late 1730s the region had attracted several of the wealthiest individuals in the Albemarle. Men like Edward Moseley and Alexander Lillington relocated their fortunes with an eye toward the Cape Fear's abundance of unclaimed land. The Cape Fear also became the residence of a small number of reasonably affluent South Carolinians, who sought to recoup their fortunes after their colony's devastating depression. In 1733 an itinerant clergyman wrote that the area had "some persons of good Substance" and

TABLE 2.1 *Distribution of Taxable Slaves among Pasquotank County Households, 1739*[5]

	Taxable Slaves (percentages in parentheses)				
	0	1–5	6–10	11+	Total
Households	180 (63.6)	90 (31.8)	13 (4.6)	— —	283

TABLE 2.2 *Distribution of Taxables among Perquimans County Households, 1740*[6]

	Taxables (percentages in parentheses)				
	1–5	6–10	11–20	21+	Total
Households	295 (91.3)	24 (7.4)	3 (.9)	1 (.3)	323

"near fifteen inhabitants with negroes." Burrington earlier reported the recent arrival of "Several . . . Men of good Estates" who had "brought with them many Negroes and other Valuable Effects." Those holding the largest numbers of slaves were Roger Moore, who owned nearly two hundred, and Edward Moseley and Maurice Moore, who each held around sixty. Eleazer Allen, Samuel Swann, James Hasell, Edward Hyrne, Archibald Hamilton, and Henry Simons each seem to have owned between thirty and forty slaves; John Porter, John Swann, and Cornelius Harnett, between twenty and thirty.[7]

Through the middle decades of the eighteenth century, the Cape Fear continued to possess a preponderance of wealthy individuals compared to other regions in the colony. But as the population grew and the economy expanded—however slowly—the social structure of the entire coastal plain gradually changed. Accompanying the expansion of commerce and agriculture was a rise in the size of personal fortunes.

The best measure of this transformation is a series of tax lists for fifteen counties during the 1760s. These present, as did the earlier Pasquotank County list, the number of slaves, twelve years and older, owned by each household. According to these lists, the level of wealth of those in the lower and middling ranks seems to have remained fairly stable in eastern North Carolina compared to what it had been in earlier years. A substantial majority of households in most eastern North Carolina counties still did not possess any taxable slaves. In Pasquotank the percentage of households without taxable slaves (65 percent) remained nearly the same as it had been in 1739 (64 percent). A shift, nonetheless, did occur in the size of slaveholdings at the opposite end of the social spectrum. Whereas in 1739 not one household owned more than ten taxable slaves in four tax districts within Pasquotank, seven households in the county held more than that number by 1769. Except in Anson County, in the distant backcountry, where holdings did not exceed ten taxable slaves, the same pattern of ample slaveholdings occurred in other counties. In Brunswick County 13 percent, or as many as twenty-six households, owned more than ten taxable slaves.[8]

Nevertheless it would be a mistake to conclude that a wealthy plantation class had emerged in eastern North Carolina by the 1760s. An extremely small number of people owned more than twenty taxable slaves, less than 1 percent of all households in most counties. Moreover, within all fifteen counties, only nine men had over fifty and eight of those lived in the counties of New Hanover and Brunswick. Even there, in the lower Cape Fear, where slaveholding was more common, only William Dry with 128, George Moore with 118, and Richard Quince with 113 owned more than 100 taxable slaves. The remainder had between fifty and seventy-three.

Some appreciation of how rare these largest North Carolina slaveholdings were can be gained through a comparison with those in Virginia and South Carolina. Available data for the 1780s suggest that approximately 6 percent of the entire adult white male population owned twenty or more slaves in the typical tidewater Virginia county, and that an even higher percentage held as many in the low-country parishes of South Carolina.[9] But in North Carolina, according to tax lists for eleven counties from the late 1770s and early 1780s, less than 1.5 percent of the adult white male population possessed twenty or more slaves in the typical eastern county. Only in New Hanover and probably in neighboring Brunswick, for which no list exists, did as many as 7 percent own this number. Equally significant is the miniscule number of people, 10 out of 6,262 taxpayers in those eleven counties, who owned fifty or more slaves.[10]

The size and distribution of landholdings in various counties afford a further perspective upon the structure of society in North Carolina around the end of the colonial period. Instead of large numbers of slaves, some North Carolinians had ample amounts of property, chiefly because of the extensive character of their agricultural and forest industries, the ever-present lure of land speculation, and the availability of cheap land. Based upon tax figures from the late 1770s and early 1780s for fifteen counties, a substantial number of men in each county owned more than one thousand acres, much of it acquired in earlier years when land was inexpensive. Carteret County was fairly average; more than 5 percent of all taxpayers held more than one thousand acres.[11] However, the values of these estates should not be overemphasized. As late as 1763, upwards of nineteen thousand acres were obtained in the Albemarle region for £100 to £200. A somewhat more common price for land, according to a contemporary estimate, ranged from £15 to £20 proclamation money per hundred acres. Despite the colony's rapid demographic growth through the mid-eighteenth century, land remained in ready supply, and its value was correspondingly low. "There is more Land," said one resident in the 1760s, "than sufficient to employ fifty times the number of Inhabitants we have at Present."[12] The lack of good port facilities also decreased the worth of these larger tracts. "It would be a valuable tract of land in any country but North Carolina," William Byrd wrote of some Albemarle property, "where, for want of navigation and commerce, the best estate affords little more than a coarse subsistence." Years later, in referring to Maryland and Pennsylvania, Governor Josiah Martin told his brother, "The advantages of those Countries with respect to navigation, and the peculiar disadvantages of this Province in that article give the lands in them a value far above those of this Colony."[13]

Additionally, much of these larger holdings consisted of marginal tracts, wasteland, or wilderness, unworked because of a shortage of labor. Consequently, as a visitor remarked in 1765, the bulk of each of these estates was of "no advantage or value for the present." Without slaves, affirmed another commentator, "Lands are of little Value." The colony's receiver general of quitrents, John Rutherfurd, wrote in 1757, "Uncultivated Lands in this Government are generally an unprofitable estate, and the value of it arbitrary and fluctuating."[14] Probably for that reason, little care was taken by testators in specifying the size and location of outlying tracts. Carolina wills were commonly vague in referring to unimproved landholdings.

Just as noteworthy as the size of individual holdings was the extent to which land was widely owned. Not only did about 70 percent of all adult white males possess landed property, but also a large majority of landowners in most counties owned more than one hundred acres. North Carolina remained predominantly a colony of small to middling farmers.

Although most of the population engaged in planting, land and slaves do not fully portray the structure of society. Some men, especially in the upper echelons, followed other pursuits, such as surveying and military service. Tavern-keeping was an especially popular secondary occupation for larger planters throughout the mid-eighteenth century. "Keeping an inn at the courthouse," J. F. D. Smyth wrote, "is scarcely thought a mean occupation here."[15]

Common primary occupations, other than planting, were commerce and the law. In some cases they also afforded planters secondary occupations, one reason perhaps why neither was very highly professionalized. North Carolina merchants not infrequently evoked the wrath of other traders because of their relative lack of business skills. The Philadelphians James and Drinker wrote, "We have long ago discovered that a careful attention to Business and a proper share of Industry is too scarce in Carolina." A ship captain agreed, observing, "Of all places I ever yett have been this is the worst either for dispatch of saile of a Cargo or the purchase of one."[16]

Equally lacking in professional attributes were members of the bar who, in the opinion of most commentators, both within and outside the colony, scarcely rose above the level of pettifoggery. "This country . . . exceeds all ever I heard of [in] the West Indies for bad Attorneys," wrote James Murray in 1736. Twenty years later, an assembly committee called attention to "the growing Number of Attornies . . . And their Mismanagement of Causes either through Ignorance of [sic] Neglect." So inept were attorneys in drawing up legal papers that the colony's vice-admiralty judge felt compelled in 1748 to inform the High Court of Admiralty in England: "When it comes to be considered how few we have here that understand the forms and practice of Civil Law Courts the want thereof will the more readily be past over and excused." Lawyers, though "bad everywhere," were "in Carolina worse than bad," according to Richard Henry Lee of Virginia.[17]

However unprofessional the people were who engaged in them, commerce and the law usually offered higher rewards than plantation agriculture. Trade proved alluring because it gave ambitious individuals the chance to profit from the growing economy. Although Carolina's exports were dwarfed by those of its neighbors, an expanding trade, sustained by rapid population growth, created new opportunities in the mid-eighteenth century. Samuel Cornell, who arrived in New Bern from his native New York in 1754, had "acquired in Trade a very considerable fortune" by the 1770s. In the Albemarle region, Thomas McKnight became a leading exporter of shingles, after arriving from Scotland in 1757. By the time of the American Revolution, he claimed commercial holdings worth about £11,000 sterling.[18] Few men, on the other hand, were so fortunate as Cornell and McKnight, who were probably the two wealthiest merchants in the colony except for John Hamilton and his partners, who traded both in Virginia and in North Carolina. Cornell and McKnight were also overseas traders, as opposed to the more numerous small retailers and country shopkeepers, and even McKnight's company was forced to struggle "long with all the difficulties attending the introduction of commerce into a new country" before it realized substantial profits. In fact, merchants in other colonies occasionally viewed their counterparts in Carolina as small-time operators who, as Henry Laurens of South Carolina put it, sometimes lacked the "Stammina [i.e. capital] to keep the branches of their Commerce in vigour."[19]

The bar offered another source of wealth, though large fortunes were usually not acquired through legal practice. Henry Eustace McCulloh counseled James Iredell in 1767, "If your Genius leads to the Bar or Trade—the first especially—you may promise yourself a fair field for Success." McCulloh also noted that North Carolina was "a most growing Country," where a demand existed for attorneys and their talents. Iredell subsequently followed McCulloh's advice, but he soon discovered that the arduous and expensive trips around the circuit to various county courts temporarily caused him to lose money. Benjamin Booth Boote encountered the same problem: "Tho my practice in the County Courts may on first sight appear very beneficial, yet when the distance of that circuit is considered, with the trouble and hardships attending it, nothing less than a real danger of wanting bread would force any person to pursue such a business." He may have exaggerated his difficulties, for those whose practices were more established seem to have fared better. Samuel Johnston, Jr., of Edenton termed his practice a "tolerable Business." Although he was "not in the way of being very Rich," he enjoyed "a prospect of making" a "Competent" fortune.[20]

Besides opportunities generated by the colony's economy, the ability of lawyers and merchants to make comparatively substantial amounts of money also stemmed from the small numbers engaged in these occupations. Unlike colonies whose professional groups were more mature, North Carolina lacked a supply of native talent. William Hooper moved to North Carolina in his early twenties because there was "no room for him" in his native Boston as a lawyer. "Professions were esteemed the first Estates and most productive," lawyer William Brimage believed, "as only few had Education for the purpose." As late as the mid-1760s, there were only about forty-five attorneys in the entire province, and only in these years did a resident mercantile community of any real significance emerge. As a result, the few members of these professions were able to capitalize on the bounty that a growing colony offered. Merchants also seem to have charged higher prices than they might have in a more competitive environment. "The trade being in few hands they take a much higher price," Arthur Dobbs wrote in contrasting North Carolina merchants with those in Charleston.[21]

During the middle decades of the eighteenth century, then, North Carolina society was gradually becoming more stratified and differentiated, especially in the east. The expanding economy made it possible for some planters to increase their holdings of land and slaves and for merchants and lawyers to profit. Nevertheless, the slow pace and checkered pattern of economic growth were not conducive to the creation of a truly wealthy elite. Few men could boast of great fortunes, and the pathways to opulence were usually narrow and uncertain, even in the 1760s and 1770s. A French traveler in 1765, who marveled at the "very great Estates" and extravagance of many Virginians, thought that there were "very few if any rich people" in North Carolina. It was, he felt, "a fine Country for poor people, but not for the rich." In describing a Cape Fear planter, Thomas Cobham commented that "he was reputed to be an industrious independant young Man, and of good Fortune for that Country which did not amount to a great deal." "The best estates in this country," Governor Tryon affirmed in 1768, "are but very moderate." Aspiring lawyer James Iredell wrote his mother in 1771, "This Country is a very poor one. I can never hope to make a Fortune here."

The distance between classes was wider on the eve of the Revolution than in earlier years, as North Carolina followed in the footsteps of its southern neighbors. But the transformation was incomplete. Unlike society in either Virginia or South Carolina, that in North Carolina was still comparatively unstratified. During a tour of the colony in 1773, Josiah Quincy, Jr., was impressed by the extent to which property was "much more equally diffused" than in its neighbor to the south. Instead of "herds of negroes and tawny slaves," he saw "husbandmen, yeomen and white laborers scattered through the country." As a visitor to New Bern affirmed, the "social system" was "still in its swaddling clothes."[22]

"The Best poor mans Cuntry"

If the provincial class structure was only gradually becoming more stratified during the mid-eighteenth century, the colonists' everyday life-style also bore the mark of a slowly evolving society. Social conditions and values in North Carolina differed markedly at times from those in other colonies. In fact, to many observers, the habits and ways of Carolinians denoted the complete absence of civilization. "The Manners of the North Carolinians in General, are Vile and Corrupt—The whole Country is a Stage of Debauchery Dissoluteness and Corruption," observed Charles Woodmason in 1765. A visiting merchant wrote his wife, "This is a Barren Desert Country—Bad Roads, Bad Lodgings Bad everything—The People in general even the best destitute of every Principle of Honour a few excepted." One commentator called it "the rudest part of the whole continent." Another simply referred to the province as "this bad part of the world." "Bona Terra Mala Gens," thought one person.[23] Numerous others shared the sentiment that North Carolina was little more than a "receptacle or Sanctuary for Out Laws and people of Despurate fortunes." Noting that "ancient Rome" had been "a city of refuge for all debtors and fugitives," William Byrd mused, "Who knows but Carolina may, one time or other, come to be the seat of some other great empire."[24]

Although it is not clear what proportion of its population consisted of fugitives from other colonies, eighteenth-century North Carolina never fulfilled Byrd's sarcastic expectations. For one thing, most of its population lived at a near-subsistence level. Less than a third of all adult white males were landless laborers or servants, but owning property by no means insured an easy existence. Possessing few, if any, slaves and a largely uncultivated tract of land, the average planter could hardly afford many finished goods of any kind—much less luxury items. He usually resided in a small log hut, which was lit only by pine-knot candles.[25] Dire poverty, however, was rare. Because of the wide ownership of land and a long growing season, most people were able to produce their own food. "Provisions here are extremely cheap and extremely good, so that people may live plentifully at a trifling expense," noted Byrd. Others echoed his observation. "In truth it is the Best poor mans Cuntry I Ever heard of," one inhabitant wrote his cousin around 1770, "and I have had the opertunity of hearing from South and north."[26]

Beyond the level of ample subsistence, however, the Carolina planter's world was self-contained, and human contact was limited. Most people in this class lived on widely scattered farms, separated by vast tracts of pine barrens, swamps, and sandy plains. J. F. D. Smyth was amazed by "the small intercourse, and very limited communication" among the people he met. Another visitor discovered a "few inhabitants scattered here and there in the forest," and Johann Schoepf estimated that individual residences were often ten to twenty miles apart.[27] The monotony of such an isolated, meager existence could be deadening. The "people," Smyth noted, "are the most wretchedly ignorant of any I ever met with. They could not tell me the name of the place, county, or parish they resided in, nor any other place in the adjacent country." Social diversions consisted mostly of drinking "killdevil" and "bombo," two variants of rum, in addition to shooting matches and frequent bouts of boxing and gouging. "Are we not able to slay Thousands, yea tens of Thousands with our Thumb-Nails . . . ," mocked a colonial humorist, "for what Men of any Nation upon Earth can cope with us at *Gouging*."[28]

Less important than these pastimes to the planter's way of life was religious worship. Because of a chronically weak Anglican church, the dispersed character of settlements, and a shortage of ministers, most planters remained on the periphery of organized religion. "No opportunity have I had since I left my Dear, Blessed, happy native Country," a 1759 visitor complained, "to hear one Sermon, or so much as to joyn in one act of Social worship, either public or private."[29] Besides a few missionaries from the Society for the Propagation of the Gospel, the exposure of planters to religion was confined to various dissenting denominations. A small number of Quakers resided in Pasquotank County, and Baptists and Methodists were scattered up and down the coastal plain. Presbyterian congregations were mostly concentrated in the upper Cape Fear county of Cumberland, where many Scottish Highlanders settled. "Every sect of religion abounds here except the Roman Catholic," reported Governor Tryon in 1765. An Anglican missionary wrote, "So large a scope for the ministry lies open before me, in a Country inhabited by many sorts of People, of various nations and different opinions, customs, and manners."[30]

Nevertheless, as countless commentators, ranging from Byrd to Josiah Quincy remarked, the majority of Carolinians probably subscribed to no particular body of religious belief at all. "As the great aim of your life is to do good by propagating the Gospel," a resident wrote George Whitefield in 1740, "there is Not a Province in America where your preaching is So Much wanted as in this." Charles Woodmason bemoaned "the Danger that not only the Church Established, but even Religion it self" would "be totally lost and destroyed."[31] Although resident ministers from the Society for the Propagation of the Gospel were occasionally worried by the presence of dissenters, an equal source of concern was the large number of people who did not belong to any sect. "We are very happy," wrote John Boyd in 1735, "in having no different sects or opinions in this part of the Country but I have great reason to complain of a Laodecean luke warmness." "There are too many," thought James Reed in 1760, "that can hardly be said to be members of any particular Christian society."[32]

Although by most standards—both contemporary and modern—their lot was necessarily primitive, rude, and perhaps, as some claimed, semibarbaric, most small planters were apparently resigned to their lives of quiet isolation. As property holders in a self-contained wilderness, they had only the most limited expectations. This was best revealed by their lack of "industry." William Byrd wryly observed, "Surely there is no place in the world where the inhabitants live with less labor than in North Carolina. It approaches nearer to the description of Lubberland than any other, by the great felicity of the climate, the easiness of raising provisions, and the slothfulness of the people." Indeed, small planter lethargy provoked frequent commentary. A Pennsylvania Quaker, who urged planters to export new and more profitable commodities, wrote, "They seem to Chuse their Old way as being less trouble." "The most Indolent lazy Drones I ever was Engaged with," voiced a visiting Scotsman. Janet Schaw, traveling in the Cape Fear, affirmed, "If they can raise as much corn and pork, as to subsist them in the most slovenly manner, they ask no more."[33]

The one significant exception to such pronounced "slothfulness" lay in the backcountry. There the steadily rising population after 1750 consisted of northerners who migrated to North Carolina in hopes of improving their lot in life. In emigrating overland from Pennsylvania and other colonies, they shared aspirations similar to those of the initial settlers of southeastern Pennsylvania and neighboring areas. As James Lemon has shown, the same concern for material improvement characteristic of Pennsylvania's early inhabitants typified later population movements to the frontier. Most of those who relocated were probably "small farmers and craftsmen" unable to keep pace in a region of diminishing land and rising prices, but they too "shared the hope of achieving success." The North Carolina backcountry attracted them because of its far-flung reputation for cheap, fertile land.[34]

The industry and sheer desire to achieve that was evinced by "settlers . . . from the northwards" were so impressive that Arthur Dobbs remarked in 1754, "None take up lands . . . but with a view to cultivate and improve them, as fast as they can, all the back settlers being very industrious, cultivating Indigo, Hemp, Flax, Corn etc. as well as breeding horses and other stock." One commentator described them as "brave Industerous people," and Bishop Spangenberg of the Moravians found "good farmers and very worthy people" among the new settlers. Yet another observer characterized them as "hardy and laborious Races of Men."[35]

Because most backcountry settlers were confirmed Protestant dissenters, they took a strong interest in religious matters. In some cases, they seem to have migrated as congregations. As early as 1756, nearly eight hundred Presbyterians from Anson, Orange, and

Rowan counties vociferously protested a provincial statute that entailed financial support for Anglican ministers. They desired, instead, to provide solely for their own clergymen, which remained a persistent backcountry demand in later years. Although lacking at times in regular clergy, local congregations did enjoy the services of itinerant ministers from the north.[36]

How did the average planter in North Carolina regard his superiors? In a society where landholding was prevalent and where wide extremes in wealth did not exist, as they did in Virginia and South Carolina, it would seem likely that deferential attitudes would not be too strong. In comparing North Carolina with its neighbor to the south, Josiah Quincy hinted as much in noting that the wider distribution of property in the former "may account for some, if not all, the differences of character of the inhabitants."[37] Byrd found that Carolinians "are rarely guilty of flattering or making any court to their governors but treat them with all the excesses of freedom and familiarity." His observation applied to the local level as well, as illustrated by the "fate of an honest justice" in Currituck: "This bold magistrate, it seems, taking upon him to order a fellow to the stocks for being disorderly in his drink, was for his intemperate zeal carried thither himself and narrowly escaped being whipped by the rabble into the bargain."[38] Some years later, Schoepf observed how the "dignity" of another gentleman justice was steadfastly ignored when he commanded two men to stop brawling outside his home. "It was more in keeping with his official worth to pass over an apparent slight, instead of taking the proud revenge which an injured self-love might demand," Schoepf commented after the justice ceased his complaints. In New Hanover County, Janet Schaw was amazed when a "set of Volunteers" descended upon the funeral services of a leading resident and proceeded to eat the food set aside for the invited guests.[39]

Although deferential attitudes were comparatively weak, less fortunate planters expressed little antagonism. If disrespectful at times, they normally accommodated themselves to the presence of their betters, not because men possessing larger fortunes had established their superiority by their style of life, but because the lot of most Carolina small planters created intense apathy and indifference. Poverty and isolation bred social stability and conservatism. As Samuel P. Huntington has written, the abject, whose aspirations are minimal, are not likely to "worry about the grand transformation of society."[40] Small planters evinced little desire to contest the authority of those who were wealthier and, in effect, did so only when their own circumscribed needs were either disrupted or demanded momentary satisfaction.

"Less of what is called politeness and good-breeding"

All North Carolinians did not experience such a limited existence, for a small number were able to enjoy the blessings of greater wealth. Leading planters, merchants, and lawyers obviously were not restricted to a semisubsistence life-style. Thus, it might be tempting to infer the existence of a small, tightly knit aristocracy. But what those at the top really represented was an emerging elite whose coherence, mode of life, and values also possessed the marks of a slowly maturing society.

The men who occupied the highest social ranks in the mid-eighteenth century constituted an extraordinarily "youthful" upper class.[41] Although a small cluster of families, such as the Harveys and Pollocks, who resided in the Albemarle region, could claim an ancestral heritage dating back to the seventeenth century, the majority of the colony's social leaders were relative newcomers to social position and were not undergirded by a long record of family precedence. In part this happenstance resulted from the rapid growth in population and settled territory that characterized the mid-1700s. In each newly settled locality, opportunities for status and position quickly arose. Significantly, the wealthier families in the Albemarle did not take wholesale advantage of the opportunities offered by the opening of new lands. That they did not stemmed from their small numbers and scant resources.

In the Cape Fear, most men of wealth and standing through the mid-eighteenth century were first-generation immigrants. Only a few individuals had come from the Albemarle counties, such as the Swanns, Edward Moseley, and Alexander Lillington. Far more numerous were the South Carolinians who began to arrive in the 1720s and 1730s: the Moores, Job How, William Dry, Eleazer Allen, and Richard Eagles, among others. But these early settlers did not establish a monopoly of social and economic resources. From the mid-1730s up to the Revolution, newcomers continued to pervade the highest circles of Cape Fear society. Coming from all parts of the Anglo-American world, this diverse group included the Quinces, John Ancrum, Lewis DeRosset, Thomas Clark, Rufus Marsden, William Faris, Benjamin Heron, James Gregory, and Joseph Eagles from England; Hugh Waddell, William Purviance, John Sampson, Frederick Gregg, and Archibald Maclaine from Ireland; and Samuel Johnston, James Murray, John Rutherfurd, Robert Hogg, Robert Schaw, Alexander Duncan, George Parker, and Thomas Cobham from Scotland. Others were William Cray and John Burgwin from South Carolina; Robert Walker and Daniel Dunbibin from New York; Jehu Davis, John du Bois, William Hill, and William Hooper from Massachusetts; and John Maultsby, James Hasell, Robert Ellis, and Thomas Lloyd from Pennsylvania. Although originally outsiders, these men represented the top crust of Cape Fear society.

Once the backcountry was settled rapidly after mid-century, social arrangements became even more fluid in the west. In contrast to Virginia, where migrant sons of gentry families extended tidewater hegemony to the frontier, the majority of social leaders in the North Carolina piedmont were first-generation immigrants from other colonies. They included, among others, Edmund Fanning from New York; Samuel Spencer and Griffith Rutherford from New Jersey; James Carter from Maryland; Thomas Polk from Pennsylvania; and the Hart brothers, Richard Henderson, and Samuel Benton from Virginia.

Social fluidity, however, was not just the product of expanding settlement patterns, for, even in the colony's older regions, the top strata of society were remarkably open to newcomers. The Pamlico Sound area, for instance, attracted a variety of immigrants: William Borden from Rhode Island; John Simpson and Michael Coutanche from Massachusetts; James Davis from Virginia; Samuel Cornell from New York; Robert Palmer from Scotland; and John Edge Tomlinson from England. The Albemarle region itself was no exception. New men like Joseph Montfort, Edward Buncombe, Francis Corbin, Thomas Child, and Henry Eustace McCulloh found few barriers to social standing. In fact, nearly every merchant and lawyer of note in the Albemarle as late as the 1760s was a first-generation immigrant: merchants such as Thomas McKnight, James Milner, Alexander Telfair, and William McCormick from Scotland; John Campbell and Richard Brownrigg from Ireland; William Lowther from New York; and Joseph Hewes from New Jersey; and lawyers such as Joshua Bodley, Alexander Elmsely, Thomas Jones, and James Iredell from England; Thomas Barker from Massachusetts; William Cumming from Maryland; and Robert Jones, Jr., John Williams, and Abner Nash from Virginia.

Several circumstances contributed to such quickly achieved prominence. Like immigrants generally, these newcomers had a heady share of ambition. Having only a "small encouragement . . . to stay" in England, James Murray traveled to the Cape Fear in 1735 intending to "push" his "fortune." Arriving from Ireland in 1746, the merchant-planter Frederick Gregg became "one of the richest Men in Wilmington" through his "industry." Some years later, Edenton's James Iredell expressed the hope that he would "be at last successful" by relying on "a steady attentive perseverance."[42]

Men like these did not usually immigrate because of North Carolina's climate, scenic beauty, or cultural attractions. Rather, they sought to better themselves materially and socially in a new land where opportunities for advancement seemed best. As Murray commented, "If I am to be *no body* I'll be that Nobody where I can have health and many other Comforts in a Degree not to be found in North Carolina." Indeed, some first-generation immigrants did not even expect to remain permanently in the colony. His original intentions are unclear, but Murray eventually moved to Boston. Other newcomers remained in North Carolina only because they apparently could not afford to pull up stakes after their expectations of quick riches failed to materialize. "I have very little right," wrote Samuel Johnston, Jr., "to hope even to be able to leave this Country and therefore take every method to make it as agreeable as possible." William Faris, who it seems had left his wife behind in England, wrote in 1750, "I had thoughts of leaving this Country; but find it almost Impracticable, and as Mrs. Faris gives me hopes of Seeing her here, determines my Setling for Life." James Iredell complained at one point that he and "all who come here" were "generally Prisoners for Life" because they could not easily make their fortunes in North Carolina.[43]

In addition to sheer ambition, other more practical circumstances aided newcomers. Some individuals, for instance, possessed a certain amount of wealth before ever setting foot in North Carolina, such as the Moores and other South Carolinians who went to the Cape Fear. Others came from families of some wealth and distinction. Robert Jones, Jr., who settled in Northampton County in the early 1750s, was the son of a Virginia assemblyman, as was Abner Nash, who practiced law in Halifax during the following decade. In fact, Nash himself had briefly served in the Virginia House of Burgesses before he moved. Merchants, in addition to whatever wealth they may have initially possessed, had some access to credit and capital through previous commercial contacts. This was true not only for Scottish traders who flocked to North Carolina, but also for other merchants, such as John Edge Tomlinson, who "brought a General Assortment of European and West India Goods" upon his arrival in New Bern in the 1760s.[44] Immigrating in 1742 as a self-made man, John Campbell of Ireland could count on trading ties with his brother, a Liverpool merchant. William Faris and Joseph Hewes similarly arrived with commercial connections and skills that helped assure their success.

A number of men also utilized political connections either in Britain or in North Carolina. Before leaving Scotland for the Cape Fear, Murray could count on the remainder of a £1,000 patrimony, trading correspondents in England and the West Indies, and the "interest" of the new governor, Gabriel Johnston, in supporting him. Arthur Benning, who served as sheriff of New Hanover County for five years, had arrived in North Carolina in the early 1760s "under the Protection" of Governor Arthur Dobbs. Hugh Waddell's Irish father left him propertyless, but provided him with a good contact in Dobbs. Other newcomers depended on their connections with either Henry McCulloh, an English merchant who owned more than a million acres of land in the colony, or with John Carteret, Earl of Granville, North Carolina's sole remaining proprietor after 1729. James Iredell was only one of several to profit from "the Natural Weight" of McCulloh's "property."[45] Francis Corbin and Thomas Child enjoyed Granville's patronage.

Although immigrants availed themselves of personal wealth, commercial contacts, and political ties whenever possible, their rapid rise was also abetted by the truncated structure of society. Because no indigenous elite of adequate strength existed to block their entrance, the pathways to social position were wide open. Had native members of the upper class been sufficiently distinguished by their wealth and education, standards of admission would have been considerably more difficult. Instead, the top stratum of society lacked cohesion well into the third quarter of the eighteenth century. Most of its members were first- or, at the most, second-generation newcomers.[46]

To some extent, marriage between new and older families blurred existing differences and added a degree of unity. In the Cape Fear a half-dozen families became linked through kinship. At the center of this group were the Moores, who had intermarried with members of the Dry, Ashe, How, Allen, and Swann families. The same phenomenon also occurred to the north. James Iredell, for instance, married the sister of Samuel Johnston, Jr., an established resident of Edenton. Another of Johnston's sisters would have married merchant Joseph Hewes had it not been for her untimely death. Yet the complex web of interrelated families so common to Virginia's upper class and other colonial elites by the mid-eighteenth century did not eventuate. Instead, small clusters of family clans came into being. As a result, the social leadership was more notable for its nascency than for its cohesion.[47]

Yet another circumstance forestalling such cohesion was North Carolina's relative safety from internal threats. After the Tuscarora and Yamassee wars early in the century, Indian conflict was limited to the backcountry. The colony's small slave population similarly guaranteed a degree of security. Elsewhere in the South, especially in the South Carolina low country, the prevalence of black slaves created an ever-present dread of insurrection that was further fueled by occasional conspiracies or rumors of conspiracies. But in North Carolina any sense of alarm was muted. In the wake of the Stono Rebellion in South Carolina, legislators did tighten up the provincial slave code in 1741. But, except for a possible rebellion in 1752 or 1753, no insurrections took place and rumors were few. As a consequence, the need was less for whites to unite in the face of an internal threat. "North Carolina," a committee of South Carolina's council remarked as late as 1769, "is secure from this danger of Negroes."[48]

Nor was North Carolina exposed like its southern neighbors to external attack. The forbidding coastline, though an obstacle to oceangoing commerce, provided a greater measure of security from French and Spanish ships. "The place by its situation," Murray claimed, "is entirely out of the power of a foreign enemy." In fact, during the Revolution, small American vessels frequently eluded prowling British warships by sailing through shallow channels in the Outer Banks. Edenton, as a consequence, even became a temporary trade entrepôt for Virginia and Philadelphia merchants.[49]

The colony's regional divisions further contributed to the diffuseness of its upper class. Because of the timing and character of its settlement, North Carolina, in contrast to neighboring provinces, was characterized by distinct regions during the mid-eighteenth century. Unlike South Carolina, it was not a highly centralized city-state; in contrast to Virginia, it did not have a homogeneous tidewater gentry, linked by ties of kinship and common economic interests, to tie disparate areas together. Rather, the colony was divided into two major sections: the north, centered chiefly in the old Albemarle counties; and the south, where the lower Cape Fear valley was the principal locus. Within each of these regions were subregions: the Pamlico Sound area, surrounding the town of New Bern in the south; and a northwestern tier, comprising the counties of Edgecombe and Northampton in the north. Later, beginning in the 1750s and especially after 1760, the backcountry became yet another distinctive region.

Few factors existed to unify the local leaders of these varying regions into a broadly based gentry, even in the east. Economic ties were almost nonexistent. The northeastern economy was geared toward tobacco, corn, shingles, staves, beef, and pork; the Cape Fear depended much more heavily on naval stores, sawed lumber, rice, and indigo. The trade of each was funneled through its ports or transported across the borders of Virginia and South Carolina. Social ties were weak. Even for the few Albemarle residents, like Edward Moseley and Alexander Lillington, who transplanted their fortunes to the Cape Fear, personal interests and acquaintances shifted to the south as well. Little intermarriage occurred among residents of the two sections, and as late as the 1760s no regular mail service linked the two—the only break in the intercolonial postal chain extending from New Hampshire to South Carolina.[50] "In this part of the Province," wrote John Barnett from Northampton County in 1770, "we have hardly any communication with

Cape Fear."[51] Nor was there a common urban center comparable to Charleston and Williamsburg that could have strengthened social bonds. The colony's seat of government shifted back and forth among Edenton, Bath, New Bern, and Wilmington. Only in 1765 was it firmly fixed at New Bern.

Although the colony's social leaders were of diverse geographic origins and resided in different regions, their style of life was similar in many respects, varying more in degree than in kind. Few men, north or south, lived ostentatiously; most dwelled in a world that had only the faint imprint of eighteenth-century gentility. "There is no difference to be perceived in Dress and Carriage," Governor Burrington complained in 1732, "between the Justices, Constables and Planters that come to a Court, nor between the Officers and Private men, at a Muster." In "no other Country but this," he remarked, was "Parity" so common.[52]

In later years, as men in the upper social echelons increased their fortunes, such parity became less common, but only a rare few enjoyed the means to live lavishly. Henry Eustace McCulloh warned James Iredell in 1768, "You must by no means suffer your imagination to dress up fairy scenes of ease, elegance, and pleasure where you are going. In a young country you must not expect the appearance of luxury or riches." Smyth, who was impressed by the aristocratic splendor of Virginia's squirearchy, noted that even the most affluent plantations in Carolina contained "a profusion of every thing, but in the coarsest and plainest style." Johann Schoepf was surprised by the lack of "exterior courtesies" exhibited both by slaves and their white masters. Upon meeting with the "principal inhabitants" of New Bern, the Venezuelan Francisco De Miranda observed that the "men dress carelessly and grossly." Not only did they smoke tobacco, he reported, but they also chewed it, and "with so much excess that some assured me they could not go to bed and reconcile sleep without having a cud in the mouth."[53]

Only in the lower Cape Fear, where individual concentrations of wealth were largest and most common, did the upper segments of society "appear . . . better dressed" and more mannerly, though even there men exhibited something less than aristocratic grandeur. Although Devereux Jaratt could speak of the awesome presence commanded by a wigged gentleman in Virginia—"*a* periwig, *in those days, was a distinguishing badge of* gentle folk"—men in the

Cape Fear seldom wore such a badge. Writing to a London wig-maker in 1752, James Murray observed, "We deal so much in caps in this country that we are almost as careless of the furniture of the outside as of the inside of our heads."[54] John Starkey, no less a figure than Murray in Cape Fear society, boasted a "bald head" and wore "a plain coat." Janet Schaw discovered a "most disgust-ing equality" during her travels through the region. More favorable, though equally revealing, were the impressions of Josiah Quincy of Massachusetts. Appalled by the aristocratic temper of the South Carolinians and the Virginians he met during his tour of the prov-inces in 1773, he found to his delight "less of what is called polite-ness and good-breeding" in "Brunswick, Wilmington, Newbern, Edenton, and so through the North province." As late as 1800, a visiting Englishman thought that North Carolinians "possessed less intelligence and suavity of manner" than Virginians and lacked the "refinement," "love of books and the arts," and the "share of polite as well as solid information" to be found in South Carolina.[55]

The plantation homes leading colonists built were no more stun-ning in appearance than their occupants. Almost invariably they were one- or two-story frame structures. A handsome brick house was "a great rarity," wrote a 1745 visitor from Pennsylvania. More than thirty years later, another traveler remarked, "There is no-body who thinks himself rich enough to live in a brick house."[56] The few brick dwellings were located chiefly in the Cape Fear, but even the famous "mansion" belonging to Roger Moore was only one story high. George Minot, in trying to sell his nearby planta-tion, claimed to live in "the best Neighbourhood in the whole place," yet he owned what a neighbor described as "two small Logg houses very indifferant." Even by the 1770s, most plantation homes in the Cape Fear remained unprepossessing. One wealthy planter was said to live in a "hovel." Another, though he hoped to build a fine house, lived in a dwelling "little better than one of his Negro huts."[57]

Estate inventories afford further evidence of the manner in which people in the upper brackets lived. Because of their small number and inconsistent quality, the inventories do not readily permit sys-tematic analysis, but they do provide some insights. For example, the majority of the colony's men of substance normally owned only a small quantity of luxury goods. Few individuals possessed rugs, clocks, pictures, or mahogany furniture. Diningware usually included few items of silver. Instead, pewter, china, stoneware, and earthenware predominated. Although he held thirty-five slaves, John Maule of Beaufort County owned only a "half Dozen Silver Tea spoons," a pair of "Silver tongs" (as well as "one Silver watch"), and dined off a "parcel of China," a "parcel of Delf ware," and some stoneware. Richard Sanderson, "Esquire," of Perquimans County owned "3 Silver Table Spoons and Punch Ladle" as well as "6 Silver Tea Spoons and 1 pair Tea Tongs," but he and his family mostly relied upon bowls, plates, and other utensils made of china, pewter, and stone.[58] The inventories of Edward Bryan and William Bartram, who owned sixteen and thirty slaves respectively, list no silver dining implements at all.[59] Some men, like Richard Eagles of Brunswick County, possessed larger quantities of silver as well as other luxury goods, but such items were usually as rare as the gentlemen who owned them.[60]

Only in their pastimes, such as an occasional ball or horse race, did Carolina's elite show a close emulation of other southern elites.[61] Such activities were ordinarily restricted to the colony's few towns and evidently did not become common until the late colonial period. Refinement was sometimes lacking. After attending a ball in Wilmington, Janet Schaw commented, "No chair, no carriage— good leather shoes need none. The ridicule was the silk shoes in such a place." Fortunately for her sake, she apparently did not encounter John Walker, a Wilmington merchant who was adept at brawling and supposedly "took the greatest delight" in pulling the teeth of his victims with a surgeon's forceps. Few men chose to duplicate his exploits, but neither were they the type to spend hours sitting for portraits. Indeed, the first known limner in North Carolina, Boyle Aldworth, did not appear until 1778.[62]

Accompanying these vagaries in the demeanor, appearance, and activities of social leaders was a limited cultural horizon. Individually and collectively, they expressed only fleeting interest in artistic or intellectual endeavors. "Their ideas are generally not very liberal," wrote one visitor. Henry Eustace McCulloh commented, "Life may be passed there very happily, without too great [an] Exercise of Philosophy."[63] Theatrical events and concerts were negligible. Although upper-class Carolinians devoted some time to reading books, the slender output of their own literary, scientific, philosophical, and political writings testifies to their inattention to intellectual pursuits.[64] Literary and scientific societies were nonexistent, as were social clubs, except for a few Masonic lodges. George Brownrigg, an Edenton merchant, submitted a paper on peanut oil to the Royal Society of London in 1769, but no North Carolinian belonged to that scientific organization—a feature shared by the inhabitants of only two other colonies, Delaware and Rhode Island. North Carolina was also one of the two colonies without at least one resident among the members of the American Philosophical Society upon its reorganization in 1769.[65]

During her travels through the Cape Fear, Schaw did happen upon one impressive "Gentleman," who was an "excellent Mathematician" and had also "studied Physic and Botany." Expecting that "this man would be prized and courted . . . that the young would refer to his experience, and those of riper years apply to his superior knowledge," she discovered to her surprise that he had "found but one man who had sense enough to understand him."[66]

As might be expected from their low level of cultural attainment, education did not figure prominently in the lives of leading Carolinians. Elkanah Watson later observed that before the Revolution "no State, perhaps, had at that period performed so little, to promote the cause of education, science, and the arts, as North Carolina." Such neglect was partially reflected by the small number of schools. "The Legislature has never yet taken the least care to erect one school, which deserves the name in this wide extended country," Governor Johnston remonstrated in 1736. A law passed in 1745 to construct a school in Edenton was never enforced, and not until 1754 was another attempt made to fund a public school in the province. When the exigencies of the French and Indian War diverted money appropriated for this purpose, educational efforts in the colony continued to lag.[67]

Finally, in 1764, residents of New Bern and the surrounding area raised a private subscription of about £120 sterling in promissory notes to construct a town schoolhouse, and in 1767 the assembly voted to help defray contingent expenses. Besides some religious instruction, the focus of the school was heavily utilitarian: "to instruct . . . children in Such Branches of useful Learning as are necessary for several of the Offices and Stations in Life." But commitment to its survival was uneven. Adequate financing was always lacking, and, when schoolmaster Thomas Tomlinson disciplined several of the local trustees' children for "very notorious offences," he was dismissed. Thereafter, what financial support remained further dwindled, and an angry Governor Martin complained that the New Bern trustees, "being ignorant and uneducated men, are as little capable of judging of the merits of a pedagogue, as [they are] inclinable to do justice."[68]

Other than the ill-fated New Bern school, educational facilities in the colony were limited. Although at least two individuals, James Winwright in 1744 and James Innes in 1760, provided funds for school construction in their wills, nothing ever came of Winwright's efforts, and Innes's school in Wilmington was not established until 1784.[69] At most, only a few schools operated in North Carolina through the mid-eighteenth century.[70] Even then, instructors did not always fit the mold of the dedicated pedagogue. Brunswick's schoolmaster, William Hill, quickly cast teaching aside in the late 1750s for a more lucrative career in commerce. James Beasley, a teacher in Bertie County, was charged in 1759 with stealing a silver snuffbox; and a schoolmaster in Chowan County, William Budd, allegedly assaulted the local sheriff.[71] Of course, some children, born to the most affluent families, were privately tutored, but this practice never became as common as in neighboring colonies.[72]

Most members of first families lacked formal education. An institution of higher learning did not exist in the province until the 1770s, when Presbyterians in the backcountry county of Mecklenburg persuaded government authorities to establish a public seminary. Only a few individuals attended institutions in other colonies. Three young men—John Ashe in 1746, John Moseley in 1757, and George Pollock in 1758—went to Harvard, and Whitmell Hill attended the College of Philadelphia in 1760. Although Williamsburg was nearby, no North Carolinian attended William and Mary until 1771.[73]

Only a paltry number studied in England. Three youths, Allen and Willie Jones and John Sitgreaves, attended Eton, but North Carolinians were conspicuously absent from the ranks of southern gentlemen attending the Inns of Court. From 1720 to 1776, over 100 southerners received instruction there: South Carolinians numbered 58, Virginians 43, Marylanders 23, and Georgians 11. At the bottom, ranking even below the newly established colony of Georgia, stood North Carolina, with 8. This handful actually did not include one native; most, like Thomas McGuire and Enoch Hall, were British natives who ultimately received places in the colony's government.[74] Nor did North Carolina's sons flock to other British centers of education. Of 58 southerners who attended Oxford or Cambridge between 1720 and 1776, not one came from the colony; Virginia sent 26, South Carolina 21, and Maryland 11.[75]

If education played only a minor role in the world of the colony's elite, so too did religion. Like less fortunate Carolinians, social leaders expressed little interest in the worldly obligations of spiritual salvation. Partly for this reason, it is difficult to determine the denominational affiliation of most men. Some were no doubt members of dissenting groups, but the majority were probably members of the Church of England.[76] Although individual expressions of piety were not unknown,[77] leading men did not do much to help bring religion to North Carolina, especially in their capacity as vestrymen. An Anglican missionary in New Hanover County in the 1760s, John MacDowell, found himself subjected to "the caprices and inconstancy of the Low minded penurious herd—be they the great, vulgar, or the small." Considering a move to the more inviting environs of Charleston, he wrote his superiors in England:

> I could give such an account of some of the Present Vestrymen here that after knowing the men . . . no body would be surprised that I am obliged to leave them[.] One of them declared that the money he is obliged to give to the maintaining a minister, he would rather give to a kind girl. Another is a person who has committed incest, with his own uncles widow and has a child by her which he owns publicly—another believes there is neither Hell or Devil, and there is here one gentleman of fortune in particular . . . whom I heard myself declare he could not believe in Jesus Christ and he despised the holy sacrament of the Lord's Supper.

John Garzia, the only Anglican minister in Beaufort County, wrote in 1742 of the problems of being "governed by twelve Vestry men, whose only endeavour is to hinder and obstruct the service of God, being performed, they themselves never coming to hear the service of God, and dissuading as much as possible others from it." He complained, in particular, that his salary amounted to only

£37 10s., and that he had not even received that for the past four years.[78]

Garzia's plight was common, for the provincial salaries allowed Anglican rectors remained low in later years. Through the efforts of Governor Dobbs, salaries were raised to £80 proclamation money in 1754, and by 1765 they amounted to £133 6s. 8d. proclamation money plus a glebe of three hundred acres or £20. Even then, however, as one minister testified, the "total amount" did not "exceed £76..13..4 sterling," a substantially smaller sum than clergymen received in other southern colonies.[79] Moreover, as illustrated by Garzia's unhappy circumstances, local notables in vestries were frequently reluctant to pay a rector's salary. John Barnett wrote that he possessed "no other security for the payment" of his stipend than his vestry's "*honor*," which he noted "is but a poor basis to build any great hopes on." James Moir, who officiated in Northampton County, complained at one point that his salary was seven years in arrears. "The establishment of a minister dependant on the caprice of a Vestry," Governor William Tryon observed in 1767, "is too precarious a device for the option of any man of real merit."[80]

Not surprisingly, given the limited funding supplied clergymen, churches also suffered from inattention and poor financing. Before 1750, public worship, when conducted, was ordinarily held in county courthouses.[81] Some structures were built in subsequent years, but as late as 1765 only five full-fledged churches existed in the entire province, and only the building in New Bern was in "good repair." Wilmington's church consisted of "walls only," Brunswick's, "only outside walls . . . and roofed." Those in Edenton and Bath were both "wanting considerable repairs."[82]

Undistinguished by spirituality, gentility, or philosophy, the men who formed North Carolina's elite shared priorities dictated by the configurations of an emerging society. More than anything else, the social leadership devoted its attention to material gain. While "the human mind, like an unweeded garden, has been suffered to shoot up in wild disorder," Jedediah Morse wrote of eighteenth-century North Carolinians, "each has been endeavouring to increase his fortune." Their "general topics of conversation" included "negroes, the prices of indigo, rice, tobacco, etc. They appear to have as little taste for the sciences as for religion." Similarly, William Dickson felt that the "Genius" of his neighbors in the upper Cape Fear was "not adapted to the study of learning and science. The most desirable object that people here have in view are interest and pleasure."[83]

Leading Carolinians were not all crude, grasping rustics. By the early 1770s, most had achieved a more cultivated life-style than their forebears had enjoyed. But they hardly constituted a mature aristocracy, even by the standards of the New World. They still devoted considerably more time to obtaining the material blessings of life than to expressing them in a genteel fashion or following other pursuits. Nathaniel Moore, who found "writing" to be "the most painfull Exercise . . . in the World," rarely did so except when "Business" was "the Object of it." William Blount's unflagging zeal for riches led him to chastise those who complained about "others, for making money to[o] fast." "I'm sure there is little Encouragement to die," wrote James Moir, "where Executors and Administrators seem to think of Nothing but dividing the Spoil." Samuel Johnston, Jr., expressed understandable caution over a currency transaction with anyone but a particular acquaintance because "very few others" could be trusted "for a large sum so long as a twelve Month." "If Dame fortune had dealt by me properly, I should have liked the trade of a Gentleman much," Henry Eustace McCulloh observed, "but hang thought and Care." Instead, he spent much of his time answering the "whisper" of "Mammon." "He is a surly Curr," he conceded, "but must be Obeyed."[84]

The roots of this acquisitive spirit are not easily identified. In some measure the weakness of such moderating influences as religion and gentility permitted it to flourish relatively unabated. Perhaps it resulted from the insecurity of an elite whose social position was at times not acknowledged by men with less wealth. Probably the continuing influx into the colony of ambitious individuals like James Murray, hoping to "push" their fortunes, also exerted an influence. This arriviste mentality introduced higher standards of achievement, and, though James Iredell thought himself and others "prisoners for life," few men, including Iredell, abandoned their quest for profits. Finally, an even more plausible possibility is that this thirst for riches was excited, but not quenched, by the contours of a slowly expanding economy that did not commonly yield large fortunes. Although small dirt farmers were not in a position to have aroused expectations, men of more wealth were particularly sensitive to the forces of an emergent commercial economy.[85] Understandably, they were not satisfied with their limited material accomplishments. Despite the growth of the economy, larger planters constantly bemoaned "the many Difficulties" they had "to struggle with."[86]

Ironically, by the 1760s, many colonial elites were beginning to lament the socially disruptive consequences of their affluence. From Virginia to Massachusetts, wealth and "luxury" were deemed to be causing a serious decline in moral standards. Provincial prosperity was thought to breed extravagance, spiritual apathy, and immorality. But North Carolina still felt the "Want of something better." Leading men worried less about their morals than about their deficient fortunes.[87]

Part II
Political Unrest

3   Property and Political Contention, 1729–1740

They engage in Party Affairs with so much Zeal.
—James Moir to [?], October 29, 1740

When North Carolina became a royal possession in 1729, its formal structure of government was fairly well defined. Established by instructions from the Lords Proprietors in 1663, the governing apparatus had been modified over the intervening decades by proprietary decree, legislative statute, and local custom. The only major change in the transition from proprietary status was that the ultimate seat of authority now lay in Whitehall and the crown.[1]

The governmental structure, though in some respects not fully matured in 1729, roughly approximated that of other royal colonies by the mid-eighteenth century. At the head of the provincial government stood the governor, who was appointed by the Privy Council as the king's direct representative. His far-ranging powers extended to judicial appointments, granting land, authenticating public documents, proroguing or dissolving local assemblies, and vetoing colonial legislation. The executive branch also included a handful of administrative officials, similarly appointed in London: a secretary, chief justice, attorney general, provost marshal, vice-admiralty judge, surveyor general, and a receiver general of quit-rents. As an advisory board of twelve members to the governor, the council also served in an executive capacity. In addition, many councillors sat as assistant justices on the General Court, the supreme judicial body, which in 1738 was joined by three circuit courts.

Appointed upon the governor's recommendation, the council further served as an upper house in the colony's bicameral legislature. The lower house, on the other hand, consisted of popularly elected representatives from counties and towns. The franchise was quite broad; voters were required to own only fifty acres of land. The lower house was less powerful in 1729 than most other colonial assemblies in relation to the governor and council, but it rose in stature over the years, particularly because of the forceful direction provided by its Speakers and other key leaders. By the third quarter of the eighteenth century, the house had largely achieved the same position of dominance in provincial affairs that its sister institutions had won elsewhere.

Local government in North Carolina revolved chiefly around county courts. Commissioned by the governor, their officers included justices of the peace, registers, clerks, coroners, and deputy provost marshals, who were replaced by sheriffs in 1738. These courts, though comparatively weak for many years, grew in competency and power during the decades following proprietary rule. Because of demographic growth and expanding settlement patterns, they acquired substantial influence by mid-century over local appointments, civil cases, grand juries, public buildings, taxation, ordinaries, and probating deeds. Another reason for their enhanced status was that many colonial leaders responsible for the assembly's steadily rising power had similarly sought to bolster provincial autonomy at the local level.

If little in its political machinery distinguished North Carolina from its fellow provinces, political configurations were notably different. Despite the panoply of institutions in the colony, it did not achieve the same degree of political institutionalization as other provinces. Government envinced little of the institutional autonomy and vitality[2] common to public life in eighteenth-century America. Especially during the early years of royal rule, North Carolina politics was characterized by frequent turmoil and intermittent violence. Disputes over land, the colony's major resource, and related controversies kept politics in a state of chronic confusion, as the commonweal fell victim to competing individuals and groups. Institutions often did not even function. When they did, they served only the narrow objectives of rival factions. Neither of the colony's first royal governors, George Burrington and Gabriel Johnston, was able to cope with the chaos, which arose partly from their conduct as self-interested servants of the crown. One was nearly shot, the other was forced to compromise his policies. Advancing their personal interests, they became both perpetrators and victims of Carolina's unruly public world.

Governor Burrington and Some Early Problems

The political life of George Burrington was anything but tranquil. He was born around 1682 in Devonshire, England, to a gentry family that expressed strong sympathies for William of Orange during the Glorious Revolution. He later became a captain in the British army, and in 1723 received an appointment as proprietary governor of North Carolina. His administration, however, was wracked by a personal dispute with Christopher Gale, the colony's chief justice, and lasted less than two years. Gale managed to arouse enough support within the provincial council to prompt Burrington's dismissal by the proprietors, who were already unhappy with his support of local interests. Burrington's second administration, as the first royal governor, extended from 1731 to 1734 and was even more turbulent. It ended with an assassination attempt and his replacement by Gabriel Johnston. Little is known of his later life in England, except that he kept a finger in Carolina politics and wrote some treatises on foreign policy and local affairs in London. In February 1759 he was murdered in a London park and his body cast into a nearby canal.[3]

Just as periodic misfortunes marred Burrington's career, so has he fared poorly at the hands of historians. One has written that he was "insolent, dictatorial, and abusive." Others have drawn attention to his "uncontrollable temper" and his "oppressive and arbitrary conduct."[4] As he certainly demonstrated on more than one occasion, especially during his second administration, he was petulant, authoritarian, and unscrupulous. But the preoccupation with his fiery style has seemed to preclude any sustained analysis of either his opponent's actions or the principal issues involved in his fall. Substantive matters, relating chiefly to land tenure, were at stake not only during Burrington's years as royal governor but also throughout the 1730s. An understanding of the ways in which many of the colony's leaders responded to these issues is fundamental to any comprehension of political configurations during the first decade of royal rule in North Carolina.

In February 1731, after a three-year stay in England, Burrington arrived in North Carolina to a favorable reception. In a special address to the king, the provincial grand jury applauded the new governor's "mildness and Generous Treatment" and "his humanity and Tenderness to all sorts of People." The Privy Council's choice was a happy one within most provincial circles. One of the major reasons was Burrington's previous efforts, in the mid-1720s, to develop the colony's uninhabited Cape Fear valley, which involved several personal trips at his own expense. In such an economically backward province, the opening of this new region had exerted a strong appeal among local leaders.[5]

Despite the apparent warmth of his welcome, a multitude of problems hampered Burrington from the very beginning. To start with, his appointment had not received the unstinting approval of all crown officers. Notwithstanding his strong ties to the powerful Duke of Newcastle, then secretary of state with jurisdiction over the colonies, some opposition had come from Martin Bladen, an active member of the Board of Trade and one of London's major patronage peddlers. Whether Bladen actually "disliked" Burrington or not, as one historian has written, he clearly saw North Carolina's change in government as a prime opportunity to reward several intimates with key posts. Bladen also had a personal interest in the colony's future, for he owned a substantial amount of property near Albemarle Sound.

In August 1730 a perplexed Burrington wrote Newcastle's secretary, "I waited upon the Lords Commissioners of Trade and shewed them my old list of Councellors without any names against Chief Justice, and Secretary, Coll: Bladen filled them up with his own hand before Mr. Pelham and Mr. Brudenell; I hope his Grace the Duke of Newcastle (my noble patron) will not be offended." For the critical offices of chief justice and senior member of the council,

Bladen had chosen William Smith, a young London attorney and an acquaintance of the secretary of the treasury, John Scrope. Only slightly less coveted was the position of provincial secretary, which Bladen gave to his brother-in-law, Nathaniel Rice, whom he also placed next in line to Smith on the council. Yet another appointment, over which Burrington exercised no control, was that of John Montgomery, a Scot, to be the new attorney general. Montgomery had been aided both by Bladen and Nathaniel Gould, an influential London banker.[6]

That Newcastle acquiesced in the face of these appointments may have stemmed from his tireless absorption in other matters at the time.[7] It is equally likely that Bladen's ample influence may have inhibited the still relatively new secretary of state from provoking a controversy within metropolitan ranks over a handful of offices that offered only modest rewards in a distant province. But Bladen's interference, by installing a trio of ambitious placemen who had direct ties to the Board of Trade firmly within Burrington's household, would exert considerable influence on the complexion of politics in North Carolina. At the very least, Bladen's appointees knew that Burrington's authority was uncertain and not above being challenged.

Another dilemma for Burrington was the necessity to confront several former enemies in the colony. Among those whose memory of earlier squabbles had not dimmed over the years were three outgoing proprietary officials: Chief Justice Gale, Receiver General William Little, and Secretary John Lovick. Probably with their aid, a last-minute effort was engineered in 1730 to prevent the governor's arrival. Expressing their fear that he would not forget "his old grudge against the Chief Justice," local residents sent an unsuccessful appeal to London authorities asking that the crown revoke its appointment. They also voiced chagrin that none of the current councillors had received places in the new administration.[8] In addition to the selections made by Bladen, other members of Burrington's new council mostly included placemen like James Stallard, Richard Eyans, and Joseph Jenoure, who lacked prior ties to the colony. Two notable exceptions, however, were Edmund Porter and John Baptista Ashe.

The son of a former proprietary official, Porter had apparently spent most of his early life in Virginia and the West Indies. He returned to North Carolina in 1725 and represented Chowan County in the lower house before obtaining the post of vice-admiralty judge in 1727. By any account, he was not a very savory character. Not only did he allegedly assault Sir Richard Everard, the colony's last proprietary governor, charge extortionate court fees, and beat a prisoner, but also in 1727 Peter Vantrump, a free black, complained that Porter had tried to enslave him.[9] Ashe had become Speaker of the lower house in the mid-1720s as a representative from Beaufort County, less than a decade after his arrival in North Carolina from England. An ambitious planter who maintained a keen interest in the Cape Fear region, he became a close friend of Burrington and managed his estate during his temporary residence in England.[10]

Still a third problem Burrington faced was that government in the colony under Governor Everard had practically come to a standstill during the final years of proprietary rule. Because of the transition to royal authority and the prospect of serving in a lame-duck administration, many provincial leaders simply neglected their customary responsibilities. A bewildering number of disputes that had plagued Everard's tenure as governor moved swiftly to the surface. "Of late years," reported one resident in 1731, "the Authority of Government has been suffered to sink so low and the Courts so much obstructed that Law and Justice seemed at a stand and but little business done." Disputes over the post of provost marshal between the governor and the council had blocked the execution of court writs and other legal documents, as had Everard's suspension at one point of Chief Justice Gale; "t'was very rare if any writt or other process by him signed were obeyed." When Benjamin Peyton, a deputy provost marshal, and a complement of eleven men attempted to arrest a ship carpenter in Bath, not only was their authority contested, but they were also set upon by a mob of twenty to thirty people. Further, the council refused to convene.

In March 1729 the governor's son, who disliked one of the General Court justices, attempted with the aid of an accomplice to kill one of the judge's friends by firing a "pistoll or pistolls" in his direction. The following year, an armed group who included John Lovick and Edmund Gale, the chief justice's brother, expressed their dissatisfaction with the conduct of Edmund Porter by breaking into his vice-admiralty court to "revel, drink, sing and dance stamp shout and alternately set up in the seat of Justice two mock Judges." Several months later, Porter and a company of men attacked Lovick's house in Edenton. It is little wonder that when Burrington finally arrived, he "found the Province in the greatest Confusion[,] the Government sunk so low that neither Peace or Order subsisted, the General Court suppressed, the Council set aside a year and half, [and] some of the Precinct Courts fallen."[11]

A final difficulty concerned two thorny issues pertaining to land that crown authorities expected Burrington to resolve. The first involved patents for immense quantities of land acquired by some of the colony's principal political leaders during the waning months of proprietary rule, despite injunctions by the proprietors that no land should be granted after 1724 except by special permission. Intended supposedly as payment for North Carolina's boundary commissioners, who had joined William Byrd in 1728 in surveying the border with Virginia, the patents were far in excess of any reasonable compensation. By 1730 not only had numerous patents for Cape Fear lands fallen into private hands, but also the exact location and amount of property in each grant was left unspecified. The culprits were "thirsty after an unreasonable Gain," according to Governor Everard. Those involved included Secretary Lovick; Receiver General William Little; Surveyor General Edward Moseley, who had played a dominant role in proprietary politics for more than twenty years as either Speaker of the lower house or as a councillor; several of Moseley's deputies, including John Baptista Ashe and Samuel Swann; and a handful of increasingly powerful South Carolinians, notably Maurice Moore and his brothers, Roger and Nathaniel.[12]

For a number of years, the Moore family had maintained an active interest in North Carolina. From 1723 to 1724, Maurice had even served in the council and in 1725 had been Speaker of the assembly. The Moores also enjoyed family ties with several prominent North Carolinians, including Moseley, Ashe, and Swann. What precipitated their involvement in the "blank patent" bonanza and their decision to carve out new estates in the Cape Fear was the devastating depression that gripped South Carolina in the mid-1720s. In 1726, when Britain temporarily ceased paying bounties for naval stores, exports sharply declined, and the colony approached a state of near-rebellion as planters faced the loss of their properties because of heavy taxes and their indebtedness to local merchants.[13]

Initially, Everard himself did not participate in the patent frauds, and in 1729 he strenuously protested the conduct of his subordinates to the crown. But anxious to capitalize on the fees accorded land grants and aware that his tenure as governor was limited, he soon cast his scruples aside. "He has . . . broke through such his Intentions," wrote a deputy official, "and now every day signs both Warrants and Patents."[14]

This massive exercise in property aggrandizement permitted a select group of men to engross "all the rich lands" in the Cape Fear. Contemporary estimates put the total at more than four hundred thousand acres. The problem became even more acute when several of the main beneficiaries began to hawk some of their patents throughout the colony. If the purchase prices were exorbitant, as later charged, the patents nevertheless carried low quitrents, ranging from 6d to 1s. per one hundred acres. Edward Moseley even attempted to sell six thousand acres to William Byrd, but the Virginian objected that the patent was probably illegal. "When a prudent man parts with his mony," he chastened Moseley, "he loves to do it safely."[15]

The blank-patent frauds alarmed royal officials, who, in their instructions to Burrington, urged that he conduct a full investigation. Because the crown had paid the imposing sum of £22,500 to the proprietors for both Carolinas, it was determined to protect its investment. Another means of achieving this goal was to strengthen the colony's dilapidated quitrent system, which had never yielded much revenue to the proprietors. The paltry sums collected had been all but absorbed by the provincial salaries of proprietary officials. But the Board of Trade now ordered Burrington to enforce the regular collection of quitrents and to establish new rents of 4s. sterling per one hundred acres. These were twice as high as the customary proprietary rate of 2s., which was also the rate in neighboring Virginia.[16]

In varying fashions, the crown's new land policies struck at the heart of North Carolina's struggling agricultural population. Land was the basis of the economy, and the imposition of new quitrents threatened an unexpected tax that many planters could ill afford to pay, especially in view of the chronic shortage of currency. Then, too, quitrents—combined with the possible invalidation of the blank patents—threatened the heady aspirations of men who viewed land aggrandizement, particularly in the Cape Fear, as a potential source of wealth in a colony not normally known for ready profits. Not only did the Cape Fear, which enjoyed comparatively better harbor facilities, offer advantages to plantation agriculture superior to those in the north, but it also afforded opportunities for land speculation, once its settlement began. "Many hundred poor People taking up small tracts of Land at a reasonable price," predicted Everard in June 1729, "will now be obliged to purchase the same at second hand and at a dear Rate, for that is the view in taking up such unreasonable Bodies of Land."[17]

Opposition Unleashed

Faced with governmental chaos, former enemies, subordinates whose loyalties extended to London, and some troublesome issues pertaining to land, Governor Burrington trod cautiously during his first months in office. Although he might have proceeded as a dutiful royal servant armed with the king's instructions, he chose instead to avoid conflict. Upon his arrival in North Carolina, he announced that he "freely forgave every body the injurys done" him "and advised others to do the same."[18] He was presented with an early opportunity, in fact, to retaliate against some of his former enemies. In the spring of 1731, with the vice-admiralty court fracas fresh in his mind, Edmund Porter solicited the governor's aid against Edmund Gale and John Lovick. Notwithstanding an earlier acquaintanceship, which culminated in Porter's recent appointment to the council, Burrington refused to take up his friend's cause.[19] Nor did he strike a stiff pose on the question of land tenure. He repeatedly expressed alarm to the crown that a 4s. quitrent would hinder the colony's growth and lessen government revenues. "It's reasonable to believe that if such Quitt Rents are advanced," he wrote the Board of Trade as early as March 1730, "the Inhabitants must of course judge themselves rather oppressed than relieved, which will deterr them from cultivating an increase of Lands."[20]

Despite Burrington's caution, a host of difficulties quickly plagued his administration. In April he convened his first assembly. The two houses at first exchanged warm greetings with the governor, who declared that they now had "a Governor that is intirely your Friend and Well Wisher." News that the crown intended to remit proprietary quitrent arrears and to accept new rents in proclamation money instead of sterling, which was much more scarce, no doubt improved the political climate. But the lower house soon insisted that quitrents be paid in provincial currency at a four to one discount to sterling or in tobacco or rice at the overrated value of "Eleven shillings per Hundred as an Equivalent for Proclamation Money." Furthermore, the house urged that the first collection not occur for nearly another two years.[21]

Equally upsetting to the harmony of this first session was Burrington's refusal to cooperate with the demands of blank-patent holders in the lower house led by Edward Moseley of Chowan County, who had been elected as Speaker. Although the governor agreed to transmit their protestations of innocence to imperial authorities, he declined to "use" his "Interest and Endeavours" to confirm their lands by provincial statute.[22] Disputes between the governor and the assembly over the appointment of a public treasurer and the payment of government fees and salaries in proclamation money only exacerbated an increasingly tense session, as did Burrington's decision not to sign warrants for the travel allowances normally permitted representatives because no law authorized those payments.[23]

Before angrily dissolving the assembly, which in five weeks did not pass a single bill, Burrington first tried to rally the council's support. But opposition within that body proved just as formidable. Miffed because Burrington had suggested that assistant judges should exercise more than mere advisory powers in the General Court, Chief Justice William Smith suddenly resigned his seat in the council on May 20. Joining Smith in his opposition to the governor were the other Bladen appointees, Rice and Montgomery, as well as John Baptista Ashe and Edmund Porter, who was irate over his earlier rebuff. "Instead of help and Assistance from His Majesty's Council and Officers . . . ," Burrington wrote in July, "I have had and still have them a weight upon me."[24]

Smith posed a particularly strong challenge to Burrington's rule. Within a matter of days after his resignation, he was soliciting funds to return to England to seek Burrington's dismissal. Not only did Smith strike a responsive chord among lower house members by voicing disapproval of a strong quitrent bill, but he also made "many Boasts of his great Interest in England." Indeed, as Burrington testily wrote the Board of Trade, "He has promised to procure the removal of myself and Several others of his Majesties officers and has already nominated our Successors."[25]

Against this backdrop of mounting opposition, Burrington suddenly found himself with little support. To make matters worse, two councillors, James Stallard and Richard Eyans, had never left England. Another, John Porter, was apparently on the verge of death, and two more, Matthew Rowan and Eleazer Allen, had yet to arrive in the colony.[26] Desperately seeking to boost his authority, Burrington turned to John Lovick and Edmund Gale, two former enemies, to whom he extended seats on the council on July 27, 1731 in violation of his instructions without the presence of a quorum in the upper house.[27]

Lovick, who had become a Chowan planter after his arrival in North Carolina during the first decade of the eighteenth century, had served as a councillor as well as provincial secretary during the 1720s. Of apparently humble English origins, he was a "man of no religion" and feared "not God nor man," according to Sir Richard Everard. Employing "his Money" as "his God," he had reportedly embezzled funds earmarked for a church in Currituck County in addition to participating in the blank-patent frauds. Nevertheless, because he was a member from Chowan in the recent assembly, his appointment to the council promised to bring Burrington some popular support.[28] Also an English native, Edmund Gale was both the brother of Christopher, the ex-chief justice, and a onetime assemblyman from Pasquotank. More significant, at least in boosting Burrington's standing in London, was Edmund's blood relation to Samuel Gale, a British customs commissioner.[29]

In return for the support of Lovick and Gale, Burrington subsequently suspended their old enemy, Edmund Porter, from his posts as councillor and vice-admiralty judge on the grounds that he had run a corrupt court. The governor also piously began to protest Lovick's innocence in the blank-patent controversy to royal authorities.[30] The new alliance was further cemented when Burrington supplemented a ten-thousand-acre estate he had acquired in

1730 from Edward Moseley with an additional forty to fifty thousand acres in blank patents, obtained apparently through Lovick's offices. Like his predecessor, Burrington succumbed to the temptations of the colony's burgeoning land market. The new tracts were situated near his older property next to the northeast branch of the Cape Fear, but they also overlapped with the claims of other blank patentees, including Moseley, Roger Moore, Samuel Swann, and several others whose strength resided in the lower house.[31]

These conflicting grants prompted an acrimonious struggle between what were now two blank-patent factions. As much as possible, Burrington attempted to undercut his adversaries' claims. In addition to making repeated complaints to crown authorities about the counterfeit titles of "Moseley and his Kindred,"[32] he aggressively contested their validity within the colony. During a tour of the Cape Fear in the fall of 1731, Burrington discovered a "logg house" on his property that a kinsman of Moseley and the Moores, John Porter, Jr., had recently erected "as an affront." He promptly ordered several slaves to set the structure afire. Upon returning to Edenton, Burrington summoned Porter, Moseley, and Maurice Moore to appear before the council in January 1732 to account for "every Tract" they possessed along the Cape Fear. He also ordered the attendance of deputy surveyors employed by Moseley when he was surveyor general under the proprietors. Only Moore and Porter appeared on the appointed day, and neither was able to satisfy the governor with their responses. For the time being the issue subsided, but in July Moseley requested a new land warrant for an additional 3,100 acres. The council approved his petition in October, but to his chagrin he did not receive the warrant for more than six months. More alarming to him still, he received title for a tract in the frontier county of Bladen, far removed from the Cape Fear River site he had requested. Meantime, according to one account, several of the governor's "creatures," including Robert Halton, a councillor, had been dispossessing Cape Fear settlers of their lands with new warrants.[33]

By late 1732, personal ambitions and popular resentment over quitrents had combined with fears over the governor's land schemes to produce a crescendo of opposition as well as several appeals to Newcastle and the Board of Trade. One of the complainants was Edmund Porter, who protested his earlier suspensions and the appointments of Lovick and Gale to the council. Porter also pointed to Burrington's fraudulent property acquisitions in the Cape Fear, as did Nathaniel Rice, John Montgomery, and John Baptista Ashe in two joint memorials. Moreover, this trio of disaffected officials, aided by Moseley and Maurice Moore, alleged numerous other instances of misgovernment. These ranged from Burrington's physical presence in council meetings to his appointment of unqualified individuals to the General Court. Undoubtedly, some of their accusations were accurate. Others, such as the charge that Burrington had confiscated some slaves stolen from the Spanish at Saint Augustine, probably had little factual basis.[34]

If their testimony is to be believed, Burrington had also personally abused several leading men who opposed him. When, for instance, Ashe complained that two of his horses had been misbranded by Burrington's servants, the governor allegedly "flew into a violent passion, and using much scurrilous and reproachful Language . . . came up with his face close to Mr. Ashe's and shaking his head at him in a jeering taunting tone and manner called him . . . pretty fellow, very pretty fellow!" Ashe was later briefly jailed after Burrington sued him for slander. Burrington evidently had Edward Moseley temporarily imprisoned as well, for remarks he had made during a session of the General Court.[35] However subdued Burrington's behavior was at first, his correspondence similarly reflected an increasing lack of tact and moderation. Once his authority had begun to decline, he became steadily more implacable and less given to conciliation. Of his nemesis, William Smith, Burrington wrote the Board of Trade in September 1731 that he had "left the Country with the Character of a Silly, rash boy, a busy fool, and engregious [sic] Sot." Burrington also suspended Smith from his post as chief justice.[36]

While his antagonists were trying to discredit the governor in London, they also kept the province in a furor in order to undermine his position at home. Ashe, Rice, and several others rarely attended meetings of the council and the court of chancery, which caused frequent postponements. When Burrington again convened an assembly in April 1732, it had to be dissolved because of the lack of a quorum in the upper house. Furthermore, each new appointment he made was hotly contested, thus impeding the effectiveness of crown officers. Perhaps for this reason, all four assistant judges attached to the General Court had resigned their commissions by the fall of 1732. As it was, crown officers were totally without salaries because Rice, the deputy receiver general, made no attempt to collect quitrents. In the meantime, some county courts had not sat, either because Rice, in his position as provincial secretary, refused to appoint qualified clerks—as Burrington alleged—or out of opposition to the governor himself.[37]

Burrington was fully cognizant of his rapidly dwindling authority, and in his letters lashed out at his opponents in England as well as those in North Carolina with a remarkable absence of restraint. "I hope," he wrote an English acquaintance at one point, "that you . . . and the rest of my friends have had an eye to my Affairs in England[,] haveing so dangerous an enemy as Bladen." He also tried to put the best face on provincial affairs. North Carolina, he reported to Newcastle in November 1732, "is now in a quiet orderly State and flourishing condition." A few months later, he assured the Board of Trade, "Peace, and good order subsist throughout the whole Province."[38]

While attempting to repair his image at Whitehall, Burrington also tried to build some local support in the lower house to counter the strength of Speaker Moseley. Burrington was hardly a populist; among other things, he commonly complained of the insufficiency of men in North Carolina fit to be government officials and contended that nonfreeholders voted in assembly elections. He, nevertheless, began to visit a number of counties, publicly attacking the characters of his adversaries. "He takes occasion at Publick Meetings of People, as at Courts, or the like, before great Audiences, of reflecting on, abusing, reviling, detracting and defaming Gentlemen without any regard to Truth," complained several who were stung by his remarks. His travels may well have aroused some sympathy, for a petition from two northern counties later applauded the "many good Offices" which he "has done for the province."[39]

In another tactic designed to augment his power, Burrington between November 1731 and November 1732 created three new counties: two in the Cape Fear valley, and one bordering the Albemarle region. Probably hoping, as his foes charged, that these counties might aid his efforts to get "a Majority of his creatures in the Lower House," Burrington called for a new house to meet the following July.[40] When it convened, however, the assembly offered little support. Of the thirty-eight representatives, sixteen were new, but Moseley remained as Speaker, and the house admitted no members from the three counties. It also castigated Burrington's arbitrary creation of these new jurisdictions, reasserted its opposition to the payment of quitrents in proclamation money or sterling, condemned the governor's appointment of "Evil and wicked Officers," and extended its gratitude to William Smith, who had recently returned from his labors in England. On top of all this, the lower house ordered the arrests of Robert Halton, for not having filed a sufficient security bond as tax collector for Port Roanoke, and William Little—whom Burrington had appointed as chief justice in October 1732—for insulting the assembly.[41]

By this time, Burrington's days as governor clearly were numbered. In fact, as early as the spring of 1732, eager place-seekers in England had begun to offer themselves in his stead. Despite the governor's efforts to minimize the colony's political chaos, the complaints of his enemies attested to a contrary set of circumstances, as did his unpopularity with the lower house. Of additional importance, no doubt, were Smith's toils in London through Martin Bladen at the Board of Trade to obtain the governor's removal.[42]

In March 1733 the Duke of Newcastle named a new governor, without even giving Burrington a chance to submit a last-minute appeal. Nonetheless, as one historian has written, "If Bladen could bring down a governor . . . , he could not make a new one." The appointment went to Gabriel Johnston, a Scottish professor of ancient languages at St. Andrews University, who had connections with Lord Anson, the Earl of Bath, and Lord Wilmington, president of the Privy Council. Because of Wilmington's support of his candidacy, Johnston experienced little difficulty in obtaining the approval of Newcastle and Bladen.[43]

Before Johnston's arrival toward the end of 1734, conditions in North Carolina deteriorated. Inasmuch as his salary of £700 per annum, like those of other provincial officials, consisted of uncollected quitrent revenues, Burrington was deeply in debt. "Haveing lived in this Province some years without receiving any mony from the King, or the Country," he wrote Newcastle, "[I] was constrained to sell not only my household goods, but even linnen, plate and Books, and mortgage my Lands, and stocks."[44] Moreover, though the assembly met again in November 1733, it had to be prorogued when an insufficient number of councillors appeared.[45] Worse still, some provincial leaders, however pleased by the news of Burrington's impending departure, chose not to wait for his successor. In the spring of 1734, a severe illness temporarily disabled the governor. So frenzied was the opposition to him that Nathaniel Rice, who was still a councillor, seized this opportunity to establish his authority over the province. On April 15 in Edenton, he appointed himself as "President and Commander in Chief" in the presence of his cohorts William Smith and John Montgomery. Although this action was patently illegal, the three cited Burrington's "departure" from the province as just cause, and Rice called for the full council to meet in May.[46]

Burrington, of course, had not left North Carolina, nor was he inclined quietly to acquiesce in such a bald grasp for power. Few records remain to suggest what happened to the reins of government during the following months except for a brief note from the governor, dated June 1, that "my escapeing death was unexpected by all who saw me." He might better have remained in bed. Toward summer's end, Rice, Smith, Montgomery, and some "confederates" tried to shoot him. Escaping the attempted assassination with the aid of some friends, Burrington immediately suspended Rice and Montgomery from their offices, and a court ordered the arrests of all three men. The provost marshal in Chowan County, who was doubtless a Burrington sympathizer, also allegedly tried to imprison and murder the culprits, but they fled across the border into Virginia. Deeply embittered, Burrington himself left the colony for England shortly after Johnston's arrival.[47]

"To perplex the Government"

The appointment of Gabriel Johnston seemed to bode well for the province. He was, after all, a distinguished academician, not a former soldier who had an authoritarian bearing like his predecessor.[48] Nor was he given to fits of temper, but instead evinced a more reasoned approach to politics. In an attempt to divorce his administration from the past, Johnston, soon after his arrival in November 1734, issued a proclamation reinstating all officers whom Burrington had suspended from their posts. Once again William Smith became chief justice and Edmund Porter vice-admiralty judge. Both men also received seats in the council, as did other local leaders such as Nathaniel Rice, Roger Moore, and Edward Moseley. Upon convening his first assembly, Johnston also openly condemned the "disorder and Confusion" Burrington's conduct had caused.[49]

For the time being, these tactics met with success. Both houses answered the governor's plea for "decency Temper and Moderation" with expressions of gratitude and promises of future support. The assembly even granted Johnston £1,300 North Carolina currency for travel and lodging expenses, though it had awarded Burrington nothing during the four years of his administration. It also voted Smith £1,000 "for his former Services . . . in Going to England."[50] But, as Johnston quickly discovered, by so confidently assuming that royal government in North Carolina merely called for exemplary leadership, he had too readily placed the entire onus of guilt upon "the unhappy conduct" of his "predecessor." "Upon my first beginning to do business here," he later lamented, "I imagined like most young beginners, that with a little assistance from home, I should be able to make a mighty change in the face of affairs."[51]

The first hint of future turmoil came later in the assembly session after Johnston had urged that past deficiencies in collections made the passage of a satisfactory quitrent law imperative. On this issue, as well as with the blank patents, the crown was as determined as ever to protect its interests. Both houses seemed willing to comply with the governor's appeal, but disagreement soon arose over the value of certain commodities that Johnston had reluctantly agreed to accept as forms of payment. More seriously, a majority of councillors withheld their approval of a lower house bill, after blank patent holders had "tryed all manner of Arts to gett a Clause in this Bill to confirm their Grants." Inasmuch as no resolution was in sight, Johnston prorogued the assembly on March 1, 1735, and in his closing address put the blame squarely on the blank patentees, whom he characterized as "a few Men who have no hopes of Screening themselves or having their Crimes pass undetected, but by keeping the Country in the same embroiled and unsettled Condition, which first gave them an Opportunity of Committing their frauds."[52]

Previous political alignments were shifting rapidly over the issue of land. Whereas property disputes had created one stumbling block for Burrington's administration, they now assumed overwhelming significance as a source of contention, not only between the governor and the lower house but also among members of the old anti-Burrington faction in the council. Smith and Rice forgot their earlier opposition to crown land policies and lined up staunchly behind Johnston and several other councillors in support of traditional imperatives relating to quitrents and blank patents. In view of London's firm insistence that these matters be resolved and in view of Johnston's strong English connections, it would have been foolhardy for the councillors to have done otherwise. In the other camp were Moseley and Moore. Both exerted considerable influence in the lower house and had a big stake in seeing that quitrents were collected only after their fraudulent patents were confirmed. So deep was the enmity between them and their former allies that in early 1735, when Smith openly expressed his disapproval of blank patents, Moseley struck his face in front of a crowd of councillors and assemblymen in Edenton. Smith returned the blow before onlookers separated them.[53]

Supported by his friends in the council, Johnston ordered Moseley's prosecution at the next session of the General Court and imposed a bond of £1,000 proclamation money. In addition, the governor embarked upon a series of measures in the coming months to compel obedience to the crown. In March he appointed a South Carolinian, Eleazer Allen, receiver general of quitrents, instead of relying upon a single collector for both Carolinas, which had been customary in the past; and made Smith chief baron of the exchequer, who was charged with prosecuting fraudulent property claims. When Johnston heard that Moseley and the Moore family were burning lightwood and boxing trees on unpatented land for tar, pitch, and turpentine, thus making "it unfit for anybody to take up," he offered a reward of £20 North Carolina currency for information leading to their arrests. Further, he announced that crown officers would begin to collect quitrents, despite the assembly's refusal to provide the necessary legislation. Finally, he wrote the Board of Trade and requested an official condemnation of all blank patents. "There wants little else to terminate all disputes about land," he counseled.[54]

At this juncture, Johnston's opposition to blank patents reflected the sincere concerns of a loyal servant of the crown. "I thank God," he commented in July 1735, "I have no Quarrel with any Body in this Country upon my own account. If I have any Enemies they are Enemies to the just Rights and Revenues of the Crown."[55] At the same time, by not acceding to the demands of his adversaries, he, like Burrington before him, was damaging his own fortune because his salary was entirely dependent upon quitrent collections. But by late 1735, the governor had acquired an additional reason for wanting the counterfeit Cape Fear titles voided.

Initially, Johnston evinced some interest in obtaining property in the colony. Insofar as he hoped to acquire tracts in the yet undeveloped backcountry, "a great way behind the settlements towards the mountains," his designs were reasonably modest. "I do not doubt getting a pretty good estate in this government," he wrote Lord Wilmington in December 1734, "without doing the least injury to any person or occasioning any complaint."[56] The governor's aspirations, however, soon changed, owing to the land scheming of a shrewd friend, Henry McCulloh, a prosperous London merchant of Scottish descent. He had helped finance Johnston's trip to the colony. Ever intent on economic gain, he also petitioned the Privy Council in February 1736 for two tracts of land in North Carolina comprising a total of 132,000 acres. The first tract lay at the head of the northwest Cape Fear, and the other bordered the river's northeast branch. Although, much to Whitehall's liking, his ostensible object was to settle hundreds of foreign Protestants on these lands and thereby spur North Carolina's growth, McCulloh clearly hoped to reap an enormous profit.

The Privy Council approved these initial grants in the spring of 1736, and in little more than a year made an even more spectacular grant of 1,200,000 acres to a group of London merchants and other investors headed by McCulloh. All these machinations received Johnston's endorsement, no doubt in part because he stood to acquire 60,000 acres himself. In fact, in November 1735, once he learned of his friend's intentions, he approved a preliminary grant of land in the Cape Fear to Samuel Woodward, McCulloh's resident agent. McCulloh then sold selected parcels to investors "who were his particular acquaintance," such as Arthur Dobbs, an Irish politician, who acquired 6,000 acres.[57]

The blank-patent holders along the Cape Fear River were under-standably suspicious of McCulloh's ambitions. Already anxious over the uncertain status of their property, they now perceived this new threat to their dominance in the valley with a mixture of "dread and confusion." James Murray, a young Scot who had re-cently arrived in the colony and enjoyed McCulloh's financial sup-port, wrote his benefactor in May 1736:

> I cannot help giving you an instance how much some gentle-men here endeavour to defeat all the Governors Designs for settling the country. Roger Moore I am told has wrote to Mr. Dobbs that it will not be his interest to concern himself in land here. . . . His view in which is that if the Irish came over here they will be a weight against him in the Assembly and will by Cultivating the land confirm Mr. Dobbs right to what he would be content to take the advantage of a lapse of, in case a new Governor should be appointed, which all the blank patent gentry are in great hopes of.[58]

In addition to this emerging rivalry over land, a related contest arose between the town of Brunswick, at the Cape Fear's mouth, where many of Johnston's opponents held property—including the Moores and Moseley, who had recently moved his residence from Chowan—and the newer port of Newton, fifteen miles upriver. First settled in 1733, Newton soon attracted a number of immi-grants—aspiring merchants and planters alike—interested in tap-ping its potential as an export center. These included William Faris and Thomas Clark from England; James Murray from Scotland; John Sampson from Ireland; Richard Eagles from South Carolina; Daniel Dunbibin and Robert Walker from New York; and various others. Governor Johnston not only approved Newton's official establishment in March 1735 and purchased a lot there, but he also subsequently ordered that several government offices, including the court of exchequer and a circuit branch of the General Court, convene in the new settlement. This fueled what one observer termed a "great emulation between the two towns."[59] Brunswick's backers had initially held great hopes for their village, which Hugh Meredith, a visitor from Pennsylvania, described in 1731 as "likely to be a Place of Trade, and the Seat of Government." At the time, however, it was but a "poor, hungry, unprovided Place, consisting of not above 10 or 12 scattered mean Houses." Newton's subsequent growth was sufficient to pose a clear menace. "The last will be first in a little time," predicted Murray in 1736.[60]

The efforts of Johnston to regulate the colony's land system achieved a measure of success inasmuch as some quitrents were collected for the first time in years. Toward the end of 1735, he enthusiastically reported to the Board of Trade, the "people pay very quietly.... The collecting his Majesty's Rents with so much Spirit as has been done in this Province is ... the best method of getting a good Quit Rent law next Assembly." "The only remains of faction in this Colony," he added, "is kept up by Mr. Moseley and the Moors, the principall proprietors of the Blank Patents." By the fall of 1736, collectors had received more than £4,200 sterling out of the arrears that had accumulated since 1729, which was "more than was Collected ... During all the time" North Carolina "was Held by the Lords Proprietors." According to one report, a frustrated Roger Moore and his family even planned to move to Virginia.[61]

But opposition to Johnston was already gaining strength. By October 1735 the blank patentees had acquired two men to represent their cause in London. One was Samuel Wragg, a Charleston merchant, who had previously been an agent for South Carolina. A more unusual spokesman was none other than ex-governor George Burrington. Embraced by his former rivals in the cause of protecting their property holdings as well as his own, he submitted a lengthy appeal to the Board of Trade attacking Johnston's administration while defending all the blank-patent claims.[62] Both Wragg and Burrington helped to stave off a definitive decision on the question, which caused Johnston to complain on several occasions that imperial authorities were dragging their feet. Acting as Johnston's representative in London, Henry McCulloh similarly urged that crown officials lend Johnston more support.[63]

Burrington was also busy on other fronts. While in London, he lobbied for the removal of William Smith as chief justice. One of Johnston's firmest supporters and Burrington's inveterate enemy, Smith made a likely target. As chief baron of the exchequer, he was also considered to be the "firebrand, and chief instrument" of the blank patentees' "hardships."[64] His intended replacement was

Daniel Hanmer, nephew of Sir Thomas Hanmer, former Speaker of the House of Commons. In the fall of 1734 Burrington had appointed Hanmer as chief justice, but upon Johnston's arrival and Smith's reinstatement Hanmer had been suspended and briefly imprisoned.[65]

Burrington's efforts to unseat Smith might have succeeded if Hanmer had not blundered badly. On October 30, 1736, at an Edenton bonfire celebrating the king's birthday, the prospective chief justice became so intoxicated that he publicly announced his claim to Smith's office. Hanmer railed that neither Johnston nor Smith, were they in England, would be "worthy to Wipe his Shoes." Even worse, he claimed to have "orders and Instructions from Mr. Burrington," and that Smith, Nathaniel Rice, John Montgomery, and Edmund Porter would all be punished.[66]

Hanmer's drunken bravado might have been ignored in more tranquil times, but in North Carolina's uncertain political climate it was tantamount to treason. Within days, Hanmer was hauled before Smith and the rest of the General Court on charges of disturbing the peace and subverting the government. What began as a hearing degenerated into a shouting match between Smith and Moseley, who, as an assistant justice, quickly rose to Hanmer's defense. Haranguing the courtroom crowd with "Great vehemence," Moseley declared that Hanmer's statements had been no worse than "what a Great Many others had Said" about the government. For his part, Hanmer claimed that crown authorities had never intended to appoint Smith in the first place.[67]

Over Moseley's protests, the General Court finally succeeded in indicting Hanmer, and, at least for the time being, Smith's position remained secure.[68] But, in the meantime, Johnston's opponents had continued to assault his authority in yet other ways. Blank-patent holders still lay claim to valuable Cape Fear lands by burning lightwood in defiance of the governor's proclamation. Further, they paralyzed the government by continuing to command majority support in the lower house. "If the Governor's friends are the majority . . . it will be a great step towards the Settling the Country," James Murray had written of assembly elections scheduled for the summer of 1736. But the new assembly remained adamant in its opposition. Because the patent issue was undecided, it refused to consider any legislation, much less the passage of a suitable quitrent act, when it met in September. Despite several requests, it even refused to meet with the governor; instead, members of the house flooded the Privy Council with complaints about his conduct. In addition, the following March the lower house ordered the arrests of crown officers who had dared to distrain on several plantations for nonpayment of quitrents, and Moseley, who had acquired the colony's quitrent records, boldly refused to relinquish them. "All business," Johnston grimly reported in June 1737, "is at a stand here."[69]

Through a variety of stratagems, the blank patentees had succeeded in substantially broadening their base of support. This came about because of a reservoir of resentment over quitrents, aggravated by assorted rumors of widespread distrainments, Johnston's impending departure, and a possible reduction in rents. Further, large numbers of counterfeit titles, carrying quitrents of only 6d. to 1s., had by that time been sold to people in northern counties. What support was not acquired through such means was perhaps gained through questionable electioneering practices, as William Smith later alleged.[70] "The bulk of the people are well inclined," remarked Eleazer Allen, "but their understandings are imposed upon by a few designing men" who "leave no stone unturned to perplex the Government."

In defending the patentees to London officials, Samuel Wragg admitted as much when he described their uncertain titles as "one of the Great Causes of the present uneasiness" in North Carolina. Johnston himself despaired by mid-1737 that without "some vigorous declaration from home, or an independent company, it will be impossible to keep things long in any tolerable order." In a letter to Lord Wilmington, he angrily declared that North Carolinians "are a standing proof that refined fraud and dextrous circumvention are not confined to courts, and the politer societies of men, but may be equally found among the meanest, most rustick and squalid part of the species." Referring to Moseley, he affirmed, "Among them a cheat of the first magnitude is treated with all the distinction and regard which is usually paid to men of merit, and conspicuous virtue in other parts of the world."[71]

So excited were his opponents now that Johnston accused the blank patentees of trying to incite a rebellion. What seems to have been a preposterous allegation gained some credence in September 1737 when a frenzied body of five hundred men from the counties of Edgecombe and Bertie started to march on Edenton, mistakenly assuming that a planter had been imprisoned for not paying his quitrents. A major confrontation within five miles of the capital was narrowly averted only after the mob learned that the arrest involved another matter and that the man had already been released. Even then, "they threatened the most cruel usage to such persons as durst come to demand any quitt rents of them for the future." Nor was any force capable of punishing the rioters available to Johnston.

Given this climate of opposition, quitrent collections noticeably suffered, declining "to a very trifle." From September 1737 to September 1738, receivers obtained only £381 sterling, less than half the sum collected during the preceding twelve months. Provincial officers, who were largely dependent on these collections for their salaries, once again found themselves in dire financial straits. Johnston himself complained that he had not received £200 sterling during his four years in North Carolina, despite a salary of £1,000 sterling.[72]

Conciliation and Renewed Strife

Although he had doggedly opposed the blank-patent men for several years, Johnston ultimately resigned himself to striking a compromise. His requests for aid had won only limited support among crown officials. In September 1735 the Board of Trade had decided to submit the blank-patent question to Attorney General Dudley Ryder. With his report still pending, the board's secretary, Allured Popple, wrote Johnston nearly two years later, "Altho' their Lordships may generally approve of your sentiments upon the subject, yet . . . My Lords do not think proper to send you any directions concerning the said Patents."[73]

If London had provided more encouragement, Johnston might have persisted in his refusal to validate the patents. But, faced with the steady erosion of his authority and worried perhaps by his dwindling finances, he could no longer permit government to remain stalemated. Further, by 1738, he had divorced himself from Henry McCulloh's land scheme in the Cape Fear, which had created an additional obstacle to any settlement with the blank-patent men. Instead of laying out 1,200,000 acres of McCulloh's property in 12,500-acre parcels in the Cape Fear as McCulloh directed, Johnston in the fall of 1737 had instructed Matthew Rowan, the surveyor general, to survey the grants in much larger tracts in the distant backcountry. The closest tract to any habitation lay a full 100 miles from the coast and nearly 150 miles above the mouth of the Cape Fear River.[74]

It is not clear why Johnston chose to defy McCulloh's instructions. Perhaps he did so with an eye toward compromise. It may also be that he sought to capitalize on the fees that would accrue from a subsequent resurveying of the land into smaller tracts. Further, Johnston might have been upset that he had yet to receive title to his own property from McCulloh. As late as March 1740, he complained to Wilmington, "I could at present dispose of the 60,000 acres of land . . . , but I have neither gott a deed for that land from Mr. Mucculloh, nor so much as his obligation which he gave."[75]

When the assembly met in February 1739, Johnston was fully prepared to seek an accommodation, as were his adversaries, who were by now no doubt less optimistic over the chances of his speedy dismissal, despite their best efforts. Under the terms of an agreement reached that session, the blank patentees were assured titles to upwards of 150,000 acres of prime land in the Cape Fear at the reduced quitrent rate of 6d. to 1s. per one hundred acres. Once that matter was resolved, the lower house approved an act establishing quitrents at 4s., payable in provincial currency at 10 to 1 to sterling or in a limited number of commodities, such as tobacco and hemp. The act represented a significant achievement for the governor because the currency to sterling exchange rate was higher than he had ever requested in the past. "We are now to Pay our Quit-rents at ten Currency for one Sterling," commented one resident, "whereas before We Grumbled at 7 for one." Also, commodities specified in the act were deliberately undervalued, so that "no person will offer any of them in payment who can . . . raise as much Gold and silver." Understandably, Johnston exulted, "The foundations of peace and good order are at last so firmly laid."[76]

Despite the accord reached by all parties, lingering animosities prevailed among members of the blank-patent faction. After achieving a limited victory, they were more confident in their opposition to the governor. "There are a certain set of Men in the Province," James Murray later asserted, "who are never to be Satisfied if they have not the Chief Management of Affairs."⁷⁷ Their enmity once again fastened upon Chief Justice Smith, who had remained one of Johnston's most loyal supporters in the council. When the assembly next met in November 1739, Maurice Moore of New Hanover County intended to propose Smith's impeachment on a multitude of grounds, ranging from jury-packing to exacting extortionate fees.⁷⁸

But, by this time, Johnston's administration had made inroads in attracting lower-house support. For one thing, settlement of the quitrent controversy deprived the blank-patent men of a popular issue. Further, Smith's antagonists would later charge that, as chief justice, he extended "distinguishing Marks" of "grace and favour" to gain adherents.⁷⁹ Outright patronage may also have been a key factor, especially in the case of the lower house's Speaker, John Hodgson of Chowan County, who six months earlier had become the colony's vice-admiralty judge to replace the deceased Edmund Porter. Hodgson had already shown that his political loyalties could be bought, when Burrington had appointed him as attorney general in September 1734, following John Montgomery's quick departure for Virginia. In any event, before the impeachment articles could even be introduced, the lower house broke up when Hodgson and three other members suddenly withdrew from the assembly chambers, thus preventing the necessary majority of representatives for a quorum. Violence may even have flared first, for Hodgson was later charged with assaulting Montgomery, who was by this time an anti-Smith representative from Tyrrell County.⁸⁰

Upon dismissing the assembly, Johnston called for new elections in hopes that Smith's backing might be augmented. The strategy proved to be successful. Smith's foes alleged that he and his friends "more or less" influenced "every Election throughout the whole Province." More enthusiastic over the outcome was one of the chief justice's backers, who observed that, though "Mr. Moore and friends" retained seats in "three Southern Counties," their "Power" elsewhere was "Declining Dayly."⁸¹

Once the new assembly convened in February 1740, the impeachment drive further stalled when Speaker Hodgson allowed only three days for the summoning of witnesses, several of whom lived more than a hundred miles away. In a last-ditch effort to salvage his cause, Maurice Moore insisted that the chamber doors of the lower house remain open so that "all the Inhabitants" could be "present to be Eye and Ear Witnesses of the Conduct of their Representatives." This attempt to arouse popular sentiment failed miserably, however, as did the subsequent publication of a pamphlet depicting the "arbitrary Attempts of Men in Power." Moore and his followers failed to understand that ordinary settlers, as in the 1737 fight over quitrents, could be aroused only when their own interests perceptibly converged with those of their leaders; otherwise, they remained indifferent to the political tempests of wealthier men. In the end, after nine hours of debate, a majority of the forty representatives in attendance voted to acquit Smith by a margin of six votes.[82]

There was one curious by-product of the abortive impeachment effort. One of its leaders, Richard Everard, Jr., a representative of Bladen County and son of the ex-governor, suggested that the house pass a bill "to prevent Bribery and Corruption in Elections." The bill might have served a useful purpose. Throughout the preceding decade, numerous allegations had been made of election irregularities, including charges recently brought against Everard himself for procuring unqualified voters and committing other illegalities. A 1735 petition from a group of settlers in Bertie and Edgecombe counties claimed that Governor Burrington's opponents had once packed "an Assembly" because "many" counties "were not Advised of their Elections Untill the very day of Electing," and Burrington himself complained that "Burgessing has been for some years a source of lyes and occasion of disturbances." But, because of a seeming lack of interest, or perhaps outright opposition, Everard's proposed bill was never even prepared, much less enacted.[83]

On the heels of the Smith controversy, a related dispute arose concerning the towns of Brunswick and Newton. During the preceding years, this contest had continued to inflame the lower Cape Fear. In 1736 Newton loyalists had tried but failed to convince the assembly to pass an act of incorporation for their town, but they were now ready to exploit their antagonists' evident weakness in the lower house. Thus, when William Bartram introduced a fresh bill granting the town, under the name of Wilmington, a seat in the assembly, it received lower-house approval. When the bill came before the upper house, however, an even split emerged between its four proponents—William Smith, Robert Halton, Matthew Rowan, and James Murray—and Brunswick's supporters—Edward Moseley, Roger Moore, Eleazer Allen, and Nathaniel Rice. On this issue, the last two men had abruptly chosen to desert their onetime allies. But, claiming that his position as senior member permitted him a second vote, Smith gave the council's assent, whereupon the bill also received the governor's approbation. The four Brunswick councillors complained vigorously both to Johnston and to the Board of Trade.[84] Meeting with no success at either level, they spent the next several years contesting their rivals within the confines of the Cape Fear, "each of them," an observer wrote in 1742, "opposing the other to the utmost of their power." One result was that the appointment of a crown officer, because of his town loyalties, was disputed; and Roger Moore even tried to obstruct the shipping of Wilmington commodities through the Cape Fear's mouth.[85]

On several fronts, then, the original blank-patent men, relegated by 1740 to a small clique associated with the town of Brunswick, had lost much of their influence over provincial politics. For a decade after the institution of royal government, they had been in the thick of factional strife. They had posed sharp challenges to Burrington, who ultimately joined their ranks; and, afterward, to Johnston, who was forced to compromise. In the following decade, they lost their identity as a distinct faction—not, however, because their zest for political combat had been exhausted, but because a realignment of forces merged their interests with those of Johnston and their Wilmington adversaries.

Sources of Disorder

If by mid-1740 politics appeared to be attaining a degree of stability, at least on the provincial level, the first decade of royal rule in North Carolina had rarely been free of disorder. One governor was nearly assassinated, whereas his successor thought a company of British troops might be necessary to restore order.

These political battles, to some degree, reflected an emerging constitutional struggle between the privileges of the colony's lower house and the prerogatives of the crown. Various scholars have noted this situation, no doubt because the lower house occasionally couched its opposition to both Burrington and Johnston in the language of local rights and liberties.[86] When Burrington, for example, attempted to establish three new counties in 1731 and 1732, an assembly committee protested that such "a Method of enlarging the Number of Assembly Men . . . is not agreeable to the Constitution" and that "the Representatives of the People are the proper Judges what Encrease is necessary."[87] On the other hand, leading men who voiced popular principles at times altered their sentiments to meet new circumstances. William Smith, who championed lower-house rights during Burrington's administration, later became an ardent defender of imperial imperatives when a change of governors occurred. Similarly, some of the same blank-patent men who joined in condemning Burrington as a source of "Tyrany and Oppression,"[88] ultimately welcomed his support. Moreover, because of the general scarcity of division lists, it is difficult to know how unified the lower house normally was. By the late 1730s, at least, it clearly was not unified—as one extant list of roll-call votes attests. For the most part, constitutional differences, when they did arise, seem to have masked more fundamental conflicts.

More disruptive of provincial stability was the political incompetence of the colony's first royal governors. Neither Burrington nor Johnston was equipped with the necessary expertise to execute London's instructions, which in themselves posed formidable problems. Because of his domineering temper and reckless actions, Burrington was especially inept. Further, despite their roles as official spokesmen for the crown, both men sought to advance their private interests, though again Burrington was more culpable in this regard than his successor. Johnston, at least, finally consented to a compromise in 1739.

Just as vexing was the problem of institutional breakdown that preceded the establishment of royal government. Ever since its founding, the colony had experienced frequent turmoil, which only increased in the late 1720s when the government nearly collapsed. Proprietary officials no longer felt any obligation to maintain even a semblance of public order. "The government there is so loose and the laws are so feebly executed," William Byrd noted, "that, like those in the neighborhood of Sidon formerly, everyone does just what seems good in his own eyes." Because of this heritage of unrest, many government institutions had already been retarded in their development; they also remained vulnerable to further disruption. "I wish you all the success in the world," Byrd wrote Burrington in 1731, "in bringing the chaos into form and reducing that anarchy into a regular government, in so doing you will deserve to [have] your statue erected, or . . . your sallary doubled."

In later years, the fragility of constituted authority continued to be a serious problem. "It is a peculiar hardship to the Gentlemen who serve the Crown in this Colony," Johnston lamented, "that it never was before brought under any order nor subject to the regulation of the Laws."[89] Indeed, coercion and violence itself were often preferred as more acceptable modes of political action than ordinary legal processes. In 1740 a lower-house member felt obliged to move that any member of the house "who shall in any wise detain" another member or "take any out contrary to his or their Inclination when the House calls for a Division on any Question" should be "Committed." Arrests and imprisonments, assaults on government officers, Burrington's attempted assassination, not to mention one assemblyman's threat to "pistol" another representative in 1739, all confirmed the frail character of existing institutions and further weakened their foundations. Following Edward Moseley's attack upon Chief Justice Smith in 1735, one observer aptly noted, "The Riots and disorder of this province can no longer appear Strange . . . when you find a Member of the Council offering an outrage to the Person of the Magistrate." Due to episodes like this, ordinary settlers, who were not inclined anyway to defer to their superiors, could hardly have been expected to obey the commands of authority or to pay quitrents for the support of a government that occasionally did not even function.[90]

Still, the weakness of institutional authority was as much an effect as it was a cause of the turbulence. Although it and other circumstances certainly contributed to political unrest, the roots of instability were also embedded in the colony's social fabric. For one thing, few men possessed the wealth, manners, and education necessary to command the respect of others and thereby lend support to public institutions. For the most part, those at the top of the political hierarchy, seventy years after North Carolina's settlement, still represented an emerging elite.

Based upon information drawn from tax lists, property rights, wills, and scattered inventories, table 3.1 presents a rough approximation of slaveholding among men who served in the assembly or in the council from 1731 to 1740. Of a total number of 126 lower-house representatives, data was available for 86. Among these, as many as 44, or 51 percent, owned ten or fewer slaves; only 6, or 7 percent, more than forty. Equally noteworthy, as shown in table 3.2, was that out of the 81 men for whom records exist, 25, or 31 percent, owned five hundred acres of land or less; and no more than 36, or 44 percent, in excess of a thousand. Just 4 individuals, Edward Moseley, Roger Moore, Thomas Pollock, and Cullen Pollock, probably owned more than ten thousand acres.

Councillors, whom a visiting Virginian in 1728 likened to a "company of pirates, vagabonds, and footmen,"[91] were more striking in their material attainments, but not overwhelmingly so. From 1731 to 1740, 20 men sat in the upper house. Of the 13 for whom data are available, 6, or nearly half, owned twenty or fewer slaves, and only 3 had more than forty. With respect to land, 5 of the 15, who could be traced, owned two thousand acres or less, and 3— again, Moseley, Moore, and Cullen Pollock—had more than ten thousand. Yet another index of how unimpressive were all these political leaders, assemblymen and councillors alike, is the fact that only two, Eleazer Allen and Richard Everard, Jr., are known to have had university educations.[92]

Given this lackluster economic and social profile, individuals

TABLE 3.1 *Slave Ownership among Provincial Officeholders, 1731–1740*[93] *(percentages in parentheses)*

Number of Slaves	Assemblymen		Councillors	
0–5	24	(27.9)	—	—
6–10	20	(23.3)	2	(15.4)
11–20	22	(25.6)	4	(30.8)
21–30	9	(10.5)	2	(15.4)
31–40	5	(5.8)	2	(15.4)
41–50	1	(1.2)	—	—
51+	5	(5.8)	3	(23.1)
	86		13	

TABLE 3.2 *Land Ownership among Provincial Officeholders, 1731–1740*[94] *(percentages in parentheses)*

Acres	Assemblymen		Councillors	
0–500	25	(30.9)	1	(6.7)
501–1,000	20	(24.7)	1	(6.7)
1,001–2,000	19	(23.5)	3	(20.0)
2,001–3,000	5	(6.2)	1	(6.7)
3,001–4,000	3	(3.7)	2	(13.3)
4,001–5,000	3	(3.7)	1	(6.7)
5,001–10,000	2	(2.5)	3	(20.0)
10,001+	4	(4.9)	3	(20.0)
	81		15	

were much more likely to contest the claim to authority of those in positions of power. Even before Burrington's arrival in 1731, the men chosen to form his council were attacked as having such "mean circumstances that put them all together their Estates . . . won't amount to £1500" and "such vile Characters and poor understandings, that it is the greatest abuse imaginable." In later years, several of these first councillors, such as John Baptista Ashe and Nathaniel Rice, found the social bearing of other officers wanting, whom they described as "very weak persons" of "bad (not to say infamous) Character." Burrington apparently recognized the problems of finding figures of authority in the colony: "It is a misfortune to this Province and to the Governor in particular that there are not a sufficient number of Gentlemen in it fitt to be Councellours, Neither to be Justices of the Peace, nor officers in the Militia." Similarly, when Johnston arrived in North Carolina, he found that the "Characters" of men in high offices "alone were sufficient to bring all Majestracy and Government into contempt and ridicule." Johnston himself was faulted at one point by Daniel Hanmer for being "a Schoolmaster and of a mean and low decent [*sic*]."[95]

In yet another respect, the social foundations of political leadership were inimical to the maintenance of public order. Because members of the provincial elite were still busy trying to achieve economic eminence, most viewed politics not as a public trust but as an opportunity to advance personal and group interests. Most leading men could simply not afford to entertain an altruistic ethic of public service comparable to that of other provincial elites by the mid-eighteenth century. Furthermore, a sizable number of leaders were first-generation newcomers to North Carolina; as a consequence, their sense of community identity was weaker than that of a more mature elite, such as Virginia's. Available information does not readily permit analysis of all assemblymen, but, of the twenty representatives who exercised key leadership roles in the lower house during the 1730s, probably fifteen were immigrants. It is even more striking that perhaps as many as seventeen of the twenty men who served in the council were also newcomers.[96] That so few were the descendants of early settlers resulted in part from the colony's continuous growth in population and settled territory, but it also stemmed from the absence of an entrenched upper class capable of blocking the movement of ambitious outsiders into the political arena.

Throughout the 1730s, provincial officeholders used political institutions to achieve private ends. Of course, both Burrington and Johnston engaged in partisan warfare to advance their respective land schemes. Just as conspicuous were the strenuous efforts of newcomers like Nathaniel Rice and William Smith to attain power at the center of government. That these individuals, using their influence at Whitehall, quickly assumed a leading role at the head of Burrington's antagonists on the strength of external connections rather than on their own merits reflected the colony's fluid political order and its essentially opportunistic orientation.

Also noteworthy in their pursuit of self-serving objectives at the expense of public stability were the blank-patent holders, who eventually whipped up a frenzy of opposition to government in order to retain their fraudulent land titles. Their ultimate success lay in the exploitation of popular resentment over quitrents, but they were hardly sincere spokesmen for the downtrodden planter. Within the Cape Fear, they did their best to corner the land market and sell property to newly arrived settlers at inflated prices or, as one newcomer stated, "screw as much as they can from a stranger for it." Those who dared to occupy vacant lands faced expulsion "by virtue of a pretended title." With some justice, Johnston called

them "men who have more squeezed and Oppressed their fellow
Subjects, and got more money for themselves and relations by the
Sale of Lands since the Year 1728, than the Lords proprietors got
during the whole sixty years they were in possession; and yet have
the insolence to foment and raise an unjust clamour against the
King."[97]

Although some of these aspiring Cape Fear magnates were above
average in wealth in comparison with other political leaders, in no
customary sense did they constitute an indigenous elite, confident
in its material circumstances. By 1732 Edward Moseley may have
owned close to sixty slaves, but, following his arrival in the province around 1704 as a young man reportedly "bred in Christ's
Hospital" in London, his career was one of steady material aggrandizement, aided by a fortuitous marriage, a profitable legal practice,
and the blank-patent frauds.[98] Similarly, the Moores were affluent
but were hardly secure in their stations. They and other South
Carolinians moved to the Cape Fear to salvage their declining fortunes from the hands of Charleston merchants and tax gatherers.
The same intense concern with their precarious material status,
which had led many of these men to the brink of rebellion in South
Carolina in 1727, underlay their later aggressiveness in the patent
controversy and the contest between Brunswick and Wilmington.

While Moseley, the Moores, and others sought to achieve dominance in the Cape Fear, they and most leading provincials manifested little interest in public concerns. Burrington met with no
success in urging the assembly to provide a modicum of support for
the colony's handful of ministers, and Johnston continually bemoaned the assembly's lack of interest in adopting measures vital
to the colony's welfare. His attempts to persuade the assembly to
lend support to the clergy, print copies of the province's laws, erect
jails, and construct schools "to polish the minds of young Persons
with some degree of learning" met with indifference at best. Such
deficiencies, he remarked bitterly, were "not reckoned grievances in
this part of the world." Nor was any noticeable concern manifested
in March 1737 when he warned of a possible Spanish naval attack
from Florida and the need to enact a stronger law for raising the
militia.[99]

In all probability, political leaders ignored many of these matters,
not only to keep a lid on spending and thus curry favor with the

electorate, but also because of a genuine lack of concern over internal improvements. North Carolinians, Johnston wrote Lord Wilmington, were "a people into whose heads no human means can beat the notion of a public interest." The missionary James Moir complained in 1740 that the colonists would not provide "a tolerable Support for a regular ministry" because "they engage in Party Affairs with so much Zeal." James Murray commented to a friend in 1736, "I wish I could write you something agreable of the country or rather the present set of inhabitants, for the place it self is well enough were it peopled by frugal, honest, industrious people who would not sacrifice the general good of the province for the obtaining their own private ends or would not be so stupid as to be led by the nose by those that would." Although he had initially resolved to avoid the fires of party combat, Murray himself succumbed to their temptation when he became a staunch council supporter of Wilmington in its rivalry with Brunswick.[100]

As North Carolina passed into its second decade under royal authority, there were signs that the turmoil of the 1730s might once again envelop provincial politics. In June 1740 Henry McCulloh urged the Board of Trade to disallow the colony's new quitrent law. Embittered over Johnston's refusal to obey his instructions and fearful that approval of the blank patents would threaten his own property holdings, McCulloh, aided by several influential London merchants who traded to North Carolina, received his wish the following month.[101] Just as ominous was the gradual rearrangement of provincial forces into two regional factions that would provoke still new animosities and again disrupt institutions of government.

4 The Politics of Regional Conflict, 1741–1754

*Tho' they do not appear in Arms, they are really in
a State of Civil Rebellion.*
—Gabriel Johnston to the Board of Trade,
    December 28, 1748

The frenzied factionalism of the 1730s gave way during the succeeding decade to the gradual emergence of northern and southern interests within the province. Economic and political differences pitted residents of the Albemarle region against settlers located predominantly in the Cape Fear valley. Regional friction, coupled with renewed efforts by Governor Johnston to obtain a satisfactory quitrent law, plunged North Carolina into a bitter political struggle beginning in 1746. After southern politicians, aided by Johnston, passed legislation highly favorable to their own region, northerners stubbornly boycotted assembly sessions and made a series of appeals to London authorities. Before tensions subsided eight years later, they had paralyzed the government and undermined the authority of the colony's basic civil institutions.

"Two different opposite States"

Although North Carolina consisted of several different regions, the primary regional division for much of the eighteenth century was between north and south, the break occurring roughly just beneath the six counties bordering Albemarle Sound. Besides having at least one principal urban center, each of these regions produced different commodities, possessed varying proportions of slave labor, and utilized different trading outlets; the south was also more recently settled and more prosperous as a whole. Regional contrasts between north and south were less sharp but still present in the intervening border zone around Pamlico Sound.

The many incongruities between north and south prompted several suggestions for separate governments. In 1727, before the Cape Fear was even fully settled, persistent rumors arose that the Moore family from South Carolina, working in concert with ex-governor Burrington, intended to establish a new colony in the lower Cape Fear. Later, in 1740, when the future location of John Lord Carteret's proprietary grant in the two Carolinas was still undecided, Carteret proposed that his tract encompass the province's northern half, that it be annexed to Virginia, and that the remainder of the colony be joined to South Carolina. In making this suggestion, he claimed to enjoy the support of "considerable Persons" not only in Virginia but in North Carolina as well. A Moravian bishop twelve years later urged that each region have its own assembly under a joint governor in the style of Pennsylvania's "upper" and "lower" counties.[1]

Compounding the regional dissimilarities was the disproportionate representation of the six Albemarle counties in the lower house of assembly. Ever since 1681, according to instructions given by the Lords Proprietors to the governor and council of Albemarle, the four counties of Perquimans, Pasquotank, Currituck, and Chowan had each assumed the right to elect five representatives. This right was reaffirmed by the biennial act of 1715. When Bertie was created out of Chowan in 1722, it also received five representatives, until nineteen years later when it lost two seats to the new county of Northampton. Tyrrell County, established from four of its older neighbors in 1729, was granted three assemblymen, but soon began to send four and five. By contrast, every other county in the prov-

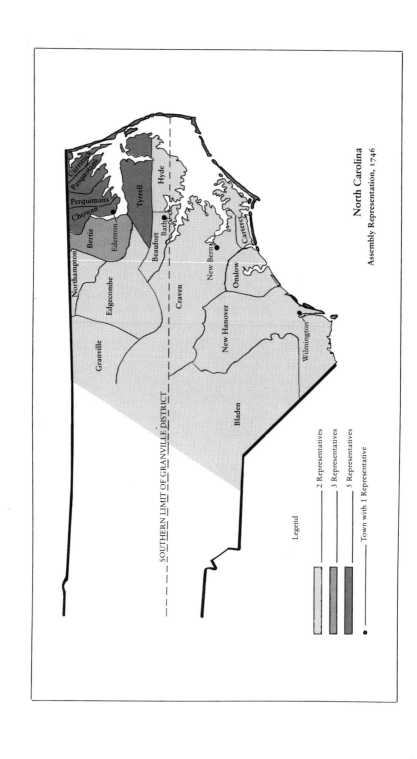

North Carolina

Assembly Representation, 1746

Legend

2 Representatives

3 Representatives

5 Representatives

Town with 1 Representative

SOUTHERN LIMIT OF GRANVILLE DISTRICT

Currituck
Pasquotank
Perquimans
Chowan
Bertie
Edenton
Northampton
Edgecombe
Granville
Tyrell
Hyde
Beaufort
Bath
Craven
New Bern
Onslow
Carteret
New Hanover
Bladen
Wilmington

ince lying to the south or west of these six elected only two assemblymen. This fundamental imbalance in lower-house representation gave the six Albemarle counties a majority of votes in the lower house; during the mid-1740s these counties and the town of Edenton in Chowan commanded twenty-nine out of fifty-two seats.[2]

Despite both the regional cleavage and the unbalanced apportionment in the lower house, political arrangements within the assembly did not result in serious antagonisms in the early 1740s, as the house routinely passed bills that benefited both regions. Thus, in August 1740, the house acted to advance the growth of Wilmington and New Bern as well as Edenton. Similarly, three years later, it approved a measure enabling county justices in Beaufort to build two warehouses together with a bill for the construction of a roadway linking Edenton to the interior of Perquimans. Moreover, northern and southern members shared positions of leadership during these years. From 1740 to 1745, leaders included such men as Samuel Swann and Richard Everard, Jr., from Onslow and Bladen counties, and John Hodgson and Thomas Barker from Chowan and Bertie. In fact, Swann became Speaker of this predominantly northern body in 1743.[3]

Yet in some respects, the south's emergence as a distinct region was already beginning to strain regional goodwill. Whatever lingering loyalty transplanted northerners like Edward Moseley and Alexander Lillington may have felt to the north had diminished by this time; only Swann had left any family members behind. Further, by the late 1730s, the movement of northerners to the Cape Fear had noticeably subsided. Coupled with the limited contact most southern settlers had with those in the north, this weakening of connections with the north contributed greatly to the creation of a separate southern interest. Also, southern unity became steadily less threatened by the bitter town rivalry between Brunswick and Wilmington. What had once polarized the lower Cape Fear elite into warring factions largely subsided by 1744 after the Moore-dominated Brunswick faction had acquiesced in the face of Wilmington's emergence as an urban center. It was perhaps more than symbolic that Maurice Moore, who had played a major role in the establishment of Brunswick, died the preceding year.[4]

By creating a faction hungry for the practical benefits of political power, the growth of a unified, self-conscious southern interest soon exerted an upsetting impact on provincial politics. Disagreement, for instance, arose over the location of the provincial assembly and related government offices. From 1736 to 1746, the assembly met in Edenton, Bath, New Bern, and Wilmington, practically trying, as Governor Johnston commented, "every Town in the Colony." Without a central capital, government documents were often lost, destroyed, or at best difficult to recover. "I am frequently obliged," Johnston complained, "to send from one end of the Province to another for them." Each region favored a place within a reasonable distance of its own center so as to avoid the hardships of prolonged travel. By 1746 southerners were firmly committed to New Bern as the future site, and northern representatives pushed for the more northern location of Bath. Nor could assemblymen agree where the General Court should sit. Upon the passage of a circuit court act in 1738, the assembly designated Bath, New Bern, and Wilmington as sites for the various circuit courts, but the General Court itself was located in Edenton, as it had been for decades. Because most of the judges, including the chief justice, were inhabitants of the lower Cape Fear, southerners favored the more central town of New Bern.[5]

Where the provincial capital was located also had major economic ramifications. Inevitably, the establishment of a permanent seat of government would bring new men and new money to the designated town and its environs.

Another flash point of discontent concerned the relative tax burden of each region. Theoretically, the inhabitants of both regions shared the burden equally: all paid a standard poll tax. Depending on how a region's particular commodity or commodities were valued as a form of payment, one area, however, could escape paying its full share. The council's overwhelmingly southern majority joined with southerners in the lower house in 1744 in an attempt to do just that by rating rice "two thirds above real value," in a money bill. As one observer later related, "The Majority of Burgesses residing in the northern Parts, where they had little or nothing to do with Rice, looked upon this as a grevious Imposition." Consequently, northern representatives in the lower house attempted to block the bill's passage both that year and the next. They could not hold out for long, however, because northern commerce was heavily dependent on Virginia merchants, who insisted that North Carolina maintain a sound currency. "Finding there was no other Way," northern assemblymen reluctantly agreed to the bill in April 1745.[6]

The pressing question of a sound medium of trade, in itself, engendered considerable disagreement between the two regions. Because of a shortage of currency and a growing economy, southern counties, particularly those in the Cape Fear, favored continued issues of paper money to lubricate their commerce. Tied to merchants in Virginia, where there was as yet no paper money, the northern counties steadfastly opposed further issues. "With regard to their private Concerns," one resident affirmed, "the Inhabitants of the Northern and Southern Division[s] Act upon different Motives[,] particularly in relation to their Currency."[7]

By the mid-1740s, North Carolina's political calm was clearly threatened, as basic economic and political differences between north and south moved swiftly to the fore. "The Southern and Northern Parts are as much divided in Their views and interests," an S.P.G. missionary wrote, "as if they composed two different opposite States." "The condition of the inhabitants varies so greatly," another commentator would remark not long afterward, "that often what is good for the southern part is bad for the northern, and vice versa."[8] The regional goodwill of previous years was quickly evaporating.

"To enflame and disturb"

Once the interests of north and south had visibly begun to diverge, Johnston moved to take advantage of the cleavage. London's repeal of the compromise quitrent act of 1739 at Henry McCulloh's urging had thrown the province once more into turmoil. Quitrent collections plummeted from £1,875 sterling in 1740 to only £776 sterling in 1742. Although Johnston renewed his struggle for a suitable bill, he again encountered considerable antagonism. This time, however, his principal opposition came from the north. Johnston entertained no desire to resume the fight against his old foes in the Cape Fear by revoking their blank patents, even though the crown invalidated them when it repealed the quitrent law; thus southerners were naturally less antagonistic toward quitrents. Northern leaders, on the other hand, remained adamant in their defiance. Hoping that Johnston would ultimately be able to persuade the crown to approve a measure similar to the repealed law, they blocked his efforts to obtain a tougher act by utilizing their commanding majority in the lower house.[9]

But Johnston was anxious for a quick solution. Assuming that southern politicians might approve a new quitrent law, he turned to southern members in the assembly and the predominantly southern council. In mid-1741 he called a session to meet in September at Wilmington in hopes that the travel distance to the meeting would dissuade northern representatives from attending. "All imaginable precautions were taken to secure the success of this Affair," he later reported to the Board of Trade. True to his expectations, northerners did boycott the session, but, to his consternation, southern members refused at this time to break from the north by passing the law Johnston wanted, and the impasse continued.[10]

The governor's frustration over the quitrent issue was further heightened two years later when he learned that John Lord Carteret, soon to be Earl Granville, was going to receive a proprietary grant from the Privy Council that would consist of the colony's northern half. This action threatened to reduce the amount of potential quitrent revenues by half. Writing to a British creditor-friend, Johnston complained, "He has not left the Crown 700l. per annum," which was £300 less than Johnston's salary. "Something must be done," he urged, "otherwise his Majesty cannot keep up the face of a government here." In a more personal vein he asserted, "If I have not justice done me before this bargain with Lord Cartret [sic] is compleated I despair of ever having it in my power to pay you or any other of my creditors, or to appear any more in life." Believing, indeed, that his personal affairs had "come to a crisis," Johnston sent two petitions to London authorities. The first asked for payment of his back salary, now at least five years in arrears because of languishing quitrent collections; the second urged the crown to send an independent company of troops to the province, a sure sign of the governor's rapidly growing desperation in his struggle with the north.[11]

Neither request was granted, and Johnston was left to continue the fight as best he could. Because of their new collective status as the Granville District, northern counties no longer owed rents to the crown. But their opposition to a province-wide quitrent measure remained the governor's chief political problem through the next few years. On several occasions, northern representatives even declined to attend assembly sessions, thereby forcing their postponement because southerners refused to meet by themselves. "The very being of Assemblies," Johnston later complained, "depended on their whim and Humour, and not on the Kings Writ."[12]

To Johnston's good fortune, however, southern leaders ultimately proved more willing to align their interests with his. In large measure, this happenstance derived from their growing alienation from the north. Johnston also successfully wooed southern politicians through two major patronage appointments. In 1743 William Faris, a leading assemblyman from Wilmington, became vice-admiralty judge, and Edward Moseley, Johnston's old enemy, assumed the office of chief baron of the exchequer. The following year, Moseley also became chief justice, succeeding William Smith, whom he and his blank-patent faction had tried to impeach five years earlier.[13]

During the spring of 1746, Johnston decided the time was ripe to employ his earlier strategy once again. Upon the close of a legislative session in June, he prorogued the assembly and called for it to meet the following November in Wilmington. When it assembled on November 18, it quickly became evident that not one representative from the six Albemarle counties had arrived. Leaders of the Albemarle faction later claimed that bad weather and poor traveling conditions had prevented their attendance. But it seems much more likely that, as Johnston anticipated, they had chosen to boycott the session out of pique over its distant location.[14]

Whatever the exact cause, Albemarle members obviously did not expect the assembly to convene without a majority, which required the attendance of at least some of them. They miscalculated. After two brief prorogations by Johnston to see if any additional representatives would appear, the lower house not only agreed to assemble but also quickly proceeded with business. Nor did southern members make any pretense about the session's chief purpose. With the governor's support, they passed two bills, neither with a suspending clause that would have delayed their implementation until the crown had granted its approval. The first measure, submitted by Rufus Marsden of New Hanover County, was entitled "An Act for the better Ascertaining the number of members to be chosen for the Several Counties." Declaring that the inequality in elected representatives between "Several of the Northern" counties and those "more Southern and western" had caused "great mischiefs and Disorders," the act limited the assembly representation of the six Albemarle counties to two members each. The second bill was no less direct in its design. Introduced by John Swann, also of New Hanover, it established the provincial seat of government at New Bern. The bill also created a new superior court system; the General Court was to sit in New Bern and circuit courts in Wilmington, Edenton, and Edgecombe County. With its principal business for the time being completed, Johnston prorogued the assembly to meet again at Wilmington in mid-January.[15]

Hoping perhaps that new elections might return less obdurate representatives from the north, Johnston subsequently decided to call a new house to meet at New Bern in keeping with the new capital act. Both he and his southern allies seriously underestimated the widespread animosity their actions had engendered in the northern counties. When writs were issued for each county to elect two members according to the representation act, the Albemarle counties returned their customary number of representatives. However, soon after the assembly opened on February 25, 1747, Johnston, upon the urgings of the lower house, met this challenge by nullifying the Albemarle elections and by having the crown clerk reissue writs for two members each. The session then proceeded with none of the Albemarle members present.[16]

Interestingly, and contrary to the assertions of various scholars, the split between the members who elected to attend the session and those who left was not simply between north and south. Representatives from the three northwestern counties of Edgecombe, Northampton, and Granville all chose to remain; they had, in fact, attended the previous assembly in Wilmington. Only the members from Edgecombe had briefly displayed uncertain loyalties by abruptly departing after passage of the representation and seat of government bills. Furthermore, representatives from all three steadfastly refused to participate in any boycott of subsequent sessions.[17]

Why these counties remained loyal to the governor and the southern faction throughout what would increasingly become a contest between two regions characterized by different economic interests is attributable to at least three factors. First, these counties had never had more than two members each and might have shared southern resentment over the inequitable representation of the Albemarle counties. Further, because many of the inhabitants of these northwestern counties were first-generation immigrants from Virginia, social and cultural ties to Albemarle residents were still in a nascent stage. In fact, of the four men who represented these counties in the lower house whose origins can be determined—Edward Jones, John Dawson, William Eaton, and John Haywood—all were newcomers to the colony.[18] Finally, Johnston seems to have valued these counties for their help in his efforts to weaken the power of the Albemarle faction, and at least in the case of Edgecombe he eventually became personally involved in local politics to insure the county's continued support. In 1750 a local missionary complained that Johnston had taken an "extraordinary Step" to obtain the county court's nomination of one of his connections for the all-important office of sheriff by adding "six new Justices to the Bench."[19]

Once they had tested Johnston's fortitude and failed, northern members in the lower house resolved to boycott future assembly sessions until their full representation was restored. They also escalated the controversy to a new level of intensity by deciding to present their case to crown authorities. A committee of six leading politicians—Peter Payne of Chowan, Mackrora Scarborough of Perquimans, Simon Byron of Pasquotank, Caleb Wilson of Currituck, Benjamin Hill of Bertie, and Stevens Lee of Tyrrell—drafted a petition to the Privy Council. The petition stoutly attacked the initial session in Wilmington as a deliberate attempt "to ensnare and entrapp" northern representatives and as an illegal breach of the rule that only a full majority of the membership constituted a quorum for meetings. In addition, the petitioners condemned the representation act as a violation of their "Ancient Rights and Priviledges" granted during proprietary rule. Asserting that they had in the past always "acted with the greatest Duty and Submission to your Majesty's Orders and Instructions," they pointedly warned that this "Law of so extraordinary and unusual Nature," passed without a suspending clause, could "only tend to enflame and disturb the Quiet and Happyness of Your Majesty's Subjects."[20]

Perhaps already aware of the petition, Johnston forwarded a

copy of the disputed representation act to the Board of Trade on March 9, 1747. Up until then, he had only hinted at the unusual nature of the Wilmington assembly session. Now he carefully defended his actions in more detail, charging among other things that northern representatives had for some time kept "Public Affairs in confusion" by refusing to attend sessions of the lower house. Only during their latest attempt to do so in November, he related, did he and the rest of the assembly finally succeed in putting an end to their schemes by passing the representation act, which, he assured the Board, violated no other statute than the long since repealed biennial act of 1715.[21]

In the meantime, southern leaders had proceeded to employ an agent to present their own case in London. Their initial choice was Samuel Wragg of South Carolina, who in the mid-1730s had served as an agent for the blank-patent holders in North Carolina. But, because he had not been paid for his earlier service, he declined the appointment. Representation of the southern cause then fell on James Abercromby, a former attorney general of South Carolina, who was aided by Joshua Sharpe, an English solicitor.[22]

Abercromby was a talented advocate, but the Albemarle counties had by then also made a shrewd selection in appointing the inveterate land speculator, Henry McCulloh, as their own agent. His long-renowned support for a strong quitrent act notwithstanding, northern leaders hoped that his influential political connections in London might substantially strengthen their cause. Although some of his early contacts, including Martin Bladen and Robert Walpole, had either died or lost their power, McCulloh had become a firmly established fixture in London over the years. He had successfully cultivated new men of influence, especially Colonel John Selwyn, Queen Caroline's treasurer and an intimate of the king, to whom he sold four hundred thousand acres in 1745.[23]

Northern politicians could also safely assume that McCulloh would zealously defend their interests, for he had strong reasons to oppose Johnston, wherever the field of battle. After the two had clashed in 1737 over the surveying of McCulloh's land claims, relations between the governor and his former patron steadily deteriorated. After obtaining a special commission from the crown in 1739, ostensibly to reform the quitrent systems in both Carolinas, McCulloh arrived in North Carolina in 1741 only to meet considerable resistance from local residents, not to mention Johnston himself. McCulloh revived his dispute with Johnston over his lands; alienated Eleazer Allen, North Carolina's receiver general, by charging him with neglect; became the target of several lawsuits; and was ultimately placed under house arrest for eighteen months. Matters further worsened for McCulloh when the Lords of Treasury suspended his lucrative salary of £600 per annum after receiving numerous complaints from North Carolina. In 1746 he finally received patents for his 1,200,000 acres, which Johnston had earlier refused to issue. But, that same year, McCulloh discovered to his horror that Johnston had authorized extension of the southern boundary of Earl Granville's proprietary district one hundred sixty miles to the west. As a result, approximately 475,000 acres of McCulloh's property now fell within the proprietary.[24]

McCulloh embarked upon his new mission as northern agent with vigor. Arriving in England in December 1747, he presented the Albemarle petition to the Privy Council, where it lay until referred to the Board of Trade in mid-January, a relatively short bureaucratic delay for the time. Once the board met and both the representation act and the Albemarle petition had been introduced, McCulloh read a prepared appeal reiterating the north's charge that each of the Albemarle counties enjoyed a constitutional right to their customary number of representatives. "Nothing," he affirmed, "can have more the force of a Law, than a Constitution so established, Continued and acted under for upwards of Fifty years." Moreover, he added, this same proprietary constitution directed that only a majority of elected representatives in the lower house could possibly constitute a quorum. As a consequence, "every Act ... done" by the Wilmington body in late 1746 "was null, void, and of no effect." McCulloh concluded his remarks by submitting relevant sections from the proprietary charter, Johnston's instructions, and the Wilmington assembly minutes.

Unhappily for the southern faction, its solicitor, Joshua Sharpe, was totally unprepared for such a detailed assault. Therefore, he tried to delay the proceedings by objecting that the provincial seal was missing from McCulloh's copy of the assembly minutes. Confident of the merits of his case, McCulloh did not contest the charge but instead urged that Johnston himself be ordered to transmit "all necessary evidence" under the proper seal. The hearing was then dissolved, and on July 14, upon the board's recommendation, the crown required both parties to gather additional materials for a subsequent session.[25]

While matters were moving slowly in London, Johnston and his provincial faction were making the most of their control of the assembly. Having assumed, as one northern leader complained, the "full power to Enact any Laws" it wanted without a majority of its membership,[26] the lower house, working in conjunction with Johnston and the council, passed two new acts in 1748 that were designed to benefit the southern counties. The first—in violation of Johnston's instructions—was a currency act that issued £21,350 proclamation money for the stated purpose of constructing forts, paying public debts, and exchanging bills of credit. No doubt southern legislators were also motivated by their long-standing desire to offset the ever-present shortage of currency afflicting the Cape Fear valley. Having failed to pass such an act in the past because of northern opposition, they now seized their opportunity, knowing full well that it would disrupt traditional northern commercial patterns.[27] Equally aggravating to the north was the prejudicial quitrent measure enacted by the assembly. Ostensibly intended to speed the formation of a rent roll for landholdings in the entire colony, the act was really geared much more heavily toward northern properties, particularly in its provision that pre-1729 proprietary grants be registered within one year.[28]

Attacks and Delay in London

While Johnston and the southern faction busied themselves with legislation, Albemarle leaders were earnestly engaged in broadening their line of attack. Impatient over the protracted length of the proceedings in London and angered by the currency and quitrent measures, they succeeded in enlisting a host of influential new supporters in their cause. Included were not only Arthur Dobbs, a prominent Irish politician and land associate of McCulloh, but also Francis Corbin, the personal agent of Earl Granville. Early in the controversy, Albemarle residents had asked Granville's help. Although he refused to take any action on the matter until it reached him as a member of the Privy Council, it is possible he chose to exercise his influence through Corbin in order to curry favor with his Carolina tenants. Corbin's support was doubly significant because of his apparent relationship with Corbyn Morris, a fast-rising English politician and an intimate of the Duke of Newcastle. It was, in fact, probably because of Morris's efforts that the Duke of Bedford, the newly appointed secretary of state for the colonies, urged the Board of Trade in January 1749 to hear the assorted complaints of Johnston's latest adversaries.[29]

On January 25 and 26 they received their opportunity. Morris himself led the assault. Armed with corroborating testimony from the others, Morris charged that Johnston had committed numerous acts of misconduct during his administration in addition to having abrogated the northern counties' "privilege of sending five Members each to the Assembly." Johnston, Morris contended, had, among other misdeeds, granted militia offices and commissions of the peace to Scottish Jacobites. Indeed, asserted Morris, Johnston had received news of the rebel defeat in 1745 at Culloden "very coldly" and "expressed a concern" that many of his former Scottish "acquaintance[s] and schoolfellows" had suffered. Further, Morris and the other complainants charged that Johnston had held infrequent sessions of the chancery court and had been negligent in his correspondence with the crown. Yet another accusation centered on his approval of the recent currency act.[30]

Once again, the governor and the southern faction were caught off guard. Obviously bewildered by this latest batch of allegations, their agent, James Abercromby, put the best face he could on the situation by responding that he had "no answer to make to accusations so extremely irregular." But both the tenor and the authors of these attacks swayed the board. On February 20 it wrote Bedford that "if the information which has been laid before us be true the Province is certainly in great disorder and confusion." Abercromby did, however, succeed in obtaining time for a rebuttal by petitioning for delays in the hearings.[31]

Embattled now on two fronts, Johnston had already written several letters to the board in which he pressed for prompt approval of the representation act and apologized for having broken his instructions by passing the money bill, even though, he added, it was desperately needed. Angered by the thinly veiled charge of treason, he also wrote Bedford that his "Enemies" may have "with the same

Justice" accused him "of Murder and Felony" as to call him a "Jacobite." "Who can there be in this wild and Barbarous Country," he asked, "that could possibly Tempt me to Abandon every Friend I have in Life and Embrace so Desperate and Profligate a Cause[?]" Johnston further proclaimed his loyalty to the crown by invoking prior political connections in London: "Before I came abroad I lived almost constantly with the late Lord President Wilmington, and have the Honour to be known for many years by the Earl of Bath, Lord Anson, the Bishop of Worcester and several other Persons of Distinction."[32]

By this point, Henry McCulloh was more anxious than ever to speed the hearings and to advance his own interests. Foremost among his objectives were obtaining the governor's removal and insuring London's continued support for his land schemes. In the spring of 1749, he again assumed the offensive. Complaining vociferously to the board of the mistreatment he had personally suffered at Johnston's hands in the past, he recited in elaborate detail how the governor had interfered with his land grants and generally made his life miserable during his six-year stay in the colony. Once the board received McCulloh's memorial, it postponed further consideration of the matter until Johnston had had sufficient time to respond.[33]

The overall investigation into the governor's administration and the regional controversy had now become seriously bogged down in an endless exchange of charges and countercharges. The next several years witnessed more of the same as each faction accused the other of preventing its witnesses in North Carolina from submitting depositions. Largely because of Abercromby's vigilance, each new allegation of misgovernment, though intended to accelerate Johnston's removal, resulted in imponderable delays designed to give Johnston and his faction more time. Moreover, the requirement that each side substantiate its assertions with depositions and other documentary evidence only further prolonged the proceedings.[34] Furthermore, the Board of Trade, under its new president, the Earl of Halifax, was currently revamping its administration of all the colonies. Notwithstanding a pronounced increase toward the late 1740s in the frequency of its meetings, it was consequently "overwhelmed by a tremendous volume of business."[35] Compounding the time-consuming nature of the entire process were the vagaries of trans-Atlantic communication, accentuated in North Carolina's case by the necessity of funneling so much of its mail through either Virginia or South Carolina.[36]

The very nature of the case also delayed its disposition. On the one hand, Johnston's opponents had been able to marshal an impressive array of arguments against both the representation act and his conduct as governor. Many of their charges were difficult to substantiate, especially the Jacobite allegation, but they at least aroused doubt in the minds of London officials as to Johnston's gubernatorial performance. In particular, the arbitrary nature of the representation act provoked considerable uneasiness. As early as September 1747, Matthew Lamb, the Board of Trade's legal counsel, reported that "however Proper and Convenient this Act may be, Yet the Governour and a Select Number of Burgesses taking upon them to Pass Any Act in any way Different from the Usuall Method . . . may be attended with great Inconveniences."[37] Just as important, Johnston had almost become an expendable commodity both because of the disorder his actions had precipitated and because of his loss of influential connections in England. Although he could recite a seemingly impressive array of London luminaries, he was sorely out of touch with the intricate and fast-changing world of royal patronage. Neither Newcastle nor Bedford was particularly fond of him. Johnston's former patron, Wilmington, was long since dead, and his friend, the Earl of Bath, was no longer in favor at Whitehall. His only remaining connection of any real influence was Lord Anson, lord of the admiralty and son-in-law of the lord chancellor.[38] In contrast, many of McCulloh's contacts in British public life were still alive and well ensconced. Upon his return to England in 1747, McCulloh had engaged a host of new acquaintances, including the Earl of Halifax, by establishing himself as an expert on colonial affairs. Although it is not known how much power he actually wielded behind the scenes during the controversy, his influence certainly made crown officials more attentive to the interests of his faction than they might otherwise have been.[39]

Despite all these handicaps, Johnston and his own provincial faction were by no means without hope in their struggle against McCulloh and the Albemarle counties. As Johnston frequently asserted, the representation act controversy stemmed in part from continued northern opposition to a strong quitrent act; thus, his actions were really in the best interests of the crown. Also, as Stanley Katz has noted, it was not an easy task for any set of provincials to remove a royal governor, "for the crown was naturally jealous of its prerogative" and supportive of its representatives. [40] Moreover, Johnston also used the quitrent issue to his advantage in neutralizing the opposition of several of his key antagonists. In April 1749, he and the assembly enacted an amendment to their quitrent act of 1748. The amendment tightened rent regulations and consequently seems to have persuaded Earl Granville's agent, Francis Corbin, as well as Corbyn Morris, to desist in pressing for the governor's dismissal. One worried Albemarle leader reported to McCulloh that Johnston had assured "his Favourites . . . that they had nothing" else to do to aid their cause "but to make such alterations in their new Quit rent Law, as it is supposed Earl Granville desires." Corbin's appointment to the council in 1751, after coming to North Carolina as Granville's representative, no doubt helped to achieve the same end. [41]

Regional Improvements and a "perfect anarchy"

The north-south conflict had severe consequences for North Carolina. While the various arguments on representation rights, majority rule, and Johnston's fitness as governor were being aired at Whitehall, the dispute continued to divide the colony's political community into warring factions. Not even a series of Spanish naval attacks on the southern towns of Beaufort and Brunswick in 1747 and 1748 diminished the rancor of the controversy. Instead, northerners merely pointed to these assaults as additional proof of Johnston's incompetence. [42] The Albemarle counties also continued to boycott assembly sessions in New Bern. Because its legal status was uncertain, conditions in the new capital were rather crude. "Nobody," Johnston complained, "cares to lay in Provisions for Man or Horse at Newbern" because "Such pains are taken to assure the People that the Seat of Government will be removed, when they get their five Members restored." As a result, "in a fortnight or three weeks time, we are obliged to separate for want of the necessaries of Life."[43]

The constraints on food and drink notwithstanding, southern politicians and, to a lesser extent, those from the maverick northern counties used the time available to them to their advantage. To weaken further the political power of the Albemarle area, the assembly created five new counties between 1750 and 1754: Duplin in the south, Cumberland and Anson in the southwest, and Orange and Rowan in the northwest. The assembly also extended a single seat in the lower house to the town of Brunswick, in New Hanover County. Equally conspicuous were steps taken to advance the social and economic growth of the non-Albemarle counties and the southern half of the colony in particular. The currency act passed in 1748 was one such measure, as some historians have noted, but there were others as well.

In an attempt to bolster the Cape Fear's languishing rice crop, the assembly attached a provision to a bill for revising the provincial laws that placed a duty on rice imported in North Carolina. The assembly also enacted inspection and export regulatory bills for the purpose of "improving the Trade and Commerce of Cape-Fear." Further, it established a public printer, who was to receive an annual salary of £160 proclamation money, in New Bern; and authorized new bridges for the southern counties of Craven and New Hanover and new towns for Carteret, Anson, and Northampton.[44] The only exception to this spate of legislation designed chiefly to benefit the south was a statute passed in 1752 for the creation of a town in Bertie County.

More common was the fate of two similar requests originating in the Albemarle region. In June 1746, during the session immediately preceding the split in lower-house ranks, the assembly received petitions from Pasquotank and Perquimans, each requesting authorization for a town. Accordingly, it ordered bills prepared, but in succeeding sessions, inasmuch as the Albemarle boycott was in force, never again considered the two requests.[45]

How southern oriented the legislature now was can be appreciated from the character of its membership. Despite the presence of representatives from the three northern counties of Edgecombe, Granville, and Northampton, the lower house, as well as the council, was predominantly southern in membership. In addition, southern representatives overwhelmingly filled leadership roles in the lower house. The Cape Fear counties of New Hanover and Onslow alone contributed six out of eleven legislative leaders.[46]

While this southern-dominated assembly enacted bills to satisfy regional priorities, affairs in North Carolina were, as Governor Johnston wrote to Abercromby, "in inexpressible confusion." The Albemarle counties, by declining to send two representatives each to the lower house, refused allegiance to the provincial government. "Tho' they do not appear in Arms, they are really in a State of Civil Rebellion," the governor observed.[47] Inhabitants of these counties, as well as those of Edgecombe, Granville, and Northampton, refused to accept the new currency issued by the assembly in their private transactions. James Moir, an S.P.G. missionary who had recently moved from Wilmington to Edgecombe, discovered that he could "get nothing for the Bills," he had received in the Cape Fear.[48] Moreover, people in the Albemarle counties refused to pay not only quitrents but also provincial taxes, thus depriving the government of more than 40 percent of its annual tax revenues.[49] An even more serious threat to the effective maintenance of provincial government and to authority in general arose when Albemarle sheriffs and jurors boycotted circuit sessions of the General Court in Edenton. Noting much "confusion" in the province, the Moravian bishop August Spangenberg wrote: "There is . . . in the older [i.e. Albemarle] counties a perfect anarchy. As a result, crimes are of frequent occurrence, such as murder, robbery etc. But the criminals cannot be brought to justice. The citizens do not appear as jurors, and if court is held to decide criminal matters no one is present." Still worse, vague rumblings of northern secession from the colony even surfaced.[50]

What was predominantly a protest against provincial authority also resulted in a more all-embracing indifference toward government. "If any one is imprisoned," Spangenberg observed, "the prison is broken open and no justice administered. In short most matters are decided by blows." Even the most basic organs of local government did not escape entirely unscathed. Some county courts met to conduct business, but, in at least one county, the court did not function for more than a year and a half. From October 1748 to April 1750, not one court convened in Pasquotank. In the end, the magistrates consented to assemble only after Johnston had threatened them with prosecution. Disruptions also occurred in those counties where courts met more regularly. During the April 1747 session of Chowan's court, for instance, both the county sheriff and the clerk failed to attend, as did the sheriff again in 1751. Tyrrell County, meanwhile, experienced problems with petit jurors who refused to attend hearings.[51]

Popular uproar in the north seems to have exerted a similar impact on institutional authority in the southern counties, for southerners began to withhold paying their own taxes and quitrents. Commissioned to collect quitrents in the three southern counties of Bladen, Johnston, and Onslow, James Murray wrote Johnston in February 1751 that his efforts had been "without Success but not without Danger." In what may have been a related incident, sometime in the early 1750s a land surveyor was shot in Bladen when he happened upon "a lawless People," consisting of fifty families who refused to take out patents or pay quitrents.[52]

However disturbing the specter of political unrest and mounting social chaos may have seemed to Johnston and the southern faction, they made no attempt to modify their stance but instead displayed a single-minded determination to wait out a ruling from London, and, in the interim, to enact legislation favorable to southern interests. Nor, for that matter, did they attempt to force northern compliance with customary political obligations. No coercive power was available to them, and, in any case, as Johnston clearly recognized, any such attempt would probably have precipitated rioting and perhaps even a full-fledged civil war.[53]

Waning Tensions

At a time when signs were few that the political tumult in North Carolina would subside and while a ruling from London was still pending, Johnston died suddenly on July 17, 1752, at the age of fifty-three. His immediate successor as chief executive was Nathaniel Rice, who, as president of the council and a leading Cape Fear planter, was a staunch partisan in the southern cause. His tenure, however, was brief. Dying slightly more than six months after Johnston, he was replaced by the next most senior member of the council, Matthew Rowan. Also a Cape Fear planter as well as a longtime associate in Johnston's land schemes, Rowan was no less firmly attached to the southern faction.

In view of the avowed partisanship of Rice and Rowan, these swift changes in executive leadership did little to alter the complexion of politics within North Carolina. But matters were beginning to accelerate in London, where Johnston's death did have an impact by removing one of the principal protagonists in the dispute. Crown authorities no longer needed to wrestle with the uncomfortable prospect of unseating a spokesman for the royal prerogative. On January 25, 1753, the crown appointed Arthur Dobbs as governor. An Irish politician who held land in North Carolina, he had extensive political connections that included Lord Hertford, Lord of the Bedchamber, as well as Henry McCulloh.[54]

Because of personal entanglements and bureaucratic delays, Dobbs did not assume office until the fall of 1754, but his appointment provided a signal as to how the Board of Trade was ultimately going to rule in the controversy. In March 1754 it submitted its recommendations to the Privy Council. They were formally adopted in April. The most momentous proposal confirmed the representation claims of the Albemarle counties. Besides suggesting that the representation act of 1746 be repealed, the board urged that both the seat of government act and the two quitrent acts be disallowed; the quitrent act of 1748, it pointedly observed, had been "partially calculated to take effect in one part of the Province only." Also, not surprisingly, McCulloh's interests were upheld when the board, in a rather needless recommendation, urged "that an Instruction should be given to" the new governor "to maintain and support the said Grantee and his Associates in their just and legal rights and in the quiet possession of their lands." Only slightly earlier, McCulloh had achieved another victory when he received credit from the Treasury Board and the auditor general for £6,200 in back salary as the crown's special quitrent agent.

Characteristic of British colonial administration, the southern faction received a few sources of consolation. One of some potential significance was the requirement that, "as the Province grows more peopled," Dobbs should "erect such and so many Towns and Counties in the Southern District" and provide them with assembly rights so "that each different district or division" may have a "reasonable and just proportion." Another recommendation, which allowed the board to reinforce the royal prerogative, ruled against the Albemarle counties' original contention that a majority of representatives was necessary for the lower house to meet. The board instead suggested a quorum of fifteen members.[55]

North Carolina's regional strife effectively came to an end shortly after the Privy Council's April rulings. When Dobbs called his first assembly in December 1754, Albemarle representatives attended the lower house for the first time in eight years. Both factions assured the new governor that, though "there may be some little sparring betwixt the parties," it would "have no effect on public affairs" nor make his "administration uneasy."[56] Various historians have largely attributed this sudden reduction in provincial animosities to the Privy Council's edicts, and, to be sure, these played a key role. Although Carolina politicians were inclined at times to defy imperial strictures, crown authority still carried some weight in colonial politics.[57]

But a variety of other circumstances also helped to reduce party passions. To ascribe such new found harmony purely to a set of pronouncements from London is to ignore the past bitterness and deep animosity that enveloped the antagonists, not to mention the fundamental imbalance in representation that the Privy Council's ruling only began to address. One prime factor was the growing possibility of hostilities between England and France in the Ohio valley. Although normally safer from external attack than its neighbors, the colony now faced a serious threat. As early as June 1753, an Indian raid occurred in the backcountry within two miles of Rowan County's courthouse. Spurred on by new alarms from London and Virginia's governor, Robert Dinwiddie, the assembly in March 1754 voted £12,000 proclamation money for two detachments to be sent to the increasingly embattled Virginia frontier as well as £4,000 for two forts on the Carolina coast and £1,000 for military supplies for the frontier.[58] Remembering their suffering at the hands of the Spanish in the late 1740s and by no means assured that taxes could be collected to finance their expenditures, southern leaders were no longer anxious to face a foreign enemy alone. Because of reports that assaults were impending from the northwest, northerners felt a similar need for reconciliation; they could no longer safely ignore what had in the past been limited to coastal attacks in the south.

A third factor behind the diminution of regional strife was the willingness by the mid-1750s of Virginia merchants to accept the colony's latest supply of paper money.[59] Perhaps even more crucial, a slave insurrection may have been attempted in 1752 or early 1753, a rarity in the colonial period among North Carolina's relatively small black population.

A fifth factor was that, by the time of the dispute's resolution, an extraordinarily large number of each faction's most inveterate leaders had succumbed to the rigors of advancing age and the dangers of an unhealthy environment. In addition to Johnston, no fewer than six of the southern faction's partisans in the council had died between 1749 and 1753: Edward Moseley, Robert Halton, Eleazer Allen, Roger Moore, William Forbes, and Nathaniel Rice. Also deceased were all six Albemarle leaders who drafted their faction's original remonstrance in 1747, as well as Thomas Pollock of Bertie County, the north's lone supporter in the council. "This has been the most Sickly and Mortal Season for Many Years; near one half of the People in and about here are dead," an Edenton resident wrote in 1754. In fact, partly because of mortality, only ten of the fifty-four men who sat in the lower house just before the boycott began were representatives once it ended in 1754.[60]

Of final significance was the degree to which leading politicians moderated their passions in order to curry favor with the new governor. Such were the mollifying effects of place-seeking that before Dobbs even obtained his appointment, he received a letter from Cape Fear planter William Faris requesting his influence for "several places of Profit." Despite Dobbs's partisan relationship with both McCulloh and the Albemarle counties, Faris was not dissuaded from pursuing a potentially profitable source of patronage. Beginning his letter by counseling Dobbs on the settlement of his Carolina property, he proceeded to request his influence with regard to the collectorships of either Brunswick or Bath, "tho'" the latter was "not near so profitable as the other." Faris noted the "Posts of Surveyor and Receiver Generals" were "also Vacant," though he feared "there will be many making Interest" for them. He then candidly expressed his wish that "our Government will be

Continued and the Measures Confirmed which have been taken in Assembly." But he also carefully concluded, "Should there be a Change, I would be glad to be one of the Council . . . in which I would also request your Interest."[61] Because of the change in government, men like Faris throughout the ranks of both factions increasingly tempered their partisanship with an eye toward future preferment.

Consequences and Considerations

The north-south struggle of the 1740s and early 1750s did not subside without leaving a diverse legacy. For example, it affected formal political arrangements within the colony in several major ways. Unhappily for the constitutional authority of the lower house, the controversy coincided with a major change in imperial administration. Under the direction of Halifax as president of the Board of Trade and of Bedford as secretary of state for the colonies, imperial officials initiated a comprehensive program to strengthen the power of colonial governors, and in 1754 exploited the reigning factionalism in North Carolina as a prime opportunity to reinforce the royal prerogative. Thus the 1746 seat of government act was disallowed partly on the grounds that only the governor could establish provincial courts. The Privy Council similarly ruled that new constituencies in the form of counties and towns could only be created by executive ordinance, in contrast to a pattern of some forty years whereby the governor and the assembly shared this power. Moreover, as stated earlier, crown officials confirmed the governor's right to convene the lower house without the presence of a majority of the representatives. Finally, the crown awarded Dobbs a yearly salary of £1,000 sterling out of the 4½ percent revenue from Barbados and the Leeward Islands. After having ignored his predecessor's need for a suitable income, London authorities finally recognized the dangers posed to public stability by forcing a governor to be dependent on quitrents for his financial support. Chiefly as a consequence, the quitrent problem would never again loom as large as it had, even though the issue remained unresolved up to the Revolution once the acts of 1748 and 1749 had been disallowed.[62]

Another important consequence was that the appointment of Dobbs gave McCulloh more influence in provincial affairs than at any time since the mid-1730s, a circumstance that substantially influenced politics during the succeeding decade. Although Dobbs was given a larger measure of authority than any previous royal governor had enjoyed, his connections with McCulloh would significantly strain his otherwise newly independent status.

On another level of consideration than the assorted by-products of this dispute is the broader meaning of the struggle itself within the context of North Carolina politics. Clearly, in one respect, it represented a clash between two distinct regions led by opposing political elites. But was it merely a regional controversy? How, for instance, did it compare with regional strife in other colonies?

As a wide array of scholars have shown, regional disputes disrupted politics in several other provinces during the eighteenth century. In New York, a "north-south, seaboard-frontier, city-country polarity" helped to make its political climate "peculiarly unstable and factious." In Connecticut conflict occurred between religious and economic factions drawn along east-west lines. Similarly, east-west divisions polarized New Jersey, and Rhode Island experienced a struggle during the 1750s and 1760s between the trading centers of Providence and Newport. Certainly regional conflict was not unique to North Carolina, though most colonies did not experience the cleavages of these five.[63]

But the scholarship on other colonies also demonstrates that in none of them did regional conflict result in such a deliberate attempt, as in the case of Johnston and the southern counties, to upset a colony's traditional governing apparatus. With some justice, McCulloh charged that the southern faction had "assumed an Arbitrary Power of New Modelling or Altering the Established Constitution of the Colony."[64] Nor did regional conflict elsewhere, however bitter it may have been at times, result in such a prolonged and serious paralysis of government, including political intransigence in the midst of foreign attack and the disruption of civil order on the local level. In its destabilizing consequences, regional strife in North Carolina was quite exceptional. Why this was so could conceivably be because of a greater polarity in regional interests in North Carolina, but, in fact, economic, cultural, and social divisions were for the most part more acute in other colonies. In New

York, for instance, ethnic, religious, and economic differences separated the downriver from the upriver interest, whereas only differing economic imperatives exerted a major influence in Carolina.

Another possibility is that Johnston's own political priorities together with his personal dispute with McCulloh significantly escalated a routine regional clash into a major dispute. These personal elements of the controversy should not be ignored. Similar factors, however, were not lacking in other colonies. Moreover, to give them too much weight would be to minimize the fundamental role both southern and northern leaders played in the Carolina controversy. In fact, it was Johnston who decided not to use force against the north, thus averting what might have turned into a civil war.

A more suitable explanation for North Carolina's exceptionalism lies in the basic features of its political system. The chaos in the north and signs of its emergence in the south demonstrate the fragile nature of institutional authority. Once governmental prestige had been weakened and Johnston's own authority challenged, institutions, as in the 1730s, had all but collapsed because of the average North Carolinian's customary indifference toward government. "Five years," Johnston complained to Whitehall in 1751, "is a long time for such a wild and uncivilized Country as this to be kept in suspense on matters so essential to the very being of Government."[65]

Just as important, the colony's political leadership still largely lacked the attributes of a conscientious, responsible ruling group by the mid-eighteenth century. The unwillingness of both sides to compromise, despite the resulting damage sustained by the colony's most basic civil institutions, stemmed from a self-interested view of government not unlike that of previous years, the one principal difference being that by the 1740s a plethora of shifting alliances had given way to two major regional interests. Only during the next decade would the conduct of leading figures begin to diverge from this near-endemic pattern of factional conflict. Until then, Carolinians had to content themselves with a political system in which the public interest was often a rare commodity.

5 Patriotism Unmasked, 1755–1765

It was frequently hinted that if I would accede to certain measures my administration might be easy and happy, which measures were tamely to be silent and let the heads of a Republican party engross the executive power of the Crown, and propose no Measures but what ultimately tended to their emolument.
—Arthur Dobbs to the Board of Trade, August 3, 1760

North Carolina enjoyed an uncommon period of political peace during the mid-1750s. The arrival of Arthur Dobbs as governor helped to insure that regional antagonisms did not reignite. Before long, however, gubernatorial patronage policies, constitutional problems, governmental corruption, and the vicissitudes of the Granville Proprietary District provoked new struggles pitting Dobbs and the council against the lower house of assembly. As a result, by 1760 Dobbs was on the brink of being recalled. Ironically, he needed to restir the embers of regional animosity to win popular support. Even more significant was the blend of opportunism and patriotism manifest in assembly opposition during much of his administration. Provincial politicians by the late colonial era acquired a heightened interest in North Carolina's welfare; they also continued to view politics as an opportunity to advance private ends.

A "Union of Affections"

Various factors contributed to the dimunition of regional strife in North Carolina. But the arrival of a new governor in late October 1754 also helped to instill a new spirit of provincial harmony. At sixty-five years of age, Arthur Dobbs was not entirely a stranger to the colony. As an Irish politician who had strong ties to Sir Robert Walpole, he became closely acquainted in the early 1730s with several enterprising London merchants, not the least of whom was Carolina land schemer Henry McCulloh. When McCulloh obtained his initial grant of land in 1735, Dobbs purchased six thousand acres, and in 1746 received an additional two hundred thousand acres from one of McCulloh's later acquisitions. The bulk of Dobb's property lay in the frontier county of Anson, and in the ensuing years, aided by several agents who resided in the province, he actively supervised its settlement.[1]

Despite his association with McCulloh and his own role in the regional controversy, the new governor eschewed partisanship during the early years of his administration. He knew that his first priority was to bring order to provincial politics and not to commit the error of his predecessor by aligning himself with a particular region. Moreover, Dobbs's previous support of the Albemarle counties had been contingent upon McCulloh's personal involvement in the dispute. Now that McCulloh's land titles once again were secure, both men looked forward to a time of stability during which they could more easily attract new settlers to their lands.[2] Further, the outbreak of the French and Indian War in 1754 posed a menace that only a united province could meet. For Dobbs, this threat seemed especially serious, not only because it could disrupt the settlement of his lands, but also because of his ardent commitment to British expansionism. As early as 1729, he had written a treatise pointing out the value of the British colonies in North America and the dangers of French imperialism. In succeeding years, he became intensely interested in the possible existence of a Northwest Passage, and argued in a lengthy essay that England could use such a link to the Pacific to increase trade and to offset the French presence in Canada. Later, he wrote a series of tracts devoted to the significance of British exploration, became deeply involved in backing several abortive expeditions to northern Canada, and actively participated in the Ohio Company of Virginia.[3]

Bearing all these imperatives in mind, Dobbs took several steps to alleviate lingering regional tensions. On December 12, 1754, he convened an assembly at New Bern, and in his opening address made only an oblique reference to the past controversy by urging representatives to adopt a "Union of Affections and Acting together for the general good of the Province." Already one symptom of renewed conflict had surfaced when northern politicians decided a few days earlier to run a candidate for the Speaker's office. "The northern members upon being restored to their Privileges," Dobbs later wrote, "wanted to shew that they were also restored to their power in the Assembly." The candidates were Samuel Swann, the current Speaker, and John Campbell, each representing regional factions. Swann, a lawyer from Onslow County, had been Speaker for the past twelve years as well as a leading exponent of southern parity in the lower house. Campbell, a Bertie County merchant, had been no less zealous in voicing his own region's interests. Each man received twenty-six votes; eight members were still due to arrive. The lower house as a consequence appealed to Dobbs, who instead of insisting upon a hasty decision wisely chose to let the contest resolve itself by postponing the election until the remaining representatives appeared. Faced by the prospect of gaining only two additional votes, Swann bowed out and Campbell became the new Speaker.[4]

Another potential problem that Dobbs encountered arose from the crown's disallowance of several provincial statutes establishing new counties and towns. In April 1754, when it voided the 1746 representation act, the Privy Council repealed twelve other laws extending assembly representation to various localities because the assembly, not the governor, had created these constituencies. The constitutional implications of the Privy Council's order notwithstanding, a more critical result would have been the disenfranchisement of numerous counties and towns, located chiefly outside the old Albemarle counties. Aware of the "confusion" this might create by reviving southern anxieties over underrepresentation, Dobbs stalled for time by not enforcing London's ruling. Fortunately, most assemblymen were not enamored of the decree. When the assembly drafted an address to the Board of Trade in protest, Dobbs quickly transmitted it along with an appeal of his own in which he warned that this ill-conceived measure could "vest the whole power of the Assembly in the few remaining Countys which might occasion a flame and again disunite the Province." In response, the crown agreed to let the assembly reestablish the towns and counties, but attached a proviso that only the governor could technically create new constituencies.[5]

By not "engaging in the little Controversies still subsisting among us," Dobbs, according to James Murray, was one of "the greatest Blessings this Province has seen of a long time." Because he helped to defuse possible sources of discord, Dobbs could justifiably claim, as he did to a longtime friend in March 1755, that he had "settled peace on the Colony" by keeping "my Self detached from any Party and giving no Countenance to any who would prevent the union in the Province."[6]

Once regional strife was effectively terminated, a new climate of tranquillity enveloped the first years of Dobbs's administration. During this time, he succeeded in obtaining much of the legislation he favored, including measures to strengthen the Anglican church in North Carolina and to improve the colony's judicial system.[7] But his major accomplishment lay in dramatizing the French threat and procuring appropriations for a province-wide counteroffensive. Before his arrival in North Carolina, he had conferred in Williamsburg with governors Robert Dinwiddie of Virginia and Horatio Sharpe of Maryland about military strategy. During his first meeting with the assembly in December, Dobbs warned that "the fire which has caught your Neighbours house has lately spread into your own." Four days later, he delivered a special address elaborating the far-flung ambitions of the "insatiable and rapacious house of Bourbon." Both the lower house and the council responded to these cries of alarm by pledging to provide all necessary funds. Before the session ended on January 15, 1755, they had granted £8,000 proclamation money to finance a force of 150 men on the Virginia and the Carolina frontier. It was not, Dobbs confessed in a letter to the Board of Trade, as large a sum as he might have wished, but, considering "the late divided state of this Province" and the debilitated condition of provincial finances, it was, he concluded, "as much as they can find ways and means to supply."[8]

The "perfect Harmony" that characterized this first session extended to future meetings. After the disastrous defeat of General Edward Braddock's Anglo-American force near the Monongahela, the assembly, meeting in September 1755, granted £9,000 for three fifty-man companies and £1,000 for a fort in the backcountry. It voted additional sums in subsequent sessions, and, though Dobbs occasionally complained that larger grants were needed, he nevertheless commended the assembly as late as May 1757 for "the constant and ready zeal" it had shown in supporting the war effort.[9]

"Personal attachments and national connexions"

Although Governor Dobbs could take satisfaction both in the assembly's support of a vigorous military effort against the French and in the stability that characterized provincial politics, he did little to insure that either would continue beyond his first years in office. Despite past years of service as high sheriff of Antrim, as a member of the Irish Parliament, and many more spent following the routes of preferment in London, he was not a particularly adept politician. He severely underestimated the possibility that the lower house could function as a coherent institution capable of blocking his policies. Although he rejoiced in the dampening of regional animosities, he continued to assume that the major threat to his administration would come from a divided house, not from a united one.[10]

Moreover, because Dobbs himself was firmly committed to the expanding interests of the British Empire, he assumed that Carolina's newly united provincial leadership naturally shared his enthusiasm beyond voting initial sums of support. For Dobbs, the principal means of enlisting the assembly's aid lay in a near endless barrage of patriotic appeals. He correctly perceived that the assembly must be "led and not drove," but he wrongly believed that leadership consisted chiefly of rhetorical flourish.[11] Instead, for men like Samuel Swann, Thomas Barker, and John Starkey, all powerful members of the lower house, political loyalty also depended on favors and benefits. When Dobbs arrived in 1754, they had anxiously looked forward to the traditional rewards by which North Carolina governors bound the interests of provincial leaders to their administrations.

Throughout the later decades of the colonial period, as in earlier years, provincial politicians displayed a keen interest in posts of profit. As Councillor James Murray described his port collectorship at Wilmington in 1740, "The advantage I have by the naval office is that it brings a great deal of ready money into my hands." Such was the lure of high office that Samuel Johnston, Jr., eagerly asked a friend's help in obtaining the attorney generalship of the province as soon as the office's present occupant was "on his last leggs or rather on none at all." When, that same year, the chief justiceship became vacant, Johnston aptly noted that there would "no doubt be a great number of Candidates for the office."[12]

Like most other colonial executives by the mid-eighteenth century, Dobbs had relatively little patronage at his disposal, but he could make some appointments, particularly because he was a wartime governor. One of his potentially most important tools consisted of awarding profitable military commissions. A major reason provincial funds voted in early 1754 for Virginia's assistance proved insufficient was because officers, eager to capitalize on their lucrative daily allowances and less than enthusiastic about combat, marched their troops so slowly that most of the money was expended before they ever reached their destination. In addition, James Murray, the paymaster, elected to take 2½ percent of the army's pay, though he was entitled to only 1 percent. One officer, later appointed to command a provincial fort at the mouth of the Cape Fear River, simply pocketed the £100 he was given to raise recruits.[13]

Although highly prized plums of patronage, most of the commands Dobbs granted were to intimates related either by blood or nationality who carried slight weight in the province. Hugh Waddell, who received command of a backcountry fort in early 1755, was originally a poor immigrant whose father had known Dobbs in Ireland. The following year, Dobbs commissioned Waddell as a major of three provincial companies ordered to join the British general John Forbes and other provincials in an attack on Fort

Duquesne.[14] Others who benefited included Dobbs's son, Edward, a former British officer, who was given command of four Carolina companies sent to New York in 1756; and the governor's nephew, Richard Spaight, who was appointed as paymaster for all the forces assembled in North Carolina.[15]

In a token attempt to forestall provincial resentment, Dobbs did grant a captaincy to the prominent Cape Fear planter Caleb Grainger for the New York expedition. But, when Grainger returned with his company to Fort Johnston on the Cape Fear and attempted to boost his salary by discharging "all the best men for money," Dobbs summarily forced his resignation, later observing that such behavior "was no encouragement . . . to employ the Country born of interest in the Province to make fortunes at the Publick expense."[16] Although Dobb's appointments may have reflected sound military judgment, they did little to sustain his early popularity.

The governor's civil appointments betrayed an equal lack of political finesse. Samuel Swann, in particular, made no secret of his desire to join his brother, John, on the council. But Dobbs ignored this and other valuable opportunities by which he might have cemented the loyalties of leading assemblymen to his administration. Past inefficiency on the part of provincial officials might partially explain his reluctance. Soon after his arrival in North Carolina, Dobbs complained about the appointment of "improper persons who know nothing of the Business, and therefore neglect it, and leave it all to their Deputies or Clerks, who only work for themselves, and not for the Publick."[17]

But Dobbs did little to remedy such problems. When council vacancies appeared, he simply appointed his son and nephew.[18] If it was possible to compound this error, he did so when he used his London connections to have his nephew appointed secretary of the colony in 1756. Two years later, he succeeded in obtaining the post of chief naval officer for his son.[19] Still worse, Dobbs rewarded the relatives of Henry McCulloh, his longtime associate. In 1755 McCulloh's cousin Henry received a seat on the council. Not long afterward, when McCulloh's nephew, Alexander, lost his office as deputy auditor, Dobbs made sure that he was reinstated. In the meantime, McCulloh himself—no doubt with the governor's approval—had been doing his best to obtain lucrative offices for himself and his relatives. Already, his cousin had held the twin posts of secretary and vice-admiralty judge up until his death in 1755; Mc-Culloh had also been instrumental in helping his nephew initially procure the deputy auditorship.[20]

The political ramifications of these varied appointments were extensive. "The Governor in his appointments and some say in his Councils," James Murray wrote in late 1755, "has had such particular Regard to his own Relations and Countrymen as to give some Jealousy."[21] Dobbs's friendship with McCulloh only made matters worse, for, though McCulloh had endeared himself to Albemarle leaders during their struggle with the south, his prestige had steadily declined following the relaxation of regional tensions. What influence he still exercised with provincial leaders deteriorated even further when a local land associate and distant relation, Speaker John Campbell, resigned his office and seat in the lower house in 1756 because of a debilitating illness.[22] No longer the hero of the Albemarle faction, McCulloh was increasingly regarded as a pariah who used his power to benefit only a small circle of friends and relatives.

One of many who lost out to McCulloh's maneuvering was Robert Jones, Jr., an assembly leader from Northampton County and the colony's attorney general who had fared well in Carolina politics after moving from Virginia. In the late 1750s he hoped to obtain yet another prize, the collectorship of Beaufort. But both this post and the collectorship of Currituck went to McCulloh, who reserved them for his son, Henry Eustace. Shortly after hearing of McCulloh's coup, James Abercromby, an intimate of Jones and other house leaders, wrote his disgruntled friend, "I do assure you I am much concerned for your Disappointment, and wish I could devise any Method to make Reprisals on McCulloch." Abercromby accurately expressed the average provincial politician's resentment over the narrow range of appointees in Dobbs's administration when he wrote Samuel Swann, Campbell's replacement as Speaker, that Dobbs had "contrived matters so, as to give himself full employment abroad" with "military promotions" and "the most advantageous and Constitutional offices of Government" going "to his personal attachments and national connexions."[23]

Restricted to a finite amount of largesse to dispense, no governor, of course, could ever have placated the ambitions of every leading provincial. But a governor could secure the tacit support of potential antagonists by giving them some reason to hope for future preferment through the judicious distribution of the limited patronage at his disposal.[24] Considering the fashion in which Dobbs used his opportunities, only the most sanguine assemblyman could entertain hopes of receiving an office.

At the same time he was making it clear that the most choice appointments in his administration would not go to house leaders, Dobbs undertook a series of ill-timed measures designed to reform government on both the local and the provincial levels. On hearing that many county justices were neglecting their duties, he issued a stern proclamation in April 1755 ordering that all offenders be suspended and only permitted to serve "in Subordinate Offices." When Robert Harris, a Granville County justice and assemblyman of eight years, apparently objected to the ruling, he lost his commission. In retaliation against Dobbs, the Granville court refused to meet in early 1756. More suspensions followed, and the remaining justices met only periodically during the next four years.[25]

In December 1757 the governor also suspended John Rutherfurd, a Wilmington merchant, from the council and from his office as receiver general on the grounds that he had permitted his close friend James Murray to pay his quitrent arrears with an illegally issued supply of paper money. Murray, who circulated several hundred pounds worth of new bills, was too suspended from the council. Rutherfurd chose to present his case to crown officials. After an initially unfavorable ruling, the matter dragged on until 1761, when he was finally reinstated in both posts.[26] The entire affair, however, had a much more immediate impact at home, where many leading politicians shared Rutherfurd's conviction that Dobbs was "determined to elbow out anybody in Places of Trust to make room for" his fellow "Countrymen." Rutherfurd also had a host of influential friends in the assembly, among whom were Speaker Samuel Swann and Councillor John Swann, his two securities as receiver general, and John Starkey, whom he unsuccessfully tried to appoint as his temporary replacement, and who was himself a prime target of the governor's zeal.[27]

"Private jobs" and Public Protest

John Starkey, a native Englishman of obscure origins who migrated to the Cape Fear around 1723, was a living testament to the region's social and political fluidity. As an aspiring planter in Onslow County, he had held numerous offices over the years and as early as 1734 obtained a seat in the lower house, where he served continuously from 1739 to 1764. His already substantial influence was significantly increased in 1750 when he was elected as one of the colony's two treasurers. It was in this post that he incurred Dobbs's ire during an assembly session in 1757. Partly because of Starkey's influence, the lower house refused to approve wartime appropriations that Dobbs had urgently requested at the opening of the session and voted only half of the 300 troops Dobbs had recommended. During the same meeting, Starkey also led a move that limited the salary of a military storekeeper at Fort Johnston to a piddling £12 per annum.[28]

Incensed by Starkey's power in the lower house, Dobbs took steps to counter it. In December 1757 he complained to the Board of Trade that Starkey's control over expenses enabled him to sway "the House against the most sensible Members in it" because "all the low Members who want a supply follow him like Chickens." Dobbs consequently urged that the board forbid passage of any future law permitting treasurers to serve in the assembly.[29] Matters between Dobbs and the treasurer worsened in 1758 when Starkey's committee of accounts disallowed a small claim filed by Secretary Spaight for expenses incurred by Dobbs in sending military dispatches. When Dobbs learned of the disallowance, he openly attacked it in a message to the lower house as the "greatest Indignity" and left no doubt as to whom his target was: "I do not lay it to the Charge of this Committee, but to the Chairman, who by aiming at a false Popularity, pretends not only to lead the Committee, but to govern the House." The house responded by denying that the claim's disallowance had been intended as an insult and by vigorously defending Starkey who, it asserted, "merited the esteem of all who wish well to the Province." Dobbs, however, continued to think otherwise. In May 1759 he asked the Board of Trade to repeal an act appointing provincial treasurers, so that the office would henceforth be held at the crown's pleasure and no treasurer would be allowed to sit in the assembly. Toward the end of the year, he also removed Starkey from his posts as justice of the peace and militia colonel.[30]

Although disturbed by Starkey's influence, Dobbs entertained another reason for wishing to bring the post of treasurer under crown control. Among the various duties attached to the office was responsibility for collecting taxes raised each year by county sheriffs. The colony's two treasurers then submitted their accounts to an assembly committee overwhelmingly composed of members from the lower house and numbering only a few from the council. As early as 1755, when political relations were still harmonious, Dobbs was compelled to declare in a message to the assembly, "I find it is become too much a Practice in this Province that those who are intrusted with the collecting or laying out the Publick Money keep it in their hands and lay it out for their benefit." Part of the problem, in his eyes, was the lower house's refusal to permit the deputy auditor to certify the treasurers' records. Assembly representatives, as Dobbs reported to a friend, were "much against the Auditors being concerned in passing their accounts."[31] Thus, when his break with Starkey occurred, the governor also complained to the board that the treasurers should submit their accounts to the governor and the council for their approval. To substantiate his point, in January 1760 he forwarded the "undigested" accounts of Thomas Barker, public treasurer for the northern half of the colony. He also complained that Starkey "has not furnished me with a Copy to send your Lordships," though "he has returned an imperfect list of Taxables and a jumbled indistinct Arrear" that were both "very irregular."[32]

London officials weighed Dobbs's allegations in June 1759, after the Board of Trade had forwarded his initial appeals to the Treasury for consideration. The response was not encouraging. In August the board asserted that "any attempt" to abrogate the assembly's privilege of appointing treasurers, "having prevailed and been acquiesced in for so long," would be "improper."[33] But, by this point, Dobbs's assault on Starkey had substantially widened to an effort to curb the activities of both treasurers, and had, at the same time, blossomed into a full-scale dispute with the lower house. The treasuers, Dobbs reported in February 1760, "are not pleased at my sending over Copies of their irregular Accounts." When the assembly met later that April, the issue occasioned an exchange in which Dobbs cited his instructions requiring the auditing of accounts and further faulted their accuracy. For its part, the lower house branded the governor's proposed change in procedure as "unprecedented and repugnant to Law."[34]

Closely related to the controversy surrounding the tenure of treasurers and the auditing of their accounts was the delicate question of how a substantial wartime grant from Parliament should be handled. In 1758 Parliament allotted £50,000 to the southern colonies for military expenses incurred during the hostilities. North Carolina's share amounted to £15,000. "Who shall have the fingering of it," as James Murray observed, became "a very knoty bone of Contention." In December the lower house drafted a bill stipulating that disposition of the grant should rest with the two public treasurers. For purposes of transferring the money from London, the bill also appointed an agent accountable to a committee of five members of the lower house. Aware by then of the governor's mounting hostility toward the treasurers, the lower house attempted to sweeten the bill by offering to enact several other measures in return for Dobbs's approval. First, it proposed to establish the provincial capital at Tower Hill, a location on the Neuse River in Craven County where Dobbs owned property, and to erect public buildings, including a governor's house, all at public expense. In addition, the house promised to reimburse Dobbs for his expenses in traveling to Philadelphia in March 1757 to attend a military conference and for the back rent of his lodgings in the colony. It was, as the governor later noted, a "fine spun scheme," but he finessed the lower house by remaining mute on the arrangement until after the representatives had approved both the grant and the capital bills. At his urging, the council then rejected the grant bill and passed the other.[35]

The governor detailed his reasons for rejecting the parliamentary aid bill in a lengthy explanation to the Board of Trade. He objected to the appointment of an agent answerable only to the lower house; he also feared the influence that disposition of the grant would give the treasurers. His strongest apprehension, however, stemmed from how the money might be received. His own proposal was that it should either be placed in the Bank of London or be used to purchase bank stock, "which upon a happy peace would rise considerably, and to remit it as wanted to this Province." According to him, however, it was the intention of the treasurers to "pass" the money by bringing it over in specie, to exchange it for inflated currency, and to distribute the excess among themselves and their friends. "Very little money," he warned, "will be raised upon the Province but for their own benefit."[36]

Rejection of the aid bill was a daring maneuver. It quickly put the lower house "all in a flame"—though, according to Dobbs, the "managers" in the house suffered the deepest disappointment.[37] Refusing to give up the fight, the house appointed James Abercromby as its agent to obtain the grant. His service as agent for the southern counties during their dispute with the north and for the entire province until 1757, as well as for South Carolina's governor, James Glen, and the Virginia council, made Abercromby well suited for the task. He was also strongly interested in the success of his mission, for his salary of £150 sterling per annum was to be drawn from the grant once it had been obtained. Moreover, he enjoyed the personal support of lower-house leaders, who recognized the value of a trusted friend in London. Although frequently unsuccessful, often against the influence of Dobbs and McCulloh, Abercromby was indefatigable in his efforts to obtain lucrative offices for his intimates. At one time or another, he used his connections in attempts to acquire the provincial posts of chief justice for Samuel Swann and chief baron of the exchequer for Thomas Barker, as well as the collectorship of Beaufort for Robert Jones. He could rightfully assert, as he did to Swann in June 1759, "I do not want full Inclination to serve my friends in North Carolina."[38]

Although hopeful of Abercromby's ultimate success in London, the lower house again sought to achieve control over the parliamentary money when it met in May 1759. At the beginning of the session, Dobbs reported the contents of a recent message from William Pitt, secretary of state for the colonies, that required the colony to appropriate a new supply for a final campaign against the French. The house promised its loyal compliance and passed an aid bill for £6,000 which the council then rejected with Dobbs's approval. Upset by the meager sum, Dobbs was even more displeased upon discovering that the bill contained several clauses empowering Abercromby to receive Parliament's grant in order to reimburse this latest expenditure.[39]

Dobbs remained steadfast in opposing the house's efforts to create what he termed "private jobs," though in early August 1759 Abercromby convinced the Board of Trade to rule that the lower house had a right to appoint an agent as well as the authority to control the parliamentary grant. The board did support Dobbs in rejecting the military aid bill, but only because of the "exceptionable" manner in which it had been drafted and its proviso that members of the council could not serve on the committee delegated to correspond with the agent. Despite that slight consolation for his efforts, Dobbs persisted in blocking the lower house on both issues. As a consequence, the money had to remain in England for the time being.[40]

While Dobbs and the lower house were sparring over treasurers, grants, and agents, another cause of friction concerned the colony's judicial establishment. In April 1759 the Privy Council disallowed seven provincial statutes. The most important of these was a judiciary act passed in 1755, which updated county court regulations and replaced the old General Court system with superior courts in Edenton, Halifax County, New Bern, Salisbury, and Wilmington. The original precipitators of what Dobbs later termed a "hasty" decision were Charles Berry, the colony's newly appointed chief justice, and Thomas Child, who was in the process of regaining his post as attorney general, which he had formerly held from 1746 to 1751. While in London, the two had made a number of charges against the act. In particular, they had asserted that the superior court provisions infringed upon the royal prerogative by not permitting the governor to establish associate judgeships for the various courts.[41]

Catching the colony by surprise, disallowance of the act officially left the province without any higher courts except one in Edenton that was sanctioned by an earlier statute. As a consequence, Dobbs, with the advice of council, delayed enforcing the repeal until the assembly could meet to enact new legislation. But, in January 1760, a prolonged dispute arose between the two houses over the question of how associate judges were to be paid, which effectively killed passage of a bill drafted by the lower house for both superior and inferior courts. The controversy assumed a new dimension when the assembly convened again in late April. A lower-court bill did not engender any serious disagreement, but the superior court bill did not fare so well. Although the question of salaries had by then been substantially resolved, the proposed act required that associate judgeships—lucrative prizes at £400 per annum—could be held only by "Attorneys of seven years Practice" in North Carolina or adjacent provinces who had been resident in the colony for a minimum of one year or by "outer Barristers of five years standing in England." Furthermore, the offices were not to be held at the governor's pleasure but during good behavior.[42]

Governor Dobbs roundly condemned the bill's provisions. The tenure stipulation constituted a violation of his instructions, which stated that associate judges should be appointed only at pleasure. Just as disturbing was the other condition, which Dobbs viewed as nothing less than an attempt to force the appointments of several of his leading antagonists in the lower house. Facing the prospect that barristers possessing five years of experience would "not come over," he might be obliged to choose Samuel Swann, the Speaker, Thomas Barker, a treasurer, and Robert Jones, yet another foe—all of whom were prominent lawyers and leading assemblymen. A final aggravation was that the lower house refused to appropriate further aid for the French and Indian War unless Dobbs consented to the bill. Interference by imperial officials had thus produced yet another issue of contention between Dobbs and the lower house.[43]

Despite the increasing unpopularity of Dobbs's administration, lower-house opposition, once it began, remained reasonably restrained for the first several years. What consisted largely of legislative skirmishes did not result in appeals to London for the governor's recall, and, though the house's rhetoric could be strident, it remained firmly within the bounds of respectful protest. However alienated men in positions of power had become from Dobbs, the assembly could do little except to discomfit his administration as much as possible. But all this changed toward the end of the decade when the lower house began a serious campaign to unseat the governor. In May 1760 it drafted resolves alleging diverse abuses of power that culminated in the accusation that he had brought the province to "the Brink of Anarchy and ruin." This rather abrupt escalation of opposition was not simply the product of political momentum or mounting dissatisfaction. Instead, the answer also lies in what has come to be known as the Enfield Riot and the complexities attending the administration of North Carolina's Granville District.

"Differences and Disputes"

When seven of the Lords Proprietors of Carolina sold their shares to the crown in 1729, John Lord Carteret, the sole remaining proprietor, chose to retain his claim. In petitioning the Privy Council for one-eighth of both Carolinas, he cited the original 1663 patent Charles II had granted his great-grandfather. Despite a favorable endorsement from the Board of Trade in May 1730, his petition elicited scant enthusiasm among council members, probably because Carteret, a prominent British politician, currently opposed the ministry of Sir Robert Walpole. The status of Carteret's claim remained unresolved throughout the 1730s, so he was forced to depend upon infrequent Carolina quitrent revenues for temporary compensation.[44]

By 1740 Carteret had grown increasingly anxious over the disposition of his petition. No quitrents at all were arriving from the Carolinas, despite an anticipated income of more than £4,000 per annum. Equally foreboding, a potential threat to his interests had arisen in the form of Henry McCulloh, who in the mid-1730s had begun to amass property in North Carolina. Fearing that further inaction by the crown would seriously jeopardize his title, Carteret sought the aid of the Duke of Newcastle. "Great Tracts of Land have been granted out to diverse Persons," he complained to Newcastle in early 1740, "to which Grants I have been no party."[45]

If Newcastle came to Carteret's assistance, his aid soon became immaterial. In early 1742 Walpole's ministry fell, and Carteret assumed the prestigious office of secretary of state for the northern department. A related consequence was that the Privy Council finally agreed in August to grant him a separate district in the Carolinas. Carteret strongly favored locating his tract next to Virginia, and formally received a proprietary grant on September 17, 1744. That same year, he became Earl Granville upon the death of his mother.[46]

The new earl's estate, the Granville District, encompassed an enormous quantity of land within the present borders of North

Carolina. The northern border was contiguous with Virginia, and the district extended nearly sixty miles south to the coastal town of Bath, at the northern latitude of 35°34'. The Atlantic formed the tract's eastern border, and the "South Seas" its western boundary, though surveyors never traveled farther inland than 350 miles. The grant contained more than 26,000 square miles.[47]

The Granville District was not a proprietary domain in any traditional sense. At no time during his negotiations with the crown did Granville express a desire to exercise governmental authority over his estate—either because of royal opposition or the sorry example of proprietary mismanagement during preceding decades. The Privy Council's grant consequently stipulated that he could not establish courts, levy taxes, or hold assemblies. Although he possessed none of the traditional privileges accorded a "country palatine," Granville did retain free rein to dispose of his property as he wished. His only remaining obligations to the crown entailed the annual payment of £1 13s. and the forfeiture of one-fourth of all gold and silver discovered on his lands.[48]

Granville clearly viewed his North American estate as a promising source of income to supplement his already impressive family fortune. The proprietary was "capable of Such improvements," he had anticipated in 1730, "as were likely to make it as valuable an Estate to my Family, as any Subject had in America." At the time of its creation, in 1744, not only did the Granville District contain a resident population of more than thirty thousand people, but ample quantities of land also lay waiting for many more settlers. Only 1,093,779 acres had already been patented. "It is not generally known on your side the water," Gabriel Johnston wrote a British acquaintance in 1743, "what a prodigious bargain my Lord Carteret has gott from the Crown. . . . It is at present better than 1,300 l. and in a few years will be worth 5,000 l."[49]

The best way to realize such profits was not, however, through imposing burdensome conditions of land tenure. North Carolinians had a long-standing hostility toward property restrictions. The Lords Proprietors frequently had failed in collecting quitrents, as did the crown after 1729. "How ever advantageous this Division may seem to be to his Lordship," Eleazer Allen warned in 1743, "I am apprehensive, he will meet with great difficultys in Collecting his rents, as well from the Scituation of the Country as from the Genius of the people, who inhabit it."[50] Granville was almost entirely bereft of powers to compel obedience from unruly settlers. Without the right to create manorial courts, he was largely dependent on North Carolina authorities to enforce proprietary regulations—a circumstance hardly designed to inspire confidence in view of the crown's own plight in collecting rents.

Whatever the temperament of resident settlers, the Granville District would really only prosper and realize its full potential if it could attract large numbers of immigrants to occupy its vacant lands, which made the establishment of liberal tenancy conditions even more imperative. As William Byrd II advised another North Carolina landlord in the mid-1730s and may later have counseled Granville: "Certainly the easier terms your lands are granted upon, the more will be granted, and the more people will remove thither. But if the conditions be as hard there, or harder than in the other colonys, men will stay where they are, rather than be at the trouble of removeing for no advantage."[51]

The Granville District also faced strong competition for prospective settlers. Besides still unoccupied sections of western Virginia and the whole South Carolina piedmont, vast quantities of unpatented land awaited immigrants in the royal half of western North Carolina. As of 1745 fewer than a hundred people had settled crown lands in the backcountry.

Probably because of all these considerations, Granville instituted a reasonably enlightened system of proprietary land tenure. Instead of offering settlers leases for a set number of years in order to profit from their improvements, he chose to grant lands in fee simple, subject to an annual quitrent of 3s. sterling or 4s. proclamation money per hundred acres, the same sums required for crown lands. For tracts settled before the proprietary's creation, quitrents were even lower, ranging from 2 to 3s. proclamation money.[52]

The price of newly patented land was similarly modest. Regardless of size, each tract cost the initial sum of £4 19s. Virginia currency, plus an additional 5s. for every 50 acres included in the patent. The price of 640 acres—normally the maximum size of a single grant to inhibit landjobbing—was only £8 4s. Virginia currency, or about £6 sterling. Moreover, patented land was not subject to such traditional manorial restrictions as alienation fees and escheat; nor did settlers need to give their landlord first refusal on buying their crops or provide several days of road work each year.[53]

Settlers were required to forfeit half of all gold and silver found on their properties, exclusive of the crown's fourth, but no controls existed for the more relevant activities of timber-cutting, fishing, hunting, and the use of waterways. Granville even omitted the mineral clause in his grants after learning in 1751 that it had "obstructed the manufacture of Iron . . . and other designs for the General Benefit of the Countrey." Furthermore, though tenant property could be seized for nonpayment of quitrents, Granville favored distraint only after "all other methods to procure payment shall have failed." Even in those instances, "Indulgence" could be shown "when it shall appear that Poverty or some unfortunate accident had disabled any Tennant from paying."[54]

In short, Granville's relationship with the tenants of his lands was overwhelmingly economic, and quite mild at that. Social and political obligations, for both parties, were nonexistent. Tenant tracts were really tantamount to freeholds. Doubtless proprietary policy was also mercenary, but Granville's interest in profits did not create onerous conditions of land tenure; it necessitated just the reverse, if his estate were ever to flourish.

Just how successful Granville's land policies actually were became evident once advertisements announcing the sale of proprietary lands had been circulated.[55] Whether as newcomers to the backcountry, which contained the largest quantity of unoccupied land, or, less commonly, as established residents, Granville District settlers eagerly purchased proprietary lands. Between 1751 and 1762, when land was being sold, agents granted almost two million acres, nearly twice the amount of property deeded within the area of the proprietary from 1689 to its creation in 1744.[56] Individual tracts were ample. Although a proprietary rent roll was never completed, a list of surveys run between 1749 and 1754 exists for several piedmont counties. As shown in table 5.1, few surveys encompassed less than two hundred acres. The typical tract ranged between three hundred and four hundred acres in Orange County, whereas most surveys in neighboring Granville contained more than four hundred. In Rowan County, surveys averaged around five hundred acres. Surveys, of course, provide conservative estimates,

TABLE 5.1 *Distribution of Granville District Land Surveys,*
1749–1754[57] *(percentages in parentheses)*

	Counties					
Acres Surveyed	Orange		Granville		Rowan	
1–100	1	(1.3)	3	(1.2)	1	(.4)
101–200	9	(12.0)	18	(7.0)	14	(6.0)
201–300	13	(17.3)	42	(16.4)	18	(7.7)
301–400	24	(32.0)	52	(20.3)	45	(19.2)
401–500	13	(17.3)	42	(16.4)	39	(16.7)
501–600	6	(8.0)	30	(11.7)	35	(15.0)
601–700	9	(12.0)	62	(24.2)	80	(34.2)
701+	—	—	7	(2.7)	2	(.9)
	75		256		234	

for they do not necessarily reflect the total acreage settlers acquired; some settlers obviously purchased multiple tracts.

Another picture of proprietary land patterns can be gained from scattered grants made in Orange County. Based upon extant land grants issued from 1751 to 1762, table 5.2 presents the minimum acreage patented by 596 Orange settlers. More than 90 percent of the patentees acquired more than two hundred acres, and nearly half received in excess of five hundred. It seems likely that more than a few newcomers even hoped to speculate in proprietary lands, for almost 15 percent patented more than one thousand acres.

None of this is to say that proprietary settlers, in purchasing substantial tracts of land, always realized their expectations of material success. Many did not. The Granville District, as well as the rest of North Carolina, suffered from a variety of economic ills. Yet, as proprietary settlers themselves understood, the land system did not hinder their material progress. Most no doubt shared Hermon Husband's conviction that "there was a good foundation a laying" in the Granville District. "I liked well the bottom of the work," he wrote Granville in 1755, after first inspecting "some of the laws and some of the deeds." Not only did large numbers of

TABLE 5.2 *Distribution of Granville District Patentees,*
Orange County, 1751–1762[58] *(percentages in parentheses)*

Acreage	Patentees	
1–100	8	(1.3)
101–200	50	(8.4)
201–300	81	(13.6)
301–400	101	(17.0)
401–500	73	(12.3)
501–600	64	(10.7)
601–700	77	(12.9)
701–1,000	54	(9.1)
1,001–2,500	74	(12.4)
2,501–5,000	8	(1.3)
5,001+	6	(1.0)
	596	

settlers invest in proprietary lands, but they also evinced a steady willingness to honor their modest obligations. "Your Lordships Tennants," a North Carolina resident assured Granville in 1749, "seem very well disposed to pay their Rents." Thomas McKnight discovered a similar "Disposition in the people to pay the Quit Rents for the time to come." Upon becoming governor in 1771, Josiah Martin was "informed on all hands" that the normal land fees had been "paid most chearfully, and without Complaint" in previous years.[59]

Considering the satisfaction of most settlers with the proprietary's liberal system of land tenure, it is worth exploring how the Granville District could quickly become a source of controversy both in England and in North Carolina. Besides causing Granville considerable distress, the proprietary experienced a series of local disputes that culminated in 1759 in the Enfield Riot. A perplexed visitor to North Carolina later commented, "My Lord Granville is proprietor, of more than one half the best of the Province, and tho' it is but an unprofitable Estate, it affects the whole, and is the means of Differences and Disputes." The answer to this riddle does not lie in the inherent features of land tenure or in a feudal revival as some scholars have recently argued.[60] One must look instead to how the Granville District was administered and to the machinations of Henry McCulloh—next to Granville himself, North Carolina's consummate land speculator.

Granville never visited his American estate. Because he remained a prominent political figure in later years, his primary concerns continued to lie in English public life, not in North Carolina. Contrary to historical opinion, however, he was not negligent toward his estate. He attached much importance to maintaining a "uniform moderate Course of proceeding," as his often detailed correspondence attests. To manage the day-to-day operation of proprietary affairs, he appointed two agents, Edward Moseley and Robert Halton, in 1746. Moseley had earlier served as a boundary commissioner, and both men were prominent North Carolina politicians.[61]

The immediate concerns of Moseley and Halton consisted of preparing a rent roll of all lands patented before 1744, granting new deeds for unpatented property, and arranging a procedure for quitrent collections. Their efforts met with minimal success. The chaos of the colony's land system was a serious impediment; another obstacle was the regional and political identities of the two men. Both were prominent proponents of representational parity for the south; they also agreed to accept as payment the new currency authorized in 1748 that northern politicians had roundly opposed. Governor Johnston even feared at one point that Moseley might be "mobbed."[62]

Matters grew more confused in 1749 when Halton and then Moseley suddenly died within a period of three months. The death of Moseley, whose years in North Carolina had been marked by a steady preoccupation with attaining the material blessings of life, was entirely in character. Johnston wrote Granville: "His eagerness to receive the fees that would accrue from doing so much Business before your Lordship could send him a colleague was what I believe pushed him to take so fatigueing a Journey in this Sultry hott Weather which neither his Years nor Constitution could bear."[63]

Granville was left without any agents and with the only papers pertaining to his concerns in a state of "Confusion and Dissipation."[64] In October he commissioned Francis Corbin and Thomas Child as replacements. Corbin had already been a deputy to Granville for several years, and in 1744 had delivered the proprietary grant to Governor Johnston. Child, the son of an English doctor, was currently North Carolina's attorney general. Significantly, in early 1749 both had helped the northern counties press their case against Johnston and the south. Granville may have felt their effectiveness as agents would be enhanced by this tie to local northern leaders.[65]

Child's stay in the colony was brief. Arriving with Corbin in late 1749, he remained for slightly beyond a year. On March 2, 1751, he was given leave by Granville to return to England to "settle his private affairs," which entailed complaining to the Board of Trade that he had not received his back salary as attorney general because of spotty quitrent collections in the southern half of the colony. Child, nevertheless, did not intend to forsake his agency, for upon returning to London, he became the earl's special counsel.[66]

During the next eight years, Corbin remained the most powerful proprietary agent in North Carolina, often despite Granville's own wishes. The proprietor strongly preferred that two men represent his interests abroad, in part because of the sheer amount of work involved in managing his estate. One agent would bear responsibility for collecting quitrents on patented lands; the second would be in charge of issuing deeds for newly surveyed tracts. Granville also seems to have felt that two men would diminish the likelihood of malfeasance because each would act as a check on the other.[67] In keeping with these priorities, Child did appoint a replacement, James Innes, to assist Corbin in his absence. But Innes resided in the Cape Fear county of New Hanover, which restricted his duties to infrequent trips to Edenton, where a land office was slowly being built. Moreover, when Innes apparently became involved in a dispute with Child, he was removed, less than three years after his appointment.[68]

Not until August 1754 was a replacement found in Benjamin Wheatley, an English placeman and chief naval officer of North Carolina. His tenure, however, resembled that of his predecessor. Intent upon controlling the land office, Corbin kept him ill informed and refused to furnish relevant land records. "We hear that Mr. Wheatly is appointed Joynt Agent . . . with equal powers," Governor Dobbs noted, "but Mr. Corbin so far denies his power, that he acts for both." In April 1756 Granville was even forced to remind Corbin that Wheatley too was an agent. Within months, however, Wheatley was relieved of his office, apparently at Child's instigation.[69]

If Corbin had been an able and loyal administrator, these interruptions in the management of the land office would have been of slight consequence. But Corbin was thoroughly untrustworthy. He complied with few of the regulations that Granville carefully formulated for the administration of his estate. In the instructions, for instance, sent Corbin and Innes in December 1751, Granville specified that all business relating to new land grants should be conducted twice each year in New Bern during the sitting of the General Court and in Edenton and Edgecombe County while circuit courts were in session. He also ordered that a land office be constructed in Edenton, that lists of all fees and grants be forwarded to London, and that a rent roll be completed.[70] Nevertheless, Corbin's attendance at the courts was erratic, and he failed to establish a permanent land office. A rent roll was never finished, and Corbin's correspondence with Granville was infrequent at best. Despite a later directive that he transmit a security bond to guard against future negligence, Corbin did so only after Granville's persistent prodding.[71]

More damaging to the proprietor's interests than Corbin's lack of diligence was his utter want of scruples. Notwithstanding the Granville District's potential as a valuable source of income, insufficient sums of money were remitted to London. As early as 1750, Governor Johnston expressed fears over Corbin's rectitude in a letter to Granville: "What that Gentlemans fortune, or Credit may be at Home I dont pretend to know, But unless both are tolerably good I am afraid He will be pretty much puzzled to make Regular Remittances." From 1751 to 1756, Corbin remitted a little more than £4,000 sterling, by no means a trifling sum but significantly less than that to which Granville was entitled. After 1756 not one shilling evidently found its way to London. The initial remittances, as a contemporary later remarked, were probably intended solely "to keep the Proprietor in humor."[72]

Fraud extended to other segments of the proprietary land system. Subagents and surveyors, working under Corbin's direction, engaged in a host of activities designed to exploit the average settler's desire for land. "There is not one single Patent," a proprietary official later concluded, "that covers the Land claimed under it, owing to the Villiany or Ignorance of former surveyors." Throughout the 1750s, local land officers charged exorbitant prices for surveying land, refused to publicize their fees, sold patents to different individuals for the same tract, and sometimes did not even issue deeds once fees had been accepted. One especially corrupt deputy was James Carter, a surveyor in the backcountry counties of Orange and Rowan; many new migrants never received deeds in exchange for the fees they paid him. Traveling to Edenton in the mid-1750s, Hermon Husband discovered that Carter had filed only "about 170 odd returns" on his surveys though "there should been near if not quite a thousand."[73]

Although some of the chicanery practiced by Carter and others may not have directly involved Corbin, he had a hand in much of it. In April 1756 an incensed Granville wrote his agents: "Great and frequent Complaints are transmitted to me of those persons you employ to receive Entries and make Surveys in the back Counties. It is their Extorsions, and not the regular Fees of Office (wholly in my Will to fix) which is the Cause of Clamour from my Tenants. Insinuations are made too, as if those Extortions were connived at by the Agents; for otherwise, it is said, They could not be Committed so repeatedly and barefacedly." Before closing his letter, Granville ordered "that effectual Methods be taken for redressing a Grievance that reflects a Scandal upon my office; as well as the Honesty of the persons employed in it." He also took the occasion to declare, "I must tell my Agents plainly, that I will have them and any others employed in my Office, not only endeavour, but actually execute all my Instructions."[74]

Corruption in the Granville proprietary, however, only continued. Whenever settlers attempted to complain directly to Corbin about his deputies, he would rise stoutly to their defense. At one point, he even reportedly encouraged the rumor that he was Granville's "natural son" so as "to impress an Opinion among the people that they could expect no Redress against him in case they applied to Lord Granville against him."[75]

If Granville entertained at least some suspicion of Corbin's malfeasance, why did he not appoint a replacement? One answer might lie in his unwillingness to disrupt further the administration of his proprietary. When informed, for example, that a minor office clerk might be suspended, Granville had written Corbin and Wheatley in 1756, "You will consider that it may not be for my Service, circumstanced as my Affairs, and office at this Time are, to dismiss Clerks upon the first Occasions, without previous Warning or any admonition."[76] In view of the rapid turnover in agents, Corbin, despite his accumulated shortcomings, was far more knowledgeable about proprietary land business than anyone who might have succeeded him. Also important, perhaps, was his friendship with Thomas Child. At a later time, Governor Dobbs even charged that Corbin acted entirely by Child's "directions."[77] Finally, Granville seems to have been optimistic about his appointment of Joshua Bodley in September 1756 as Corbin's new coagent. A London attorney, Bodley was sent to North Carolina to bring Corbin to account and, in the process, to restore order to proprietary affairs. Among his other duties, he was instructed to "make out from the Records and Papers of" Granville's "Office the Amount or Sum Total of the Quit Rents yearly due to" the proprietor and to make "a compleat Account of the Quit Rents that have been received by Messrs Corbin, Innes and Wheatley." Granville further instructed both Corbin and Bodley that they were "punctually [to] obey all" his "Instructions, without any Remonstrance, Delay or Excuse What ever." Unhappily for Granville, however, Bodley, like his predecessors, failed to assume control over Corbin's activities.[78]

While Corbin was reaping handsome profits from his proprietary office, he became involved in an increasingly acrimonious dispute with Henry McCulloh. Of the more than 1,000,000 acres McCulloh had acquired since 1736, approximately 475,000 fell within the boundaries of the Granville District. Both McCulloh and Granville were eager to resolve what could have grown into a protracted and damaging dispute, and in the late 1740s they began negotiations to settle the conflicting claims. Nevertheless, shortly after his arrival in North Carolina, Corbin authorized proprietary grants of McCulloh territory. When Granville learned of these sales, he wrote Corbin and Wheatley: "You having made Entries, and granted some Deeds of the forfeited Lands, that were late Mr. McCulloh's . . . has thrown a Difficulty upon me, as Mr. McCulloh is in Treaty with me for my Permission to settle them, if He can." Corbin, however, continued to grant the disputed property, and at the same time made it clear that he opposed an agreement with McCulloh. Even

Child felt obliged to write his friend in late 1753, "Whether it will be proper for his Lordship to enter into that Agreement, is a Point that must be wholly referred to his own Judgement and Good Pleasure."[79]

Because of Corbin's interference, negotiations over the conflicting claims slowed considerably. An angry McCulloh charged in a petition to the Board of Trade that Granville's agents were forcing his tenants to pay quitrents. Many settlers, he asserted, had already deserted their properties because of the prevailing confusion. Corbin's defiance became even more unsettling when a small party of men commissioned by McCulloh and an English associate traveled to Rowan County in June 1755 to survey a tract of one hundred thousand acres. Before completing their chores, they were set upon by fifteen armed men who ordered them to stop. The attackers, probably either Granville settlers or opportunists taking advantage of the land chaos, threatened to "Break their Bones," which frightened the surveyors into retreat.[80]

Still anxious to conclude an agreement, Granville assured McCulloh that proprietary agents were not acting under his authority. Although a settlement was reached on the strength of these assurances,[81] Corbin continued to sell patents to anyone wishing to buy them. Even a subsequent lawsuit had slight effect. In July 1757 McCulloh directed his nephew Alexander, then deputy auditor of the province, and John Campbell, ex-Speaker of the assembly and a friend, to sue Corbin for £8,000 sterling for intimidating his tenants with what he described as "sordid wiked and avaritious Intentions." Matters so deteriorated the following year that McCulloh wrote Granville in November, "I can by no means tamely Submit to the Injury's I daily receive from those who have the conduct of your Lordship's Affairs." Not long afterward, McCulloh threatened that "Things are now brought to a Crisis."[82]

The growing enmity Corbin engendered as Granville's agent was not confined solely to proprietary settlers and Henry McCulloh but also extended to Governor Dobbs. Shortly after his arrival in the colony, Corbin had been given a seat on the council by Dobbs's predecessor, Gabriel Johnston. For the next few years, Corbin maintained a low profile in his new position, and in 1753 managed to win a commission as an associate judge of the General Court. When Dobbs arrived, however, Corbin soon informed Granville that the new governor was granting crown patents for proprietary lands. Although Granville then wrote Dobbs requesting that any such patents be revoked, he also wrote Corbin in June 1755: "If you, Mr. Corbin coud have depended on your Intelligence of the Governour's having granted Lands, which lie in my District, you should have instantly stated the Facts in a paper by Way of Representation to him, and desired him to Recal and cancel those Patents." What scant evidence Corbin actually possessed became clear when he denied to Dobbs ever having made any accusations to the proprietor.[83]

Over the next few years, relations between Dobbs and Corbin grew more strained when Corbin finally promised to present a copy of his letter to Granville before the council to show that no accusation had ever been made, and then continually failed to do so. Yet another source of irritation was Corbin's overall conduct as proprietary agent. In what was doubtless a sincere expression of concern for settlers who had been abused, Dobbs had already complained to Granville about his agent's chicanery. In December 1758 matters came to a head when Dobbs suspended Corbin from his posts as associate judge and colonel of the Chowan County militia. Anxious not to offend Granville, he appointed Joshua Bodley to the vacant judgeship, and, for the time being at least, refrained from dismissing Corbin from the council.[84]

For most of Francis Corbin's tenure as agent, his administration of the Granville proprietary did not exert a visible impact on the public arena. Some early signs, however, indicated that the myriad antagonisms he and his deputies incurred would have far-reaching ramifications. Besides Corbin's dispute with Dobbs, which was confined to the council chambers, the surveyor James Carter quickly became the victim of several court suits because of his chicanery.[85] Beyond that, a committee in the North Carolina assembly charged Corbin and his "substitutes" in 1755 with numerous frauds, ranging from exorbitant fees to voiding entries that had been approved prior to Corbin's agency. Significantly, the Speaker of the house was John Campbell, whose close connections to McCulloh may have influenced the committee's accusations.[86]

After Campbell resigned as Speaker in 1756, the assembly remained mute on the issue that its own committee had raised. This happenstance probably suggests that Corbin, despite the growing number of his enemies, actually wielded a substantial amount of power in the lower house. Proprietary posts were highly valued, and Corbin used his patronage as agent wisely by appointing local leaders as deputies in the outlying counties. James Carter, who was both a Rowan assemblyman and a deputy surveyor, was one beneficiary. Another surveyor was William Churton, who served as Orange County's register of deeds and also an assemblyman from 1754 to 1762. In Bertie County, Benjamin Wynns, a county clerk and assemblyman, was a Corbin deputy, as was John Clayton, a Perquimans County justice of the peace, and Colonel John Edwards, a court clerk in Northampton County. Still another deputy was Richard Caswell, an assemblyman from 1754 to the 1770s from Johnston County. Foremost in Corbin's entourage was Colonel John Haywood, a former assemblyman and probably the most powerful man in Edgecombe County. All these individuals and other deputies were influential both in the lower house and in their counties. Some, it would seem, also used their proprietary posts to enhance their power. Hermon Husband claimed that in the counties of Orange and Rowan the "most leading men" and James Carter's "perticular favourites who voted him an assemblyman" experienced no trouble getting deeds to the best lands but "others were continually put off."[87]

But there were limits to how long Corbin's malfeasance could be ignored. In late 1758 an unknown number of planters urged Attorney General Robert Jones to prosecute Corbin and his deputies. Unwilling to assume the responsibility, Jones suggested that they petition the assembly or Granville himself. After the lower house convened on November 23, legislators were greeted by the sobering spectacle of five hundred men demanding that their grievances be redressed. The assembly hastily formed a committee, which on December 22 submitted a report that was at best ambivalent. It confirmed numerous fraudulent acts on the part of proprietary surveyors as well as McCulloh's charge that some of his property had been granted illegally. Yet Corbin was absolved of any guilt. In fact, when Francis Brown, a representative from Perquimans, accused Corbin of exacting an extortionate quitrent fee, he was expelled from the house. Nor did the committee or, for that matter, the assembly take any steps to discipline representatives who were surveyors or to correct existing abuses through legislation. If Governor Dobbs is to be believed, the committee and its chairman, Thomas Barker, found "it more for their Interest to make up matters with Corbyn" in exchange for "a valuable consideration."[88]

In response to the assembly's investigation, Corbin did post a table of land fees, but this belated concession only confirmed fears of past extortions. When his chief deputy, John Haywood, suddenly died, local residents unearthed his body to make sure his rumored death was not just a trick to avoid prosecution. Then on the night of January 25, 1759, less than five weeks after the assembly adjourned, a group of from twenty to twenty-five men assembled from the counties of Edgecombe, Halifax, and Granville. Taking Corbin by surprise at his Edenton residence, they carried him seventy-five miles to the small village of Enfield, in Halifax County. For four days, the band kept him confined, together with his coagent Bodley, who had also been seized. Both men eventually agreed to open all land records for public inspection and to dismiss corrupt deputies. "Frightened out of his wits," Corbin also signed a bond for £2,000 Virginia currency that guaranteed his May appearance in Enfield to remit the illegal fees he and his underagents had received.[89]

The Enfield rioters, interestingly enough, did not constitute a class-conscious mob of impoverished tenants. Of the eight whose identities are known, most seem to have been middling planters and one, William Hurst, was a Granville County justice of the peace.[90] Moreover, the rioters' complaints faulted the corrupt behavior of local officials, not the structural features of land tenure in the Granville District. They did not, in fact, express the least dissatisfaction with proprietary land policy.

But, in one significant respect, Corbin's kidnapping did involve more than a momentary outburst of popular indignation over short-term grievances. The Enfield Riot, in all likelihood, represented a dispute between rival land magnates as much as an expression of settler disaffection. A chief participant, and probably the kidnappers' leader, was none other than Alexander McCulloh, nephew of Henry, deputy auditor of North Carolina, and a militia colonel in Edgecombe County. McCulloh would later head a list of defendants charged with having "imprisoned and evilly treated" Corbin for the "Spell of four days."[91]

His precise motives remain hidden, but it seems likely that Mc-Culloh was acting in the best interests of his uncle. Gabriel Johnston once remarked that the younger McCulloh "never takes one step without" his uncle's "direction." Clearly, Henry McCulloh by early 1759 had lost all patience with Corbin for continuing to settle his lands. His nephew probably chose to exploit popular discontent to expose Corbin's corruption once and for all. If in fact he employed this strategy, he certainly succeeded. Once Granville learned of his agent's humiliation, he quickly suspended both Corbin and Bodley and appointed Thomas Child in their stead.[92] No longer could Granville permit obstructions in the management of his estate.

In the riot's immediate aftermath, Corbin approached the attorney general for relief. Jones, a leading member of the house as well as attorney general, set aside his earlier scruples over intervening in proprietary matters and agreed to prosecute the kidnappers. But he himself was soon threatened by a group of men in Granville County and was even forced to carry a pistol for protection. When the assembly met in May, Jones also applied for relief. Dobbs and the council agreed to offer a reward of £25 proclamation money for information leading to the arrest of the rioters, but it was the lower house that chose to champion Corbin's plight. Chiding the governor for not having taken effectual measures in the past, it dramatized the kidnapping as a traitorous conspiracy. It also urged that Dobbs do more than offer a reward by dismissing any officials who might have been involved and that he alert county militia units in the event of further violence.[93]

Hoping perhaps that the entire matter would fade away, Dobbs complied with neither of the lower house's requests. But the issue did not subside, for the rioters had become local heroes in their counties. In the ensuing months, when some were captured and confined for trial, the jails were raided and the men released. "The Distraction of the People had been so great," one resident later wrote, "that they had been without law[,] quite Lawless at Times." Meanwhile, Dobbs had made no attempt to suspend Alexander McCulloh from his posts as deputy auditor and colonel of the Edgecombe militia.[94] Increasingly, lower house leaders—however sincere their alarm over the disturbances and their empathy for Corbin—must have sensed that they now had a prime opportunity to push for the governor's dismissal. Their older grievances against

Dobbs were not insubstantial, but none was so potentially damaging as the charge that he was abetting rioters. Ironically, the man who ultimately led the effort to oust Dobbs was not a member of the lower house or a provincial of long standing, but Thomas Child, Francis Corbin's longtime friend and his newly appointed successor as resident agent of the Granville District.[95]

A "flame [of] opposition"

There seemed to be precious little to endear Thomas Child to the lower house. He was an English placeman; upon being commissioned by Granville to return to North Carolina in April 1759, after an absence of nine years, he used his London connections to regain his provincial post as attorney general. While still in England, he also helped to persuade the Board of Trade to disallow the 1755 superior court statute, partly on the grounds that it interfered with the royal prerogative. Indeed, convinced that Child would add a measure of strength to his administration, Dobbs unwittingly recommended in January 1760 that he be given a seat on the council to replace Corbin, whom he had finally suspended. Dobbs also seems to have thought that by rewarding Child he could dispel any misapprehensions that his treatment of Corbin was intended as an attack on Granville.[96]

Whatever aid Child might have contributed to the governor's beleaguered administration shortly evaporated. In fact, just before Child left England, James Abercromby wrote Samuel Swann, "Whatever part he may act on your side the water, I can assure you that he is no Partisan of the Governors."[97] While Corbin had for the most part been willing to confine his energies to landjobbing, Child's ambitions extended more into the political realm. To be sure, as later evidence would show, Child exploited Granville's trust by embezzling proprietary revenues just as his predecessor had done.[98] But Child also hoped for nothing less than to win the governorship of the province. In previous years, through his position as Granville's chief adviser, he had maintained contact with several house leaders. In December 1754 one of Child's resident attorneys, Thomas Barker, had even tried to see that he was appointed as agent for the province. Before Child's return in 1759, Samuel Johnston, Jr., a Chowan County representative, wrote Barker that a recent letter from Child requested "a House of his own" reserved "immediately" and that "his coming over may be a secret."⁹⁹

Knowing full well that the governor's position was becoming more and more tenuous, Child decided by early 1760 to cast his lot with the lower house. In doing so, he reestablished his old ties to Barker by making him a quitrent receiver for the Granville District. Child also became a close friend of other house leaders, like Robert Jones, Jr., who was ultimately rewarded with the post of proprietary agent. Indeed, when the assembly met in April 1760, Child left no doubt where his loyalties lay, for he quickly became embroiled in the superior court controversy. Having acquired a seat in the house from Chowan County, he launched a violent attack on Dobbs's administration in a speech accusing his adherents of being "Pimps and Hangers." Further, in his capacity as attorney general, he joined the chief justice of the colony in urging Dobbs to ratify the lower house's court acts, despite his earlier pronouncements to the contrary to the Board of Trade.¹⁰⁰

But it was in his position as Granville agent that Child posed the strongest threat to the governor. According to Dobbs, Child promised house leaders that the governor would be removed through his influence with Granville. Once that was accomplished, Child and his new allies would procure "the Government . . . and every lucrative employment . . . for themselves and their friends." Samuel Swann, for one, was to be an associate judge, and Richard Spaight claimed that his own office as provincial secretary had already been earmarked for Robert Jones.¹⁰¹

Dobbs and Spaight were not impartial observers, but Child clearly helped raise a "flame [of] opposition" that precipitated what James Murray characterized as "a tryal of Strength between the Governor on one side and Mr. Child supported by the general Voice of the people on the other." A more detached commentator was George Pollock, a Bertie County planter, who afterwards noted that "the assembly had been drawn in to Severall most rediculous Things by [a] Disigning and interested Person."¹⁰² The "Things" Pollock had in mind transpired shortly after Child allied himself with assembly leaders. On May 23 the house took the extraordinary step of meeting in closed session, in which each member was sworn to secrecy upon threat of permanent expulsion. Before the house completed its business in five hours, it had charged Dobbs with numerous abuses of power. Addressed to the king, the list of fifteen complaints extended from the alleged exaction of extortionate fees by Dobbs and James Hasell, a former chief justice, to the issuance of illegal election writs. Specially indicative of lower house disgruntlement were the large number of resolves—five out of the fifteen—that pertained to appointments Dobbs had made over the previous years. Several resolves, for instance, alleged various acts of malfeasance committed by Spaight in his twin capacities as secretary and military paymaster. Another condemned the granting of "military Commissions . . . to Persons of little Weight and Interest in the Province." With obvious reference to the suspensions of Corbin and John Starkey, among others, the house also condemned the removal of "Gentlemen of unexceptionable Characters and distinguished worth." Child figured prominently in the resolutions by receiving a vote of gratitude for having urged passage of the court bills and thereby saving the province "from imminent danger of Anarchy and ruin."

It was this threat of impending disorder that formed the most persistent theme of the resolutions. The lower house attributed it to various acts of malfeasance committed by Dobbs and his cohorts, but the most damaging allegation was that the governor had openly condoned the turmoil in the Granville District. The assembly declared:

> That tho' the Governor was Addressed by the Assembly in June last to take necessary Measures to suppress the several Mobbs, and Insurrections which for many months in Open Violation of all Law have with Impunity Assembled in great Numbers in different Counties[,] Erected Sham Jurisdiction and restrained men of their liberty[,] Broke open Gaols[,] released Malefactors[,] dug up the Dead from the Graves and Committed other Acts of rapine and violence, but no Effectual Steps have been taken to check the Torrent of their Licentious Extravagances notwithstanding their having since repeated those Outrages. On the contrary some of their Principal Leaders and known Conductors have been preferred to the Magistracy and honoured with Commissions in the Militia.[103]

Before the meeting had adjourned, copies of the resolves together with an address to the king and accompanying letters written by Speaker Swann were ordered sent to Granville, Secretary Pitt, and the Earl of Halifax. None of the letters have survived except that to Granville, in which Swann asked his "immediate Interposition for removing the Cause of our Sufferings." Otherwise, he warned, the result would be "the Ruin of the Country, already become a Scene of Tumult and unrestricted Licentiousness." Meantime, the lower house had chosen Anthony Bacon, an English merchant, as its new agent and assigned him specific responsibility for presenting these grievances to Pitt. In addition to having important connections in London, Bacon was a close associate of Child.[104]

Upon learning of the lower house's actions, Dobbs quickly wrote to the Board of Trade defending his administration and attacking Child as the likely "Contriver" of most of the resolutions. However, Dobbs was forced to postpone a more detailed account, for a more immediate problem demanded his energies once the secret meeting had adjourned. He and the assembly were still at odds over two crucial pieces of legislation, a superior court bill and allocation of aid for the war. Already, he had offered a proposal whereby he would approve the house's court bill if it were limited to two years. The house balked but, after being prorogued for three days, finally assented to the compromise on May 26. The aid bill, however, met the governor's rejection, and the assembly was prorogued until September. The bill, Dobbs angrily wrote to Pitt, was "so Crude and Undigested and so long Before the Men Could be raised, Armed and Disciplined [that it] would be of no Service to his Majesty."[105]

Rejecting the aid bill was a dangerous risk. Added to his obvious lack of control over the lower house, Dobbs gave the ministry even more reason to accede to demands for his dismissal. Aware of the precariousness of his position, he decided to call a June meeting of the assembly in Wilmington. As he probably anticipated, Child and "his Northern Junto," piqued over the hastily called session and the long travel distance, boycotted the meeting in the hope that southern representatives would similarly refuse to meet. This strategy met with no more success than it had fourteen years earlier. Attracting only a handful of representatives from the old Albemarle counties, the lower house not only convened with less than a majority of its membership, but it also proved more open to Dobbs's entreaties.

Thus the governor could afterward write the Board of Trade, "They have passed an Aid Bill . . . without the restrictions and exceptionable Clauses in the former rejected Bill." Expressing even more delight, Dobbs reported, "The Northern Junto have been disappointed in all their schemes, and are now breaking in pieces[,] the speaker and their southern friends having broke from them."[106]

Now that the crown's requests for more military aid were satisfied, Dobbs poured his energies into writing a rebuttal to the lower house's numerous allegations. It was a masterful defense of his administration and a searing critique of his antagonists. Many of Dobbs's arguments were not strikingly novel, particularly his rendition of his troubles with the assembly, though he did persuasively impugn Child's motives as a lower house leader. But what enhanced the document's persuasiveness was its painstaking detail in contrast to the vague charges of his adversaries. More than thirteen thousand words in length, it confronted each of the lower house's allegations with a host of specifics.[107]

Because of the skillfulness of Dobbs's report and royal inhibition about removing a governor, lower-house efforts to unseat him failed. The crown turned a deaf ear not only to the May assembly resolves but also to a petition in late 1760 or early 1761 from Anthony Bacon, the assembly's new agent, requesting that a special commission of provincial leaders hear charges against Dobbs's administration.[108] Other factors were probably also involved in Dobbs's vindication. Proprietary disturbances, for one thing, subsided in 1760. Although Child reaped a substantial harvest in defrauding Granville, he seems to have learned from Corbin's troubles not to exact extortionate fees from local settlers, and instead initiated a number of reforms in proprietary administration. Furthermore, Child made no effort to renew the past controversy with McCulloh, who negotiated a new accord with Granville in 1761.[109] Yet another reason for the governor's triumph was that Granville apparently did not attempt to take up the assembly's cause. Perhaps because his health was declining at this time or because he shared Dobbs's assessment of Corbin's behavior, Granville shunned any personal involvement in North Carolina's political turbulence.

"Reconciliation"

Once Dobbs was again secure as governor, the remaining four years of his administration witnessed a return to relative political tranquillity. The lower house made no further attempts to seek his dismissal; when a lieutenant governor was appointed by the crown in April 1764, it was because the aged Dobbs had petitioned for a leave of absence to return to England. Of course, most of his earlier disputes with the assembly continued, but more often than not they either ended in compromise or were settled by a definitive ruling from the Board of Trade, which was usually sympathetic to the assembly's point of view.

The divisive issue of the parliamentary grant money was resolved in late 1763 when the board ruled that the lower house should have full authority over its disposition despite Dobbs's continued protestations that house leaders intended to manipulate the currency for their own profit.[110] Similarly, the board in May 1763 strongly reiterated an earlier ruling that the governor could not interfere in the appointment of provincial treasurers. After the act appointing treasurers expired later that year, Dobbs did not contest the matter, but instead approved a new act once the lower house had agreed to limit its duration to three years.[111]

In one instance, the crown actually imperiled a previous settlement. In December 1761 it disallowed the superior court act passed in 1760 on the grounds that the appointment of judges should be made at pleasure, not during good behavior as the bill stipulated. Within a year, however, the lower house agreed to compromise and passed a new court bill that left the manner of judicial appointment unspecified.[112]

Only two issues continued to provoke controversy. The provincial agent dispute was temporarily resolved during a legislative session in March 1761. Hard pressed once again to obtain an adequate military supply from the assembly, Dobbs consented to an aid bill containing a clause appointing an agent responsible only to a joint committee of five representatives and three councillors. Out of deference to Dobbs's wishes, the lower house agreed to drop the appointment of Anthony Bacon and instead chose Couchet Jouvencal, a clerk to William Pitt. Before long, however, Dobbs began to object that the councillors on the committee had no voice in corresponding with Jouvencal, and in March 1764, when the agent's first term expired, the council actively joined the fray by insisting on more influence in the committee. After the council defeated a new agent bill, the lower house simply appointed Jouvencal to a new term of one year together with a committee of correspondence composed of five representatives.[113]

Similarly, the issue of the treasurers' accounts was never settled to the satisfaction of the governor. Although he finally consented to the lower house's right to appoint public treasurers, he refused to drop his demand that the crown be allowed to audit their accounts. In February 1763 he again resorted to forwarding copies of the accounts to London in order to let the "Lords of the Treasury . . . see how slightly they are passed by the Assembly." In particular, Dobbs complained that the treasurers had not tried to compile an adequate listing of taxes due from county sheriffs. Although encouraged by the Board of Trade to press his case, he never did succeed in wresting this right from the lower house.[114]

Despite these and a few more minor disputes that surfaced from time to time, relations between Dobbs and the lower house became significantly less heated after 1760. Lower-house opposition waned in part because he proved more amenable to making compromises. Receiving limited support from London, Dobbs was at times constrained to bow to the assembly's demands. Moreover, the ranks of his opponents shifted over the years, and his new adversaries proved to be less antagonistic. In early 1761 the lower house lost one of its more able leaders when Thomas Barker, for reasons that are not clear, suddenly chose to leave the province. Not returning to North Carolina for seventeen years, he lived in England and devoted much of his energy to place-seeking for himself and his friends. At one point, his intimate, Samuel Johnston, Jr., wrote him: "Your Business in London is a matter which engrosses the Attention of most people here who have any Connections there and there is scarcely an Officer in the Country who does not apprehend himself in danger from you as they think you have been too long accustomed to business to be intirely Idle in so convenient a Scene of Action."[115]

Less than two years after Barker's departure, Thomas Child, the governor's inveterate foe, also left for England, never to return to Carolina. His fortunes steadily plummeted after 1760, beginning when Joshua Bodley, the ex-proprietary agent, sued him for fraud.

Perhaps because of this embarrassment, Child met with little success when he then attempted to have Granville obtain for him the provincial office of clerk of the pleas. Child also became involved in a dispute with Robert Jones over the terms of Jones's appointment as his successor as proprietary agent. "Child Sails soon for Europe[,]" Samuel Johnston wrote Barker in 1762. "Jones gives out that he and Child are acting in Concert and have come to agreement about the Land Office but whither they have or not is impossible to know as there is no believing a word that either of them says."[116] Jones was not entirely without problems of his own. Besides his dispute with Child, he failed to win reelection to the lower house in 1762; and, though he regained his position as attorney general, he was accused in 1764 of obstruction of justice and attempted rape.[117]

Not only did the shifting leadership of the lower house prove to be less hostile, but, more importantly, Dobbs was able to exploit a slowly recurring rift between the assembly's southern and northern representatives. Although the party fires of regionalism had subsided significantly after 1754, bitterness still lingered. Southern leaders, if less passionate than their predecessors of a decade earlier, still resented the north's commanding majority in the lower house. Even though the assembly had established after 1754 the two central counties of Dobbs and Pitt, it had also created two new counties in the northeast.[118] Northern control over the lower house was thus never in serious jeopardy. Then, in April 1761, the lower house refused to divide New Hanover County in the lower Cape Fear because, as Dobbs related to the Board of Trade, the "five Member Northern Counties and a few adjoining" desired to "Keep down the numbers of the Southern District."[119]

Because Dobbs had already succeeded once in reaching an accord with southern members, he was determined to exploit what he sensed was a prime opportunity to split his opposition. Ironically, though he had been instrumental in dousing regional fires, he now rekindled them. As a resident of the Cape Fear since the 1750s, he began to cement his neighborly ties. Beside decrying the injustice of northern domination to London officials, in mid-1761 he married the young daughter of an influential Cape Fear planter. What one historian has too hastily described as the "supreme folly" of "old age"[120] had noteworthy political consequences, especially during an assembly session in December 1762. Upon urging that the lower house petition the crown to revoke the governor's instructions relating to the appointment of superior court judges, Samuel Johnston of Chowan County met substantial opposition from southern leaders. "The Truth of the Case," he informed Barker, "is that since the Governor's Marriage there has been a Reconciliation between him and [Samuel] Swann," with "Starkey . . . included in the Treaty." Consequently, he added, "They are very cautious how they give offence."[121]

Despite the measure of success Dobbs enjoyed in procuring a suitable court bill that session, the southern treaty did not permanently silence lower-house opposition, probably because of its preponderantly northern membership. But the governor's alliance with the south again served his advantage when he convened the assembly in Wilmington in early 1764. Although most northern representatives refused, as before, to attend out of protest, the lower house agreed to meet. To Dobbs's delight, it approved "several good Bills," including the long overdue bill to divide New Hanover, the compromise treasurer's act, and an extension of the expired superior court act—all of which the governor attributed to the "absence of these Northern Members." The growing rift within the lower house was such that one observer feared that "old quarrels will be renewed[,] old grievances repeated and the whole Province disunited and divided into the old Parties of North and South."[122]

That a full-scale rupture between north and south did not occur on the scale of their earlier clash resulted partly from the soothing effects of William Tryon's appointment as lieutenant governor. Because of Dobbs's impending departure and sudden death in March 1765, leading provincials once again cooled their tempers in expectation of future preferment. Moreover, southern representatives were now bereft of an influential patron. Determined not to display partiality "to any particular Spot of the Country or people," Tryon convened his first assembly in New Bern. "By siding with no party," Tryon, a visiting Englishman observed, "will greatly reconcile the heats and Animosities, which have long subsisted, between the Northern and Southern Interests."[123]

Another reason for the calming of regional conflict was that by the latter half of 1764 a division had occurred within southern ranks. By the 1760s, the town of New Bern had grown rapidly as a commercial center. Tied to the Cape Fear in their opposition to northern overrepresentation in the assembly, politicians in the surrounding area had nevertheless become increasingly resentful over Wilmington's threatened dominance as the colony's capital. When Tryon first arrived in the province, New Bern residents offered the lieutenant governor sumptuous accommodations to counter the offer of a house in Wilmington. When Tryon did, in fact, decide to reside in New Bern, James Davis, printer of the town's *North Carolina Magazine*, exuberantly declared: "Mourn, Mourn ye *Wilmingtonians*, and put on Sack cloth and Ashes, for the Measure of thy Good Things is full, and the evil Day is coming upon thee! Mr. T R Y A N . . . is coming to live in P E A C E among us, and deliver us from unleveued Bread."[124]

A final consideration was that both the north and the south would, within a matter of a few years, face a serious challenge arising from the backcountry. Although it did not dampen regional fires entirely, the Regulation helped to unify members of North Carolina's political elite by questioning their very right to govern.

A "mask of patriotism"?

The reemergence of regional interests in the lower house was a clear sign that provincial factionalism had not died in North Carolina. Indeed, as late as 1774, Josiah Martin described the province as "composed of parts that have been evermore heterogeneous and discordant to the last degree in their Politics[,] which in the Northern and Southern districts of this Country have been immemorially and uniformly adverse . . . as their local situations are opposite."[125]

But the revival of regional conflict should not obscure the impressive degree of unity that the lower house manifested during its struggles with Governor Dobbs. At no previous time in the colony's history had the lower house achieved such internal harmony as it did from the mid-1750s to the early 1760s, except, perhaps, in the first decade of royal rule during its conflicts with Burrington and Johnston. Traditionally, historians have ascribed this accord to an all-consuming concern for the constitutional rights of an increasingly powerful assembly in its struggle with a governor sworn to uphold the prerogatives of the crown. The various controversies dating from 1759, according to Jack P. Greene, arose from "Dobbs's attempt to challenge the power of the House." In Greene's opinion, this particular set of disputes was part of a much larger effort in which lower houses of assembly in the colonies were trying to acquire "political influence," to "strengthen their authority," and to "reduce to a minimum the amount" of royal or proprietary supervision within their political systems. At the same time, the lower house assumed the self-perceived "task of defending men's rights and property against the fraud and violence of tyrannical executives." Similarly, Hugh T. Lefler and William S. Powell have written that the legislature in its battles with Dobbs "operated under the sincere conviction that it was fighting the battles of constitutional, traditional, and representative government."[126]

This interpretation, which has achieved widespread currency, possesses considerable merit. Dobbs himself remarked upon the "republican spirit of Independency" he found in the lower house. "The Assembly," he complained in 1760, "think themselves entitled to all the Priviledges of a British House of Commons." Along these lines, the lower house assumed certain ceremonial attributes absent in previous years. In 1756 it acquired a mace-bearer for the first time, and in the mid-1760s it began to provide officers, such as the Speaker, clerk, and doorkeepers, with robes from London.[127]

This growing interest on the part of North Carolina's political elite in preserving local rights and autonomy appears to have been part of a broader concern over internal affairs and matters of public consequence. Displaying a degree of responsibility unknown in previous decades, the lower house between 1754 and 1765 enacted laws establishing bounties for the cultivation of hemp and flax as well as quality-control regulations for the improvement of numerous commodities in order to stimulate the provincial economy. In 1760 it passed a law to make assembly elections more orderly and less corrupt than they had previously been. Further, its Committee of Propositions and Grievances became more active in its assigned task of calling attention to local problems. Although it filed only two reports from 1729 to 1754, it submitted three over the next ten years.[128]

The average politician's concern for local projects, such as schools and churches, did remain fairly weak or "crusty," as Dobbs commented in 1757. Not only were many legislators still unconvinced of the need for internal improvements, but keeping taxes low was a favorite way to insure public favor. "The most Popular men among us," wrote James Murray, "are the most penurious and they will do all they can to defeat the Honest views of others."[129] As revealed by an account of funds used for public expenditures from 1754 to 1765 (table 5.3), the assembly allocated almost three-quarters (72 percent) of its combined appropriations of £101,206 for military defense. Public debts and the normal contingencies of government, such as salaries, made up roughly 10 percent and 4 percent respectively. Only 15 percent of all money raised from 1754 to 1765 went for social services and public improvements. The assembly appropriated £6,000 for public schools, which was later diverted for defense; £7,200 for churches and ministerial salaries; and £2,000 for public buildings.

On the other hand, in 1754 alone, before the exigencies of the French and Indian War were fully felt, as much as 38 percent of the assembly's budget consisted of local-improvement funding. From 1755 to 1765, largely because of the war, no money was expended for local improvements. But in later years, up until the Revolution, the assembly would attempt to establish a public seminary in Mecklenburg County and a provincial postal system. During the third quarter of the eighteenth century, it also provided periodic financing for a public printer to publish the colony's laws, assembly journals, and other public documents.[130]

Reflective of this new sense of public responsibility, the colony's governing apparatus fared better than it had in the past. Political

TABLE 5.3 *Public Expenditures, 1754–1765*[131]
(in proclamation money; percentages in parentheses)

	Military Defense	Local Improvements	Public Debts	Contingencies of Government	Total
1754–1765	£72,706 (71.8)	£15,200 (15.0)	£9,700 (9.6)	£3,600 (3.6)	£101,206
1754	£17,000 (42.5)	£15,200 (38.0)	£4,200 (10.5)	£3,600 (9.0)	£40,000

institutions, of course, were no longer so young and vulnerable, and North Carolina's provincial elite, which was now wealthier than ever before, probably provided an added measure of authority. Yet, just as important, the sort of damaging interference by political leaders with the colony's civil institutions that had characterized earlier decades did not occur in these years. Although lower-house opposition to Dobbs grew sufficiently intense by 1760 for leaders to petition London for his removal, they did not attempt to undermine the normal political process by resorting to violence or by paralyzing government in their efforts to protect popular liberties from external usurpation. The only instance comparable to the events of earlier years occurred when Granville County justices refused to hold court during the late 1750s in opposition to Robert Harris's removal from the bench.

Still, to view the governor's problems entirely within the context of a much larger, colony-wide, fundamentally constitutional struggle initiated by an increasingly powerful and concerned assembly is to obscure equally basic features of North Carolina's political system. For one thing, some of the unity within the lower house was probably a direct consequence of the French and Indian War. It is significant that regional animosities were revived once the war had subsided and the threat of any enemy attack had grown less pressing. Equally important was the crucial role Dobbs's clumsy distribution of patronage played in fomenting lower-house opposition to his policies. The essentially constitutional issues raised during his disputes with the lower house were in themselves a major source of contention, but it is doubtful that they would have reached such a pitch if Dobbs had brought key leaders, like Swann, Starkey, and Barker, into his administration. Although Barker once denigrated a county clerkship by commenting, "I always thought it a happyness to be independent of men in power," he and others were confirmed office-seekers.[132]

Furthermore, Dobbs in all likelihood would not have faced the danger of dismissal in 1760 if it had not been for the appealing patronage schemes of Corbin and Child, two outsiders who nonetheless wielded substantial influence among local leaders. Indeed, though Dobbs at times attributed the actions of his adversaries to mounting republicanism, he always insisted that the origins of their drive for power lay in a more self-interested wellspring. "It was frequently hinted," he typically reported to the Board of Trade in 1760, "that if I would accede to certain measures my administration might be easy and happy, which measures were tamely to be silent and let the heads of a Republican party engross the executive power of the Crown, and propose no Measures but what ultimately tended to their emolument."[133]

In nearly every major issue of discord between himself and the assembly, Dobbs discerned a mercenary motive in its behavior. Moreover, in his view, the line between profit-seeking through government patronage and undiluted varieties of corruption was at best blurred for the Carolina politician. In opposing lower-house control over the parliamentary grant money, he asserted that house leaders, acting in league with their agent James Abercromby, intended to "sink" the "surplus" into "their pockets." On another occasion he asserted that "the old Junto had begun the grand scheme of dividing the Bear's skin, the dividend of our share of the £50,000 amongst them" and "their friends." Similarly, in his contests over the treasurers' membership in the lower house and the crown's right to audit their accounts, he repeatedly expressed alarm that the treasurers' accounts were highly irregular and that their vast influence arose from making "payments" to their "favourites" and "rewarding" their "friends." In all these instances, he affirmed that the policies of lower-house leaders were simply "self interested projects disguised under the mask of patriotism."[134]

Dobbs, of course, lacked proof to substantiate many of his allegations, and, in fact, the crown did not always find them sufficiently plausible to lend its support. Yet it is difficult to dismiss his accusations as mere examples of special pleading by an embattled governor. The problems of the Granville District demonstrated that some leading politicians still thirsted for illegal gain. Further, in the matter of the parliamentary grant, the integrity of at least one participant in Dobbs's scenario, James Abercromby, was suspected by others than just himself. Although Abercromby was an industrious agent for the provinces he represented, Virginia's lower-house-controlled committee of correspondence in 1759 appointed a coagent for him to "make sure he did not lay his grasping hands on" that colony's share of the parliamentary grant and "to ascertain as well the commissions charged by other agents in order to determine whether Abercromby's had been exorbitant." That North Carolina's lower house entertained no such suspicions may say more about the rectitude of its leaders than it does about the caution of their Virginia counterparts.[135]

Somewhat greater credence is lent the governor's charges concerning the treasurers by an investigation completed in 1770 into the accounting of provincial taxes. The investigation disclosed that for the period from 1754 to the late 1760s, tax gatherers were in arrears to the public £64,013, well over half of all taxes collected during these years. As one inhabitant commented not long afterward, "In no Country have the Public Accounts been in greater Confusion than in this." In 1767, Governor William Tryon asserted that "more than one half of the public money" had been embezzled. On the basis of these and other findings, one historian has found that 25 percent of all poll taxes were embezzled by local sheriffs, plus additional sums by officials on the provincial level, notably by the treasurers. Such was the degree of corruption that a student of taxation in the South has concluded that the colony's tax system was the "most corrupt" in the region.[136]

In several respects, North Carolina's leadership was still a new political elite, susceptible to opportunistic considerations such as patronage and even corruption.[137] As a consequence of the colony's slow economic growth, provincial politicians by the last decades of the colonial era had outdistanced their predecessors in their level of personal wealth, but few had achieved substantial affluence. Table 5.4 presents available slaveholding figures for 60 of the 79 men who sat in the lower house from 1764 to 1765, the last assembly of Governor Dobbs's administration. Although a higher proportion of representatives owned more than twenty slaves than during the 1730s (38 percent compared to 23 percent), the majority still held twenty slaves or less. Only 5 men had more than forty. In contrast, the average assemblyman in the Chesapeake colonies of Virginia and Maryland during the 1760s owned forty slaves, and in South Carolina he probably held more than a hundred.[138]

Rough landholding figures, as shown in table 5.5, are also available for 60 men who served in the 1764–65 assembly. Of these, 34, or 57 percent, owned over a thousand acres, compared to 44 percent of the 1730s representatives. But only 20 men, or 33 percent, had more than two thousand acres, and only 2, or 3 percent, more

TABLE 5.4 *Slave Ownership among Assemblymen,*
1764–1765 [139] *(percentages in parentheses)*

Number of Slaves	Assemblymen
0–5	10 (16.7)
6–10	11 (18.3)
11–20	16 (26.7)
21–30	11 (18.3)
31–40	7 (11.7)
41–50	2 (3.3)
51+	3 (5.0)
	60

than ten thousand. By comparison, the average 1760s assembly-man owned from fourteen hundred to eighteen hundred acres in the Chesapeake colonies, where land was more valuable, and more than two thousand acres in South Carolina.[140]

Also notable was the large number of provincial politicans who, as late as the third quarter of the eigtheenth century, were new-comers to the colony, including those men who rose to the upper-most levels of the lower house. Of the 42 representatives who served as house leaders from 1754 to 1775, the native origins of 35 can be approximated. Probably 24 of these, or over two-thirds, were first-generation immigrants. Among others, John Starkey, Thomas Barker, Robert Jones, Jr., John Campbell, and Francis Corbin, not to mention Thomas Child, though strictly speaking he was not an assembly leader, were all newcomers to North Carolina. In all probability, they possessed a weaker sense of public service and community identity than would characterize the descendants of established families. Of Virginia's assembly leaders, during the en-tire period from 1720 to 1776, nearly four-fifths came from families that had settled in Virginia before 1690.[141]

Corruption, of course, was not new to North Carolina, for nu-merous instances had taken place in the past, of which the blank-patent bonanza of the late 1720s was the most conspicuous. Local officials periodically embezzled funds marked for public buildings

TABLE 5.5 *Land Ownership among Assemblymen,*
1764–1765 [142] *(percentages in parentheses)*

Acres	Assemblymen	
0–500	11	(18.3)
501–1,000	15	(25.0)
1,001–2,000	14	(23.3)
2,001–3,000	8	(13.3)
3,001–4,000	5	(8.3)
4,001–5,000	2	(3.3)
5,001–10,000	3	(5.0)
10,001+	2	(3.3)
	60	

and ministerial salaries, and provincial officers were not infrequently charged—albeit sometimes because of partisan politics—with bribery, taking extortionate fees, and other abuses of power.[143] "All the officers there," wrote William Byrd in 1736, "are as hungry as hawks, and like them make a prey of every poor creature that falls into their pounces."[144]

What was new was that Dobbs, more than any of his predecessors, openly opposed the corruption he found rooted in the political system. Moreover, it had never before reached such extensive proportions. In the past, it had normally been the preserve of a particular individual or provincial faction. In this respect, Dobbs may have been right when he suggested that the joint contrivance by provincial treasurers and other assembly leaders was an additional factor in forging lower-house unity by linking potentially discordant interests in a common division of the spoils. As a consequence, corruption in North Carolina probably served a vital function by contributing to political integration through the creation of bonds of mutual interest.[145] Southern and northern leaders, to the extent that they and other representatives seem to have been involved, had yet another reason for muting the lingering grievances dividing their regions. Additionally significant, North Carolina's territorial expansion during this period had resulted in large migrant populations in the inner coastal plain and the piedmont. Often of different religious and ethnic identities than their eastern counterparts, the political leaders of these groups, who might otherwise have formed new regional interests whose cultural as well as economic orientations differed, perhaps became less prone to contest eastern domination in the assembly by being wedded to the existing political system through corruption.

Corruption can be functional in yet another respect by tying the interests of talented individuals to government service and, in fact, to the public interest. As David Bayley has observed of many underdeveloped countries, "The corrupt are not always unable; nor are they always unpatriotic."[146] This may well have been so in North Carolina, where some provincial leaders were eminently capable of defending popular liberties and provincial autonomy and, at the same time, dipping their hands in the public till. The former need not have been solely a conscious mask for the latter. Certainly, it is simplistic for historians to erect rigid conceptual barriers in all cases between self-interest and a larger public interest. These barriers, to be sure, existed in the eighteenth-century mind, particularly in such colonies as Virginia and South Carolina, but in North Carolina they may have been substantially less clear, especially by the late 1750s. The assembly's defense of popular liberties did not entail the complete subjugation of private ends, but, in fact, may have depended, at least in part, upon their continued pursuit. This was the larger meaning of Arthur Dobbs's administration. The unity and very thrust of the opposition to him in the lower house stemmed not from patriotism or from self-serving ends, but from a blend of both.

6   "Justice to Poor Carolina," 1766–1771

Our only Crime with which they can charge us is virtue in the very highest Degree, Namely to risque our All to save our Country from Rapine and Slavery.
—Orange County Petition, October 19, 1770

Governmental corruption can be a highly functional means of political integration. Depending on its extent and "the degree of tolerance" a "culture has developed toward such acts," however, it can also undermine a political system's authority.[1] In North Carolina, corruption probably furthered provincial unity in the assembly, but beginning in the mid-1760s it also helped fuel the Regulator riots, which, on May 16, 1771, ended in the largest single instance of collective violence in early American history. For four years, these disturbances disrupted local and provincial politics. They also caused North Carolina to enter the era of the American Revolution in a divided and embittered state. In an age that extolled virtue at the expense of private interest in public life, the right of its provincial elite to govern had been called into serious question.

"Harmony and good understanding"

Shortly after leaving North Carolina in 1771, William Tryon would be hailed with cries of "Long Live Governor Tryon." His departure stood in sharp contrast to the inauspicious beginning of his administration six years earlier. Early in May 1765, less than three months after Tryon, an English army officer, had succeeded Arthur Dobbs as chief executive,[2] opposition against the stamp tax had first appeared in the colony. From then until June 1766, when Tryon officially announced news of the repeal of that tax, the colony experienced several heated demonstrations. The Stamp Act crisis also soured his relations with the lower house. When the first assembly met under his administration in May 1765, he hastily adjourned it as soon as he learned that its members intended to elect delegates to the upcoming Stamp Act Congress in New York. He did not reconvene the legislature until after the act had been repealed.

No region in the colony favored the stamp tax, but most of the resistance centered in the lower Cape Fear, where the province's lone "Sons of Liberty" association was located. A crowd of several hundred in Wilmington forced the newly appointed Stamp Master William Houston to resign his commission on November 16. Later, on February 21, 1766, after three vessels bearing unstamped clearances had been seized downriver in Brunswick harbor, sixty opponents, headed by Cornelius Harnett and other leading residents of the area, forced William Pennington, comptroller of the port, to relinquish his office after surrounding both him and Tryon in the latter's local residence. The presence of Houston and Tryon in Brunswick made the lower Cape Fear the natural locus of resistance. Inhabitants of more northern towns, in addition, may have moderated their tempers because of Tryon's decision to fix the capital in New Bern, much to their delight and the anger of Cape Fear residents.[3]

Once the stamp tax dispute ended, political stability returned to the province, and Tryon entered into a relatively harmonious relationship with both houses of assembly. Except for occasional skirmishes between the council and the lower house relating to provincial appointments, salaries, and a few more minor issues, the only other immediate threat to the peace of Tryon's administration arose from his efforts to reform the assembly's accounting procedures for public funds. Sharing his predecessor's concern over the embezzlement of large sums of provincial taxes, he urged the lower house on several occasions to adopt stricter measures in regulating both its own treasurers and the county sheriffs. He did not, however, insist upon Dobbs's more severe proposal that the crown should appoint public treasurers.[4]

Tryon was strongly disposed to maintain a close relationship with the lower house. Only in his mid-thirties, he was nevertheless more politically astute than most of his predecessors. He did not, like Dobbs for instance, threaten provincial leaders with suspensions from office. He even recommended for a seat in the council Samuel Swann, who, Tryon admitted, had "not always supported the measures of government." He showed a similar penchant for accommodation by appointing Robert Howe, a prominent Cape Fear politician, to a superior court judgeship and by urging the crown to appoint him as chief baron of the exchequer for North Carolina. Tryon also recommended the restoration of council membership for Francis Corbin, Dobbs's old adversary, who had by then built a base of support in Chowan County, despite his earlier dismissal as Earl Granville's agent.

Tryon, over the entire course of his administration, only disciplined one leading political figure, Maurice Moore, Jr., whom he temporarily suspended from his post as superior court judge for "his intemperate zeal and conduct in opposition to the Stamp Act." But the risks in that instance were minimal. Although Moore was "a leading man" in the Cape Fear, Tryon was fully aware that he enjoyed "no great share of popularity in other parts" of the province. Given such political tactfulness, an Anglican missionary could understandably write in 1767, "We have a Governor who rules a willing People with the Indulgent Tenderness of a Common Parent, who desires rather to be Beloved, than Feared by them, and takes the truest care toward securing their utmost Love."[5]

The most telling mark of this spirit of mutual goodwill occurred in December 1766 when the lower house voted £5,000 North Carolina currency for the construction of a governor's mansion in New Bern. This appropriation was followed in January 1768 by the additional allocation of £10,000. Except for southern representatives—probably still upset over the capital's location—lower house members overwhelmingly approved the construction of "Tryon's

Palace," which a resident soon predicted would "exceed for magnificence and architecture any edifice on this continent." In view of the colony's perennial shortage of public monies, such a massive expenditure—to benefit a royal governor—was extraordinary, all the more so because an extra £8,000 needed to be borrowed to complete the edifice. As a visitor from the West Indies later commented, "It cost £1150 Sterling [*sic*]—a Sum rather disproportioned to the abilities of this Infant Province"; John Joachim Zubly, the Georgia cleric, thought it a "sumptuous needless building."[6]

For the first few years of his administration, the governor, as one assemblyman noted, remained "very popular." "This province seems to be very flourishing and happy, under the present administrations [*sic*] of Governor Tryon," a visitor, John Whiting, reported in April 1767. Tryon himself was no less sanguine. He reveled in late 1766 in "the Harmony and good understanding that so generally subsists in all ranks through this Province." The following summer, he toured the rapidly growing backcountry, where he found "a spirit of industry and harmony diffused among the inhabitants"; "It was with a very sensible satisfaction I found on those hilly or back settlements a race of people, sightly, active, and laborious, and loyal subjects to his Majesty."[7]

One year later, Tryon revisted western North Carolina not, however, to extend his favor, but to lead a military force of one thousand troops. Ironically, the very qualities he had earlier admired in the local settlers had by then already propelled thousands of them into what one observer would later term "the most formidable and dangerous rebellion that ever arose in America."[8]

Facts, Figures, and Forensics

Beginning in August 1766 with the establishment of the Sandy Creek Association in Orange County, the Regulator crusade soon spread across the backcountry. At the heart of the movement lay the efforts of western settlers to arrest an epidemic of corruption by bringing local authorities "under a better and honester regulation."[9] Although small disturbances broke out in the counties of Granville, Mecklenburg, and Johnston, most of the discontent was confined to Orange and the two other principal backcountry counties, Rowan and Anson. Settlers from these three counties addressed numerous petitions to provincial authorities, refused to pay taxes, engaged in various acts of violence, and systematically disrupted both county and superior courts.

The first major disturbance took place at Hillsborough, the county seat of Orange, on May 3, 1768, shortly after Edmund Fanning, a county official, had ordered the arrests of Hermon Husband and another Regulator leader for having encouraged nearly 100 men to fire guns at his home. In retaliation, 700 armed Regulators forced the release of the 2 without any loss of life or serious property damage. The following September, bloodshed in Hillsborough was again narrowly averted when upwards of 3,700 settlers from Orange and neighboring counties confronted 1,419 militiamen under Tryon's command.

By this time, 100 Regulators had forcibly disrupted inferior court proceedings in Anson County, and a similar, though smaller, disturbance had occurred in Johnston County. The next major riot took place again in Hillsborough in September 1770. At that time, 150 Regulators, headed by Husband, James Hunter, and several others, stormed the superior court and assaulted officers and attorneys, including Fanning, whose house was also destroyed. Finally, in the spring of 1771, Governor Tryon and 1,185 well-armed provincial militia marched to the backcountry, and, aided by artillery, defeated 2,000 to 3,000 Regulators at Alamance on May 16. This victory, which resulted in approximately 30 deaths, 200 casualties, and 7 executions, formally ended the Regulator movement.[10]

Throughout these disturbances, the Regulators were a fluid organization, whose chains of command periodically shifted. Several individuals, however, assumed key leadership roles, notably Hermon Husband, the principal spokesman, and James Hunter, the "General." Participants in the movement numbered in excess of six thousand and accounted for nearly three-quarters of the backcountry's adult white male population. Indeed, when Tryon's force reached Orange County in May 1771, it discovered that "it was impossible to obtain" any reliable "intelligence relative to the insurgents" because "the people round about" were "generally disaffected to government."[11]

The Regulators also represented a fairly balanced cross section of the backcountry's truncated wealth structure. No doubt, some were truly impoverished at the time of the movement's inception. But most were small to middling planters, and at least several were well-to-do, even wealthy.[12] Husband patented 10,948 acres of land in Orange and Rowan counties after arriving in the backcountry and later invested in a gristmill.[13] John Pryor, another resident of Orange County, owned upwards of 3,500 acres and twenty-one slaves by 1772.[14] Benjamin Dumas, who held nine taxable slaves, was one of Anson County's largest slaveholders as of 1763. He owned more than 2,000 acres of land as well.[15] Other substantial Regulators included John Wilcox, a Cumberland County merchant and sawmill proprietor,[16] Lodwick Clapp of Orange, whose personal estate in 1778 was worth in excess of £1,600,[17] and William and Hermon Cox, who received grants for land totaling 4,705 and 2,026 acres respectively.[18] The wealthiest Regulator, as well as one of the most affluent men in the piedmont, was Thomas Person of Granville County, who by 1769 owned twenty-three taxable slaves and land grants for more than 20,000 acres.[19] After the riots had ended, many of the lands formerly belonging to outlawed Regulators were reported to be of "great value, being perhaps the best lands on this continent." Such men being involved, it is not surprising that a New Bern newspaper account attested that "men of considerable property" led the 1770 Regulator assault on the Hillsborough superior court or that another commentary described them as "regulating gentry."[20]

This brief sketch of the riots and composition of the Regulators only begins to explain the origins and meaning of their movement, a task that has occupied numerous historians of North Carolina. The Regulation is in fact one of the few events in the state's early history that has aroused any significant level of historiographical debate. It began in the nineteenth century, when Whig historians, such as George Bancroft and John Fiske, portrayed the riots as an early protest against British tyranny.[21] But, toward the end of the century, John Spencer Bassett published his classic sectional analysis of the riots. Citing differences in economic development, social structure, and political behavior between the backcountry and the coastal plain, he argued that the ensuing contest occurred between two fundamentally different regions. The west's subsistence economy, featuring small farms, contained a broad middle class of husbandmen committed to a democratic way of life and Protestant sectarianism. By contrast, the east, whose large plantations were peopled with slaveowning, Anglican aristocrats, cared little for democracy. Although the backcountry counties contained a majority of the colony's total white population, easterners dominated politics on the provincial level through overrepresention in the assembly. Moreover, Bassett argued, transplanted easterners occupied the highest positions in the governments of western counties, which they exploited by engaging in various kinds of corruption. This combination of injustices, he concluded, aroused piedmont farmers to a pitch of protest and riot that ended with their devastating defeat at the hands of a predominantly eastern army.[22]

Bassett's sectional interpretation achieved widespread popularity among succeeding generations of scholars, and continues to command acceptance in many circles.[23] In the mid-1950s, however, Elisha P. Douglass offered a modification of the sectional argument in his study of North Carolina's revolutionary era. Focusing largely on differences in class between the Regulators and their opponents, he asserted that the "yeoman farmers" rioted "not only as inhabitants of the piedmont but also as common men against gentlemen."[24] More critical attacks against Bassett and his adherents followed. In reviewing Bassett's major contentions, Marvin Kay argued that contrasts in social structure, religion, and commercial growth between east and west were not substantial. Whatever differences existed were more a matter of degree than of type, for commercial agriculture and the presence of both a wealthy elite and some Anglicans also characterized the backcountry. More to the point, Kay also asserted that the force of the Regulator protests was directed not at the eastern power structure but rather at the extortionate practices of an indigenous ruling class in the west, consisting of political officeholders, lawyers, merchants, and land speculators. Excluded from this elite were poor planters, or the "producer class," who suffered consequently at the hands of an "acquisitive" minority of "non-producers." The riots then represented a populist protest against abuses of power committed by a moneyed clique.[25]

Kay's attack on the sectional school has recently received ready acceptance by James Whittenburg. Eschewing a simple class analysis, Whittenburg, however, has argued that the Regulator movement actually contained two discernible levels of protest. Particularly in its early stages, the Regulation represented not much more than an old-fashioned contest for power. Ambitious planters such as Hermon Husband felt deprived of their rightful station on the top tier of backcountry society because a "super class," consisting of merchants and lawyers, had by the mid-1760s acquired a substantial number of local political offices in the west. As a consequence, corruption, Whittenburg suggests, was not a sincere grievance but a propaganda device used to attract popular support within the backcountry. In this, Husband and his amorphous group of ambitious planters were successful, Whittenburg believes, for before long they had mobilized vast numbers of more humble farmers into action against this new backcountry elite. Once aroused, the farmers soon acquired control over the direction of the protest. This permitted them to clamor for democratic reforms, which, Whittenburg has concluded, were truly radical given the normally deferential spirit of early American politics.[26]

Although Kay and Whittenburg have both demonstrated some major inaccuracies in the earlier sectional interpretation, a host of disturbing problems relating to selective use of evidence and ill-conceived definitions seriously weaken their arguments. Further, neither one has sufficiently appreciated the dynamic character of backcountry society. That the west was still in many respects a rapidly growing frontier in the 1760s determined in no small way that men would assemble in protest over a variety of grievances. As a consequence, elementary questions basic to an understanding of the Regulation remain unanswered. What was the character of backcountry officialdom and why was political corruption so rampant? What was the nature of governmental authority in the west? What were the principal aspirations and ideals of the Regulators? How did they perceive the behavior of their officials? Finally, what was the significance of the Regulator movement within the context of both colonial North Carolina and early American politics?

"Adventurers in the perenial pursuit of gain"

Governmental corruption in North Carolina was rooted partly in the upper echelons of the assembly insofar as provincial treasurers profited from the embezzlement of public taxes. But sheriffs and their county-court connections also reaped handsome rewards on the local level, where an important regional variation existed. According to the 1770 investigation into public taxation, which produced a county-by-county listing of insolvent sheriffs over the previous 17 years, corruption reached its highest levels in the west. From 1754 to 1768, when large numbers of settlers began withholding their taxes, the three principal backcountry counties of Orange, Rowan, and Anson experienced a median of 9 and a mean of 10 years during which county officials embezzled public taxes. Embezzlement in coastal plain counties, in contrast, occurred during a median of 2 and a mean of 2.6 years over this same 15-year period. Indeed, the backcountry also experienced an epidemic of other forms of malfeasance, such as extortionate fee-taking by county registers and clerks, which does not seem to have occurred in the east. A favorite tactic was that used by sheriffs in collecting taxes. If an individual was unable to pay the required sum, the sheriff would seize some of his property, which would be sold later below its actual value to his friends and political associates.[27]

That the west experienced more frequent abuses of power by local officials than the east stemmed from the west's more fluid social system. Neither region featured an indigenous aristocracy with a deeply ingrained sense of public responsibility, but the backcountry's elite was considerably more homespun in its origins, less conspicuous in its wealth, less experienced in politics, and, in all probability, more avaricious in its temperament. Upon settling in the west in the mid-1750s, Hermon Husband noted that "the rogueish sort as had been forced to fly the law" had been "active to gain all offices and posts of profitt."

One official who nearly fitted this description was James Carter, the notoriously corrupt proprietary surveyor and Rowan County's reigning political leader. He had probably been born in Bucks County, Pennsylvania. He later became a carpenter and a millwright as well as a tenant farmer in Maryland. As of 1740 he was a "languishing prisoner" in a Cecil County, Maryland, debtors' jail. After being befriended by William Rumsey, an influential Cecil County planter, Carter subsequently moved to the Shenandoah valley of Virginia and during the late 1740s was among the first to settle in the North Carolina backcountry. Once Rowan was established in 1753, Carter became a justice of the peace, a major in the county militia, and a surveyor for the Granville proprietary. After being elected to the assembly, he was forced to resign his seat after he and several cronies embezzled £500 proclamation money appropriated for arms and ammunition for county residents during the French and Indian War.[28]

Other backcountry officials whose origins were not so obscure that they cannot be easily traced include Thomas Polk, a representative for Mecklenburg County for eight years beginning in 1766. He had migrated from Pennsylvania to western Carolina around 1753 "to seek his fortune" because he "could not bear the dull pursuit of a Pennsylvania farmer."[29] Thomas Hart, one of Orange County's most powerful justices in the 1760s, moved from Virginia in 1757 with his five brothers after the death of their father, who was at most a middling planter.[30] John Dunn was a Scotch-Irish immigrant and either a tenant farmer or a servant in Maryland before moving to Rowan, where he reputedly made shoes, kept school, and studied law. He became the county's first court clerk, was colonel of the Rowan militia, and served in the assembly in 1762 and from 1769 to 1771.[31] Another Scotch-Irishman, Griffith Rutherford, represented Rowan from 1766 to 1775 and served as county sheriff in 1767. He had come to North Carolina from New Jersey around 1753 as a poor orphan.[32] Richard Henderson of Granville County moved with his family to the province about 1740 from Virginia. A "self-made man and, largely, a self-taught man," he later became a lawyer and in 1768 a superior court justice in the backcountry.[33] Another leading resident of Granville was Philemon Hawkins. Born in 1717 in Virginia, he was orphaned as a youth and in the mid-1730s came to North Carolina "poor in purse, but rich in spirit."[34]

Not all backcountry officials were of such lackluster origins. Anson County's court clerk in the mid-1760s, Samuel Spencer, was a recent graduate of the College of New Jersey when he first settled in the west, as was also Alexander Martin, a justice of the peace and crown attorney in Rowan. Similarly, Edmund Fanning, a native of New York who served as register of deeds and militia colonel in Orange and sat in the assembly in the years 1766–68 and 1770–71, studied at both Yale and Harvard. But none of these individuals came from particularly prominent families. Spencer originated from an apparently humble background, where "more than likely" he "had scrounged in his youth to make ends meet." Martin was the son of an Irish immigrant who taught school, ran a farm, and served as a justice of the peace in New Jersey. For his part, Fanning, the fifth son of a captain in the British army, was described as having been a poor man upon his backcountry arrival at the age of twenty-three.[35] Moreover, all three were clearly atypical in their education. Few of their fellow officers had anywhere nearly so much to recommend them for their posts; virtually none came close to meeting traditional eighteenth-century criteria for public office. The backcountry's elite was overwhelmingly nouveau riche. Of local sheriffs, an Anglican missionary in Rowan County commented that they were "Persons in low circumstances." "Yet the Sheriff who was in poor circumstances before," he added, "would become possessed of Negros and a trading man" through his corruption. The traveler J. F. D. Smyth later observed of the region's leading planters, lawyers, and merchants, "Almost every man in this country has been the fabricator of his own fortune."[36]

Once in the backcountry, many officials continued to live in a relatively humble, if not entirely rude, manner. A 1759 traveler from eastern North Carolina discovered "a strange infatuation in the Devil possessing the Courts of Rowan and Anson," and resolved "never . . . if possible," after one more trip, "to visit the Western Regions" again. Justices of the peace, another contemporary wrote, "frequently bring down upon themselves, the contempt they deserve." A visitor from Virginia found that the justices in Granville County "appeared like Gladiators . . . Ready for fighting" and that the "Debates of the Lawyers was rather Obscene than Learned." Upon riding on "to Orange Court house," he discovered "sundry people assembled" whose "appearance did not prejudice" him "much in their favour but" he "soon understood they were j_____ces of this Court which disapated" his "fears a little."[37] The visitor's fears were warranted, for backcountry justices were commonly a rough lot and were not infrequently charged with disorderly conduct, theft, assaults, and other criminal offenses.

When in 1755 a neighbor rebuked John Martin, a justice of the peace in Granville County, for permitting several people to "quarrell and dance and Riot in" his house on the Sabbath, Martin replied, "I'll be damned if any body can hurt me . . . for I am part Judge in Court part Judge in Hell and Part Judge in heaven." Later, after the neighbor swore out a warrant for his arrest, he was warned by the justice's wife: "I don't know but if any of your family should come [here], . . . if he should be in Drink . . . Death would be your Portion." Robert Harris, another Granville justice and an assembly-man from 1747 to 1768, demonstrated his own peculiar respect for law and order during a drunken brawl in 1760 when he and several others bound a public-spirited constable by his "neck and heels." Before the festivities were over, they had smeared "human order" on the victim's face. Another malefactor in Granville was Robert Hicks. Although charged by his own brother with robbing him of £4 at the point of knife in 1758, he was appointed as a justice of the peace two years later.[38]

A few officials, such as the planter John Frohock, amassed quick fortunes and presumably did not live so crudely. A Rowan assembly-man from 1760 to 1768 and county court clerk in the 1760s, he owned 38 slaves and several thousand acres of land by 1768 and was probably the wealthiest man in the west except for Thomas Person, the Regulator leader, and possibly Edmund Fanning.[39] Much more representative, however, was Samuel Benton, the Gran-ville court clerk and an assemblyman from 1760 to 1768, who died in 1770 owning only 6 slaves.[40] Indeed, in the three principal coun-ties of Regulator activity, Anson, Orange, and Rowan, few local leaders, the vast majority of whom were planters, owned even as many slaves as this. Table 6.1 presents the median and mean num-bers of taxable slaves owned by justices of the peace in these coun-ties for the years for which tax and justice of the peace lists are available. The normal county justice did not own as many as 2.

Equally basic to an understanding of why the west was prone to such a high level of corruption is the fact that none of its local officials are known to have enjoyed any experience in public office before migrating to North Carolina beyond, in a few instances, holding such posts as tax assessor and constable.[41] Further, because of the continuing influx of migrants during the 1760s and the re-gion's fluid political order, few county justices had acquired much experience in the backcountry. Of Orange County's 26 justices of the peace as of November 1766, 22, or 85 percent, had served less than 10 years, and 16, or 62 percent, less than 5 years. In Rowan, 18 men out of 26, or 69 percent, had served less than 10 years in office, and 15, or 58 percent, under 5 years. Even more striking was

TABLE 6.1 *Slave Ownership among Backcountry Justices of the Peace*[42]

County	Date of Tax List	Date of Justice of the Peace List	Verifiable Justices of the Peace on Tax List	Percentage of Total Justices of the Peace	Mean No. of Taxable Slaves	Median No. of Taxable Slaves
Anson	1763	1764	9	81.8	1.9	1
Orange	1755	1755	13	81.3	1.4	0
Rowan	1768	1768	11	39.3	1.1	0

the political inexperience of Anson County's 14 justices, of whom only 1 as of November 1766 had served more than 2 years. As shown in table 6.2, the median and mean number of years served for justices of the peace in these three counties was very small.

A final factor behind the avarice of local officials was that virtually all were migrants from other colonies. None, except for the Orange assemblyman John Gray,[43] was a native of North Carolina, much less a native of the backcountry. As a consequence, their sense of community attachment was of recent origin and probably not yet strong, and their primary identification with the west was

TABLE 6.2 *Years of Experience for Backcountry Justices of the Peace, 1766*[44]

County	No. of Justices of the Peace	Mean Years	Median Years
Orange	26	8.2	2.5
Rowan	26	6.5	4
Anson	14	1.7	2

overwhelmingly one of material fulfillment. Most members of the backcountry's elite were men of middling if not, as in a number of instances, poor social origins, who viewed the piedmont primarily as a place to improve their fortunes. They gravitated to public office not out of any sense of responsibility bred by prior generations of identification with the land and its inhabitants or out of past political experience. Rather, officeholding offered an attractive, though not always legal, means of making quick money. They came to the backcountry, as one contemporary observed, as "adventurers in the perenial pursuit of gain."[45]

The Fragility of Authority

Corruption was a fundamental cause of the Regulator disturbances because it further undermined the legitimacy of a group of officials whose claim to authority was necessarily already tenuous. Several circumstances, intrinsic to the backcountry's settlement, prevented local political institutions from achieving widespread public affirmation. Fluid social arrangements and the unimposing stature of backcountry officialdom corrosively affected popular perceptions of government. The rough-hewn, newly rich character of local officials created an obvious disjunction between customary concepts of sociopolitical deference and the actual conditions of political life. Backcountry settlers, in fact, frequently recognized this situation when criticizing county officers. George Sims wrote of Samuel Benton, Granville County's court clerk and assemblyman: "View him but in his former, and then view him in his present capacity, and make an estimate of the services he has done you, in requital for the favour you did him by taking him out of prison, or what was next door to it [i.e., the poorhouse], and sending him Burgess. He was universally esteemed a person calculated for what is called a poor mans Burgess."[46]

Three years later, Anson residents castigated their county justices as poor and ignorant men, and Regulators sang ballads depicting the newly achieved affluence of their inveterate enemies, Edmund Fanning and John Frohock:

When Fanning first to Orange came
He looked both pale and wearworn

An old patched coat upon his back
An old mare he rode on.
Both man and horse won't worth five pounds
As I've been often told
But by his civil robberies
He's laced his coat with gold.

Says Frohawk to Fanning to tell the plain truth
When I came to this country I was but a youth
My father sent me I wasn't worth a crop.
And then my first study was to cheat for a horse.
I quickly got credit and straight ran away.
And Haven't paid for him to this very day.[47]

As in other societies whose political systems temporarily suffer from the destabilizing effects of large-scale immigrations, the rapid influx of northern settlers into the backcountry further weakened the nascent foundation supporting its political hierarchy. The very nature of this migration, occurring as it did in the 1750s and 1760s, meant that most new settlers were entirely unfamiliar with most of their officials. Initially, this circumstance worked to the advantage of ambitious officeholders like James Carter and Samuel Benton, for, as Orange Regulators later lamented, such men had "practised upon our ignorance and new settled situation."[48] But, in the long run, as soon as a common awareness of governmental malfeasance arose, backcountry residents were inclined to challenge their officials, partly because their leadership was not sanctioned by years of familiarity, as in more settled areas of colonial America.

The migrant character of backcountry society helped to forestall the legitimation of political power in another respect. Critical to the support of any government is what Max Weber termed "the authority of the eternal yesterday"; or, in Michael Kammen's words, "the traditionalism which emanates over a long period of time from a system larger than any individual and faithful to 'original principles.'"[49] Established traditions were sorely lacking in the backcountry, for often considerable legal, constitutional, and procedural differences existed between North Carolina and the migrants' parent colonies, most notably Pennsylvania, where the majority of new settlers originated. As the Moravian bishop August Spangenberg discovered "from the law book" of North Carolina during a journey from Bethlehem, Pennsylvania, settlers needed to adjust to "many" unfamiliar "rules and laws." Statutes, with which the average migrant might have been previously unfamiliar, included laws against shooting deer out of season and herding livestock across streams at certain places.[50]

More fundamental discrepancies probably also perplexed settlers from the north. North Carolina's poll-based system of taxation, for instance, varied significantly from the systems in Pennsylvania and other northern colonies, where estates, real and personal, formed the fundamental units of taxation.[51] In addition, differences of both a statutory and an informal nature existed in the respective systems of government. Election balloting in North Carolina was viva voce, not secret as in Pennsylvania. Voters did not instruct their assemblymen as they occasionally did in the North, nor were assembly votes published in North Carolina.[52]

Yet another problem stemmed from the long unsettled boundary line between the western regions of the two Carolinas. Beginning in the 1750s, disturbances had broken out whenever either of the provinces had attempted to collect quitrents and taxes, or when militia duty was compelled. In fact, when Governor Arthur Dobbs visited the disputed area in 1762, he was nearly assaulted by a justice of the peace from South Carolina. Compounding the chaos, some settlers took advantage of the confusion by "pretending" that they belonged to either province, thus creating "a kind of sanctuary" for "Criminals and Vagabonds." A more powerful consequence was the crisis in provincial loyalty afflicting many settlers who were uncertain as to which colony was entitled to their allegiance.[53] Moreover, many backcountry farmers in North Carolina seem to have favored annexation to their southern neighbor, where much of their trade flowed, so that they would no longer have to pay costly South Carolina duties on their exports. After the boundary between the two provinces was extended farther west in 1764, settlers as far north as Rowan County continued to assert their fealty to South Carolina. During the Regulator riots, one Mecklenburg settler protested that the "connections and trade" of the "back settlements" will "ever . . . centre in South Carolina." Another observer noted "that the general dissatisfaction in Anson, Rowan, Mecklenburg, and Dobbs counties, has been much heightened, by the course" of the "boundary line between the two provinces, the people of those counties have always expected to fall into the fourth [i.e., South] province."[54]

A final factor in unsettled attitudes toward government in the west was the backcountry's chaotic land system. The South Carolina boundary dispute kept property titles in confusion for years. Thus a party of settlers in Mecklenburg County who held South Carolina patents attacked several agents employed by Henry Eustace McCulloh in the spring of 1765 when they attempted to survey his lands.[55] Conditions were hardly better to the north of the disputed territory, where widespread fraud in the Granville District during the 1750s had prevented large numbers of migrants from procuring property. In 1755 Hermon Husband observed that without "a shure foundation and title" the "people like Israll of old begin to wish themselves back to Pennsylvania . . . and had rather rent land there from year to year than live under a gover[n]ment where they thought themselves not fairly used." Others simply chose to remain in expectation of eventual relief. Thomas Child's arrival as proprietary agent in 1759 insured that many settlers received grants, but when the proprietary land office closed in 1763 upon Earl Granville's death, matters once more grew confused as thousands of new migrants resorted to squatting.[56]

Both the Granville and the South Carolina land troubles meant that large numbers of expectant settlers were unable to obtain legal titles to property. Consequently, in an age when the ownership of land was synonymous with a stake in society, many backcountry inhabitants were not inclined to obey the strictures of authority. The provincial governors were well aware of the connection between property disputes and discontent in the backcountry. Tryon noted, in reference to the Regulator turmoil, that "the restless dispositions of the inhabitants of Rowan and Orange Counties are in some measure occasioned by Lord Granvilles Land Office having been shut up." When "great bodies of the inhabitants from the northern colonies" came afterward "to take up land" and found when they arrived that no land was available, they were "under a necessity to set down on vacant land." As a result, "they become discontented and unwilling to pay a proportion to the exigencies of that government in which they have no more interest than they can move out of it perhaps in a few days." Josiah Martin, Tryon's successor as governor and a strong sympathizer with the Regulators, later concurred with this assessment by observing that "the superior excellence of the soil" in the Granville District "invites emigrants from all the northern Colonies, who many of them bring money to take up Lands but Lord Granville having impowered no person here to give them titles they set themselves down where they please and because they cannot establish freeholds under these circumstances, they refuse to pay Taxes." This, he concluded, was "a very principal cause of the discontents that have so long prevailed in this Country."[57]

"Few People on earth were more industrious than we"

The Regulation arose in opposition to abuses of power committed by men whose claim to authority and position in North Carolina's newly settled backcountry was extremely fragile. The Regulator movement, however, constituted more than a merely reflexive expression of indignation, for an underlying strain of anxiety bordering at times on hysteria characterized its protests. The language of the Regulators was deeply apprehensive and obsessed by fears of an impending apocalypse. Orange Regulators referred to the "anguish of our Souls." Petitioners in both Orange and Rowan warned of their "Common Destruction" with "Thousands of other honest industrious familys." George Sims demanded: "Does not daily experience shew us the gaping jaws of ruin, open, and ready to devour us?"[58]

Although the Regulators' alarm was not entirely groundless, the nature of their expectations in settling the backcountry fanned their anxieties. Just as local officials, such as Edmund Fanning, had migrated to the piedmont in the hope of improving their lot in life, so too had thousands of other new settlers, in response to the backcountry's reputation for cheap, fertile land. "The people," Arthur Dobbs remarked, "are industrious and are desirous to cultivate as much as they can accomplish to turn to account." Backcountry settlers were not grasping individualists, for family and religious values also helped to shape their existence. But neither were they content with the meager rewards of "subsistence only," partly, in fact, because, as Tryon noted, they hoped to make "provision for their children."[59]

Few of the migrants left records describing their expectations in moving to the backcountry, but some accounts have survived. John Ramsour, a Pennsylvania German who ultimately joined his father and three brothers in Anson County in the mid-1750s, kept a memorandum book during his travels. It reveals that he was an ambitious, commercially minded man. Before settling for good, he made at least two journeys to the backcountry, presumably to inspect the land market. According to the careful account he kept of his expenses, during one of his trips he made a profit of £10 on furs purchased in North Carolina, which he sold in Pennsylvania.[60]

Visions of material betterment also lured Hermon Husband, who was to become the Regulator leader. He was the elder son of a prosperous planter in Cecil County, Maryland. He joined relatives and friends in Orange County in 1755 after two previous visits to North Carolina. The backcountry's "first settlers," Husband noted, consisted principally of "the dole and the poor," but increasingly "Numbers of honest industrious people" appeared among the immigrants. These newcomers, "many of which were the better sort of people," had begun to purchase land from the others, "who was generally unpractised in cultivateing lands." The hopes of these settlers were such that Husband boasted, "Though the lower parts [of North Carolina] have been long settled and still remain poor that makes no rule with us for we are want to smile with secret pleasure and pity when we here [*sic*] of or behold their manner and method." Northern settlers, he observed, "by far have in a few years convinced the Publik that they would soon out do the old Natives of Carolina in husbandry affairs."[61]

That these expectations of profit and prosperity were not fulfilled was attributable to a variety of circumstances. First, from the mid-1750s to the early 1760s, the backcountry experienced frequent Indian raids related to the French and Indian War that resulted in widespread property damage. Between 1757 and 1760 alone, the Moravians in Rowan County offered protection to more than 220 refugees. The worst attacks occurred during the latter year when the Cherokees assaulted Fort Dobbs and many outlying settlements in the backcountry. Not until 1762, however, did many of the planters return to their farms.[62]

Piedmont settlers also suffered from outlaw gangs. Crime conditions were never as bad as they were in the South Carolina backcountry, but they still caused considerable alarm. In the mid-1750s, as many as seventy settlers banded together to attack an outlaw fort, but highwaymen and other criminals continued to infest the west in later years.[63]

A third obstacle to the success of commercial agriculture concerned mercantile arrangements in the backcountry. Despite the region's fertile soil and mild climate, the high costs of overland transportation inevitably lowered profits for local agricultural commodities and raised the cost of imported finished products. "It cannot be expected that the back Lands in his Lordship's District will fetch a great price at any period," wrote the colonial postmaster, Hugh Finlay, in 1774 of Rowan and Orange counties, "for the Farmer there will ever labour under the disadvantage of an expensive Carriage of his produce to market." In describing some western lands, one eastern resident even asserted that their situation "so far back in the Country" rendered them "of as little value as if in the middle of the Ocean."[64]

Fourth, the varied problems of land tenure not only resulted in a crisis of identity and a general disinclination to honor the normal responsibilities of citizenship; but they also imposed an unexpected burden upon migrants coming to the backcountry to obtain cheap land.

On top of everything else, a series of natural disasters plagued local planters from the mid-1750s on. Drought, disease, and unusually harsh winters resulted in crop failures, loss of livestock, and even occasional food shortages. The scarcity of grain was so severe during the winter of 1765–66 that the Moravians, who distributed free bread when possible, reported, "At present we hear of many . . . thefts here and there, and it is probably so, for there is a shortage of food everywhere." During the following summer, a severe drought, accompanied by uncommonly high temperatures, afflicted the backcountry as well as other parts of the colony.[65]

Notwithstanding all these handicaps, backcountry planters persistently expended their resources by purchasing finished goods and other items. Even in 1770, in the midst of the Regulator riots, the Moravians, who owned several stores in Rowan County, noted in their diary, "We have this year had more [people] than ever coming to sell and to buy, and many have complained that they could not get all they wanted." The natural consequence of these expenditures was that settlers became increasingly indebted to local merchants. In 1766 the Moravians alone estimated that six hundred individuals owed them a total of more than £1,800. Merchants frequently resorted to court suits in an attempt to recover these debts, which only added to the planters' troubles.[66]

Backcountry settlers responded in varying fashions to the manifold problems that confronted them in their quest for material improvement. A few probably moved to new frontiers or returned to their original communities; some may have simply resigned themselves to a less profitable existence. Still, other settlers attempted to strengthen their commercial ties by establishing roads and ferries, and some even sought government incentives. Displaying an impressive awareness of commercial trends, Orange and Rowan Regulators later wrote provincial authorities:

> We beseech you to consider of some proper Staple or Staples of the Manufactures, or produce of the Country to answer foreign Demands, would not (with Submission) pot Ash be a fine Article, to answer the British Markets; and in a Country abounding in wood, the very Ashes now thrown away, might with encouragement (if manufactured) be a saving, or rather gain, of some Thousands per annum to the province, and render Voyages to Riga, Narva, and Danzick, from Great Britain, for that useful commodity needless.[67]

But by far the most common response of backcountry residents to their economic woes was a mixture of anxiety and deep frustration, accompanied by a seething hostility toward local officials, merchants, and lawyers, who seemed to be acquiring overnight fortunes at the average settler's expense. The people of Orange County, Husband asserted, were "good industrious labouring Men; who knew the value of their property better than to let it go to enrich, Pettyfogging Lawyers, extortionate and griping publicans or Tax gatherers."[68]

The wrath of backcountry planters was not entirely misplaced, for county officers surely engaged in widespread acts of extortion and fraud. No doubt, too, some local merchants, as subsequently alleged, instituted rigorous credit policies, though probably they were simply taking advantage of a large-scale demand for a finite amount of products in a noncompetitive market; in nearby Virginia, more intense competition among Scottish merchants encouraged relatively easy credit terms.[69] As for lawyers, who were also targets of Regulator animosity, the fee books of two backcountry attorneys do not indicate that extortionate fees were exacted, though this may have occurred.[70] Whatever the extent of corruption among all three of these related groups, it is also true that such men represented both the most obvious and the most accessible target upon which thousands of backcountry settlers could vent their frustrations. The Regulator riots did not break out among a settled population long dulled by years of poverty, but among a migrant population whose aspirations toward material betterment had been steadily stymied by a variety of circumstances, of which corruption was only one, yet the most visible. Orange County Regulators exclaimed with frustrated pride in 1768, "While we held anything we could call our own few People on earth were more industrious than we[,] but alas the iron hand of tyranny has displayed its baneful influences over us with impunity[.] How has dejection, indifference and mealancholy and Chagrin diffusively spread themselves far and wide among us."[71]

Precipitants

By the mid-1760s, frustrated expectations, widespread hostility toward government, and corruption had converged to create considerable malaise in the backcountry. But two other factors helped trigger the Regulator movement. The first concerned the economic consequences of the French and Indian War. Because of large military expenditures made by North Carolina, provincial poll taxes rose appreciably from 1s. 8d. in 1754 to a yearly average of 8s. 1d. between 1755 and 1763. As late as 1765, the annual tax amounted to 6s. Coupled with this was the severe shortage of currency created by the war. In December 1765 Governor Tryon noted, "There is little or no specie circulating in the maritime counties of this province, and what is in circulation in the back counties is so very inconsiderable." Many westerners, lacking paper as well as hard money, were not only unwilling but also simply unable to pay their taxes, as Tryon later appreciated when he wrote to Lord Shelburne in 1768 of "the great inconveniences his subjects here labor under . . . for want of a medium to pay the public taxes."

Indeed, the currency shortage underlay the proposal subsequently voiced by the Regulators that commodities be accepted as taxes at public-inspection warehouses in the backcountry.[72]

A second precipitant of the Regulator movement was Hermon Husband. In 1766 he helped to organize, if in fact he was not the sole mover in, the Sandy Creek Association, the progenitor of the Regulators. Throughout the subsequent disturbances, he also served as their chief spokesman and was consequently the major target of government opposition. Governor Tryon termed Husband "their principal," and James Hasell, president of the council, labeled him as "the Chief Ring Leader."[73]

Husband's leadership among the Regulators derived partly from his indefatigable energy. The traveler Johann David Schoepf later commented that he possessed a "restless and enterprising spirit." But more important was his ability to mobilize opinion by making public orations and writing pamphlets, notably "An Impartial Relation." Contrary to recent assertions, he did not seek to enhance his own political power; indeed, no evidence suggests that, before the Regulator riots, Husband had ever sought public office of any sort, even though he was one of the wealthiest men in the backcountry. More intensely moral than most individuals, he was able to define the major issues at stake in the backcountry and to articulate grievances based upon common experience and widely shared assumptions about the nature of political authority. He was, as one backcountry settler later recalled, a "firebrand amongst the people."[74]

"Save our Country"

Ultimately the most vital ingredient in the Regulator movement was the set of values and attitudes by which its adherents perceived their world. As in other societies undergoing intense cultural, social, and psychological adjustment, ideological activity assumed a fundamental significance in the backcountry by providing the Regulators with a map of "problematic social reality" that explained both their own social situation and that of their adversaries.[75] Although the ideological component of their protest was not in itself wholly determinative, it exerted enormous power in shaping some of their perceptions and helping to intensify their anxieties. As a consequence, it exercised a strong influence on the goals and the scope of their protest.

In recent years, a growing number of historians have argued that crowd movements in mid-eighteenth-century America often expressed an emerging "popular" or "protoproletarian" ideology. Rather than sharing with early American elites the values of "Country" or "radical Whig" ideology, as delineated by J. G. A. Pocock, Bernard Bailyn, and others, mobs in both urban and rural settings frequently opposed wealthy individuals and upper-class rule.[76]

The Regulators have been especially attractive subjects for those who find ideological divisions in colonial society. Elisha Douglass, Marvin Kay, and James Whittenburg have all in varying fashions asserted that the Regulators' scorn for their county officials, lawyers, and merchants embodied a fundamental antideferential, class-conscious spirit of democracy. For Douglass, the Regulation was a conflict between classes as well as sections. More recently, Kay has written that the Regulators "proposed democratic reforms to implement [lower] class rule," and Whittenburg has argued that "the Regulation was as radical a movement as the age produced."[77] But just how radical were the Regulators? Did they, for instance, propose that the poor or even the middling classes should rule? Or, for that matter, precisely how far did their ideology diverge from that of colonial elites in America?

Various studies mistake a pervasive commitment among the Regulators to the chief tenets and assumptions of Country thought for a radical democratic spirit. Admittedly, most Regulator expressions of Country ideology were never so stylized or replete with classical references as the elegant writings of a James Otis or a Josiah Quincy, Jr.; at one point, the leading rioter, James Hunter, wrote that he did not know the identities of Cicero and Demosthenes.[78]

But the Regulator commitment to the central tenets of this body of thought was no less powerful. Most backcountry settlers were migrants from other colonies, notably Pennsylvania, where Whig values had exerted a significant impact on indigenous political cultures for several decades.[79] Moreover, the overwhelming majority of these settlers were Protestant dissenters, which no doubt sharpened the appeal of Country principles. Above all, migrant expectations of material betterment heightened their attraction. By extolling the virtues of economic independence and personal liberty and by emphasizing the perils of governmental power, Country thought was especially appealing for those anxious to better their lives in a new society. Indeed, it was this fundamental relationship between "LIBERTY! thou dearest Name! and PROPERTY! thou best of blessings!"[80] which persuaded the Regulators that corruption threatened not only their status as prospering planters but also their ability to function as free men.

In this respect, Country ideology considerably accentuated the apprehensions underlying their movement and played a decisive role by convincing backcountry settlers that the corrupt activities of their officials would result in their enslavement. Anson petitioners declared themselves already "slaves to remorseless oppression. . . . How relentless is the breast without sympathy, the heart that cannot bleed on a View of our calamity; to see tenderness removed, cruelty stepping in; and all our liberties and priviledges invaded and abridged." "Death itself is better than such slavery," James Hunter exclaimed, and Husband asked his fellow backcountrymen, "How long will ye in this servile Manner subject yourselves to Slavery?"[81]

The terminology of the Regulators, in other respects, reflected their deep attachment to Country principles. In their petitions, pamphlets, and letters, they frequently invoked the good of the "Country" as a moral justification for their actions. They often referred to themselves as the "Country" as opposed to the "Court Party," which encompassed their antagonists.[82] To a minor degree, these rhetorical categories may have reflected an actual division between an agrarian interest and a county court interest, but these terms assumed a much broader, more vital significance to the Regulators. Orange petitioners in 1770 exclaimed, "Our only Crime with which they can charge us is virtue in the very highest Degree, Namely to risque our All to save our Country from Rapine and Slavery." Similarly, Husband urged settlers to favor the "man who is the choice of the country, and not one who sets up himself, and is the choice of a party; whose interest clashes with the good of the publick." George Sims prefaced his famous "Nutbush Address" to the people of Granville County with Alexander Pope's exclamation, "'Save my country, Heaven!' shall be my Last."[83]

The Regulators' devotion to Country thought was manifest in their primary assumptions and values. As a consequence, their liberties under Britain's "ancient constitution," with its mixed form of government, served as the fundamental source of authority for their actions. Anson petitioners, in presenting their complaints in 1769, declared, "Permit us to conceive it to be our inviolable right to make known our grievances, and to petition for redress; as appears in the Bill of Rights passed in the reign of King Charles the first, as well as the act of Settlement of the Crown of the Revolution." Sims exhorted others "to throw off the heavy yoke, which is cast upon our necks, and resume our ancient liberties and priveleges, as free subjects." The Regulators arose "not to protect any particular or private property whatsoever." Rather, James Hunter declared, "I can truly say it is out of pure love to ourselves, our neighbors and our posterity, that we contend unwearied for our constitutional rights and privileges." As the Regulators asserted time and time again, they were not rebelling against the British constitution, but were instead acting stoutly in its defense. In case any one remained ignorant of their rights, they promised in January 1768 "to inform one another and to learn, know and enjoy all the Priviledges and Liberties that are allowed us and were settled on us by our worthy Ancestors the founders of the present Constitution in order to preserve it in its ancient Foundation that it may stand firm and unshaken."[84]

Danger to their liberties under the constitution, according to the Regulators, derived almost wholly from the corrupt conduct of their local leaders. Backcountry residents were not oblivious to the growing American outcry against British colonial policy, but they discovered that their own officials posed a similar threat to their rights that was just as ominous, even more immediate, and especially barefaced. Thus, observed the first Regulator protest in August 1766, "Whereas that great good may come of this great designed Evil the Stamp Law while the sons of Liberty withstood the Lords in Parliament in behalf of true Liberty let not Officers under them carry on unjust Oppression in our own Province . . . as there is many Evils of that nature complained of in this County of Orange in private amongst the Inhabitants therefore let us remove them (or if there is no cause) let us remove the Jealousies out of our minds." A second protest, published that same month, asserted, "Though you should see all those Sons of Liberty (who has just now redeemed us from tyranny) set in Offices," they would soon "oppress" the people "if they were not called upon to give an account of their Stewardship." One set of Regulators even declared, "Every one of our Enemies here are utter Enemies to W I L K E S, and the Cause of Liberty."[85]

The underlying source of these internal evils was clear. The Regulators did not oppose concentrations of wealth per se. What was at issue were the corrupt ways in which men of power in the backcountry had acquired and used their affluence. Like other adherents of Country ideology, the Regulators focused their scorn on "ignorant and unworthy" men "dependant in their Fortunes," "cringing Vassals," "Creatures," "pentioners," "Courtiers," and "tools," who had "crept into Posts of Office" and were "leagued together" to "sacrifice the Interest of the Community to the Idol Self."[86]

Into this "joint confederacy"[87] they lumped the vast majority of their local officers—county justices, clerks, and registers—as well as their assembly representatives. Included less frequently were lawyers, who allegedly exacted extortionate sums for their services or who held political office; and merchants, particularly Scottish merchants, whose chief crime seems to have been their stringent credit terms, which helped to subject increasing numbers of people in the backcountry to indebtedness and court suits. Other than these grievances and the hostility their comparative affluence created, members of both professions did not fit the Country tradition of landed independence in what was overwhelmingly an agrarian society.

But Regulator opposition to lawyers and merchants should not be exaggerated. Much of the antilawyer sentiment arose not as an original grievance but only after attorneys appeared hostile to the Regulator cause. Husband, in fact, initially consulted attorneys for aid. Even later, he still distinguished between "pettyfoggers" and a "Great lawyer" such as Sir John Holt, a seventeenth-century Country hero. Similarly, though some rioters ultimately denounced all lawyers, one set of Regulators in the final stages of the protest declared with reference to those serving in the lower house, "That such old experienced members as have been true to the Interest of their Country, by all Means keep in, and such Men as have studied the Law from a Motive purely for the Good of their Country; but such as have studied and learnt the Law for Gain, it is contrary to Nature and their Interest to preserve our Liberties as they ought to be Preserved."[88]

The Regulators attacked merchants with even less ferocity. Despite the assertions of some historians that the Regulators opposed the introduction of traders into the backcountry, Husband complained at one point that a consequence of continuing corruption among officeholders was the damage done to backcountry commerce, "for men of public generous spirits, who have fortunes to promote trade, are discouraged from coming among you." Because of their commercial-mindedness and expectations of profit from planting, the Regulators objected not so much to merchants as to the penurious credit policies of backcountry traders.[89]

In explaining why some individuals acquired fortunes through illegal or quasi-legal means, the Regulators pointed in part to their "own blind stupid Conduct." As Husband put it, "The indolence of a people is a temptation to governors to turn usurpers." Beyond that, of course, was the persistent problem of man's inherent depravity and lust for power. Orange Regulators advanced the "maxim that while men are men" even patriotic individuals if "vested with power . . . would soon corrupt again." "There is Certainly very few Men put into Power," thought Husband, "who are not ambitious for it, and daily serve their own Wills."[90]

Equally important, the initially impoverished circumstances of many local officials helped to explain backcountry corruption. Men born without property, the Regulators said in echoing Country writers, were more easily tempted to try to achieve it through corrupt means. Thus, in their ballads, they lampooned the humble circumstances of Edmund Fanning and John Frohock upon their arrivals in the backcountry. Orange and Rowan petitioners railed that their officers, "intent on making their own fortune," were "blind to, and solely regardless of their Country's Interest." "Has not the Publick Money," asked Husband, "been intrusted in Hands of insufficient Persons, without sufficient Securities." George Sims castigated Samuel Benton of Granville County as a "poor mans Burgess" who was elected to the assembly shortly after being imprisoned for debt. Widening his attack to include other court officers, Sims declared that their primary object was "to reduce us down to that despicable state whence they rose." "It is," he continued, "a received maxim among the unhappy subjects of electoral Dominions, that they have the most to fear from a King who hops from the dunghill to the throne."[91]

The continuing poverty of some officers was a complementary source of antagonism for the Regulators, for such men were thought to be ignorant and susceptible to corruption at the hands of those who had already achieved their wealth through unscrupulous means. Anson Regulators condemned their justices as acting the "Magistrate parte through fear as fearing to offend the Persons who conferred the Honors on them, and part ignorance as not knowing what to do, they being a number of very poor ignorant and almost illiterate men." John Stringer, also of Anson, pointed to "the stupidity of our County's being ignorantly guided by such illetorate ignorant Magistrates as we have at our Court."[92]

All their officials, poor and newly rich alike, the Regulators believed, did not serve the public interest, but were, instead, scheming "to enrich themselves" and their "Creatures." "Mark any clerk, lawyer or Scotch merchant," Husband warned, "or any sect of men, who are connected with certain companies, callings, and combinations, whose interests jar with the interest of the publick good."[93]

Contrasted with the self-interested placeman in the Regulator mind was the "disinterested, public spirited" patriot of independent property who lived by "the principles of virtue and honesty." Orange and Rowan petitioners pleaded that the government "pass an Act to call in all the now acting Clerks, and to fill their places with Gentlemen of probity and Integrity." "Where there is no virtue," Husband averred, "there can be no liberty; it is all licentiousness." He also urged his fellow backcountrymen to favor such men "as have been unblamable in Life, independent in their Fortunes, without Expectations from others; let them be such as enjoy no Places of Benefit under the Government; such as do not depend upon Favour for their Living, nor do derive Profit or Advantage from the intricate Perplexity of the Law. In short, let them be Men whose private Interest neither doth nor can clash with the Interest or special Good of their Country."[94]

Indeed, the significance that Regulators attached to having men of independent fortunes serve their interests was further reflected in the candidates they elected to the lower house during assembly elections in 1769 and 1770. Of the five representatives identifiable as either Regulators or pro-Regulator, all were above average in their personal wealth. As a "relatively well-to-do" farmer, Christopher Nation of Rowan County held land grants for at least 846 acres.[95] Charles Robinson of Anson had, by 1771, purchased 740 acres of land and may have owned several slaves.[96] Moreover, Hermon Husband and John Pryor, who represented Orange County, and Thomas Person of Granville were all affluent.

If the Regulators supported men of independent means for political office, both in theory and in practice, what, then, was their attitude toward the poor and their role within society? Significantly, they did not voice the grievances of servants nor did they ask that suffrage requirements or property qualifications for elected officials be extended to include the propertyless. Moreover, though they occasionally described themselves as "the wretched poor" and even as "peasants," they clearly viewed themselves first and foremost as otherwise honest, industrious farmers—the backbone of any free government—who had suffered from the corrupt machinations of their adversaries. "Several Hundred of the industrious Farmers and Planters of North Carolina, some of whom were in good circumstances," wrote a self-styled "Planter," "have been entirely ruined by the Malpractices of the public Officers of Government." "The consequence of not bringing these Men Subject to the Law," affirmed Orange petitioners in a reference—replete with their status anxiety—to European peasants, "is wooden Shoes and uncombed Hair."[97]

Poverty was also deemed by the Regulators to be a fundamental threat to liberty. Along with traditional proponents of radical Whig thought, they feared that corrupt leaders could easily manipulate the dependent poor for their own evil purposes. Thus, they mocked the cowardly servility of their county justices. Similarly, when Tryon raised an army to march against the Regulators in spring 1771, one Regulator sympathizer noted, "He has collected, out of the meaner sort, an army of 1500 or 2000 men, by way of enlisting for bounty money and high wages, and promises of equal share of plunder."[98]

Many of the demands which Regulators presented to provincial authorities in petitions and remonstrances reflected not only a practical response to governmental corruption but also adherence to the principles of Country ideology. Seeking to curb the excesses of self-interested men, they urged that officials begin an investigation into the tax arrears of local sheriffs; that clerks and—a less frequent demand—lawyers be prohibited from holding assembly seats; that corrupt county justices and clerks be removed from office; that clerks be paid salaries, not fees, to render them more independent; and that restrictions be placed on attorney fees. Further, in what was probably an effort to eradicate the threat to liberty posed by poverty as well as a more practical attempt to ease the financial burdens of some Regulators, they favored a more equitable tax system, in which each person would "pay in proportion to the profits arising from his Estate." Finally, to reduce the likelihood that even the most virtuous public servant might succumb to the temptations of power, the Regulators urged that voters instruct their representatives, that the secret ballot be instituted for assembly elections, that roll-call votes of the assembly be published, and that copies of those votes be sent to every county justice of the peace.[99]

There was a complementary dimension to the Country protest of the Regulators. Although Country ideology served as a general source of values and attitudes, the Regulators' more distinctive frame of reference lay in their understanding of how political institutions functioned in their parent colonies. Many of their demands, though new to North Carolina, had long been institutionalized in more northern colonies, in Pennsylvania especially, where they overlapped with the dictates of Country thought. Underlying the Regulator movement, as a result, was a basic desire to reshape the backcountry not only in strict accordance with Country precepts, but also in the image of past experience. In 1766, when Orange Regulators first sought to enforce their right to confer with their assemblymen and other officers "in matters of weight and moment," they observed that this practice was "somewhat new in the County though practised in older Governments." Similarly, such measures as secret balloting, the right to instruct assemblymen, an ad valorem tax system, and the publication of assembly votes had all been practiced in some of the colonies whence they came. Emblematic of this nostalgic urge was the proposal made by Anson Regulators that Benjamin Franklin or "some other known patriot" be appointed "to represent the unhappy state of this Province to his Majesty, and to solicit the several Boards in England." The recommendation of Franklin probably derived not only from his reputation as a leading patriot but also from his visibility as the foremost son of Pennsylvania, the colony so many of them had just left to come to North Carolina.[100]

In voicing the tenets of Country thought and attempting to re-create political institutions in the image of the past, the Regulators did not resort to radical innovations to cope with the threatening world in which they found themselves. Social tensions of the sort depicted by a growing number of historians played little role in backcountry North Carolina. Some Regulator demands, such as the right to instruct assemblymen, were standard Country reforms voiced in moments of crisis, which carried the potential for a more democratic polity. But backcountry settlers did not actively seek to overturn social arrangements by instituting lower, or even middle-class rule. At the same time, they retained a firm belief in the virtues of the British constitution. Like other Country followers throughout early America, they attempted to restrict the excesses of government by substituting public-spirited, independent proprietors for self-interested officeholders. On a more general level, they demanded greater responsibility and responsiveness from their political system, and thereby sought to bring North Carolina into the mainstream of eighteenth-century political life. Unhappily for the Regulators, they consequently posed a challenge not only to their own local officials, but also to the entire governing apparatus of the colony.

"Knaves alike"

What began as a protest against abuses of power in the backcountry was quickly transformed into an all-encompassing attack on the character of political leadership within the entire province. At first, the Regulators confined their allegations of governmental corruption and other acts of malfeasance to their own county officials. Before long, however, they considerably broadened the scope of their charges. During the summer of 1768, the Regulators learned that Tryon had recently compelled the assembly to pass an act to make it more difficult for sheriffs throughout the province to embezzle public funds. As a consequence, they became increasingly fearful that local officials in other counties and a majority of the assembly were also guilty of corruption. A Regulator committee in August wrote Tryon that it intended to "obtain justice" and "detect fraudulent practices in the officers which has been so common in this Province that it is mentioned in many Public Acts of Assembly." Hermon Husband later recalled, "We found by the Journals of the House, that the Publick Accounts were really unsettled; by a Motion from the Governor to them on that Head."[101]

Compounding their suspicions of widespread chicanery was the construction of the governor's palace in New Bern. News that the assembly had appropriated £5,000 in late 1766 probably reached the backcountry soon afterward, though it seems not to have evoked immediate opposition. But the additional appropriation of £10,000 in January 1768 caused the palace to assume a new and highly symbolic importance in the Regulator mind. One writer sarcastically referred to it as "this famous house." Another declared, "We want no such House, nor will we pay for it." Although the Regulators resented the building's cost, they also depicted it as yet another sign of corruption and as evidence of courtly intrigue involving Tryon himself. There was "in the breasts of many," one writer noted, "a suspicion that there was a design concerted, in which the Governor was a principal Character, and the Palace a Principal object." They now suspected that Tryon "and Fanning with the rest of the civil officers" may have been "leagued together, Knaves alike, to fleece the people that they might build palaces etc." As in other states threatened by tryannical rulers, North Carolina's leaders seemed to the Regulators to be systematically impoverishing the province to satisfy their gluttony for riches. At the time of the Battle of Alamance, one backcountry report even circulated that Tryon had sold "the whole land to the French."[102]

Interestingly, Tryon's alleged involvement was not attributed to "ministerial influence" from his superiors in England. Although he was considered a "principal Character," he was also viewed as the unwitting victim of his own corrupt officials. Husband declared:

> How unfortunate is that Prince, who is sorely wounded
> thro' the side of base designing wretches, who prostitute all
> things sacred and civil to deceive their King, and to get
> into places of important trust; and because they have spent

> much time in basely sycophanting to a noble Lord, and
> prostituting the honour and virtue of their family connections,
> when in place, run hard to bring up lost time, and the King's
> good subjects are made their beasts of burden and of prey.

Husband contrasted Tryon with the "Prince" who "is a wise and
good man, and one who knows the bound of the peoples privilege,
and limits of the rulers power." "Should not they who are thus
happy," Husband added, "prize and love such an one, and in every
instance avoid giving him pain, remembering his anxiety and solicitude, for the prosperity of the King, his Master's subjects."[103]

Regulator apprehensions that their entire government was
steeped in corruption further mounted when Tryon and provincial
leaders did not respond to their insistent calls for reform. Shortly
after Anson County settlers had threatened violence and openly
questioned their officials' honesty during the spring of 1768, Tryon
and the council ordered their dissolution for having committed
"several outrages in open violation of the Laws of their Country."[104]
Militia units in eight counties were also mobilized for a march to
Orange County. This angry response from provincial authorities set
the stage for a series of measures designed to quell the Regulators
and compel their obedience to the obligations of citizenry—in particular, the payment of provincial taxes that the Regulators steadfastly opposed until proper assurances could be given that their
money would not be embezzled. Tryon and the assembly, over the
next several years, promised the Regulators that their grievances
would be heard; more frequently, they continued to insist that their
assemblages were illegal and to demand that taxes be paid. In the
meantime, Tryon had demonstrated his willingness to use force
when necessary, notably in September 1768 when he marshaled
upwards of 1,400 militiamen to protect the superior court at Hillsborough.[105]

All these steps suggested to the Regulators that Tryon and the assembly were united in a corrupt conspiracy against their liberties
and willing to use force to maintain control. But two measures, in
particular, seemed to leave no doubt that a despotic tyranny truly
ruled in the highest echelons of provincial government. The first
concerned Hermon Husband. On December 20, 1770, the lower
house expelled him for allegedly libeling superior court justice

Maurice Moore. Later that same day, law officials arrested and imprisoned Husband in New Bern to prevent his return to the backcountry. He was subsequently released on February 2, 1771; his treatment, nonetheless, considerably heightened Regulator fears.[106]

Not long after Husband's arrest, the assembly had taken a second even more infuriating step. On January 15, 1771, it passed a riot act that Samuel Johnston, Jr., of Edenton had introduced in the lower house. This "spirited Bill," as one approving observer described it, made riotous behavior a felony without benefit of clergy, and, in certain cases, even made it treasonous. Rioters could be tried in any of the province's six superior courts, regardless of where the alleged offense took place. Moreover, the bill gave indicted offenders sixty days in which to present themselves for trial. "If at the end of that time," as Johnston later observed, the subject "failed to appear he was deemed Guilty of the Offence and might be killed or destroyed with impunity."[107]

To the Regulators, the act constituted a fundamental threat to their liberties as Englishmen. Styling themselves "True Friends to Government," Orange County petitioners charged that the assembly had violated "that Bullwark of life the habeus Corpus." Another commentator later voiced a widespread belief that the act had given the governor "as arbitrary a power as the King of France has." Meanwhile, in Mecklenburg County, one Regulator had hysterically declared to a crowd, "assenting to and affirming the Truth of what was said":

> The Assembly have gone and made a Riotous Act, and the
> people are more inraged than ever, it was the best thing that
> could be for the Country for now We shall be forced to kill all
> the Clerks and Lawyers, and We will kill them and I'll be
> damned if they are not put to Death. If they had not made that
> Act We might have suffered some of them to live. A Riotous
> Act! there never was any such Act in the Laws of England
> or any other Country but France, they brought it from
> France, and they'll bring the Inquisition.[108]

Passage of the act, combined with Husband's incarceration, put the Regulators in a frenzy. In Orange, as one sympathizer observed, "the publication of this act, together with the account of Husband being in gaol, set the whole country in an uproar." Shortly afterward, Regulator leaders sought to broaden their ranks by enlisting additional support in several nearby counties. From Halifax County, a compatriot wrote James Hunter in February, "I have animated the people here to join the Regulation . . . come 2 weeks they are to have a meeting for that purpose[,] if it once takes a Start here it will run into the neighbouring County's of Edgcomb, Bute and Northampton and this will undoubtedly facilitate Justice to poor Carolina."[109]

Upon learning of Regulator intentions, Tryon embarked on his famous western campaign to suppress the rioters. As he correctly discerned, the Regulators were now firmly at odds with the colony's entire governmental establishment. Less apparent to him and, for that matter, to most provincial leaders was that the Regulators were more convinced than ever that North Carolina was quickly descending into the barest species of tyranny. The power of this conviction soon propelled thousands of aroused backcountry settlers into a desperate military confrontation with a British governor and his heavily armed force—a confrontation that offered the Regulators little, if any, hope of victory.

"This Land of perpetual Strife and Contention"

The response of provincial authorities to the Regulator protest was at best ambivalent. Some leaders did expressly sympathize with them. Maurice Moore, the superior court justice and one of the wealthiest planters in the Cape Fear, was initially well disposed. However, he seems to have been repelled by Regulator violence, or, as Husband later alleged, perhaps intimidated into silence by Edmund Fanning and Tryon.[110] Others remained sympathetic throughout the struggle. Two years after the Battle of Alamance, Josiah Quincy, Jr., during a visit to North Carolina, characterized wealthy Cape Fear planter William Dry as a "friend to the Regulators." Not long thereafter, Alexander Schaw, himself affluent, wrote that the "rapacity" and "oppression of pettyfogging attorneys . . . had been the original cause of the rebellion." Besides these expressions of support, the assembly evinced a measure of responsiveness, if only because of Regulator pressure. In December 1768 it appointed the clerk of the council, John Burgwin, to conduct an investigation into the state of the public accounts, even though in a subsequent session it refused to accept Tryon's reform proposal to audit public funds after the model of Virginia's accounting system. In 1771 the assembly also passed a bill to restrict the fees of lawyers and court clerks.[111]

Although eastern political leaders, including Tryon, displayed some degree of sympathy with backcountry grievances, the overall response of the provincial government was much less favorable. Tryon's stance seems to have stemmed from the traditional priorities that most governors embraced in trying to administer their colonies. He himself was concerned about the corruption he found in North Carolina and not infrequently rebuked the lower house for its complicity in the embezzlement of public taxes. But public malfeasance became much less important to him once the Regulators posed a threat to provincial stability. His foremost concern became his ability to preserve order, command respect for government, and thereby convince London officials that peace could be quickly and firmly restored in the province.

More complex in motivation was the response of colonial leaders who supported such strong measures as Husband's expulsion from the lower house, the Johnston Riot Act,[112] and the hangings of seven Regulators after the Battle of Alamance. In fact, subsequent to the Hillsborough confrontation in September 1768, many lamented that Tryon had not adopted a harsher course of action in response. As the wife of William Hooper, a Wilmington attorney, wrote to a friend, "People imagine they have been too passive with them[;] if the Governor had been well he would have pursued more vigorous measures and have humbled them sufficiently." Probably some who might have been sympathetic were, like Moore, alienated by the violent tactics of the Regulators. Such fears were no doubt heightened by reports in late 1770 that they planned to march on New Bern to release Husband from jail. Indeed, in the months immediately preceding Alamance, the Regulator threat seemed to be lurking everywhere. One Cape Fear planter wrote his brother in March, "Mr. Maurice Moores kitchen and Study with all His Books Are burnt and the poor Regulators are Blamed when God knows It Much more Probably happened by the neglegence of His Servants."[113]

But real or unfounded apprehensions of violence do not adequately explain why most provincial leaders from the very beginning were so unresponsive to the Regulators' protests. Moreover, violence, though ultimately helping to weaken some of their support, played a significant role in making some provincial politicians more attentive.

Another possible circumstance underlying the repressive actions of the elite was the clear challenge that the Regulators represented to the lower house of assembly. By undertaking extralegal acts, backcountry settlers not only undermined the authority of the lower house, but also, in the later stages of their protest, threatened it outright with their allegations of widespread malfeasance—this at a time when the assembly had become an immensely powerful institution in the province. As Jack P. Greene has noted, the lower house in North Carolina by mid-century, as in other colonies, exhibited "a soaring self-confidence and a willingness to take on all comers."[114] Thus, the house in December 1770 characterized the rumored Regulator march on New Bern as "a Daring Insult offered to this House," and the Regulators were later condemned for having committed "plain Usurpations of the Power of the Legislature."[115]

Still, concern for the rightful powers of the lower house does not fully explain the anti-Regulator response of provincial leaders. In particular, it does not explain why their foremost grievance, corruption, failed from the beginning to arouse a deeply passionate moral response. Throughout the disturbances, political leaders remained fundamentally oblivious to the numerous charges of corruption emanating from the backcountry. Both in their public and private discussions of the Regulators, provincial leaders rarely referred to their allegations of corruption,[116] and, when they did, dismissed them as either "nominal grievances," or, however real and flagrant, insufficient to justify violence.[117] Such insensitivity may have partly stemmed from crude self-interest, but this explanation seems more applicable to local officials in the backcountry, where avarice reached its highest levels. More perplexing is the case of leading eastern politicians, a number of whom in all likelihood did not stand to reap any personal gain from the malfeasance of others.

Opposition to the impassioned protests of the Regulators ultimately resulted from the degree to which self-serving and even corruption were accepted as regular features of North Carolina's political system. For decades, politics in the province had revolved around conflicting private, group, and regional interests, resulting at times in the breakdown of civil institutions: land squabbles in the 1730s, the north-south clash of the succeeding decade, the problems of the Granville District, and Governor Dobbs's efforts to root out corrupt practices in the province in the late 1750s and early 1760s. "I must ingenuously confess, I am heartily weary of living in this Land of perpetual Strife and Contention," an Anglican missionary wrote in 1774; such he had found it during his entire twenty-year stay in the colony.[118] Even the patriotic stance taken by the assembly in its confrontation with Dobbs involved a substantial degree of self-interest. All these episodes not only highlighted the extent to which North Carolina still deviated from many of its sister colonies, which by the mid-eighteenth century were enjoying responsible government and internal stability, but also prevented leading North Carolinians from understanding the Regulators' anguish over corruption.

Self-seeking activities were never formally legitimatized within the political culture, and some leaders occasionally voiced the rhetoric of radical Whig thought, though less frequently than in other colonies.[119] Leaders also deplored factionalism and private gain as threats to the common good. But few men missed opportunities to engage in party strife or to pursue selfish ends. In the early 1760s, Henry Eustace McCulloh, who though a relative newcomer to the colony was immensely popular with the provincial elite, lamented: "Oldfather chaos seems resolved to establish a perpetual Empire here." However heartfelt his concern, he was also eminently capable of furthering his own interests and those of his friends at the expense of the public welfare. He even boasted, "Before I came into this Country, I answered the Description of Horace's Imberber Juvenis etc. pretty well, but now, I doubt whether there is a stock-jobber in Exchange Alley that takes more pains about the Universal Catholicon [i.e., money] than I do."[120] McCulloh might bemoan that "Pleasure, pomp, or power, rule the human Race," but he and others largely accepted these frailties as inevitable. "Connections in this Life," he acknowledged, "are generally formed by the Universal Cement of Interest." "Interest that more or less biases all Mankind," Josiah Martin claimed, "among a rude ignorant people such as the Inhabitants of this Country are, governs more than principles of Justice."[121]

While their greater tolerance of self-interest in politics made it difficult for provincial leaders to share the Regulators' hysterical concern over corruption, it also prevented them from viewing the Regulators as public-spirited patriots. Instead, they were seen as little more than a factious mob headed by a self-interested clique intent on exploiting the issue of corruption to further their own ends. Thus the council in December 1770 characterized the Regulators as "a deluded People under the Direction of . . . Seditious Leaders." A grand jury in New Bern deemed them "a Number of unthinking and deluded People . . . under the Influence and Direction of several wicked, seditious, evil designing, and disaffected Persons." What made them so intolerable in the eyes of provincial leaders, and thereby different from other factional interests, was that the Regulators threatened to disrupt North Carolina's entire political system.[122]

"Rigour and Egyptian Austerity!"

The degree to which the conduct of North Carolina's political leadership did not reflect the values of Country thought was widely recognized outside the province. Other colonists were nearly universal in their sympathy for the rioters, though such a stance entailed criticism not only of an English governor but also of North Carolina's political elite. For the vast majority of observers in other colonies, the Regulator riots signified neither a radical democratic spirit nor levelism but rather a protest in defense of liberty against a corrupted government. Ezra Stiles, the future president of Yale, exclaimed in his diary: "What shall an injured and oppressed people do, when their Petitions, Remonstrances and Supplications are unheard and rejected, they insulted by the Crown Officers, and Oppression and Tyranny (under the name of Government) continued with Rigour and Egyptian Austerity!" Richard Henry Lee of Virginia wrote to his brother William, "In truth [the] whole of this business was dirty work in the mildest view of it. . . . Grieved . . . without being able to obtain redress, the people were at length driven by repeated injuries to do what otherwise they would never have thought of."[123]

Such private expressions of sympathy were echoed in colonial newspapers, to the virtual exclusion of support for the Regulators' adversaries except for reprinted editorials from North Carolina. In Rhode Island, the *Newport Mercury* asked: "Is it possible for any Man, unless he possess the Soul of a Canibal, to wish Success to an Administration so corrupt, so absolutely void of Humanity, and every christian Virtue, as that of North-Carolina!?" A correspondent in the *Pennsylvania Journal* declared, "When those who are entrusted with the conduct of the affairs of the public, oppress the people . . . they, and not the people who resist them, are Rebels." Although admitting that the Regulation may have been too violent, the *Virginia Gazette* asserted, "It ought to be a lesson for all good Governments to suffer no Set of Men, under the Sanction of Authority, to fleece the People." "Humanus" in the *Massachusetts Spy* averred that "These people have suffered a series of the most cruel extortions and illegal plunderings that ever men under any shadow of civil government were subjected to."[124]

Most of these and other commentators pointed to the original grievances of the Regulators in their criticism of North Carolina authorities. Then, too, most also condemned the new steps of "oppression" taken by the provincial government in opposition to the rioters. Although corruption in its own right was alarming, such measures as the Johnston Riot Act and the post-Alamance executions were similarly depicted as grievous abuses of power. No doubt equally appalling were the steps taken by Tryon, and approved by his provincial supporters, to capture Husband, Hunter, and other fugitive "Chiefs" after the battle. Offering a reward of 1,000 acres of land and 100 dollars for return of each, Tryon "permitted several of the Regulators . . . to go in quest of them, on leaving their children hostages."[125]

The offenses of North Carolina's political leadership against the prevalent civic morality of the American colonies were capped when numerous "Gentlemen" and the county sheriff assembled in New Bern on July 31, 1771, for the common hangman's public burning of the *Massachusetts Spy*, "Number 17," which had criticized Tryon and his "Banditti of Robbers."[126] That this extraordinary act of retaliation should be taken by a group of Americans was not lost

upon the *Spy*'s editor, who, in a pointed reference to the celebrated
ordeal of the English radical John Wilkes, responded, "In humble
imitation of your betters at home, you gave the poor harmless
paper the same fate as the famed *North-Briton*, to be burnt by the
common hangman." "Thank God," affirmed a correspondent in
the *Boston Gazette*, "these instances of savage joy are confined to
the brutish inhabitants of the howling wilderness, and the J[us-
tice]s L[awyer]s and S[heriff]s of NORTH CAROLINA."[127]

To whatever degree provincial authorities in North Carolina had
in the past been guilty of what were viewed as abuses of power in
the context of Country thought, they had, indeed, resorted to even
more extreme measures in their efforts to suppress the Regulators.
Basic propensities within the colony's political environment, accentuated by fear, had given way to oppression and violence. When
Tryon was promoted to be governor of New York in 1771, ending
what New Bern residents hailed as "one of the mildest Administrations in America,"[128] the colony's political elite found itself in the
position of having sanctioned measures that other colonials associated with "prerogative-subjects," "Stuartizing Loyalists," and
"Court sycophants."[129] At no previous time in North Carolina's
history had its divergence from the political values and habits of its
sister colonies been so starkly visible.

7 The Regulator Legacy, 1772–1776

This summer our new governor has been up with us and given us every satisfaction we could expect of him . . . , and I think our officers hate him as bad as we hated Tryon.
—James Hunter to William Butler, November 6, 1772

The Battle of Alamance sealed the Regulators' fate. Never again did backcountry settlers mass to reform their political system as they had from 1766 to 1771. But the legacy of their abortive efforts was substantial. The fact that many backcountry grievances remained unredressed, coupled with the arrival of a new governor, created a volatile atmosphere and a serious crisis for provincial leaders. In several major respects, North Carolina's role in the American Revolution was shaped by the still-rumbling waves of Regulator turbulence.

"To purge the country"

North Carolina received its new governor in August 1771. For Tryon's replacement, imperial authorities had selected Josiah Martin, a firm supporter of crown imperatives. As the son of a wealthy Antiguan sugar planter, he had initially chosen the British army for a career. After serving in the Seven Years' War, he rose to the rank of lieutenant colonel, but became disillusioned with army life because of its meager financial rewards and because his protests over a salary scandal among fellow officers were ignored. His fortuitous nomination as governor of North Carolina was the handiwork of his older brother, a powerful English politician who had ties to Lord Hillsborough, secretary of state for the colonies. At the time of his appointment, Martin was living in New York with his father's financial assistance.[1]

Although imperial relations had deteriorated up and down America's eastern seaboard, Martin inherited a colony whose political leaders still celebrated the conduct of their last royal governor. For the time being, victory at Alamance over the Regulators transcended local resentment over British transgressions. Prospects for the new governor also appeared promising. Upon convening an assembly in November, Martin expressed pleasure that Tryon's "unwearied endeavours" for "restoring the peace" had been "so well seconded by the Legislature." In return, both houses promised a happy administration, as the glow of Tryon's "Spirited Conduct" continued to warm both governor and governed.[2]

Martin had first learned of the Regulator disturbances while in New York. Awaiting his departure for North Carolina, he lamented that "the nice limits and prescriptions of our constitution . . . allow little latitude for such vigorous exertion" as might be needed. An ardent champion of British authority during the New York Stamp Act riots, he held no brief for provincial insurgents. On the other hand, he later thought Tryon's triumph at Alamance "a sacrifice—like a slaughter of defenceless, deluded sheep."[3] More important, Martin became convinced, once he had arrived in the colony, that local authorities had indeed committed serious abuses of power. His attitude toward the Regulators did not immediately change, but he increasingly came to suspect that some of their grievances might have been legitimate.

The embezzlement of public taxes especially disturbed the new governor, much as it had backcountry settlers and his two predecessors. In November he expressed concern to the assembly, as he did in later correspondence with royal officials. By his estimation not even a third of £66,000 still owed by county sheriffs and other collectors would ever be paid into the provincial treasury. For that reason, Martin took the bold step of posting the public accounts for the past seventeen years on the doors of churches and courthouses throughout the colony. These not only listed the counties from which taxes were still owed but also identified guilty tax collectors by name.[4]

The conduct of other government officers seemed just as culpable. Besides suspending a customs collector at Port Currituck for misconduct, Martin charged county clerks with exacting extortionate fees, and concluded that justices of the peace were as "corrupt" as they were "ignorant." Both clerks and magistrates, he wrote Hillsborough, were united by "reciprocal countenance of malversation." Indeed, only eight of thirty-four clerks complied with Martin's proclamation ordering them to post fee tables to minimize the possibilities of corruption.[5]

While Martin tried to remedy some of the original causes of the Regulator riots, flash fires of discontent continued to burn in the backcountry. In early 1772 James Hunter, the outlawed ex-Regulator leader, brazenly appeared at a backcountry court, yet no one dared arrest him. Public appearances by still other outlaws and the possibility that more serious problems lay in store convinced Martin to take a western trip to inspect backcountry conditions firsthand.[6] From June to September, he resided in Hillsborough, visiting nearby counties and talking to scores of settlers, including Hunter and other former leaders. The trip effectively converted his "indignation" over past riots to "pity." His worst suspicions about local officials were also confirmed. "My progress through this Country," he wrote, "hath opened my eyes exceedingly with respect to the commotions and discontents that have lately prevailed in it. I now see most clearly that they have been provoked by insolence and cruel advantages taken of the peoples ignorance by mercenary tricking Attorneys, Clerks and other little Officers who have practiced upon them every sort of rapine and extortion."[7]

British officials in America commonly denigrated the political qualifications of local elites, but Martin became especially disdainful toward North Carolina's ruling group. Genuine sympathy for former Regulators, combined with traditional notions of British superiority and a rather tactless temperament made him outwardly contemptuous of provincial officers and their capacity for public service. In making his trip to the backcountry, Martin not only urged the assembly to pardon most of the outlawed Regulators, but he also suspended several backcountry officials on the spot. A delighted James Hunter wrote an old friend in November 1772:

> This summer our new governor has been up with us and given us every satisfaction we could expect of him . . . , and I think our officers hate him as bad as we hated Tryon only they don't speak so free. He has turned Colonel [John] McGee out of commission for making complaint against out-lawed men—and he has turned out every officer that any complaint has been supported against. In short I think he has determined to purge the country of them.[8]

Such was his zeal for political reform while in the backcountry that Martin projected several sweeping changes in the structure of local government. Knowing that the current county court law would expire at an upcoming assembly session, he sent Whitehall several proposals designed to undermine the power of local authorities. For one thing, he desired a stronger role as governor in the appointment of county sheriffs. Rather than be forced to select one of three candidates normally nominated by each county court, Martin wanted the right to make an independent choice should any of the three refuse his appointment. Under the old system, he complained, county magistrates often preelected favorites by nominating two candidates on the "assurance that they will decline the office."

Martin also wished to establish new restrictions on the membership of county courts. Believing that "very few of the present Inhabitants are qualified for such important trust," he favored a law limiting county commissions to only five justices. Three of these would constitute a quorum for routine business, and all five a quorum for more important duties, such as approving tax accounts. Martin himself would appoint the five magistrates from each county's full roster of justices of the peace. The remaining justices would serve in a nonjudicial capacity as "mere Conservators of the Peace." All these measures, he wrote Hillsborough in July 1772, would "increase" the "dignity and utility" of the courts and "would call forth to the public service the ablest and best men" rather than "the ignorant and vulgar people who in the present circumstances of things must be a majority in every County's commission of the peace."[9]

Martin's proposals had radical implications. County authorities, who had steadily increased their power during the mid-eighteenth century, represented bastions of strength by the eve of the Revolution. Besides numerous powers they had acquired over the years, they were represented by ever-loyal spokesmen in the assembly. Most representatives, in fact, were themselves county justices, "whose policy and aim it had ever been," as Martin himself realized, "to usurp to the County Courts as much power as possible."[10] He wished not only to curtail local influence over the key office of sheriff, but also to restrict drastically the number of justices who could serve on county courts.

Whether Martin expressed his views to assembly leaders as openly as he did to London officials is not known. But colonial politicians could not have misinterpreted his sentiments. When the assembly convened in January 1773, a confrontation was probably inevitable. In addition to befriending former Regulators, Martin had championed some of their foremost grievances in the spirit of political reform—"to the great grief and shame of our gentry," as James Hunter said of Martin's attack on the "extortionate actions" of local leaders.[11]

In his opening remarks to the assembly, Martin raised several sensitive issues. Besides calling attention to the "perplexity and disorder" of the provincial finances, as well as to the "malversation" of county sheriffs and other abuses, he urged that the assembly take special care in drafting new laws for the provincial judicial system. The assembly promised compliance, but passed a law for superior and inferior courts that all but eclipsed the session's other business. The bill represented a stunning blow to Martin's plans for judicial reform. The governor opposed it partly because it gave North Carolinians the right to attach the property of foreigners for debt, in open violation of his instructions. But just as upsetting, if not more so, was that the bill set no quorum for the number of magistrates allowed to sit as county justices. "This Establishment of mine," he feared, "is mutilated and destroyed." Moreover, the assembly had extended the jurisdiction of county courts from £20 to £50 sterling in civil causes, a considerable expansion of authority at the expense of superior courts. To make matters worse, the court act provided that county court clerks be appointed not at the governor's pleasure but during good behavior. All these steps, in Martin's view, clearly threatened an end to the "reformation" of what he later called "those little prostitute judicatures."[12]

After considerable haggling with the assembly, Martin reluctantly agreed to the court bill after it was passed with a suspending clause delaying implementation until the crown had granted its approval. In the meantime, the colony had been left without any superior courts because of the expiration of an earlier act. When Martin exercised his royal prerogative to establish temporary courts of oyer and terminer, relations with the assembly continued to deteriorate. Indeed, up until the demise of royal authority, when Martin fled from New Bern in May 1775, the issue of courts remained the single greatest source of discord between himself and local leaders.[13]

To a significant degree the court controversy represented the culmination of Martin's efforts to cleanse North Carolina's governing apparatus of corruption. Almost immediately upon arriving in the province, he had sought to remedy lingering abuses of power by government officers, which his later tour of the backcountry had only seemed to confirm.

None of this is to suggest that the Regulator riots and Martin's response to the problems they raised single-handedly pushed leading North Carolinians toward revolution. Resistance to British authority, though initially milder than in many provinces, had arisen as early as the mid-1760s in response to the Sugar Act and the Stamp Act. Besides these and other imperial measures that excited opposition throughout the colonies, several issues largely peculiar to North Carolina, such as the foreign attachment controversy and the appointment of a provincial agent, further fueled anti-British sentiment.[14] Whether most provincial leaders believed that a corrupt conspiracy was afoot in London to enslave America is less certain. Compared to that on other colonial elites, the impact of radical Whig thought on leading North Carolinians remained weak. This body of related political assumptions was doubtless of no more significance to political leaders now than it had been in explaining the Regulator protests.

Yet any understanding of North Carolina's role in the Revolution, whatever the exact influence of these other considerations, cannot ignore the strong challenge Martin's policies posed to local leaders. Attacks against the embezzlement of public funds, extortionate clerks' fees, and the corrupt actions of many county courts—

all seriously impugned the conduct of North Carolina's governing elite. British rule significantly undermined the status of American elites everywhere on the eve of the Revolution—by shutting colonial leaders off from metropolitan sources of political preferment, threatening the power of colonial assemblies, and denigrating the professional competence of indigenous rulers.[15] But probably nowhere was this threat sharper and more keenly felt than in North Carolina, where British officialdom openly confronted an already deeply troubled elite. In 1771 leading provincials had just survived the greatest assault upon their power and prestige in the eighteenth century; for four years, thousands of backcountry settlers had defied their authority and vigorously protested their public conduct. Not only did Martin, after his arrival, openly sympathize with the Regulators, but he also increasingly echoed many of their complaints. As had many North Carolinians, he repeatedly questioned the authority of local leaders and found it wanting. In contrast to William Tryon's years as governor, Martin's administrative priorities resulted in the progressive alienation of leading provincials from imperial authority.

Revolutionary Allegiances

Whereas one result of the Regulator riots was increased friction between leading North Carolinians and British rule, an equally weighty consequence was that North Carolina remained deeply divided as it prepared for war. The riots had left a large, embittered population in the backcountry with ambivalent allegiances during the growing imperial crisis. On the one hand, the Regulators had not infrequently voiced opposition to British policies during their own struggle in the backcountry;[16] and in the years following Alamance, customary Regulator grievances were often expressed side by side with protests against crown rule. In the instructions, for instance, sent Orange County representatives in 1773, local residents protested both the judicial fee system and the creation of special prerogative courts, notably the oyer and terminer tribunals established by Martin.[17] Certainly leading eastern Whigs recognized the value of backcountry support against the British. In August 1775 the Third Provincial Congress, meeting in Hillsborough, arranged a conference with disgruntled ex-Regulators, as did the Continental Congress three months later in Philadelphia.[18] In fact, probably because of the Whig need for western backing, a few old Regulator demands, like elections by secret ballot and a reformed public treasury, were incorporated into the North Carolina constitution in 1776. In this way, backcountry settlers ultimately exerted some statutory influence, however slight, on their political system.

Yet, by that time, Governor Martin, in thoroughly antagonizing leading provincials, had made firm friends with many former Regulators. Not only had Tryon been replaced, but western settlers now had a British governor who was openly sympathetic to their interests, thereby winning him "their highest confidence and esteem." "The country," declared James Hunter after Martin's visit to the backcountry, "is as much master now as ever."[19] Moreover, many former Regulators remained fearful of again contesting British authority, especially after they had been compelled to take an oath of allegiance to the king upon their defeat at Alamance. Joining the Whig cause also meant embracing many of their former enemies. For all these reasons, more than five hundred backcountry residents in early 1775 signed addresses of loyalty to the British crown. "I have no doubt," Martin wrote, "that the people in the Western Counties of this Province . . . will generally unite in support of Government."[20]

Because of insufficient records, historians may never be able to determine the revolutionary allegiances of most former Regulators once hostilities actually commenced. Their principal leader during the riots, Hermon Husband, was an avid Whig, but he opposed British authority from an exile residence in Pennsylvania, a province whose leaders had always been much more to his liking than North Carolina's.[21] As for his former compatriots, no stampede to the Whig banner took place. Many former Regulators, perhaps a majority, simply decided to sit the Revolution out as best they could. For them, the conflict with Britain probably seemed at best anticlimactic to their earlier struggle on behalf of freedom and true liberty. Still others became Loyalists. When violence erupted at Moore's Creek Bridge in February 1776, one to two hundred former Regulators were among those defeated by Whig forces. Asked about the role the common people played in the Revolution, John

Adams asserted that "the back part of North Carolina" afforded the chief instance of people rising "in large bodies" against Whig authority. He attributed this to "particular" causes and the "hatred" former Regulators felt "towards their fellow-citizens."[22] In few other colonies did revolutionaries go to war with so little popular support.

Part III
Conclusion

8   The Origins of Instability

It is small wonder that North Carolinians approached the American Revolution so deeply divided. Throughout the eighteenth century, internal squabbles had beset the colony's public world and produced what Gabriel Johnston once called "a great deal of unprofitable strife and contention." "In this Country," Josiah Martin echoed in 1772, "there prevails a proneness to contention without example."[1]

North Carolina, of course, was not alone in its factious political life. Recent scholarship has suggested that the middle provinces in America and possibly others by the end of the colonial period were beginning to exhibit an "interest" system of politics. The growing differentiation of early American society, according to this view, spawned a multiplicity of new ethnic, religious, regional, and economic groups that increasingly saw politics in relation not to a broader public interest but to their own narrow concerns. Foremost among these especially heterogeneous colonies whose political life foreshadowed the emergence of republican pluralism, full-scale political parties, and open competition was New York, which had always featured a contentious political system but where the pursuit of interest was now becoming an accepted norm of political behavior. "The growing legitimacy . . . of self-interest as a public concept," Patricia Bonomi has written of New York, "may well have been the sharpest single innovation of colonial politics."[2]

A key question raised by Bonomi's analysis and similar studies is whether late colonial factionalism, if indeed a common occurrence, diverged, other than in its growing acceptance, from earlier political turbulence. Was the factional strife that New York, Pennsylvania, and New Jersey exhibited in the 1760s and early 1770s similar to that which plagued most colonies in the seventeenth century? If so, did the middle colonies show no signs of political growth over the course of nearly a hundred years?

It is significant that political strife in the three colonies, however bitter at times, did not normally produce the same sort of civil breakdown, violence, uncompromising intransigence, and unbridled opportunism characteristic of earlier years. Politics in all three was comparable to that in the more stable provinces of Virginia and South Carolina insofar as their political processes remained more noteworthy for restraint than for recklessness. Ironically, this circumstance may have stemmed in part from the presence of proto-political parties that served to temper the divergent interests they represented.[3]

Of those colonies that experienced internal strife during the late colonial period, North Carolina probably most closely typified the seventeenth-century pattern of political disorder. No parties were yet emerging in North Carolina. Further, politics remained a highly vulnerable arena for the self-serving interests of individuals, groups, and entire regions. Political controversy also frequently escalated into civil disorder and produced violent and destabilizing consequences for the basic institutions of government. James Murray, who moved to Boston in 1765, appreciated this fact in writing a North Carolina acquaintance three years later: "We have our disturbances as well as you have yours with this Difference[—]that our People are more Civilized."[4] In fact, the very legitimacy of provincial authorities was challenged on more than one occasion— during the land squabbles of the 1730s, in the north-south controversy, and again during the Regulator riots.

Several principal factors contributed to North Carolina's disorderly public life. To begin with, political institutions were still reasonably immature when the colony came under royal authority in 1729. Major organs of government on the provincial and local levels did not have the sophistication and regularity of political structures in other colonies. For at least the first decades of royal rule, they consequently remained susceptible to disruption.

Second, the colony's sale to the crown brought it under closer scrutiny from an outside authority than it had ever been before. Direct royal control occasioned new restrictions, such as stiffer quitrents in the 1730s, and, after 1754 stronger efforts to bolster executive authority. On the other hand, Britain also attempted to strengthen its authority over proprietary colonies in the later decades of the colonial period, so that, in the long run, North Carolina's loss of proprietary status probably did not matter very much.

Nor was the crown's involvement after 1729 uniformly negative. Royal control insured some degree of external guidance and coherent policymaking, which had been seriously wanting during the proprietary period. In several instances, imperial authorities even helped to resolve provincial conflicts, as in the early 1750s during the north-south struggle and a decade later when they acceded to several of the demands of North Carolina's lower house of assembly, which in itself periodically exerted a divisive influence. Especially by the French and Indian War, the assembly's struggle for political dominance was beginning to strain political relations on the provincial level.

Also disruptive were the policies and personalities of the colony's governors. Neither Burrington nor Johnston was above seeking personal aggrandizement. And, whatever their objectives, all of North Carolina's chief executives knew how to employ hard-nosed tactics. Although they initially manifested a proclivity toward compromise, Burrington, Johnston, Dobbs, and Martin did not shrink from confrontations with local factions. Tryon valued harmony more than did other governors, but he could have avoided his costly displays of military prowess and made stronger efforts to mollify the Regulators.

All these essentially political circumstances were important, but they should not be overemphasized. Most studies of colonial North Carolina have inevitably focused upon the conduct of some governor, the impact of an imperial ruling, the demands of an increasingly powerful assembly, or other institutional factors to explain political configurations that normally originated in a deeper wellspring. Still more significant were the ways in which the varied contours of North Carolina society affected the character of politics. For one thing, North Carolina, whose religious establishment was weak, did not experience the calming effects that religion sometimes produced in other colonies. Both the Quaker influence in

Pennsylvania and Puritanism in New England, while sufficiently strong, helped to discourage political bickering. North Carolinians could also afford a factious brand of politics partly because of their relative physical security from both foreign attacks and Indian warfare. In addition, the comparative absence of slavery and the racial fear that accompanied it elsewhere in the South meant that yet another major limit on party strife was missing in North Carolina. Political leaders also may have neglected the interests of lesser planters partly for the same reason. It might be more than coincidental that the colony's elite became more preoccupied with internal concerns as the number of slaves grew, except of course in the backcountry where slavery was less widespread and official venality reached its highest levels.

North Carolina's rapid expansion during the mid-eighteenth century also created politically upsetting consequences. The opening of new areas of economic opportunity and the influx of new groups whose appetites were large, particularly in the Cape Fear, or whose expectations were high, as in the backcountry, severely strained the colony's political system. Backcountry settlers who ultimately formed the Regulator movement not only arrived with high material hopes but also felt few allegiances to governing authorities and even tried to introduce new standards of conduct into Carolina politics. Moreover, rapid territorial growth, in the case of the north-south clash, created sources of regional antagonism.

Of related significance was the crucial role North Carolina's nascent elite played in provincial affairs. Although lesser men, as in the 1730s uproar over quitrents and again during the Regulator riots, exercised occasional influence in the public realm, the colony's upper class determined for the most part the course of provincial politics. Members of this predominantly nonnative, achieving elite aggressively contested with each other over land as well as local and regional supremacy, repulsed efforts by Governor Dobbs to rid the government of corruption, and remained indifferent to similar attempts by his successor. Although public malfeasance toward the end of the colonial period probably contributed to both elite integration and a heightened interest among political leaders in the colony's deficiencies, it soon plunged North Carolina once again into internecine strife. Nor could men in positions of authority, because of their often lackluster credentials, always command the respect of those beneath them, especially during the 1730s and later during the Regulator riots.

North Carolina's most fundamental problem during the mid-eighteenth century lay in its slowly growing economy. Because of limited economic progress, incentive was lacking to maintain an orderly political life. But, more important, the colony's economic exigencies left men's expectations unfulfilled, except in the case of the isolated dirt farmer. North Carolinians did not clash over conflicting religious or ethnic values, though cultural differences existed among settlers, but rather over predominantly economic concerns, such as access to land, town supremacy, regional development, posts of profit, and the disposition of public funds. If the economy had yielded better returns, such matters would have loomed less large.

That the colony was not totally destitute only exacerbated this happenstance. Besides growing in population and settled territory, North Carolina was within sight of economic prosperity because of an expanding trade sector. Leading planters consequently demonstrated a heartier appetite for profit than they would have in a desolate backwater. They also had more incentive to war over economic benefits, which in themselves were more substantial than in previous years. "If poor countries appear to be unstable," Samuel P. Huntington has observed, "it is not because they are poor, but because they are trying to become rich. A purely traditional society would be ignorant, poor, and stable."[5]

Although North Carolina's relatively impoverished state meant that public affairs would be anything but tranquil, its experience was not very different from those of other British colonies, where economic ambitions frequently kept provincial affairs in turmoil for the first several generations. Political strife still occurred in eighteenth-century North Carolina principally because social and economic conditions, which normally insured a stable public world in colonial America, remained in an early stage of development.

Not until the late eighteenth and early nineteenth centuries did North Carolina's social fabric prove more conducive to a peaceful commonweal. Among other factors, a healthier economy, a prospering elite united by ties of nativity and kinship, improved regional integration in the east, and a growing and threatening number of black slaves all contributed to a more tranquil political atmosphere and reduced disruptive consequences for institutions of government. Although the emergence of political parties, western sectionalism, and republican pluralism in the Revolutionary era meant that political currents remained somewhat turbulent, episodes of violence and civil disorder, punctuated by basic challenges to governmental authority, lay firmly in the past. In the wake of the Revolution, North Carolina not only joined a new nation, but it also moved closer to the mainstream of American politics.

Appendix

TABLE A.I *Distribution of North Carolina Landholders, 173*

	Acres Owned (percentages in parentheses)				
County	1–100	101–250	251–500	501–1,000	1,00 2,00
Currituck	19 (27.5)	18 (26.1)	22 (31.9)	8 (11.6)	1 (1.5
Pasquotank	74 (31.9)	63 (27.2)	61 (26.3)	26 (11.2)	8 (3.5
Perquimans	43 (19.3)	73 (32.7)	60 (26.9)	36 (16.1)	10 (4.5
Chowan	42 (18.8)	78 (34.8)	51 (22.8)	36 (16.1)	14 (6.3
Tyrrell	17 (25.8)	16 (24.2)	11 (16.7)	12 (18.2)	8 (12.1
Bertie	33 (12.0)	62 (22.6)	70 (25.5)	79 (28.7)	17 (6.2
Edgecombe	12 (18.8)	25 (39.1)	19 (29.7)	6 (9.4)	1 (1.6

es Owned (percentages in parentheses)				
001–000	3,001–4,000	4,001–5,000	5,001+	Total Landholders
1 (1.5)	— —	— —	— —	69
— —	— —	— —	— —	232
1 (.5)	— —	— —	— —	223
2 (.9)	— —	— —	1 (.5)	224
— —	— —	— —	2 (3.0)	66
6 (2.2)	4 (1.5)	3 (1.1)	1 (.4)	275
1 (1.6)	— —	— —	— —	64

ᴿCES: Quitrent Lists, June 12, 1735, NCCR, 22:240–58.

T A B L E A.2 *Distribution of Land among Households in North Carolina, About 1780*

County	Acres Owned (percentages in parentheses)					
	0	1–100	101–250	251–500	501–1,000	1,0 2,0
Pasquotank	189 (29.4)	230 (35.8)	147 (22.9)	55 (8.6)	15 (2.3)	(1
Perquimans	158 (28.3)	138 (24.7)	168 (30.1)	66 (11.8)	21 (3.8)	(1
Chowan	134 (28.7)	161 (34.5)	70 (15.0)	49 (10.5)	33 (7.1)	❙ (3
Hertford	168 (27.1)	116 (18.7)	143 (23.0)	97 (15.6)	61 (9.8)	❩ (3
Halifax	359 (30.6)	155 (13.2)	262 (22.3)	213 (18.1)	112 (9.5)	⸗ (4
Tyrrell	112 (20.7)	131 (24.3)	168 (31.1)	71 (13.2)	41 (7.6)	❙ (2
Beaufort	126 (23.4)	106 (19.7)	119 (22.1)	83 (15.4)	66 (12.3)	⸗ (4
Carteret	131 (29.0)	115 (25.4)	78 (17.3)	68 (15.0)	35 (7.7)	❙ (3
New Hanover	94 (26.2)	43 (12.0)	50 (13.9)	57 (15.9)	56 (15.6)	⸗ (9
Brunswick	75 (30.2)	47 (19.0)	37 (14.9)	41 (16.5)	19 (7.7)	❙ (9
Bladen	250 (20.7)	225 (18.6)	264 (21.8)	195 (16.1)	169 (14.0)	⸗ (6
Cumberland	223 (27.5)	157 (19.3)	152 (18.7)	128 (15.8)	103 (12.7)	⸗ (3
Granville	400 (32.7)	94 (7.7)	272 (22.2)	227 (18.5)	143 (11.7)	❙ (9
Orange	342 (29.0)	102 (8.7)	327 (27.7)	239 (20.3)	117 (9.9)	⸗ (3
Surry	557 (30.9)	218 (12.1)	451 (25.0)	355 (19.7)	141 (7.8)	⸗ (2

SOURCES: Francis Grave Morris and Phyllis Mary Morris, "Economic Conditio North Carolina about 1780, Part I, Landholdings," *NCHR* 16 (1939): 118–29 "Economic Conditions in North Carolina about 1780, Part II: Ownership of ❙

	Acres Owned				
(percentages in parentheses)					
01–00	3,001–4,000	4,001–5,000	5,001+	Acreage Unknown	Total Households
—	—	—	—	—	643
—	—	—	—	—	
—	1 (.2)	—	—	—	559
—		—	—	—	
4 9)	1 (.2)	—	—	1 (.2)	467
2 3)	1 (.2)	—	—	9 (1.5)	621
2 0)	5 (.4)	3 (.3)	4 (.3)	—	1,174
2 4)	—	—	—	—	540
5 9)	3 (.6)	1 (.2)	6 (1.1)	—	538
5 1)	—	—	2 (.4)	2 (.4)	452
1 1)	4 (1.1)	2 (.6)	6 (1.7)	2 (.6)	359
6 4)	6 (2.4)	—	4 (1.6)	—	248
8 5)	3 (.3)	4 (.3)	4 (.3)	—	1,209
9 1)	4 (.5)	—	2 (.3)	2 (.3)	812
6 3)	4 (.3)	1 (.1)	3 (.3)	—	1,225
7 6)	1 (.1)	—	1 (.1)	5 (.4)	1,179
4 2)	2 (.1)	1 (.1)	2 (.1)	26 (1.4)	1,802

, Slaves, and Cattle," *NCHR* 16 (1939): 296–98. Town lots were included in
–100 acre category.

TABLE A.3 *Distribution of Taxable Slaves among Households in North Carolina, 1760s*

County	Taxable Slaves (percentages in parentheses)						Total Households
	0	1–5	6–10	11–20	21–50	51+	
Pasquotank	501 (64.7)	249 (32.2)	17 (2.2)	5 (.7)	2 (.3)	— —	774
Perquimans	253 (46.3)	235 (43.0)	40 (7.3)	19 (3.5)	— —	— —	547
Chowan	220 (47.2)	192 (41.2)	37 (7.9)	13 (2.8)	4 (.9)	— —	466
Bertie	344 (61.3)	170 (30.3)	32 (5.7)	11 (2.0)	4 (.7)	— —	561
Beaufort	206 (65.0)	97 (30.6)	10 (3.2)	3 (1.0)	1 (.3)	— —	317
Craven	623 (64.2)	262 (27.0)	49 (5.1)	25 (2.6)	10 (1.0)	1 (.1)	970
Pitt	365 (74.3)	112 (22.8)	11 (2.2)	2 (.4)	1 (.2)	— —	491
Onslow	358 (66.9)	153 (28.6)	17 (3.2)	4 (.8)	3 (.6)	— —	535
New Hanover	171 (49.3)	117 (33.7)	28 (8.1)	11 (3.2)	16 (4.6)	4 (1.2)	347
Brunswick	110 (55.8)	44 (22.3)	17 (8.6)	12 (6.1)	10 (5.1)	4 (2.0)	197
Bladen	254 (64.6)	112 (28.5)	13 (3.3)	8 (2.0)	6 (1.5)	— —	393
Dobbs	685 (70.8)	247 (25.5)	30 (3.1)	5 (.5)	1 (.1)	— —	968
Cumberland	451 (77.5)	117 (20.1)	11 (1.9)	3 (.5)	— —	— —	582
Granville	482 (63.7)	225 (29.7)	39 (5.2)	9 (1.2)	2 (.3)	— —	757
Anson	279 (90.0)	28 (9.0)	3 (1.0)	— —	— —	— —	310

SOURCES: See Bibliographical Essay.

T A B L E A.4 *Adult White Males Owning Twenty or More and Fifty or More Slaves in Eastern North Carolina, About 1780 (percentages in parentheses)*

County	Adult White Males	20+		50+	
Pasquotank	643	7	(1.1)	—	—
Camden	601	4	(.7)	—	—
Perquimans	559	5	(.9)	—	—
Chowan	467	20	(4.3)	2	(.4)
Gates	578	9	(1.6)	—	—
Hertford	621	8	(1.3)	—	—
Tyrrell	540	7	(1.3)	—	—
Halifax	1,174	48	(4.1)	6	(.5)
Jones	268	4	(1.5)	—	—
Carteret	452	5	(1.1)	1	(.2)
New Hanover	359	25	(7.0)	1	(.3)

SOURCE: Morris and Morris, "Economic Conditions in North Carolina about 1780, Part II," *NCHR* 16 (1939): 305, 308–9. Camden was formed from Pasquotank in 1777, Gates from Chowan, Hertford, and Perquimans in 1779, and Jones from Craven in 1779. David L. Corbitt, *The Formation of North Carolina Counties, 1663–1943* (Raleigh, 1950), 56, 105, 134.

Notes

Abbreviations

AASP	*Proceedings of the American Antiquarian Society*
Add. MSS	Additional Manuscripts, British Library, London, England
AHR	*American Historical Review*
AJPH	*Australian Journal of Politics and History*
A.O.	Audit Office, Public Record Office, London
Boston Gaz.	*Boston Gazette*
C.O.	Colonial Office, Public Record Office, London
Conn. Cour.	*Connecticut Courant* (Hartford)
DAB	Allen Johnson, ed., *Dictionary of American Biography*, 20 vols. (New York, 1928–37)
DNB	Leslie Stephen and Sidney Lee, eds., *Dictionary of National Biography*, 63 vols. (London, 1885–1900)
DNCB	William S. Powell, ed., *Dictionary of North Carolina Biography* (Chapel Hill, 1979–)
EHR	*English Historical Review*
H.C.A.	High Court of Admiralty, Public Record Office, London
JAH	*Journal of American History*
JSH	*Journal of Southern History*
JSHP	*James Sprunt Historical Publications*
Mass. Hist. Soc.	Massachusetts Historical Society, Boston
Mass. Spy	*Massachusetts Spy* (Boston)
Moravian Records	Adelaide L. Fries, ed., *Records of the Moravians in North Carolina*, 8 vols. (Raleigh, 1922–54)
N.H. Gaz.	*New Hampshire Gazette* (Portsmouth)
N.C. Archives	North Carolina State Department of Archives and History, Raleigh
N.C. Biog. Hist.	Samuel A. Ashe, Stephen B. Weeks, and Claude L. Van Noppen, eds., *Biographical History of North Carolina*, 8 vols. (Greensboro, N.C., 1905–17)
N.C. Gaz.	*North Carolina Gazette* (New Bern and Wilmington)
NCB	*North Carolina Booklet* (journal)
NCCR,	William L. Saunders, Walter Clark, and Stephen B. Weeks, eds., *The*

NCSR	*Colonial and State Records of North Carolina*, 30 vols. (Raleigh, Winston, Goldsboro, and Charlotte, N.C., 1886–1914)
NCHR	*North Carolina Historical Review*
Pa. Jour.	*Pennsylvania Journal and Weekly Advertiser* (Philadelphia)
PMHB	*Pennsylvania Magazine of History and Biography*
P.R.O.	Public Record Office, London
Reg. Doc.	William S. Powell, James K. Huhta, and Thomas J. Farnham, comps. and eds., *The Regulators in North Carolina: A Documentary History, 1759–1776* (Raleigh, 1971)
S.P.G.	Society for the Propagation of the Gospel in Foreign Parts
S.C. Gaz.	*South Carolina Gazette* (Charleston)
S.C. and Am. Genl. Gaz.	*South Carolina and American General Gazette* (Charleston)
South. Hist. Coll.	Southern Historical Collection, University of North Carolina, Chapel Hill
T.	Treasury, Public Record Office, London
Va. Gaz.	*Virginia Gazette* (Williamsburg)
Va. State Lib.	Virginia State Library, Richmond
VMHB	*Virginia Magazine of History and Biography*
WMQ	*William and Mary Quarterly*

Introduction

1. See Bibliographical Essay.

2. For all works on early North Carolina referred to on xvi–xvii, see Bibliographical Essay.

3. James Murray to David Nicoll, Feb. 20, 1755, Murray Letter Book, 1735–60, 303, James Murray Collection, Mass. Hist. Soc.; Johnston to Duke of Bedford, [1749], NCCR, 4:919; Upper House Journals, Dec. 18, 1754, NCCR, 5:224.

4. George Burrington to Commissioners of Customs, July 20, 1736, NCCR, 4:172; William Borden, "An Address to the Inhabitants of North Carolina . . . ," 1746, in William K. Boyd, ed., *Some Eighteenth Century Tracts concerning North Carolina* (Raleigh, 1927), 72; Adam Boyd to Isaiah Thomas, Dec. 2, 1769, D. L. Corbitt, ed., "Historical Notes," NCHR 4 (1927): 315. See also Upper House Journals, Jan. 17, 1735, NCCR, 4:78; Council Journals, Mar. 24, 1741, NCCR, 4:591; G. Johnston to Earl of Granville, Jan. 26, 1749, Arthur Dobbs to Granville, Feb. 10, 1755, Hermon Husband to Granville, 1756, Library of the Marquess of Bath, Longleat, England (microfilm, Granville District Papers, English Records, N.C. Archives); James Murray to Richard Oswald & Co., Feb. 28, 1755, Murray Letter Book, 1735–60, 310; Dobbs to Secretary Fox, July 12, 1756, NCCR, 5:601; "Leonidas," *Mass. Spy*, Aug. 1, 1771; "Atticus," Oct. 1771, Purdie and Dixon's *Va. Gaz.*, Nov. 7, 1771; James Iredell to Margaret Iredell, Oct. 3, 1771, in Don Higginbotham, ed., *The Papers of James Iredell* (Raleigh, 1976), 1:80.

5. Rednap Howell to James Hunter, Feb. 16, 1771, in Council Journals, Mar. 18, 1771, *Reg. Doc.*, 373; Daniel Earl to Sec. of S.P.G., May 5, 1760, NCCR, 6:241; Mark A. De Wolfe Howe, ed., "Journal of Josiah Quincy, Junior, 1773," Mass. Hist. Soc., *Proceedings* 49 (1915–16): 462; Henry Eustace McCulloh to Edmund Fanning, [1762?], Fanning-McCulloh Papers, N.C. Archives. See also Upper House Journals, July 11, 1733, NCCR, 3:552; Upper House Journals, Jan. 21, 1735, NCCR, 4:84; G. Johnston quoted in James Abercromby to Board

of Trade, [1750], *NCCR*, 4:1224; Matthew Rowan to Samuel Smith, Sept. 19, 1751, Arthur Dobbs Papers, Public Record Office of Northern Ireland, Belfast (microfilm, reel 2, South. Hist. Coll.); Petition of Orange County Inhabitants, May 15, 1771, *Reg. Doc.*, 454; Cullen Pollock to Aaron Lopez, Mar. 9, 1773, in *Commerce of Rhode Island, 1726–1800* (Mass. Hist. Soc., *Collections*, 7th Ser., 9 [Boston, 1914]), 1:429.

6. Hugh Williamson, *The History of North Carolina* (Philadelphia, 1812), 1:xii; James Murray to Ann and Jean Bennet, Aug. 4, 1760, Murray Letter Book, 1760–61; Marquis De Chastellux, *Travels in North America in the Years 1780, 1781, and 1782*, ed. Howard C. Rice, Jr. (Chapel Hill, 1963), 2:437.

7. Williamson, *History of North Carolina*, 1:viii; John MacDowell to Sec. of S.P.G., Aug. 17, 1760, *NCCR*, 6:238.

1. The Limits of Growth

1. Hugh Jones, *The Present State of Virginia*, ed. Richard L. Morton (Chapel Hill, 1956), 104; Thomas Lowndes to Secretary of Board of Trade, Feb. 16, 1729, *NCCR*, 3:11; Lowndes to Board of Trade, Dec. 8, 1729, *NCCR*, 3:49–50; Peter Wood, *Black Majority: Negroes in Colonial South Carolina from 1670 through the Stono Rebellion* (New York, 1974), 258–59; George Burrington to Board of Trade, Jan. 1, 1733, *NCCR*, 3:433; David L. Corbitt, *The Formation of North Carolina Counties, 1663–1943* (Raleigh, 1950); Lawrence Lee, *The Lower Cape Fear in Colonial Days* (Chapel Hill, 1965), 101–2.

2. Harry Roy Merrens, *Colonial North Carolina in the Eighteenth Century: A Study in Historical Geography* (Chapel Hill, 1964), 53, 147–55; Louis B. Wright, ed., *The Prose Works of William Byrd of Westover: Narratives of a Colonial Virginian* (Cambridge, Mass., 1966), 207. In 1739 "precincts" in North Carolina were renamed "counties." However, for purposes of clarity, the term "county" will be used for the entire royal period when referring to these localities. Corbitt, *Formation of North Carolina Counties*, xviii.

3. Edmund and Dorothy Berkeley, eds., " 'The Manner of Living of the North Carolinians,' by Francis Veale, Dec. 19, 1730," *NCHR* 41 (1964): 242; Burrington's Remarks, [1731], *NCCR*, 3:185; Burrington to Board of Trade, Jan. 1, 1733, *NCCR*, 3:433; Upper House Journals, Jan. 17, 1735, *NCCR*, 4:78; Proposals by Henry McCulloh, Feb. 1736, *NCCR*, 4:156.

4. Dr. [?] Douglass, "A Discourse Concerning the Currencies of the British Plantations in America," 1740, in Andrew McFarland Davis, ed., *Colonial Currency Reprints, 1682–1751* (New York, 1911), 3:324; Rice to Board of Trade, Aug. 1, 1752, *NCCR*, 4:1314. For population figures, I have relied on the sources and procedures outlined in Merrens, *Eighteenth-Century North Carolina*, 194–201, with one exception. In several computations, Merrens used a multiplier of 2 in converting the number of black taxables into the total number of blacks. I have used a multiplier of 1.75 for several reasons. First, black taxables in North Carolina included all blacks twelve years and older, as opposed to sixteen years and older in Virginia, where historians have also utilized a multiplier of 2. North Carolina needed to have had an extremely young slave population for half of its slaves to have been under twelve years. Second, inventories listing slave children and adults suggest that a ratio of .5 children for every 1 adult is much more accurate than 1 child for 1 adult. See, for example, J. Bryan Grimes, ed., *North*

Carolina Wills and Inventories (Raleigh, 1912). Finally, a 1779 Hertford County tax list, rare in listing black taxables by several age categories, yields a ratio of .63 children under eleven years for each black eleven years and older. See also Marvin Lawrence Michael Kay, "The Institutional Background to the Regulation in Colonial North Carolina" (Ph.D. diss., University of Minnesota, 1962), 28, 15n.

Most population figures are conservative estimates because they come chiefly from county tax lists, which commonly excluded such nontaxpaying adults as delinquents and insolvents. According to a recent study, nontaxpaying adults in most counties made up from 5 to 15 percent of the taxpaying population. Although both the scarcity and the fluctuating nature of available figures do not permit any sort of systematic allowance for this missing segment of the population, this bias should be taken into account regarding all discussions in this study involving data from tax lists. See Alan D. Watson, "County Fiscal Policy in Colonial North Carolina," *NCHR*, 55 (1978): 299, 305.

5. [Arthur Dobbs], "The Colony, Its Climate, Soil, Population, Government, Resources, Etc.," [1761], NCCR, 6:614; Richard J. Hooker, ed., *The Carolina Backcountry on the Eve of the Revolution: The Journal and Other Writings of Charles Woodmason, Anglican Itinerant* (Chapel Hill, 1953), 81. See also "Colonel [Robert] Halton's Paper concerning My Lord Granville's Estate in North Carolina," Jan. 11, 1746, Granville District Papers; Alan D. Watson, "Household Size and Composition in Pre-Revolutionary North Carolina," *Mississippi Quarterly* 31 (1978): 557.

6. John MacDowell to Sec. of S.P.G., Mar. 26, 1763, NCCR, 6:978; William Hooper to James Iredell, July 15, 1778, in Griffith J. McRee, ed., *Life and Correspondence of James Iredell* (New York, 1857), 1:399; Pierce Butler to Iredell, May 5, 1783, in Sarah McCulloh Lemmon, "Parson Pettigrew of the 'Old Church': 1747–1807," *JSHP* 52 (Chapel Hill, 1970), 10; John Duffy, "Eighteenth-Century Carolina Health Conditions," *JSH* 18 (1952):302. For other contemporary descriptions of disease conditions, see, for example, "Journal of a French Traveller in the Colonies, 1765, I," *AHR* 26 (1920–21):735; John S. Ezell, ed., and Judson P. Wood, trans., *The New Democracy in America: Travels of Francisco de Miranda in the United States, 1783–1784* (Norman, Okla., 1963), 9–10; Johann David Schoepf, *Travels in the Confederation,* [1783–1784], trans. and ed. Alfred J. Morrison (Philadelphia, 1911), 2:114–16.

7. Merrens, *Eighteenth-Century North Carolina,* 53–62; Lee, *Lower Cape Fear,* 96–102; Hugh T. Lefler and William S. Powell, *Colonial North Carolina: A History* (New York, 1973), 89–112; Carl Bridenbaugh, *Myths and Realities: Societies of the Colonial South* (Baton Rouge, 1952), 119–39; A. Roger Ekirch, "'A New Government of Liberty': Hermon Husband's Vision of Backcountry North Carolina, 1755," *WMQ*, 3d Ser., 34 (1977): 632–46; Robert W. Ramsey, *Carolina Cradle: Settlement of the Northwest Carolina Frontier, 1747–1762* (Chapel Hill, 1964). Pennsylvania Council quoted in ibid., 20. Franklin quoted in Merrens, *Eighteenth-Century North Carolina,* 54.

8. See works cited in note 7, above. Burrington to Board of Trade, Jan. 1, 1733, NCCR, 3:432; Stella H. Sutherland, *Population Distribution in Colonial America* (New York, 1936), 211; Hugh Meredith, *An Account of the Cape Fear Country, 1731,* ed. Earl G. Swem (Perth Amboy, N.J., 1922), 8; James Murray to Andrew Bennet, May 13, 1735, in Nina Moore Tiffany, ed., *Letters of James Murray, Loyalist* (Boston, 1901), 18; Husband quoted in Ekirch, "New Gov-

ernment of Liberty," *WMQ*, 3d Ser., 34 (1977): 638; T. W. J. Wylie, ed., "Franklin County One Hundred Years Ago: A Settler's Experience Told in a Letter Written by Alexander Thomson In 1773," *PMHB* 8 (1884): 322.

9. Corbitt, *Formation of North Carolina Counties*; James Moir to [?], Oct. 24, 1740, S.P.G., London, B Manuscripts, 9, 145 (microfilm, Library of Congress).

10. G. Johnston to Earl of Granville, Mar. 13, 1750, Granville District Papers; *Conn. Cour.*, Nov. 30, 1767, quoted in Merrens, *Eighteenth-Century North Carolina*, 54.

11. Johnston quoted in Charles M. Andrews, *Colonial Folkways: A Chronicle of American Life in the Reign of the Georges* (New Haven, 1919), 38; Diary of August Gottlieb Spangenberg, entry of Sept. 25, 1752, *Moravian Records*, 1:38; Hooper quoted in L. H. Butterfield, ed., *Diary and Autobiography of John Adams* (Cambridge, Mass., 1961), 2:246–47.

12. Murray to James Abercromby and Captain Forsyth, Dec. 26, 1755, Murray to Sarah Allen, Feb. 11, 1757, Murray to Mrs. Bennet, Nov. 25, 1758, Murray Letter Book, 1735–60, 319, 362, 392; Samuel Johnston, Sr., to Samuel Johnston, Jr., Oct. 5, 1755, Hayes Collection, reel 2, 38 (microfilm, South. Hist. Coll., made from the manuscripts owned by John Gilliam Wood, Hayes, Edenton, N.C.); Petition of Tanners and Merchants to Governor Dobbs and Assembly, [1757], *NCCR*, 5:745–46; *S.C. Gaz.*, Sept. 12, 1741; S. Johnston, Jr., to Thomas Barker, Aug. 20, 1766, Hayes Collection, reel 2, 45; Lefler and Powell, *Colonial North Carolina*, 154; Letter from "A Carolina Planter," *N.C. Gaz.*, New Bern, Dec. 5, 1777. Quote is from a letter from Thomas Howe, Sept. 10, 1769, *NCCR*, 8:75.

13. Murray to John [Murray], James Murray Papers, 1760–86, N.C. Archives (transcript). See also Murray to Andrew Douglas, Jan. 6, 1747, Murray to [James] Innes, July 21, 1747, Murray Letter Book, 1732–47; Murray to Alneas and Hugh Mackay, Sept. 12, 1749, Murray to George Dunbar, Jan. 27, 1757, Murray Letter Book, 1735–60, 200, 347; William Faris to [Dobbs], Feb. 8, 1750, Dobbs Papers, reel 2; Murray to Mrs. Bennet, Mar. 25, 1758, Murray Letter Book, 1735–60, 377; Petition of Merchants and Traders to Governor Dobbs, Council, and Assembly, Dec. 9, 1758, Legislative Papers, 1689–1764, N.C. Archives.

14. S. Johnston, Jr., to [Barker], Oct. 2, 1765 [1766?], Hayes Collection, reel 2, 45; Murray to his Sister, [early 1760s], Murray Papers, N.C. Archives. See also Murray to Thomas Campbell, Mar. 1, 1757, James Murray Robbins Collection, Mass. Hist. Soc.; George Pollock to Bridgen & Waller, Aug. 20, 1762, G. Pollock to Granville, [1761?], Pollock Letter Book, 1708–1761, N.C. Archives. For the background of currency in North Carolina, see John J. McCusker, *Money and Exchange in Europe and America, 1600–1775* (Chapel Hill, 1978), 215–19; Leslie V. Brock, *The Currency of the American Colonies, 1700–1764: A Study in Colonial Finance and Imperial Relations* (New York, 1975), 106–13, 428–46; Charles J. Bullock, *Essays on the Monetary History of the United States* (New York, 1900), 125–204; Jack P. Greene, *The Quest for Power: The Lower Houses of Assembly in the Southern Royal Colonies, 1689–1776* (Chapel Hill, 1963), 115–18; Joseph Albert Ernst, *Money and Politics in America, 1755–1775: A Study in the Currency Act of 1764 and the Political Economy of Revolution* (Chapel Hill, 1973), 199–200, 296; Robert M. Weir, "North Carolina's Reaction to the Currency Act of 1764," *NCHR* 40 (1963): 183–99.

15. Murray to [H. McCulloh], Nov. 6, 1736, in Tiffany, ed., *Murray Letters*, 35;

S.C. Gaz., June 6, 1743; Lida T. Rodman, ed., "Journal of a Tour to North Carolina by William Attmore," *JSHP* 17 (1922): 38–39. For the recognized importance of slaves, see also Murray to H. McCulloh, May 11, 1741, in Tiffany, ed., *Murray Letters*, 64; G. Johnston to Granville, Jan. 26, 1749, Granville District Papers; Dobbs to Board of Trade, Mar. 29, 1764, *NCCR*, 6:1026; Report by Frederic William Marshall, Aug. 3, 1770, *Moravian Records*, 2:614.

Perhaps because of their persistent need for labor, residents of North Carolina reputedly offered sanctuary to many runaway slaves from Virginia and South Carolina during the eighteenth century. Gerald W. Mullin, *Flight and Rebellion: Slave Resistance in Eighteenth-Century Virginia* (New York, 1972), 110–12; Wood, *Black Majority*, 258–59; Wright, ed., *Byrd Prose Works*, 186; Jeffrey J. Crow, *The Black Experience in Revolutionary North Carolina* (Raleigh, 1977), 41–42.

For North Carolina's fledgling slave trade, see Elizabeth Donnan, ed., *Documents Illustrative of the History of the Slave Trade to America* (New York, 1969), 4:235–37. For indentured servants, see Lewis Cecil Gray, *History of Agriculture in the Southern United States to 1860* (New York, 1941), 1:349; Bridenbaugh, *Myths and Realities*, 168; Watson, "Household Size," *Mississippi Quarterly* 31 (1978): 559.

16. Robert Rogers, *A Concise Account of North America* (New York, 1966), 134.
17. Tax Lists, 1755 and 1767, *NCCR*, 5:575, 7:539. Because the 1755 list does not distinguish between white and black taxables in Bertie, Cumberland, and Johnston, figures for these counties were obtained from 1754 and 1756 lists. Similarly, 1767 figures for Bertie, Chowan, and Perquimans were taken from 1765 and 1766 lists. *NCCR*, 5:320, 603, 7:145–46, 288–89. For converting black taxables into black population figures, see note 4, above.
18. Committee Report of South Carolina Council, [1769], *NCCR*, 8:559. See also Charles Garth to Board of Trade, [1771], *NCCR*, 8:571; Howe, ed., "Quincy Journal, 1773," Mass. Hist. Soc., *Proceedings* 49 (1915–16): 462.
19. R. C. Simmons, *The American Colonies: From Settlement to Independence* (New York, 1976), 177.
20. Merrens, *Eighteenth-Century North Carolina*, 108–24, 134–40. See also James F. Shepherd, "Commodity Exports from the British North American Colonies to Overseas Areas, 1768–1772: Magnitudes and Patterns of Trade," *Explorations in Economic History*, 8 (1970): 5–76.
21. Merrens, *Eighteenth-Century North Carolina*, 93–107.
22. Ibid., 85–92; Charles Christopher Crittenden, *The Commerce of North Carolina, 1763–1789*, Yale Historical Publications, *Miscellany* 29 (New Haven, 1936), 53–58.
23. Tryon to Board of Trade, Feb. 2, 1767, Kings Manuscripts, 206, 115, British Library (transcripts, Library of Congress); Converse D. Clowse, *Economic Beginnings in Colonial South Carolina, 1670–1730*, Tricentennial Studies 3 (Columbia, S.C., 1971), 243; Justin Williams, "English Mercantilism and Carolina Naval Stores, 1705–1776," *JSH* 1 (1935): 169–85; Wood, *Black Majority*, 111; G. Johnston to Board of Trade, Dec. 12, 1734, *NCCR*, 4:5; Murray to Andrew Bennet, Feb. 28, 1755, Murray Letter Book, 1735–60, 308; Murray to Robert Palmer, Mar. 31, 1768, Murray Letter Book, 1764–69, 236; Letter from New Bern, June 10, 1768, *S.C. and Am. Genl. Gaz.*, July 29, 1768. See also Burrington to Board of Trade, Feb. 20, 1732, *NCCR*, 3:337; Thomas Stephens to

Thomas Hancock, Mar. 16, 1762, Preston Davie Collection, South. Hist. Coll.;
Extract of letter from Wilmington, Mar. 6, 1768, *S.C. Gaz.*, Mar. 14, 1768;
Howe, ed., "Quincy Journal, 1773," Mass. Hist. Soc., *Proceedings* 49
(1915–16): 462.

24. Bridgen & Waller and Hindley & Needham to Earl of Hillsborough, Mar. 31,
1770, NCCR, 8:186–90. For other complaints about the quality of naval stores
from North Carolina, see Joseph Squire to Lord North, Aug. 23, 1771, T. 1/486,
and John Robinson to Lancelot Grave Berry, Oct. 2, 1771, T. 28/1 (transcripts,
N.C. Archives); [?], "A View of the Polity . . . ," [1767], NCCR, 7:489; Gray,
Southern Agriculture, 1:428.

25. James Reed to Sec. of S.P.G., July 10, 1765, NCCR, 7:99; Meredith, *Account of
Cape Fear*, ed. Swem, 20; Merrens, *Eighteenth-Century North Carolina*, 126;
James M. Clifton, "Golden Grains of White: Rice Planting on the Lower Cape
Fear," *NCHR* 50 (1973):365–69.

26. Laurens to Rawlinson & Davison, Dec. 10, 1755, in Philip M. Hamer et al., eds.,
The Papers of Henry Laurens (Columbia, S.C., 1968–), 2:31; Murray to
Abercromby, Feb. 26, 1755, Murray Letter Book, 1735–60, 298–99; Merrens,
Eighteenth-Century North Carolina, 127.

27. Merrens, *Eighteenth-Century North Carolina*, 127; Murray to Lady Don [?],
Nov. 25, 1758, Murray Letter Book, 1735–60, 389; Schoepf, *Confederation
Travels*, trans. and ed. Morrison, 2:121. See also Dobbs to Board of Trade, Mar.
29, 1764, NCCR, 6:1029; Hugh B. Johnston, ed., "The Journal of Ebenezer
Hazard in North Carolina, 1777 and 1778," *NCHR* 36 (1959): 374; Harry J.
Carman, ed., *American Husbandry*, Columbia University Studies in the History
of American Agriculture 6 (New York, 1939): 244.

28. Murray to Richard Oswald & Co., Nov. 16, 1752, Murray Letter Book,
1735–60, 288.

29. Letter from Wilmington, Mar. 6, 1768, *S.C. Gaz.*, Mar. 14, 1768.

30. J. F. D. Smyth, *A Tour in the United States of America* (London, 1784),
1:234–35; Crittenden, *North Carolina Commerce*, 1–9; [Dobbs], "The Colony," [1761], NCCR, 6:608; Dobbs to Board of Trade, Mar. 29, 1764, NCCR,
6:1027–28. See also Spangenberg Diary, entry of Sept. 25, 1752, *Moravian
Records*, 1:38; Carman, ed., *American Husbandry*, 240; Josiah Martin to
Samuel Martin, Mar. 3, 1772, Add. MSS, 41361, 235.

31. C. Pollock to Nathaniel Duckinfield, Dec. 20, 1741, C. Pollock to Nathaniel
Bethune, July 4, 1743, Pollock Letter Book. See also G. Johnston to Granville,
May 7, 1751, Granville District Papers; Crittenden, *North Carolina Commerce*,
8–13, 109; Schoepf, *Confederation Travels*, trans. and ed. Morrison, 2:125.

32. Tryon to Board of Trade, Jan. 30, 1767, NCCR, 7:429; Crittenden, *North
Carolina Commerce*, 13.

33. Laurens to Abraham Parsons, Sept. 14, 1764, in Hamer et al., eds., *Laurens
Papers*, 4:425. See also John Campbell to Granville, May 18, 1749, Granville
District Papers.

34. Murray to Campbell, Mar. 1, 1757, James Murray Robbins Collection;
Meredith, *Account of Cape Fear*, ed. Swem, 29; MacDowell to Sec. of S.P.G.,
Apr. 17, 1760, NCCR, 6:236; Alexander Stewart to Sec. of S.P.G., June 1768
[1767], NCCR, 7:496; Reed to Sec. of S.P.G., July 10, 1765, NCCR, 7:98–99.
See also Clement Hall to Sec. of S.P.G., June 19, 1746, NCCR, 4:793; Hall to
Sec. of S.P.G., May 1, 1751, S.P.G., B MSS, 19, 126; MacDowell to Sec. of
S.P.G., Feb. 23, 1763, NCCR, 6:966; Iredell to Francis Iredell, Sr., July 20, 1772,

in Don Higginbotham, ed., *The Papers of James Iredell* (Raleigh, 1976), 1:106; Martin to Samuel Martin, Oct. 11, 1771, Add. MSS, 41361, 226; Lelia Sellers, *Charleston Business on the Eve of the American Revolution* (Chapel Hill, 1934), 38.

35. Merrens, *Eighteenth-Century North Carolina*, 116, 240, 62n, 63n; Crittenden, *North Carolina Commerce*, 75–76, 88; "Journal of a French Traveller, 1765," *AHR* 26 (1920–21): 737–38; "Ettwein's Visit to Governor Tryon . . . ," 1766, Wachovia Diary, entries of Oct. 27, Nov. 22, 1767, *Moravian Records*, 1:338–46, 356.

36. Crittenden, *North Carolina Commerce*, 76; Merrens, *Eighteenth-Century North Carolina*, 240, 63n, 142–67; Schoepf, *Confederation Travels*, trans. and ed. Morrison, 2:145; Smyth, *Tour in the United States*, 2:87.

37. Burrington to Commissioners of Customs, July 20, 1736, *NCCR*, 4:172; Murray to John Murray, Jan. 10, 1737, in Tiffany, ed., *Murray Letters*, 37; Upper House Journals, Dec. 21, 1773, *NCCR*, 9:730. See also Gray, *Southern Agriculture*, 1:43; Upper House Journals, Jan. 20, 1735, *NCCR*, 4:82; Petition of Merchants, Traders, and Planters in North Carolina to Board of Trade, [1754], *NCCR*, 5:322; Tryon to Board of Trade, Jan. 27, 1766, *NCCR*, 7:155; Stewart to Sec. of S.P.G., June 1768 [1767], *NCCR*, 7:496.

38. "An Account of the number of Ships . . . for the Years 1739 and 1740," Add. MSS, 33028, 400 (transcripts, Library of Congress); "An Account of the Number of Vessells . . . between the 5th of January, 1770 and the 5th of January, 1771," in John Lord Sheffield, *Observations on the Commerce of the American States*, [1784] (New York, 1970), plate 7.

39. James F. Shepherd and Gary M. Walton, *Shipping, Maritime Trade, and the Economic Development of Colonial North America* (Cambridge, 1972), 47; [H. McCulloh] to Board of Trade, Sept. 17, 1736, *NCCR*, 4:258.

40. Martin to Hillsborough, Mar. 8, 1772, *NCCR*, 9:270; Howe, ed., "Quincy Journal, 1773," Mass. Hist. Soc., *Proceedings* 49 (1915–16): 462.

41. Carman, ed., *American Husbandry*, 248; Alexander Cluny, *The American Traveller . . .* (London, 1769), 65; Lord Adam Gordon, "Journal of an Officer's Travels in America, and the West Indies, 1764–1765," in Newton D. Mereness, ed., *Travels in the American Colonies* (New York, 1916), 402. See also Lower House Journals, Nov. 14, 1760, *NCCR*, 6:476.

42. Compilations are adapted from Shepherd and Walton, *Economic Development of Colonial North America*, 47, table 3.2. The value of exports shipped through North Carolina ports was doubled and approximate corresponding amounts subtracted from Virginia and South Carolina export values. A slightly different figure was used for North Carolina's white population.

43. C. Pollock to Aaron Lopez, Mar. 9, 1773, in *Commerce of Rhode Island, 1726–1800* (Mass. Hist. Soc., *Collections*, 7th Ser., 9 [Boston, 1914]), 1:429; Murray to Palmer, July 21, 1769, Murray Letter Book, 1764–69, 286.

2. Carolina Society and Culture

1. Louis B. Wright, ed., *The Prose Works of William Byrd of Westover* (Cambridge, Mass., 1966), 212, 74, 237, 39–336 passim.

2. See Appendix, table A.1. In those few instances in which an individual owned land in two or more Albemarle counties, the acreage has been combined and the total listed under the county of residence.

3. Burrington to Board of Trade, Feb. 20, 1732, Jan. 1, 1733, *NCCR* 3:337, 430; Perquimans County Tax List, 1720, in William P. Johnson, ed., *North Carolina Genealogy* 16 (1970): 2484–89; Barbara Lathroum-Wilson, "The Structure of Wealth in Early Eighteenth-Century Albemarle," (Seminar Paper, The Johns Hopkins University, 1977), 14.

4. Craven County Tax List, 1719, in Johnson, ed., *North Carolina Genealogy* 19 (1973): 2835–36.

5. Pasquotank County Tax Lists, 1739, Pasquotank County Lists of Taxables, 1735–99, N.C. Archives. It should be noted that this and the other tax lists discussed in this chapter, except for those for the late 1770s and early 1780s, only included property in the county where the list was taken. However, so few people owned land and slaves outside their home counties, the bias is not very great.

6. Perquimans County Tax List, 1740, in W. P. Johnson, ed., *The North Carolinian* 1 (1955): 117–19.

7. Richard Marsden to Bishop of London, June 20, 1733, quoted in Fleming H. James, "Richard Marsden, Wayward Clergyman," *WMQ*, 3d Ser., 11 (1954): 587; Council Journals, Oct. 18, 1732, C.O. 5/309, 168 (unless otherwise noted, all citations to collections in the P.R.O. refer to microfilmed materials at the Library of Congress); Council Journals, Nov. 2, 1732, May 21, 22, 23, Sept. 23, 1741, May 6, 1742, Nov. 20, 1744, *NCCR*, 3:426, 4:594, 595, 596, 617, 705.

8. See Appendix, table A.3.

9. Jackson Turner Main, *The Social Structure of Revolutionary America* (Princeton, N.J., 1965), 55, 57–58.

10. See Appendix, table A.4.

11. See Appendix, table A.2.

12. Deposition of William McCormick, May 12, 1785, in Hugh E. Egerton, ed., *The Royal Commission on the Losses and Services of American Loyalists, 1783–1785: Notes of Daniel Parker Coke* (Oxford, 1915), 363; Memorandum on the value of lands and slaves in the South, [1784?], A.O., 13/85 (transcripts, N.C. Archives); Samuel Johnston, Jr., to Mr. Farriar, [1760s], Hayes Collection, reel 2, 60. See also Alexander Stewart to Sec. of S.P.G., June 1768 [1767], *NCCR*, 7:495; Memorandum by Henry Eustace McCulloh, May 2, 1770, Dobbs Papers, reel 2; J. F. D. Smyth, *A Tour in the United States of America* (London, 1784), 1:152–53; Harry J. Carman, ed., *American Husbandry*, Columbia University Studies in the History of American Agriculture 6 (New York, 1939), 240–41; Hugh T. Lefler and William S. Powell, *Colonial North Carolina: A History* (New York, 1973), 152.

13. Wright, ed., *Byrd Prose Works*, 184; Martin to Samuel Martin, Oct. 23, 1773, Granville District Papers. See also Norman K. Risjord, *Chesapeake Politics, 1781–1800* (New York, 1978), 55.

14. "Journal of a French Traveller in the Colonies, 1765, I," *AHR* 26 (1920–21): 738; Couchet Jouvencal to Board of Trade, [1762], *NCCR*, 6:745; John Rutherfurd to Arthur Dobbs, [1757], *NCCR*, 5:937. See also Dobbs to Board of Trade, Jan. 4, 1755, *NCCR*, 5:315; Memorandum by Joshua North, Sept. 15, 1783, A.O. 12/107 (transcripts, N.C. Archives); Johann David Schoepf, *Travels in the Confederation*, [1783–1784], trans. and ed. Morrison (Philadelphia, 1911), 2:132; Harry Roy Merrens, *Colonial North Carolina in the Eighteenth Century: A Study in Historical Geography* (Chapel Hill, 1964), 131; Lawrence Lee, *The Lower Cape Fear in Colonial Days* (Chapel Hill, 1965), 186; Alice Elaine Mathews, *Society in Revolutionary North Carolina* (Raleigh, 1976), 21.

15. Alan D. Watson, "Ordinaries in Colonial Eastern North Carolina," *NCHR* 45 (1968): 71; Smyth, *Tour in the United States*, 1:114.
16. Quoted in Arthur L. Jensen, *The Maritime Commerce of Colonial Philadelphia* (Madison, Wis., 1963), 80–81.
17. Murray to David Tullideph, Mar. 31, 1736, in Nina Moore Tiffany, ed., *Letters of James Murray, Loyalist* (Boston, 1901), 27; Lower House Journals, Jan. 9, 1755, NCCR, 5:300; Joseph Anderson to Dr. Samuel Sabon Plummer, Oct. 26, 1748, quoted in Carl W. Ubbelohde, Jr., "The Vice-Admiralty Court of Royal North Carolina, 1729–1759," *NCHR* 31 (1954): 522; Lee to William Lee, June 19, 1771, *Reg. Doc.*, 482. See also Anton-Hermann Chroust, *The Rise of the Legal Profession in America* (Norman, Okla., 1965), 1:311, 322, 331; Ernest H. Alderman, "The North Carolina Colonial Bar," *JSHP* 13 (1913): 6; Smyth, *Tour in the United States*, 1:162.

    The colony's small community of doctors was no more professional than lawyers and merchants. William Cathcart, a doctor in North Carolina, advised a patient to seek medical assistance in Williamsburg because doctors there "must be much more capable than any this way." Cathcart to S. Johnston, Jr., Feb. 29, 1770, Hayes Collection, reel 2, 70. See also Martin to Earl of Dartmouth, Sept. 1, 1774, NCCR, 9:1061.
18. Martin to Dartmouth, Apr. 6, 1774, NCCR, 9:973; Deposition of Thomas McKnight, in D. L. Corbitt, ed., "Historical Notes," *NCHR* 2 (1925): 521. See also Deposition of William Brimage, A.O. 13/117.
19. Deposition of James Parker, June 4, 1784, A.O. 13/121; Laurens to William Freeman, Dec. 11, 1767, in Philip M. Hamer et al., eds., *The Papers of Henry Laurens* (Columbia, S.C., 1968–), 5:501.
20. H. E. McCulloh to Iredell, Sept. 11, 1767, Iredell to Francis Iredell, Sr., July 20, 1772, in Don Higginbotham, ed., *The Papers of James Iredell* (Raleigh, 1976), 1:7, 106; Deposition of Benjamin Booth Boote, A.O. 13/117; S. Johnston, Jr., to Farriar, [1760s], Hayes Collection, reel 2, 60.
21. Murray to William Tryon, Sept. 24, 1765, Murray Letter Book, 1764–65; Deposition of Brimage, A.O. 13/117; Dobbs to Board of Trade, Aug. 24, 1755, NCCR, 5:356; [?], "A View of the Polity . . . ," [1767], NCCR, 7:486; Martin to Samuel Martin, Mar. 3, 1772, Add. MSS, 41361, 235.
22. "Journal of a French Traveller, 1765," *AHR* 26 (1920–21): 743, 738; Deposition of Dr. Thomas Cobham, Feb. 3, 1790, A.O. 13/118; Tryon to Earl of Shelburne, Mar. 21, 1768, NCCR, 7:699; Iredell to Margaret Iredell, Oct. 3, 1771, in Higginbotham, ed., *Iredell Papers*, 1:80; Mark A. De Wolfe Howe, ed., "Journal of Josiah Quincy, Junior, 1773," Mass. Hist. Soc., *Proceedings* 49 (1915–16): 462; John S. Ezell, ed., and Judson P. Wood, trans., *The New Democracy in America: Travels of Francisco de Miranda in the United States, 1783–1784* (Norman, Okla., 1963), 5. See also Martin to Dartmouth, May 27, 1773, NCCR, 9:647.
23. Richard J. Hooker, ed., *The Carolina Backcountry on the Eve of the Revolution: The Journal and Other Writings of Charles Woodmason, Anglican Itinerant* (Chapel Hill, 1953), 80–81; John Simpson to Peggie Simpson, Mar. 16, 1786, William Ross Papers, Library of Duke University, Durham, N.C.; *S.C. Gaz.*, June 8, 1765; John MacDowell to Sec. of S.P.G., July 3, 1761, NCCR, 6:567; Eleazer Allen quoted in Murray to Alneas and Hugh Mackay, Sept. 12, 1749, Murray Letter Book, 1735–60, 200. See also Gabriel Johnston to Earl of Granville, May 1, 1751, Martin to Anthony Todd, Dec. 1, 1774, Granville District Papers.

24. Robert Pringle to Thomas Burrill, June 11, 1740, in Walter B. Edgar, ed., *The Letterbook of Robert Pringle* (Columbia, S.C., 1972), 1:219; Wright, ed., *Byrd Prose Works*, 186. See also Hugh Jones, *The Present State of Virginia*, ed. Richard L. Morton (Chapel Hill, 1956), 83, 104; Thomas Lowndes to Board of Trade, Dec. 8, 1729, *NCCR*, 3:49; Thomas Child to Duke of Bedford, received Dec. 15, 1748, *NCCR*, 4:928; Spangenberg Diary, entry of Sept. 25, 1752, *Moravian Records*, 1:40–41; "Journal of a French Traveller, 1765," *AHR* 26 (1920–21): 738.

25. See, for instance, Wright, ed., *Byrd Prose Works*, 206; "William Logan's Journal of a Journey to Georgia, 1745," *PMBH* 36 (1912): 9; Winslow C. Watson, ed., *Men and Times of the Revolution; or, Memoirs of Elkanah Watson . . . 1777 to 1842* (New York, 1857), 46; Hugh B. Johnston, ed., "The Journal of Ebenezer Hazard in North Carolina, 1777 and 1778," *NCHR* 36 (1959): 370; Smyth, *Tour in the United States*, 1:103.

26. Wright, ed., *Byrd Prose Works*, 207; Alexander McAllister to his Cousin, [1770?], Alexander McAllister Papers, South. Hist. Coll. See also Hugh Meredith, *An Account of the Cape Fear Country, 1731*, ed. Earl G. Swem (Perth Amboy, N.J., 1922), 29; Hooker, ed., *Woodmason Journal*, 81; S. Johnston, Jr., to Farriar, [1760s], S. Johnston, Jr., to Robert Cathcart, Nov. 28, 1774, Hayes Collection, reel 2, 60, reel 3, 87.

27. Smyth, *Tour in the United States*, 1:110; Watson, ed., *Elkanah Watson Memoirs*, 47; Schoepf, *Confederation Travels*, trans. and ed. Morrison, 2:103. See also James Moir to Sec. of S.P.G., Apr. 22, 1742, *NCCR*, 4:605; James Reed to Sec. of S.P.G., Dec. 26, 1761, *NCCR*, 6:595; "Journal of a French Traveller, 1765," *AHR* 26 (1920–21): 734; "The Journal of Thomas Coke, Bishop of the Methodist Episcopal Church," *The Arminian Magazine* (Philadelphia, 1789–90), 1:341.

28. Smyth, *Tour in the United States*, 1:104; Wright, ed., *Byrd Prose Works*, 205; Evangeline W. and Charles M. Andrews, eds., *Journal of a Lady of Quality; Being the Narrative of a Journey from Scotland to the West Indies, North Carolina, and Portugal, in the years 1774 to 1776* (New Haven, 1923), 153; N.C. *Gaz.*, Wilmington, Mar. 24, 1775. In 1752 Governor Johnston told the assembly: "I desire of you in a Special manner, to take into your consideration the barbarous and inhuman manner of boxing which so much prevails among the lower sort of people. . . . I have been informed of no less, than four persons, who within these Two years, have come to a violent death by This atrocious Custom." Upper House Journals, June 12, 1752, *NCCR*, 4:1318. Two years later, provincial authorities passed an act "to Prevent Malicious Maiming and Wounding," which included the cutting out of tongues, putting out of eyes, slitting of noses and lips, and the biting off of any "Limb or Member." Laws, *NCSR*, 23:420. See also Schoepf, *Confederation Travels*, trans. and ed. Morrison, 2:123–24; Jedidiah Morse, *The American Geography; Or A View of The Present Situation of the United States of America* (London, 1792), 418; A. R. Newsome, ed., "Twelve North Carolina Counties, 1810–1811," *NCHR* 6 (1929): 88.

29. John Whiting to [Ezra Stiles?], June 28, 1759, Francis Nash Collection, N.C. Archives (typescript).

30. Tryon to S.P.G., July 31, 1765, *NCCR*, 7:102; MacDowell to Sec. of S.P.G., Apr. 17, 1760, *NCCR*, 6:236. For general treatments of religion in North Carolina, see Sarah M. Lemmon, "Genesis of the Protestant Episcopal Church in North Carolina, 1701–1823," *NCHR* 28 (1951): 426–62; Paul Conkin, "The Church

Establishment in North Carolina, 1765–1776," *NCHR* 32 (1955): 1–30; Gloria
Beth Baker, "Dissenters in Colonial North Carolina," (Ph.D. diss., University of
North Carolina, Chapel Hill, 1970); *Sketches of Church History in North
Carolina* (Wilmington, N.C., 1892); Robert M. Calhoon, *Religion and the
American Revolution in North Carolina* (Raleigh, 1976).

31. Murray to Whitefield, June 24, 1740, in Nina Moore Tiffany, ed., *Letters of
James Murray, Loyalist* (Boston, 1901), 66; Hooker, ed., *Woodmason Journal*,
76. See also Edmund and Dorothy Berkeley, eds., " 'The Manner of Living of the
North Carolinians,' by Francis Veale, Dec. 19, 1730," *NCHR* 41 (1964): 242,
244; Louis B. Wright and Marion Tinling, eds., *Quebec to Carolina in 1785–
1786. Being the Travel Diary and Observations of Robert Hunter, Jr., a Young
Merchant of London* (San Marino, Calif., 1943), 271; Morse, *American Geography*, 216–17; Howe, ed., "Quincy Journal, 1773," Mass. Hist. Soc., *Proceedings* 49 (1915–16): 462.

32. Boyd to Bishop of London, Apr. 12, 1735, *NCCR*, 4:7; Reed to Sec. of S.P.G.,
June 26, 1760, *NCCR*, 6:265. See also Clement Hall to Sec. of S.P.G., May 19,
1752, S.P.G., B MSS, 20, 133.

33. Wright, ed., *Byrd Prose Works*, 204, passim; "William Logan's Journal, 1745,"
PMHB 36 (1912): 7; Simpson to Mrs. Simpson, Dec. 30, 1786, Ross Papers;
Andrews and Andrews, eds., *Lady of Quality Journal*, 153. See also William
Byrd to Burrington, July 20, 1731, *NCCR*, 3:194; August Spangenberg to [?],
Sept. 12, 1752, *NCCR*, 4:1312; "Journal of a French Traveller, 1765," *AHR* 26
(1920–21): 733.

34. James T. Lemon, *The Best Poor Man's Country: A Geographical Study of Early
Southeastern Pennsylvania* (Baltimore, 1972), 85, 218, passim; Merrens,
Eighteenth-Century North Carolina, 53–74. See also Matthew Rowan to
Samuel Smith, Sept. 19, 1751, Dobbs Papers, reel 2; Deposition of H. E.
McCulloh, A.O. 13/117, 450; Russell Sage Nelson, Jr., "Backcountry Pennsyl-
vania (1709 to 1774): The Ideals of William Penn in Practice" (Ph.D. diss.,
University of Wisconsin, 1968), 80.

35. Dobbs to Board of Trade, Nov. 9, 1754, *NCCR*, 5:149; Matthew Rowan to Earl
of Holdernesse, Nov. 21, 1753, *NCCR*, 5:25; Spangenberg to [?], Sept. 12,
1752, *NCCR*, 4:1312; G. Johnston to Granville, May 1, 1751, Granville District
Papers. See also Rowan to Smith, Sept. 19, 1751, Dobbs Papers, reel 2; John
Campbell to John Hanbury, June 24, 1749, Dobbs Papers, reel 2; Morse,
American Geography, 415; Newsome, ed., "Twelve North Carolina Counties,"
NCHR 6 (1929): 296.

36. Four petitions of "His Majestie's Most Dutiful Subjects, Protestant Dissenters,
and Your Lordships Most Dutiful Tennants . . . " to Granville, [1756?], Gran-
ville District Papers; Theodorus Swaine Drage to Sec. of S.P.G., Feb. 28, 1771,
NCCR, 8:505. See also A. Roger Ekirch, " 'A New Government of Liberty':
Hermon Husband's Vision of Backcountry North Carolina, 1755," *WMQ*, 3d
Ser., 34 (1977): 632–46; works cited in note 30, above.

37. Howe, ed., "Quincy Journal, 1773," Mass. Hist. Soc., *Proceedings* 49
(1915–16): 462.

38. Wright, ed., *Byrd Prose Works*, 207, 212.

39. Schoepf, *Confederation Travels*, trans. and ed. Morrison, 2:123–24; Andrews
and Andrews, eds., *Lady of Quality Journal*, 171.

40. Samuel P. Huntington, *Political Order in Changing Societies* (New Haven,
1968), 53. See also Seymour Martin Lipset, *Political Man: The Social Bases of*

Politics (New York, 1963), 47–48; Manfred Hildermeier, "Agrarian Social Protest, Populism, and Economic Development: Some Problems and Results from Recent Studies," *Social History* 4 (1979): 323; Edward C. Banfield, *The Moral Basis of a Backward Society* (New York, 1958).

41. For biographical data used in the following section, see Bibliographical Essay.

42. Murray to Andrew Bennet, May 13, 1735, in Tiffany, ed., *Murray Letters*, 17; Deposition of Thomas McGuire, A.O. 12/36; Deposition of Frederick Gregg, A.O. 13/119; Iredell to Francis Iredell, Sr., July 20, 1772, in Higginbotham, ed., *Iredell Papers*, 1:108; David C. McClelland, *The Achieving Society* (New York, 1976), 316–17.

43. Murray to John [Murray], July 18, 1761, Murray Papers, N.C. Archives; S. Johnston, Jr., to [Barker], Aug. 29, 1765, Hayes Collection, reel 2, 54; Faris to [Dobbs], Feb. 18, 1750, Dobbs Papers, reel 2; Iredell to Margaret Iredell, Oct. 3, 1771, in Higginbotham, ed., *Iredell Papers*, 1:80.

44. Deposition of Rigdon Brice, A.O. 12/36.

45. Tiffany, ed., *Murray Letters*, 16; Murray to Bennet, May 13, 1735, ibid., 17–19; Deposition of Arthur Benning, A.O. 13/117; H. E. McCulloh to Iredell, Sept. 11, 1767, in Higginbotham, ed., *Iredell Papers*, 1: 7.

46. Because of this circumstance, the three signers of the Declaration of Independence from North Carolina, the first five state governors, and the first two attorneys general were all nonnatives.

47. See James Kirby Martin, *Men in Rebellion* (New Brunswick, N.J., 1973), 109, table 4.5.

48. Committee Report of South Carolina Council, [1769], NCCR, 8:559; Alan D. Watson, "Impulse Toward Independence: Resistance and Rebellion Among North Carolina Slaves, 1750–1775," *Journal of Negro History* 63 (1978): 317–28. Matthew Rowan wrote in 1753 that "Negroes" had "lately attempted an insurrection among us." Rowan to William Wilkins, Feb. 1, 1753, Governors Papers, 1753–54, N.C. Archives. The only other hint of massed resistance for the colonial period that the author has found was a 1769 report in New Hanover County of twenty armed runaway slaves. New Hanover County Court Minutes, entry of Sept. 1767, N.C. Archives. Not until the very eve of the American Revolution did more rumors begin to arise. Andrews and Andrews, eds., *Lady of Quality Journal*, 199–200; Crow, *The Black Experience in Revolutionary North Carolina* (Raleigh, 1977), 55–59.

49. Murray to Bennet, May 13, 1735, in Tiffany, ed., *Murray Letters*, 19; Norman C. Delaney, "The Outer Banks of North Carolina During the Revolutionary War," *NCHR* 36 (1959): 1–16; Schoepf, *Confederation Travels*, trans. and ed. Morrison, 2:112.

50. Lefler and Powell, *Colonial North Carolina*, 173.

51. Barnett to Sec. of S.P.G., Sept. 15, 1770, NCCR, 8:229.

52. Burrington to Board of Trade, Feb. 20, 1732, NCCR, 3:333.

53. H. E. McCulloh to Iredell, Sept. 5, 1768, in Higginbotham, ed., *Iredell Papers*, 1:19; Smyth, *Tour in the United States*, 1:105, 172; Schoepf, *Confederation Travels*, trans. and ed. Morrison, 2:118; Ezell, ed., *Travels of Miranda*, 6. See also the impressions of John Macrae, a Scottish immigrant, in Charles Dunn, "A North Carolina Gaelic Bard," *NCHR* 36 (1959): 473–75.

54. Ezell, ed., *Travels of Miranda*, 14; Schoepf, *Confederation Travels*, trans. and ed. Morrison, 2:118; Jaratt quoted in James Henretta, *The Evolution of American Society, 1700–1815: An Interdisciplinary Analysis* (Lexington, Mass., 1973),

94; Murray to William Guyther, Mar. 20, 1752, in Tiffany, ed., *Murray Letters*, 23. Such carelessness seems to have been common elsewhere. James Iredell of Edenton wrote his father, "I almost always wear my hair without dressing." Iredell to Francis Iredell, Sr., July 20, 1772, in Higginbotham, ed., *Iredell Papers*, 1:106.

55. Dobbs to Board of Trade, Dec. 27, 1757, *NCCR*, 5:948; Andrews and Andrews, eds., *Lady of Quality Journal*, 153; Howe, ed., "Quincy Journal, 1773," *Mass. Hist. Soc., Proceedings* 49 (1915–16): 462; John Bernard, *Retrospectives of America*, ed. Bayle Bernard (New York, 1887), 205, 209. See also Murray to John Murray, Feb. 9, 1757, Murray Letter Book, 1735–60, 354; La Rochefoucauld-Lian-Court, *Voyage Dans Les Etats-Unis D'Amerique. Fait En 1795, 1796, Et 1797* (Paris, 1799), 248.

56. "William Logan's Journal, 1745," *PMHB* 36 (1912): 10; Schoepf, *Confederation Travels*, trans. and ed. Morrison, 2:129. See also Wright, ed., *Byrd Prose Works*, 207. The residence of Jacob Blount, a Craven County justice of the peace during the late colonial period, was probably typical. For a 1911 photograph of his home, see Alice Barnwell Keith, ed., *The John Gray Blount Papers* (Raleigh, 1952), 1: xv. See also Bayard Wooten and Archibald Henderson, *Old Homes and Gardens of North Carolina* (Chapel Hill, 1939); Julia Cherry Spruill, "Virginia and Carolina Homes Before the Revolution," *NCHR* 12 (1935): 332; J. Bryan Grimes, "Some Notes on Colonial North Carolina, 1700–1750," *NCB* 5 (1905): 111.

57. Lee, *Lower Cape Fear*, 188; George Minot, "Some Observations on my Plantation . . . on the North East Branch of Cape Fear River," [1747?], William Lithgow to Joshua Crump, May 23, 1747, in Samuel B. Doggett, ed., "A Plantation on Prince George's Creek, Cape Fear, North Carolina," *New-England Historical and Genealogical Register* 52 (1898): 469–73; Andrews and Andrews, eds., *Lady of Quality Journal*, 178, 185. See also "A New Voyage to Georgia. By a Young Gentleman. Giving an account of his travels to South Carolina, and part of North Carolina . . . ," *Georgia Historical Society Collections* 2 (1842): 55–58; Burrington to Board of Trade, Oct. 13, 1735, *NCCR*, 4:305; *S.C. Gaz.*, Feb. 25, 1745; Col. A. M. Waddell, "Historic Homes in the Cape Fear Country," *NCB* 2 (1903): 20; Spruill, "Virginia and Carolina Homes," *NCHR* 12 (1935): 335.

58. Inventories of John Maule, Beaufort County, Dec. 22, 1773, Richard Sanderson, Perquimans County, July 17, 1772, in J. Bryan Grimes, ed., *North Carolina Wills and Inventories* (Raleigh, 1912), 513–14, 543–44. See also inventories of John Hodgson, Chowan County, 1747, Tillie Bond Manuscripts, I, N.C. Archives; David Henderson, Bertie County, [?], Bertie County Record of Estates, 1728–44; James Castellaw, Bertie County, 1749, Bertie County, Estates, Box 16; George Wynns, Bertie County, 1751, Bertie County, Estates, Book 6, 1750–58, 18; Joseph Howell, Edgecombe County, Aug. 17, 1750, Edgecombe County Inventories and Accounts of Sales of Estates, 1733–53; Timothy Ward, Chowan County, [1771?], Chowan County Estates; Richard Ward, Onslow County, 1774, Onslow County Estate Records, 1735–1910, N.C. Archives; Martin Francks, Craven County, June 14, 1745, John Gray, Bertie County, Feb. 14, 1751, Caleb Wilson, Currituck County, Aug. 30, 1754, Jeremiah Vail, Craven County, June 17, 1760, David Shepard, [?], Mar. 1, 1775, in Grimes, ed., *North Carolina Wills and Inventories*, 494–98, 498–99, 567–69, 561–64, 544–47.

59. Inventories of William Bryan, [?], Mar. 15, 1750, William Bartram, Sr., [?], in

Grimes, ed., *North Carolina Wills and Inventories*, 478–79, 469–70. See also the inventories of Simon Jeffreys, Bertie County, [?], Thomas Bryant, Bertie County, Aug. 1741, Bertie County Record of Estates, 1728–44, N.C. Archives; James Millikin, [?], Apr. 27, 1737, Inventories of Estates, 1728–41, North Carolina Executive Records (microfilm, Library of Congress); Richard Lovett, Craven County, Jan. 7, 1754, John Peyton Porter, [?], Mar. 13, 1755, in Grimes, ed., *North Carolina Wills and Inventories*, 508–13, 534–35.

60. Inventory of Richard Eagles, Brunswick County, Mar. 29, 1769, in Grimes, ed., *North Carolina Wills and Inventories*, 486–90. Interestingly, the inventory of Cullen Pollock, Sr., who owned 150 slaves, listed only furniture constructed of walnut, cedar, and pine, and a comparatively small quantity of silverware: four teaspoons, one strainer, one tea tong, two salt sellers, two cups, one pepper box, one porringer, sixteen spoons, and two tankards. Inventory of Cullen Pollock, Tyrrell County, Sept. 1751, ibid., 531–34.

61. For references to such activities, see Bertie County Court Minutes, entry of Aug. 9, 1732, N.C. Archives; George Pollock to Allan Pollock, June 20, 1761, Pollock Letter Book; Whiting to [Stiles?], Apr. 8, 1767, Nash Collection; "The Diary of James Iredell," entry of Jan. 1, 1773, in Higginbotham, ed., *Iredell Papers*, 1:204; Deposition of [?], Oct. 4, 1730, General Court Records, Criminal Papers, 1730, N.C. Archives; Purdie and Dixon's *Va. Gaz.*, Oct. 15, 1772; Henry Lewis, "Horses and Horsemen in Northampton before 1900," *NCHR* 45 (1968): 309; Wesley H. Wallace, "Cultural and Social Advertising in Early North Carolina Newspapers," *NCHR* 33 (1956): 298; W. C. Roberts, "Cockfighting: An Early Entertainment in North Carolina," *NCHR* 42 (1965): 309. In 1756 Governor Dobbs complained that a British vessel, assigned to protect the Cape Fear coastline from enemy privateers, had sailed to Charleston because "no balls or entertainments" were available in Brunswick or Wilmington. Dobbs to Board of Trade, Oct. 31, 1756, *NCCR*, 5:639. See also Murray to Captain Forsyth, Dec. 26, 1755, Murray Letter Book, 1735–60, 317.

62. Andrews and Andrews, eds., *Lady of Quality Journal*, 154; Griffith J. McRee, ed., *Life and Correspondence of James Iredell* (New York, 1857), 2:11; Wallace, "Cultural and Social Advertising," *NCHR* 33 (1956): 294. For the few portraits of North Carolinians before the American Revolution, see Laura MacMillan, comp., *The North Carolina Portrait Index, 1700–1860* (Chapel Hill, 1963).

63. Ezell, ed., *Travels of Miranda*, 5; H. E. McCulloh to Iredell, Sept. 11, 1767, in Higginbotham, ed., *Iredell Papers*, 1:6.

64. For the reading habits of leading North Carolinians, see S. B. Weeks, "Libraries and Literature in North Carolina in the Eighteenth Century," *Annual Report of the American Historical Association for the Year 1895* (Washington, D.C., 1896), 169–267; Helen R. Watson, "The Books They Left: Some 'Liberies' in Edgecombe County, 1733–1783," *NCHR* 47 (1971): 245–257; Iredell Diary, 1770–73, in Higginbotham, ed., *Iredell Papers*, 1:171–217 passim. For the contrast between the sparse writings of Carolinians with those of other southern colonials, see Richard Walser, *Literary North Carolina: A Brief Historical Survey* (Raleigh, 1970); William K. Boyd, ed., *Some Eighteenth Century Tracts concerning North Carolina* (Raleigh, 1927); Jay B. Hubbell, *The South in American Literature* (Durham, N.C., 1954), 79–82, 153–59; Richard Beale Davis, *Intellectual Life in the Colonial South, 1583–1763*, 3 vols. (Knoxville, Tenn., 1978); Richard Beale Davis, *Literature and Society in Early Virginia: 1608–1840* (Baton Rouge, 1973), 149–67; Leo J. A. LeMay, *Men of Letters in*

Colonial Maryland (Knoxville, Tenn., 1972); David Curtis Skaggs, "The Flowering of the Chesapeake," *Reviews in American History* 1 (1973): 493–99.

65. Raymond Phineas Stearns, *Science in the British Colonies of America* (Urbana, Ill., 1970), 293, and "Colonial Fellows of the Royal Society of London, 1661–1778," *WMQ*, 3d Ser., 3 (1946): 208–68; Lester J. Cappon, ed., *Atlas of Early American History: The Revolutionary Era, 1760–1790* (Princeton, N.J., 1976), 35.

66. Andrews and Andrews, eds., *Lady of Quality Journal*, 165.

67. Watson, ed., *Memoirs of Elkanah Watson*, 290; Upper House Journals, Sept. 22, 1736, *NCCR*, 4:227; Daniel Earl to Sec. of S.P.G., May 5, 1760, *NCCR*, 6:241; Dobbs to Sec. of S.P.G., Mar. 30, 1762, *NCCR*, 6:709.

68. R. D. W. Connor, "Genesis of Higher Education in North Carolina," *NCHR* 38 (1951): 2–4; [Tryon?] to S.P.G., [1765], S.P.G., B MSS, 5, 1; Reed to Sec. of S.P.G., July 10, 1765, July 2, 1771, Feb. 15, 1772, *NCCR*, 8:98, 9:6, 238–43; Tomlinson to Sec. of S.P.G., Feb. 20, 1772, *NCCR*, 9:245–48; Martin to Bishop of London, June 20, 1772, *NCCR*, 9:306. See also John Calam, *Parsons and Pedagogues: The S.P.G. Adventure in American Education* (New York, 1971), 178–87; Charles Lee Raper, *The Church and Private Schools of North Carolina: A Historical Study* (Greensboro, N.C., 1898), 24–27.

69. Lefler and Powell, *Colonial North Carolina*, 211; Charles M. Andrews, *Colonial Folkways: A Chronicle of American Life in the Reign of the Georges* (New Haven, 1919), 141.

70. Cullen Pollock to Mr. Fraisor, Jan. 19, 1741, Pollock Letter Book; Faris to [Dobbs], Feb. 18, 1750, Dobbs Papers, reel 2; Lemmon, "Episcopal Church," *NCHR* 28 (1951): 441; Wallace, "Cultural and Social Advertising," *NCHR* 33 (1956): 288, 292; Louis B. Wright, *The Atlantic Frontier: Colonial American Civilization, 1607–1763* (Ithaca, N.Y., 1959), 289.

71. *N.C. Biog. Hist.* 2:176; Presentment against James Beasly, Mar. 1759, Presentment against William Budd, May 20, 1763, Superior Court Records, Criminal Papers, 1759, 1763.

72. Lemmon, "Parson Pettigrew," *JSHP* 52 (1970): 7; Andrews, *Colonial Folkways*, 141.

73. Connor, "Genesis of Higher Education in North Carolina," *NCHR* 28 (1951): 4–7; Clifford K. Shipton, *Sibley's Harvard Graduates* (Cambridge, Mass., 1933–), 12:3–12, 14:191–92, 307–8; *University of Pennsylvania: Biographical Catalogue of the Matriculates of the College . . . , 1749–1893* (Philadelphia, 1894), 4; *The History of the College of William and Mary: From Its Foundation, 1660, To 1874* (Richmond, 1874), 92.

74. J. G. de Roulhac Hamilton, "Southern Members of the Inns of Court," *NCHR* 10 (1933): 273–86; E. Alfred Jones, *American Members of the Inns of Court* (London, 1924); Chroust, *Legal Profession in America*, 1:322–23.

75. Willard Connely, "Colonial Americans in Oxford and Cambridge," *The American Oxonian* 30 (1942): 6–17, 75–77. See also William L. Sachse, *The Colonial American in Britain* (Madison, Wis., 1956), 3, 228.

76. See, for instance, Martin, *Men in Rebellion*, 143.

77. See, for instance, Murray to Whitefield, June 24, 1740, in Tiffany, ed., *Murray Letters*, 66–67, and James Iredell's two essays on religion, [ca. 1768?] and Sept. 17, 1769, in Higginbotham, ed., *Iredell Papers*, 1: 8–11, 36–39. Even Iredell, though, was less than scrupulous in observing the Sabbath. See his Diary, 1770–73, ibid., 171–217 passim.

78. MacDowell to Sec. of S.P.G., Apr. 16, 1761, *NCCR*, 6:556; Garzia to Sec. of S.P.G., Apr. 16, 1742, *NCCR*, 4:604. See also Moir to Sec. of S.P.G., Mar. 26, 1745, *NCCR*, 4:754–56; Moir to Sec. of S.P.G. [?], Nov. 9, 1747, S.P.G., B MSS, 15, 165.

79. Reed to Sec. of S.P.G., July 10, 1765, *NCCR*, 7:99; Lemmon, "Episcopal Church," *NCHR* 28 (1951): 428–29. For comparative salaries, see Main, *Social Structure of Revolutionary America*, 97. In his discussion of salaries in North Carolina, Main, however, mistakenly assumes that £133 6s. 8d. proclamation money equaled £100 sterling. During the 1760s, rates of exchange fluctuated between £166 and £200 proclamation money to £100 sterling. John J. McCusker, *Money and Exchange in Europe and America, 1600–1775* (Chapel Hill, 1978), 218–19. See also Stewart to Sec. of S.P.G., June 1768 [1767], *NCCR*, 7:493–95.

80. John Barnett to Mr. Waring, Feb. 1, 1766, *NCCR*, 7:162; Moir to Sec. of S.P.G., Oct. 2, 1764, *NCCR*, 6:1052; Tryon to Bishop of London, Apr. 30, 1767, *NCCR*, 7:456. See also Boyd to Bishop of London, Apr. 12, 1735, *NCCR*, 4:7; Marsden to Bishop of London, July 7, 1735, *NCCR*, 4:12; Reed to Sec. of S.P.G., Dec. 27, 1762, S.P.G., B MSS, 5, 138; Reed to Sec. of S.P.G., July 10, 1765, *NCCR*, 7:97; Moir to Sec. of S.P.G., Oct. 13, 1766, *NCCR*, 7:265; Stewart to Sec. of S.P.G., June 1768 [1767], *NCCR*, 7:494–95.

81. Wright, ed., *Byrd Prose Works*, 207, 210; Entries of Dec. 25, 30, 1739, in William Wale, ed., *George Whitefield's Journals . . .* (Gainesville, Fla., 1969), 375, 378; Moir to Sec. of S.P.G., Sept. 4, 1742, *NCCR*, 4:607.

82. Tryon to S.P.G., July 31, 1765, *NCCR*, 7:103.

83. Morse, *American Geography*, 417–18; Dickson to Robert Dickson, Nov. 30, 1787, in James O. Carr, comp. and ed., *The Dickson Letters* (Raleigh, 1901), 34.

84. Moore to [?], Jan. 27, 1770, Miscellaneous Papers, 1697–1912, I, N.C. Archives; Thomas Hart to Blount, Jan. 25, 1780, in Keith, ed., *Blount Papers*, 1:8–9; Moir to Sec. of S.P.G., April 21, 1747, S.P.G., B MSS, 15, 164; S. Johnston, Jr., to Alexander Elmsley, Nov. 7, 1770, Samuel Johnston Papers, N.C. Archives; McCulloh to Edmund Fanning, May 4, 1764, Apr. 21, 1763, Fanning-McCulloh Papers, South. Hist. Coll.

85. See Norman S. Buchanan and Howard S. Ellis, *Approaches to Economic Development* (New York, 1955), 407–8; McClelland, *Achieving Society*, 425–26; Emile Durkheim, *Suicide* (Glencoe, Ill., 1965), 246–54.

86. Murray to Mr. Forsyth, Jan. 3, 1756, Murray Letter Book, 1735–60, 328. See also chapter 1.

87. Thomas Stephens to Thomas Hancock, Mar. 16, 1762, Preston Davie Collection. For elite anxiety over the social problems caused by affluence, see Jack P. Greene, "Search for Identity: An Interpretation of the Meaning of Selected Patterns of Social Response in Eighteenth-Century America," *Journal of Social History* 3 (1970): 189–220.

3. Property and Political Contention, 1729–1740

1. For North Carolina's governmental structure, see Charles L. Raper, *North Carolina, A Study in English Colonial Government* (New York, 1904); Jack P. Greene, *The Quest for Power: The Lower Houses of Assembly in the Southern Royal Colonies, 1689–1776* (Chapel Hill, 1963); Florence Cook, "Procedure in

the North Carolina Assembly, 1731–1770," *NCHR* 8 (1931): 258–83; Paul M. McCain, *The County Court in North Carolina Before 1750*, Historical Papers of the Trinity College Historical Society 31 (Durham, N.C., 1954); William Guess, "County Government in Colonial North Carolina," *JSHP* 11 (1911): 5–39. For a general analysis of colonial government, see Leonard W. Labaree, *Royal Government in America: A Study of the British Colonial System before 1783* (New Haven, 1930).

2. On this point, see Samuel P. Huntington, *Political Order in Changing Societies* (New Haven, 1968), 12.

3. For biographical information on Burrington, see *N.C. Biog. Hist.*, 1:203; *DAB*, s.v. "Burrington, George."

4. R. D. W. Connor, *History of North Carolina* (Chicago, 1919), 1:217; Hugh T. Lefler and William S. Powell, *Colonial North Carolina: A History* (New York, 1973), 88; Herbert L. Osgood, *The American Colonies in the Eighteenth Century* (Gloucester, Mass., 1958), 2:410. See also William S. Price, "A Strange Incident in George Burrington's Royal Governorship," *NCHR* 51 (1974): 149–58.

5. Address of the Grand Jury for North Carolina, Apr. 1, 1731, *NCCR*, 3:134–35. For Burrington's early Cape Fear activities, see Lawrence Lee, *The Lower Cape Fear in Colonial Days* (Chapel Hill, 1965), 92–96.

6. Price, "Burrington's Royal Governorship," *NCHR* 51 (1974): 150; Burrington to [Charles Delafaye], Aug. 8, 1730, *NCCR*, 3:85; William Byrd to Martin Bladen, June 13, 1729, in Marion Tinling, ed., *The Correspondence of the Three William Byrds of Westover, Virginia, 1684–1776* (Charlottesville, Va., 1977), 1: 405–6. See also James Henretta, *"Salutary Neglect": Colonial Administration under the Duke of Newcastle* (Princeton, N.J., 1972), 116–19; *DNCB*, s.v. "Montgomery, John"; Philip Haffenden, "Colonial Appointments and Patronage under the duke of Newcastle, 1724–1739," *EHR* 78 (1963): 419, 429; Burrington to Newcastle, July 1, 1731, *NCCR*, 3:139.

7. Haffenden, "Newcastle Appointments," *EHR* 78 (1963): 429.

8. Address of the Inhabitants of North Carolina, [1730], *NCCR*, 3:121–24; John L. Cheney, Jr., ed., *North Carolina Government, 1585–1974: A Narrative and Statistical Analysis* (Raleigh, 1975), 74, 94n; William S. Price, Jr., "'Men of Good Estates': Wealth among North Carolina's Royal Councillors," *NCHR* 49 (1972): 79.

9. Will of Mary Porter, Chowan Precinct, Nov. 12, 1717, in J. Bryan Grimes, ed., *Abstract of North Carolina Wills* (Raleigh, 1910), 296–97; Jacquelyn H. Wolf, "The Proud and the Poor: The Social Organization of Leadership in Proprietary North Carolina, 1663–1729," (Ph.D. diss., University of Pennsylvania, 1977), 99, 41n; Deposition of Edward Moseley, April 1733, *NCCR*, 3:503; Address of Inhabitants of North Carolina, [1730], *NCCR*, 3:123; Cheney, ed., *North Carolina Government*, 15, 35, 58; General Court Minutes, entry of Oct. 29, 1726, Feb. 3, 1727, *NCCR*, 2:669–70, 702–3; Presentment against Edmund Porter et al., Oct. 1731, General Court Records, Criminal Papers, 1731; Council Journals, May 12, 1731, *NCCR*, 3:224–32.

10. Cheney, ed., *North Carolina Government*, 25; *N.C. Biog. Hist.*, 4:36; Burrington to Board of Trade, Nov. 14, 1732, *NCCR*, 3:371; *DNCB*, s.v. "Ashe, John Baptista."

11. William Little to Burrington, [Aug. 1731], *NCCR*, 3:200; William Badham to Burrington, Aug. 2, 1731, *NCCR*, 3:197–98; Deposition of Benjamin Peyton,

Aug. 13, 1730, General Court Records, Criminal Papers, 1730; General Court Minutes, entry of Apr. 2, 1729, *NCCR*, 3:60–61; Narrative of Edmund Porter, Aug. 15, 1733, *NCCR*, 3:511–12; Presentment against Edmund Porter et al., July 1731, General Court Records, Criminal Papers, 1731; Burrington to Duke of Newcastle, July 2, 1731, *NCCR*, 3:142.

12. Everard to Newcastle, June 18, 1729, *NCCR*, 3:18–19; Edmund Porter to Newcastle, Jan. 24, June 15, Dec. 29, 1729, *NCCR*, 3:8, 17–18, 51–52; Everard to [Newcastle], [1729], *NCCR*, 3:26–27; Burrington to Board of Trade, Jan. 1, 1733, *NCCR*, 3:431; Burrington to Council, [1733], *NCCR*, 3:460–61; Lower House Journals, Nov. 8, 1733, *NCCR*, 3:618–19; Board of Trade to King, Mar. 14, 1754, *NCCR*, 5:95; Lee, *Lower Cape Fear*, 102–3.

13. Mabel L. Webber, comp., "The First Governor Moore and His Children," *South Carolina Historical and Genealogical Magazine* 37 (1936): 12–22; Cheney, ed., *North Carolina Government*, 34; Lee, *Lower Cape Fear*, 97–102. For South Carolina's economic and political troubles, see also Converse D. Clowse, *Economic Beginnings in Colonial South Carolina, 1670–1730*, Tricentennial Studies 3 (Columbia, S.C., 1971), 236–39.

14. Porter to Newcastle, Dec. 22, 1729, *NCCR*, 3: 51–52. See also Porter to Burrington, Nov. 30, 1729, *NCCR*, 3:49; Board of Trade to Newcastle, May 1, 1730, *NCCR*, 3:83.

15. Opinion of Attorney and Solicitor Generals, Feb. 11, 1738, *NCCR*, 4:320; Burrington to Council, [1733], *NCCR*, 3: 460; Byrd to Moseley, Feb. 12, 1729, in Tinling, ed., *Byrd Correspondence*, 1:390; Remarks upon Instructions to the Governor of North Carolina, [1733], *NCCR*, 3:495; Eleazer Allen to Board of Trade, Mar. 29, 1737, *NCCR*, 4:246–47; Gabriel Johnston to Board of Trade, Oct. 15, 1736, *NCCR*, 4:175; Upper House Journals, Mar. 1, 1735, *NCCR*, 4:114; James Murray to William Ellison, July 10, 1736, Murray Letter Book, 1735–60, 32.

16. Beverly Bond, *The Quit-Rent System in the American Colonies* (New Haven, 1919), 113–18; Instructions to Burrington, Dec. 14, 1730, *NCCR*, 3:101–2, 95.

17. Everard to Newcastle, June 18, 1729, *NCCR*, 3:19.

18. Burrington to [?], July 1, 1731, George Burrington Papers, Library of Duke University.

19. Burrington to Board of Trade, [July 1, 1731], *NCCR*, 3:141; Burrington to Newcastle, July 2, 1731, *NCCR*, 3:148.

20. Burrington to Board of Trade, Mar. 1730, *NCCR*, 3:78. See also Burrington to [Newcastle], July 1, 1731, *NCCR*, 3:139–40; Burrington to Newcastle, July 2, 1731, *NCCR*, 3:150, 155.

21. Lower House Journals, Apr. 14, 18, 21, May 8, 15, 17, 1731, *NCCR*, 3:288, 292–93, 294–95, 312–13, 320–21, 324; Burrington to Newcastle, July 2, 1731, *NCCR*, 3:142–46.

22. Lower House Journals, May 5, 7, 1731, *NCCR*, 3:311–12; Burrington to Newcastle, July 2, 1731, *NCCR*, 3:149; Burrington to Board of Trade, Feb. 20, 1732, *NCCR*, 3:332.

23. Lower House Journals, Apr. 13–May 17, 1731, *NCCR*, 3:285–325 passim.

24. Council Journals, May 15, 18, 20, 1731, *NCCR*, 3:233, 237–43; Burrington to Board of Trade, [July 1, 1731], *NCCR*, 3:141. See also Burrington to [Newcastle], July 1, 1731, *NCCR*, 3:139–40.

25. Burrington to Board of Trade, Sept. 4, 1731, *NCCR*, 3:203; Burrington to Newcastle, July 2, 1731, Nov. 15, 1732, *NCCR*, 3:143–44, 374.

26. Burrington to Board of Trade, Sept. 4, 1731, NCCR, 3:204, 209.

27. Council Journals, July 27, 1731, NCCR, 3:250–51.

28. Cheney, ed., *North Carolina Government*, 16–17, 21, 36; Everard to Bishop of London, Apr. 14, 1729, NCCR, 3:16; Burrington to Board of Trade, Jan. 1, 1733, NCCR, 3:433–34. See also Louis B. Wright, ed., *The Prose Works of William Byrd of Westover: Narratives of a Colonial Virginian* (Cambridge, Mass., 1966), 57.

29. Cheney, ed., *North Carolina Government*, 33; Burrington to Board of Trade, Sept. 4, 1731, NCCR, 3:205–6; *DNB*, s.v. "Gale, Samuel."

30. Council Journals, Jan. 20–22, 1732, NCCR, 3:405–13; Burrington to Board of Trade, Sept. 4, 1731, NCCR, 3:205.

31. Porter to Sec. of Board of Trade, Aug. 15, 1733, NCCR, 3:501–2; Lower House Journals, Nov. 8, 1733, NCCR, 3:617–19; Price, "Men of Good Estates," NCHR 49 (1972): 75.

32. Burrington to Board of Trade, Sept. 4, 1731, Feb. 20, 1732, NCCR, 3:205, 208–9, 332–33; Burrington to Board of Trade, Jan. 1, May 19, Oct. 5, 1733, NCCR, 3:434, 488, 529.

33. Lower House Journals, Nov. 8, 1733, NCCR, 3:618; Council Journals, Nov. 4, 1731, Jan. 18, 19, Nov. 2, 1732, NCCR, 3:254, 401, 403, 426; Burrington to Board of Trade, Feb. 20, 1732, NCCR, 3:333; Moseley to Board of Trade, with enclosures, [Apr. 20, 1733], NCCR, 3:466–72; Nathaniel Rice et al. to Newcastle, Sept. 16, 1732, NCCR, 3:363–64.

34. Porter to Board of Trade, Feb. 19, 1732, NCCR, 3:325–28; Rice et al. to Newcastle, Sept. 16, 1732, NCCR, 3:356–68; Rice et al. to Board of Trade, Nov. 17, 1732, NCCR, 3:375–82.

35. Rice et al. to Board of Trade, Nov. 17, 1732, NCCR, 3:376–79.

36. Burrington to Board of Trade, Sept. 4, 1731, NCCR, 3:203.

37. Council Journals, July 26, Aug. 31, Nov. 3, 4, 23, 1731, Mar. 28, Apr. 3, May 16, July 25, Oct. 7, 18, 1732, NCCR, 3:250–56, 415–17, 420, 422, 423; Rice et al. to Newcastle, Sept. 16, 1732, NCCR, 3:359; Affidavit of William Dry, [1735], T. 1/289 (transcripts, N.C. Archives); Burrington to Board of Trade, Jan. 1, 1733, NCCR, 3:436; Burrington to Newcastle, Nov. 15, 1732, Mar. 1, 1733, NCCR, 3:374, 437; Lower House Journals, Nov. 8, 1733, NCCR, 3:620; Upper House Journals, Jan. 17, 1735, NCCR, 4:77. The lack of court minutes for the counties of Tyrrell, Pasquotank, and Perquimans for most of Burrington's administration might be partly attributable to judicial breakdowns. See also Carteret County Court Minutes, June 1731, Dec. 1732, June 1734, N.C. Archives.

38. Burrington to [?], Feb. 27, 1732, Burrington Papers; Burrington to Newcastle, Nov. 15, 1732, NCCR, 3:374; Burrington to Board of Trade, Jan. 1, 1733, NCCR, 3:429.

39. Burrington to [Board of Trade?], [1731], NCCR, 3:181; Burrington to Board of Trade, Sept. 4, 1731, Feb. 20, 1732, NCCR, 3:207, 332–33; Rice et al. to Board of Trade, Nov. 17, 1732, NCCR, 3:381; Petition of the Inhabitants of Bertie and Edgecombe Counties, [Oct. 1735], NCCR, 4:19.

40. Council Journals, Nov. 23, 1731, Nov. 1, 1732, NCCR, 3:256, 425; Statement by Burrington, Dec. 26, 1732, NCCR, 3:442; Rice et al. to Board of Trade, Nov. 17, 1732, NCCR, 3:380.

41. Cheney, ed., *North Carolina Government*, 36–37; Lower House Journals, July 3–18, 1733, NCCR, 3:561–611 passim.

42. Henretta, *Salutary Neglect*, 152–55.

43. Newcastle to Board of Trade, Mar. 27, 1733, *NCCR*, 3:438; Henretta, *Salutary Neglect*, 155.

44. Burrington to Newcastle, June 1, 1734, *NCCR*, 3:625.

45. Lower House Journals, Nov. 8, 1733, *NCCR*, 3:613.

46. Council Journals, Apr. 15, 1734, *NCCR*, 3:633. Although it wrongly concludes that Burrington was not ill but had gone to South Carolina, see Price, "Burrington's Royal Governorship," *NCHR* 51 (1974): 155–56.

47. Burrington to Board of Trade, June 1, Sept. 17, 1734, *NCCR*, 3:625, 627; Warrant for Thomas Sherwin, Dec. 14, 1734, General Court Records, Criminal Papers, 1734; Burrington to Newcastle, Oct. 7, 1734, *NCCR*, 3:628; Burrington to King, [1736], *NCCR*, 4:165.

48. For biographical information on Johnston, see *N.C. Biog. Hist.*, 5:187–93; Mary Shaw Robeson Cunningham, "Gabriel Johnston, Governor of North Carolina," (M.A. thesis, University of North Carolina, Chapel Hill, 1944), 1–15.

49. Council Journals, Nov. 2, 1734, *NCCR*, 4:1–2; Upper House Journals, Jan. 17, 1735, *NCCR*, 4:77.

50. Upper House Journals, Jan. 17, 20, 21, 1735, *NCCR*, 4:77, 80–85; Lower House Journals, Feb. 27, 1735, *NCCR*, 4:150–51.

51. Johnston to Lord Wilmington, Dec. 16, 1734, Feb. 10, 1737, *Wilmington Manuscripts* (Historical Manuscripts Commission, *Eleventh Report*, Pt. IV), 3: 258, 263.

52. Instructions for Johnston, July 18, 1733, *NCCR*, 3:498; Lower House Journals, Feb. 11, 12, 26, 1735, *NCCR*, 4:132–35, 147–48; Johnston to Board of Trade, May 25, 1735, *NCCR*, 4:8.

53. Lower House Journals, Feb. 12, 1735, *NCCR*, 4:134–35; Charles G. Sellers, Jr., "Private Profits and British Colonial Policy: The Speculations of Henry McCulloh," *WMQ*, 3d Ser., 8 (1951): 536–37; Council Journals, Jan. 29, 1735, *NCCR*, 4:32. For a full description of Moseley's assault, see Council Journals, Jan. 29, 1735, C.O. 5/309, 53–56.

54. Council Journals, Jan. 29, Feb. 13, Mar. 6, 22, 1735, *NCCR*, 4:33, 36–37, 39–45; Johnston to Board of Trade, May 25, 1735, *NCCR*, 4:8–10.

55. Johnston to Board of Trade, July 10, 1735, *NCCR*, 4:15.

56. Johnston to Wilmington, Dec. 16, 1734, *Wilmington Manuscripts*, 3:258.

57. Matthew Rowan to Johnston, [1744], *NCCR*, 4:697; Sellers, "Private Profits," *WMQ*, 3d Ser., 8 (1951): 535–40. For McCulloh, see also John Cannon, "Henry McCulloch and Henry McCulloh," *WMQ*, 3d Ser., 15 (1958): 71–73.

58. James Murray to David Tullideph, Jan. 10, 1737, Murray to McCulloh, May 3, 1736, in Nina Moore Tiffany, ed., *Letters of James Murray, Loyalist* (Boston, 1901), 29, 31.

59. Lee, *Lower Cape Fear*, 120–23; Murray to Ellison, Feb. 14, 1736, in Tiffany, ed., *Murray Letters*, 24.

60. Hugh Meredith, *An Account of the Cape Fear Country, 1731*, ed. Earl G. Swem (Perth Amboy, N.J., 1922), 15; Murray to Ellison, Feb. 14, 1736, in Tiffany, ed., *Murray Letters*, 26.

61. Johnston to Board of Trade, Dec. 5, 1735, *NCCR*, 4:24; Johnston to Newcastle, Dec. 5, 1735, C.O. 5/309,353; Johnston to Board of Trade, Oct. 15, 1736, *NCCR*, 4:177; Murray to Tullideph, Dec. 15, 1735, Murray Letter Book, 1735–60, 111.

62. Board of Trade Journals, Oct. 14, 17, 31, 1735, *NCCR*, 4:29–30; Burrington to

Board of Trade, Oct. 13, 1735, *NCCR*, 4:299–307; Johnston to Board of Trade, Oct. 15, Nov. 29, 1736, *NCCR*, 4:176, 203; Johnston to Sec. of Board of Trade, Oct. 6, 1737, *NCCR*, 4:265–66. For Wragg, see Ella Lonn, *The Colonial Agents of the Southern Colonies* (Chapel Hill, 1954), 284.

63. Johnston to Board of Trade, Oct. 15, 1736, *NCCR*, 4:173; Johnston to Sec. of Board of Trade, Mar. 11, 1737, *NCCR*, 4:243; McCulloh to Sec. of Board of Trade, Jan. 17, 1737, *NCCR*, 4:241–42.

64. William Byrd to [?], July 22, 1736, in Tinling, ed., *Byrd Correspondence*, 2:497.

65. Burrington to [Newcastle], Oct. 7, 1734, *NCCR*, 3:628; Petition of Bertie and Edgecombe Counties to Johnston, Oct. 1735, *NCCR*, 4:19–20; *DNB*, s.v. "Hanmer, Sir Thomas."

66. Depositions of Peter Young, Thomas Lowther, and Joseph Anderson, [1736], General Court Records, Criminal Papers, 1736.

67. Warrant for Daniel Hanmer, Nov. 1, 1736, Trial Memorandum, [1736], General Court Records, Criminal Papers, 1736.

68. Petition of Daniel Hanmer, Mar. 29, 1737, General Court Records, Criminal Papers, 1737.

69. Murray to Ellison, July 10, 1736, Murray Letter Book, 1735–60, 33; Upper House Journals, Sept. 21–Oct. 12, 1736, *NCCR*, 4:225–41 passim; Privy Council Committee Minutes, May 8, 1739, Sir Thomas Phillips Collection, 5–8, Library of Congress; Council Journals, Mar. 4, 1737, *NCCR*, 4:272; Johnston to Board of Trade, Oct. 15, 1736, Oct. 6, 1737, *NCCR*, 4:173, 268; Johnston to Wilmington, June 2, 1737, *Wilmington Manuscripts*, 3:264.

70. Johnston to Board of Trade, Oct. 15, Nov. 29, 1736, *NCCR*, 4:176–77, 203; Johnston to Sec. of Board of Trade, Mar. 11, 1737, *NCCR*, 4:243; Allen to Board of Trade, Mar. 29, 1737, *NCCR*, 4:246–47; Council Journals, Nov. 19, 1739, *NCCR*, 4:352.

71. Allen to Board of Trade, Mar. 29, 1737, *NCCR*, 4:246; Wragg to Board of Trade, received July 12, 1738, *NCCR*, 4:324; Johnston to Wilmington, June 2, Feb. 10, 1737, *Wilmington Manuscripts*, 3:264, 262.

72. Johnston to Sec. of Board of Trade, Mar. 11, Oct. 6, 1737, *NCCR*, 4:243, 267; Johnston to Board of Trade, Apr. 15, 1741, C.O. 5/296, 20; Abstract of Quitrents in North Carolina from Sept. 29, 1729 to Mar. 25, 1742, by Eleazer Allen, Lansdowne Manuscripts, 1215, 163, British Library (photostats, Library of Congress); Johnston to Board of Trade, Apr. 30, 1737, *NCCR*, 4:251.

73. Popple to Johnston, Apr. 22, 1737, *NCCR*, 4:248; Board of Trade Journals, Sept. 3, 1735, *NCCR*, 4:29. See also Board of Trade Journals, Nov. 9, 1736, *NCCR*, 4:214.

74. Sellers, "Private Profits," *WMQ*, 3d Ser., 8 (1954): 541–42.

75. Ibid.; Johnston to Wilmington, Mar. 1, 1739 [1740], *Wilmington Manuscripts*, 3:264.

76. Johnston to Board of Trade, Jan. 28, 1740, *NCCR*, 4:415–17; McCulloh's Remarks on Quitrent Act, [1740], *NCCR*, 4:425–34; Murray to McCulloh, Jan. 30, 1740, in Tiffany, ed., *Murray Letters*, 55; Johnston to Newcastle, Apr. 10, 1739, *NCCR*, 4:337.

77. Murray to McCulloh, Apr. 12, 1741, in Tiffany, ed., *Murray Letters*, 62.

78. "A True and Faithful Narrative of the Proceedings of the House of Burgesses of North Carolina . . . ," 1740, in William K. Boyd, ed., *Some Eighteenth Century Tracts concerning North Carolina* (Raleigh, 1927), 9–10.

79. Ibid., 15.

80. Council Journals, Mar. 6, 1739, *NCCR*, 4:345; Burrington to Board of Trade, Oct. 7, 1734, *NCCR*, 3:629–30; "True and Faithful Narrative," 1740, in Boyd, ed., *Eighteenth Century Tracts*, 9–10, 14; Depositions of Catherine Routledge, Thomas Lovick, Benjamin Hill, John Blount, [1748–49], *NCCR*, 3:1190, 1201, 1207–9; Recognizance Bond for John Hodgson, Dec. 29, 1739, General Court Records, Criminal Papers, 1739.

81. "True and Faithful Narrative," 1740, in Boyd, ed., *Eighteenth Century Tracts*, 11; Murray to McCulloh, Jan. 30, 1740, Murray Letter Book, 1735–60, 103.

82. "True and Faithful Narrative," 1740, in Boyd, ed., *Eighteenth Century Tracts*, 13–53; Council Journals, June 5, 1740, *NCCR*, 4:459; Lower House Journals, Feb. 11–13, 1740, *NCCR*, 4:500–504.

83. Lower House Journals, Feb. 16, 8, 1740, *NCCR*, 4:507, 494–95; Petition of Bertie and Edgecombe Counties to Johnston, Oct. 1735, *NCCR*, 4:19; Upper House Journals, July 18, 1733, *NCCR*, 3:560. See also Johnston's Observations on Several North Carolina Acts, Dec. 5, 1735, *NCCR*, 4:25; Lower House Journals, Apr. 14, 1731, *NCCR*, 3:288–89; Lower House Journals, Feb. 8, 1739, Feb. 9, 11, 1740, *NCCR*, 4:384, 499–500; Deposition of Patrick Ryan, Oct. 23, 1734, General Court Records, Criminal Papers, 1734.

84. Lee, *Lower Cape Fear*, 123; Lower House Journals, Feb. 20, 25, 1740, *NCCR*, 4:510, 515; Upper House Journals, Feb. 20–25, 1740, *NCCR*, 4:482–87; Council Journals, May 22, June 5, 1740, *NCCR*, 4:448–53, 455–60; Rice et al. to Board of Trade, July 3, 1740, *NCCR*, 4:462–70.

85. James Moir to Sec. of S.P.G., Sept. 4, 1742, *NCCR*, 4:607; New Hanover County Court Minutes, entry of Dec. 11, 1740; Donald R. Lennon and Ida Brooks Kellam, eds., *The Wilmington Town Book, 1743–1778* (Raleigh, 1973), xxiii, 23n.

86. See, for instance, Greene, *Quest for Power*, 6, passim; Lefler and Powell, *Colonial North Carolina*, 116–19; Raper, *North Carolina Colonial Government*, 100, 219–20, passim; Connor, *History of North Carolina*, 1:213–22.

87. Lower House Journals, July 7, 1733, *NCCR*, 3:575.

88. Lower House Journals, Jan. 21, 1735, *NCCR*, 4:119.

89. Wright, ed., *Byrd Prose Works*, 212; Byrd to Burrington, July 20, 1731, in Tinling, ed., *Byrd Correspondence*, 2:446; Johnston to Sec. of Board of Trade, Mar. 11, 1737, *NCCR*, 4:242–43. For similar comments, see Burrington to Newcastle, Nov. 15, 1732, *NCCR*, 3:374; Byrd to Johnston, Dec. 21, 1735, in Tinling, ed., *Byrd Correspondence*, 2:466; Johnston to Sec. of Board of Trade, Oct. 6, 1737, *NCCR*, 4:267–68. See also Donna J. Spindel, "The Administration of Criminal Justice in North Carolina, 1720–1740," *American Journal of Legal History*, forthcoming. I am indebted to Ms. Spindel for allowing me to see an early draft of this article.

90. Lower House Journals, Aug. 19, 1740, Feb. 27, 1739, *NCCR*, 4:569, 399; Council Journals, Jan. 29, 1735, *NCCR*, 4:32; Harry Eckstein, "On the Causes of Internal Wars," in Eric A. Nordlinger, ed., *Politics and Society: Studies in Comparative Sociology* (Englewood Cliffs, N.J., 1970), 299.

91. Wright, ed., *Byrd Prose Works*, 87.

92. Clifford K. Shipton, *Sibley's Harvard Graduates* (Cambridge, Mass., 1933–), 8:6, J. G. de Roulhac Hamilton, "Southern Members of the Inns of Court," *NCHR* 10 (1933): 279.

93. See Bibliographical Essay.

94. See Bibliographical Essay.

95. Address of Inhabitants of North Carolina, [1730], *NCCR*, 3:123; Rice et al. to Newcastle, Sept. 16, 1732, *NCCR*, 3:359; Rice et al. to Board of Trade, Nov. 17, 1732, *NCCR*, 3:376; Burrington to Board of Trade, Feb. 20, 1732, *NCCR*, 3:332–33; Upper House Journals, Jan. 17, 1735, *NCCR*, 4:77; Deposition of Thomas Lowther, [1736], General Court Records, Criminal Papers, 1736.

96. For assembly leaders and the manner in which they were determined through committee assignments, see Greene, *Quest for Power*, 463–64, 466, 489–92. See Bibliographical Essay for background information.

97. Murray to Ellison, Feb. 14, 1736, in Tiffany, ed., *Murray Letters*, 26; Upper House Journals, Sept. 22, 1736, Mar. 1, 1735, *NCCR*, 4:229, 114. See also Murray to Ellison, July 10, 1736, Murray Letter Book, 1735–60, 32.

98. Council Journals, Nov. 2, 1732, *NCCR*, 3:426; Wright, ed., *Byrd Prose Works*, 54; *DNCB*, s.v. "Moseley, Edward"; Price, "Men of Good Estates," *NCHR* 49 (1972): 81. See also D. H. Hill, "Edward Moseley: Character Sketch," *NCB* 5 (1906): 202–8.

99. Burrington to [Board of Trade?], [1731], *NCCR*, 3:180; Burrington to Bishop of London, Mar. 15, 1732, *NCCR*, 3:339; Upper House Journals, July 4, 1733, Jan. 17, 1735, Sept. 22, Oct. 7, 1736, *NCCR*, 3:541, 4:78, 227–28, 239; Johnston to Board of Trade, Oct. 15, 1736, Mar. 11, 1737, *NCCR*, 4:178, 243; Council Journals, Mar. 4, 1737, *NCCR*, 4:272; Johnston to Board of Trade, Apr. 30, 1737, *NCCR*, 4:250; [Alexander] Garden to Bishop of London, Sept. 6, 1737, *NCCR*, 4:264–65.

100. Johnston to Wilmington, Feb. 10, 1737, *Wilmington Manuscripts*, 3:262; Moir to [Sec. of S.P.G.], Oct. 29, 1740, S.P.G., B MSS, 9, 145; Murray to McCulloh, Nov. 6, 1736, in Tiffany, ed., *Murray Letters*, 35. Murray wrote in early 1736 that he intended "to concern my self with neither" of the two towns. Murray to Ellison, Feb. 14, 1736, in Tiffany, ed., *Murray Letters*, 24.

101. McCulloh's Remarks on Quitrent and Cultivation Acts, [1740], *NCCR*, 4:425–34; Board of Trade Journals, June 4, 5, 10, 11, 12, 19, 25, July 1, 1740, *NCCR*, 3:436–38; Order in Council, July 31, 1740, *NCCR*, 4:434–35; "The Case of Gabriel Johnston, Esquire, Governor of North Carolina," [1743], Historical Manuscripts Commission, *Report on the Laing Manuscripts Preserved in the University of Edinburgh* (London, 1925), 2:339; Sellers, "Private Profits," *WMQ*, 3d Ser., 8 (1951): 543.

4. The Politics of Regional Conflict, 1741–1754

1. Lawrence Lee, *The Lower Cape Fear in Colonial Days* (Chapel Hill, 1965), 100–101; Lord Carteret to Duke of Newcastle, Jan. 21, 1740, Add. MSS, 32693, 39–40; Spangenberg Diary, entry of Sept. 14, 1752, *Moravian Records*, 1:35. See also *S.C. Gaz.*, June 6, 1743.

2. Jack P. Greene, *The Quest for Power: The Lower Houses of Assembly in the Southern Royal Colonies, 1689–1776* (Chapel Hill, 1963), 174–78; Lawrence F. London, "The Representation Controversy in Colonial North Carolina," *NCHR* 11 (1934): 264; John L. Cheney, ed., *North Carolina Government, 1585–1974: A Narrative and Statistical Analysis* (Raleigh, 1975), 41, 43; Board of Trade to King, Mar. 14, 1754, *NCCR*, 5:88; Deposition of Abraham Blackall, Apr. 13, 1749, *NCCR*, 4:1173.

3. Laws, *NCSR*, 23:136–43, 146–49, 212–15; Greene, *Quest for Power*, 489–92.

4. Lee, *Lower Cape Fear*, 117–18, 330; Will of Samuel Swann, Perquimans County, Jan. 8, 1753, in J. Bryan Grimes, ed., *Abstract of North Carolina Wills* (Raleigh, 1910), 368.

5. Lower House Journals, Nov. 16, 1744, *NCCR*, 4:735; Johnston to Board of Trade, Dec. 17, 1740, *NCCR*, 4:423–24; London, "Representation Controversy," *NCHR* 11 (1934): 258–59; Laws, *NCSR*, 23:127.

6. James Moir to Sec. of S.P.G., Apr. 16, 1750, S.P.G., B MSS, 18, 179; Laws, *NCSR*, 25:234–35.

7. [McCulloh] to Board of Trade, n.d., *NCCR*, 4:1217; London, "Representation Controversy," *NCHR* 11 (1934): 261–62; John Campbell to Earl of Granville, May 13, 1749, Granville District Papers.

8. Moir to Sec. of S.P.G., Mar. 26, 1745, *NCCR*, 4:756; Spangenberg Diary, entry of Sept. 14, 1752, *Moravian Records*, 1:35.

9. Eleazer Allen to [?], 1743, James Abercromby Letter Book, 1743–51, N.C. Archives; Abstract of Quitrents, Lansdowne MSS, 1215, 163; Henry McCulloh to Board of Trade, Aug. 19, 1742, C.O. 5/369 (microfilm, N.C. Archives).

10. Johnston to Board of Trade, Dec. 21, 1741, *NCCR*, 4:584–85; Cheney, ed., *North Carolina Government*, 40.

11. Johnston to [Bishop of Worcester?], Dec. 3, 1743, Johnston to [William] Adair, Dec. 3, 1743, "The Case of Gabriel Johnston, Esquire, Governor of North Carolina," [1743], Historical Manuscripts Commission, *Report on the Laing Manuscripts Preserved in the University of Edinburgh* (London, 1925), 2:336–40.

12. Johnston to Board of Trade, Mar. 9, 1747, Dec. 28, 1748, *NCCR*, 4:1153, 1164.

13. Cheney, ed., *North Carolina Government*, 58; Council Journals, July 26, 1743, *NCCR*, 4:637; Greene, *Quest for Power*, 490.

14. Petition of Peter Payne et al. to King, [1747], *NCCR*, 4:1158–60; Johnston to Board of Trade, Mar. 9, 1747, *NCCR*, 4:1152–53.

15. Lower House Journals, Nov. 21–Dec. 5, 1746, *NCCR*, 4:838–43; Laws, *NCSR*, 23:251–67.

16. Johnston to Board of Trade, Mar. 9, 1747, *NCCR*, 4:1152–53; Lower House Journals, Mar. 3, 1747, *NCCR*, 4:857–58.

17. Cheney, ed., *North Carolina Government*, 44–45; Depositions of William Herritage and Abraham Duncan, [Apr. 1749], *NCCR*, 4:1176, 1178. For accounts emphasizing a strictly north-south split, see, for instance, London, "Representation Controversy," *NCHR* 11 (1934): 255–70; Hugh T. Lefler and William S. Powell, *Colonial North Carolina: A History* (New York, 1973), 121–24; "Prefatory Notes," *NCCR*, 4:xviii–xx.

18. W. C. Allen, *History of Halifax County* (Boston, 1918), 12; A. R. Newsome, ed., "Twelve North Carolina Counties, 1810–1811," *NCHR* 6 (1929): 69; Manly Wade Wellman, *The County of Warren, North Carolina, 1586–1917* (Chapel Hill, 1959), 19; *DNCB*, s.v. "Dawson, John"; Anton-Hermann Chroust, *The Rise of the Legal Profession in America* (Norman, Okla., 1965), 1:322; "Virginia Council Journals, 1726–1753," *VMHB* 36 (1928): 230; *N.C. Biog. Hist.*, 3:164; J. Kelly Turner and John L. Bridges, Jr., *History of Edgecombe County, North Carolina* (Raleigh, 1920), 435.

19. Moir to Sec. of S.P.G., May 15, 1750, S.P.G., B MSS, 18, 180. In 1751 Johnston further cemented his ties to Northampton County by recommending the appointment of its leading politician, John Dawson, to the council. Johnston to Board of Trade, Sept. 3, 1751, *NCCR*, 4:1075.

20. Petition of Peter Payne et al., [1747], *NCCR*, 4:1158–60.
21. Johnston to Board of Trade, Mar. 9, 1747, *NCCR*, 4:1152–53. For his earlier account, see Johnston to Board of Trade, Jan. 20, 1747, *NCCR*, 4:844.
22. Nathaniel Rice et al. to Samuel Wragg, June 17, 1747, Joshua Sharpe Papers, South. Hist. Coll.; James Abercromby to Johnston, Nov. 16, 1747, Abercromby Letter Book, 1743–51, N.C. Archives. For Abercromby, see Michael G. Kammen, *A Rope of Sand: The Colonial Agents, British Politics, and the American Revolution* (Ithaca, N.Y., 1968), 323; Ella Lonn, *The Colonial Agents of the Southern Colonies* (Chapel Hill, 1954), 78–79, 286; *DNCB*, s.v. "Abercromby, James."
23. Charles G. Sellers, Jr., "Private Profits and British Colonial Policy: The Speculations of Henry McCulloh," *WMQ*, 3d Ser., 8 (1951): 544; Alan D. Watson, "Henry McCulloh: Royal Commissioner in South Carolina," *South Carolina Historical Magazine* 75 (1974): 41. For Selwyn, see *DNB*, s.v., "Selwyn, George Augustus."
24. McCulloh to Board of Trade, received June 8, 1749, *NCCR*, 4:1076–81; Johnston to Board of Trade, Apr. 16, 1750, *NCCR*, 4:1082–90; McCulloh to Board of Trade, received June 12, 1751, *NCCR*, 4:1137–52; Sellers, "Private Profits," *WMQ*, 3d Ser., 8 (1951): 544–45.
25. Board of Trade Journals, May 11, 1748, *NCCR*, 4:880–81; [McCulloh] to Board of Trade, [1748], *NCCR*, 4:1156–58; Order in Council, July 14, 1748, *NCCR*, 4:1161–63.
26. Cullen Pollock to Roger Moore, Jan. 15, 1747, Pollock Letter Book.
27. Laws, *NCSR*, 23:292–96; Johnston to Granville, May 15, 1749, Granville District Papers; McCulloh to Board of Trade, n.d., *NCCR*, 4:1217; London, "Representation Controversy," *NCHR* 11 (1934): 262.
28. Laws, *NCSR*, 23:301–3.
29. Abercromby to Johnston, Nov. 16, 1747, Abercromby Letter Book, 1743–51, N.C. Archives; Francis Corbin and Isaac Arthand to Duke of Bedford, Dec. 14, 1748, Thomas Child to Bedford, Dec. 15, 1748, *NCCR*, 4:925–28; "Observations on the Colony of North Carolina together with the Conduct of the Present Governour," by Corbyn Morris, [1748], Add. MSS, 32715, 172. For Corbin see *DNCB*, s.v. "Corbin, Francis." For Morris, see *DNB*, s.v. "Morris, Corbyn"; James Henretta, *"Salutary Neglect": Colonial Administration under the Duke of Newcastle* (Princeton, N.J., 1972), 263–66; William Tryon to Board of Trade, Feb. 1, 1766, *NCCR*, 7:160.
30. Board of Trade Journals, Jan. 24, 25, 26, 1749, *NCCR*, 4:936–41.
31. Board of Trade Journals, Jan. 26, Feb. 7, 14, 15, 1749, *NCCR*, 4:942–43; Board of Trade to Bedford, Feb. 20, 1749, *NCCR*, 4:930–35; Abercromby to Johnston, Jan. 15, 1749, Abercromby Letter Book, 1743–51, N.C. Archives; Lonn, *Southern Agents*, 79.
32. Johnston to Board of Trade, May 17, Dec. 28, 1748, Apr. 4, 1749, *NCCR*, 4:868–70, 1163–66, 919–23; Johnston to Bedford, [1749], *NCCR*, 4:918.
33. McCulloh to Board of Trade, received June 8, 1749, *NCCR*, 4:1076–81; Board of Trade Journals, July 6, 7, 1749, *NCCR*, 4:943–44.
34. Board of Trade Journals, July 14, 19, 27, 1749, Mar. 21, 23, 26, Apr. 3, 4, May 10, 11, Aug. 31, Sept. 1, Oct. 23, 31, Dec. 11, 1750, Jan. 11, Feb. 6, 8, 14, 18, 22, Mar. 13, 15, 20, 29, May 9, June 4, 12, 14, 18, 19, 27, 1751, *NCCR*, 4:944–45, 1028–31, 1225–37.
35. Jack P. Greene, "'A Posture of Hostility': A Reconsideration of Some Aspects of the Origins of the American Revolution," *AASP* 87 (1977): 44–48.

36. Johnston to Board of Trade, Oct. 24, 1748, C.O. 5/296, 104. As late as 1765, Governor William Tryon observed, "The arrival of Dispatches from the public Boards is extremely uncertain here at all times." Tryon to Seymore Conway, Dec. 26, 1765, *NCCR*, 7:144. See also Ralph R. Tingley, "Postal Service in Colonial North Carolina," *The American Philatelist* 62 (1949): 310–12.

37. Lamb to Board of Trade, Sept. 25, 1747, *NCCR*, 4:1156.

38. Alison Gilbert Olson, *Anglo-American Politics, 1660–1775* (New York, 1973), 154; Henretta, *Salutary Neglect*, 294; *DNB*, s.v. "Anson, George."

39. Sellers, "Private Profits," *WMQ*, 3d Ser., 8 (1951): 548–49.

40. Stanley Nider Katz, *Newcastle's New York: Anglo-American Politics, 1732–1753* (Cambridge, Mass., 1968), 101.

41. Laws, *NCSR*, 23:310–12; Benjamin Hill to McCulloh, July 23, 1750, *NCCR*, 4:1099; Council Journals, Sept. 26, 1751, *NCCR*, 4:1245; Abercromby to Johnston, Dec. 15, 1749, Abercromby Letter Book, 1743–51, N.C. Archives.

42. Lee, *Lower Cape Fear*, 232–34; Johnston to Board of Trade, Apr. 4, 1749, *NCCR*, 4:922–23; John Campbell to Bedford, June 1, 1748, "Complaints against Gabriel Johnston Esquire Governor of North Carolina," [1748?], Add. MSS, 32715, 140–41, 170–71.

43. Johnston to Board of Trade, Dec. 28, 1748, *NCCR*, 4:1166.

44. Laws, *NCSR*, 23:268–72, 314–15, 342–44, 346, 352–58, 383–86, 390, 398–99, 25:252–54, 272–73. The assembly also gave Johnston £950 proclamation money between 1748 and 1751 for his expenses. Greene, *Quest for Power*, 140.

45. Laws, *NCSR*, 25:248–49; Lower House Journals, June 20, 24, 1746, *NCCR*, 4:827, 829.

46. Cheney, ed., *North Carolina Government*, 18; Greene, *Quest for Power*, 489–92.

47. Johnston quoted in Abercromby to Board of Trade, [1750], *NCCR*, 4:1224; Johnston to Board of Trade, Dec. 28, 1748, *NCCR*, 4:1166.

48. Moir to Sec. of S.P.G., May 2, 1749, *NCCR*, 4:923. See also Moir to Sec. of S.P.G., Nov. 22, 1748, *NCCR*, 4:878; Campbell to Granville, May 13, 1749, Granville District Papers; Clement Hall to Sec. of S.P.G., June 25, 1751, S.P.G., B MSS, 19, 126.

49. Johnston to Board of Trade, Dec. 28, 1748, *NCCR*, 4:1166; Table of North Carolina Taxes, 1748–70, [1770], in William K. Boyd, ed., *Some Eighteenth Century Tracts concerning North Carolina* (Raleigh, 1927), 416.

50. Spangenberg to [?], Sept. 12, 1752, *NCCR*, 4:1311–12. See also Assize Court Summons, Edenton, Oct. 13, 1750, General Court Papers, II, 1717–54, N.C. Archives; Assize Court Minutes, Edenton, entries of Oct. 1753, Apr. 1754, Minute Dockets, 1680–1754, N.C. Archives; Assize Court Minutes, Edenton, entry of Oct. 1754, General Court Papers, III, 1751–87, N.C. Archives; Depositions of John Rutherfurd and Enoch Hall, May 8, 1750, *NCCR*, 4:1222–23. For the possibility of northern secession, see Abercromby to Samuel Swann, Oct. 7, 1751, James Abercromby Letter Book, 300, Va. State Lib.

51. Spangenberg to [?], Sept. 12, 1752, *NCCR*, 4:1312; Pasquotank County Court Minutes, entry of Apr. 10, 1750, N.C. Archives; Chowan County Court Minutes, entries of Apr. 16, 1747, Oct. 17, 1751, N.C. Archives; New Action Docket, Sept. 1751, Tyrrell County Court Minutes, N.C. Archives.

52. Arthur Dobbs to Board of Trade, Jan. 11, 1755, *NCCR*, 5:326; Murray to Johnston, Feb. 8, 1751, Murray Letter Book, 1735–60, 242; County Militia Returns, [1754], *NCCR*, 5:161. See also Lee, *Lower Cape Fear*, 129.

53. Johnston to Board of Trade, Dec. 28, 1748, NCCR, 5:1166.
54. Desmond Clarke, *Arthur Dobbs, Esquire, 1689–1765: Surveyor-General of Ireland, Prospector, and Governor of North Carolina* (Chapel Hill, 1957), 97–100.
55. Clarke, *Arthur Dobbs*, 100–105; Board of Trade to King, Mar. 14, 1754, NCCR, 5:81–108; Alan D. Watson, "The Quitrent System in Royal South Carolina," *WMQ*, 3d Ser., 36 (1976): 204.
56. Dobbs to Board of Trade, Dec. 19, 1754, NCCR, 5:154. See also Upper House Journals, Dec. 17, 1754, NCCR, 5:217–19; Lower House Journals, Dec. 16, 1754, NCCR, 5:237–38.
57. See, for instance, London, "Representation Controversy," *NCHR* 11 (1934): 268; Lee, *Lower Cape Fear*, 129–30; Lefler and Powell, *Colonial North Carolina*, 123–24.
58. Matthew Rowan to Earl of Holdernesse, Nov. 21, 1753, Rowan to Board of Trade, Mar. 19, 1754, NCCR, 5:25, 108–9; Laws, NCSR, 23:392–98.
59. Dobbs to Board of Trade, Dec. 19, 1754, NCCR, 5:154–55.
60. Francis Corbin to Granville, Mar. 19, 1754, Granville District Papers; Cheney, ed., *North Carolina Government*, 18, 43–46.
61. William Faris to [Dobbs], Feb. 18, 1750, Dobbs Papers, reel 2. With or without Dobbs's help, Faris received the office of vice-admiralty judge in 1756. Letters Patent, May 13, 1756, H.C.A. 50/11 (transcripts, N.C. Archives).
62. Greene, "Posture of Hostility," *AASP* 87 (1977): 44–56; Greene, *Quest for Power*, 338, 181–82, 145–46; Beverly Bond, *The Quit-Rent System in the American Colonies* (New Haven, 1919), 300–317.
63. Patricia U. Bonomi, *A Factious People: Politics and Society in Colonial New York* (New York, 1971), 40, 55, passim; Richard Bushman, *From Puritan to Yankee: Character and the Social Order in Connecticut, 1690–1765* (New York, 1970), 122–34, 235–66; Oscar Zeichner, *Connecticut's Years of Controversy, 1750–1776* (Chapel Hill, 1949); Richard P. McCormick, *New Jersey: From Colony to State, 1609–1789* (Princeton, N.J., 1964), 58–79; Larry R. Gerlach, *Prologue to Independence: New Jersey in the Coming of the American Revolution* (New Brunswick, N.J., 1976), 23–36; David S. Lovejoy, *Rhode Island Politics and the American Revolution, 1760–1776* (Providence, 1958); Mack E. Thompson, "The Ward-Hopkins Controversy and the American Revolution in Rhode Island: An Interpretation," *WMQ*, 3d Ser., 16 (1959): 363–75.
64. [McCulloh] to Board of Trade, n.d., NCCR, 4:1216.
65. Johnston to Sec. of Board of Trade, Sept. 16, 1751, NCCR, 4:1076.

5. Patriotism Unmasked, 1755–1765

1. For background information on Dobbs, see Desmond Clarke, *Arthur Dobbs, Esquire, 1689–1765: Surveyor-General of Ireland, Prospector, and Governor of North Carolina* (Chapel Hill, 1957), 9–106. See also Caroline Robbins, *The Eighteenth-Century Commonwealthman: Studies in the Transmission, Development, and Circumstance of English Liberal Thought from the Restoration of Charles II until the War with the Thirteen Colonies* (New York, 1968), 149–52.
2. At the height of the north-south clash, Dobbs's land agent in North Carolina had written, "The Irregularities of our government is the only discouragement . . .

that deters men of considerable Fortunes to the northward from coming to our Country. They who can fully inspect into our proceedings . . . fear Impositions in taking up Lands." Matthew Rowan to Samuel Smith, Sept. 19, 1751, Dobbs Papers, reel 2.

3. Clarke, *Arthur Dobbs*, 31–35, 44–94.

4. Upper House Journals, Dec. 14, 1754, NCCR, 5:216; Dobbs to Earl of Granville, Jan. 3, 1755, Granville District Papers; Dobbs to Board of Trade, Dec. 19, 1754, NCCR, 5:154.

5. Dobbs to Board of Trade, Jan. 11, 1755, NCCR, 5:326–28; Jack P. Greene, *The Quest for Power: The Lower Houses of Assembly in the Southern Royal Colonies, 1689–1776* (Chapel Hill, 1963), 181–82.

6. Murray to James Abercromby, Feb. 26, 1755, Murray Letter Book, 1735–60, 298–99; Dobbs to Alexander McAuley, Mar. 17, 1755, Dobbs Papers, reel 2.

7. Lower House Journals, Jan. 14, 1755, NCCR, 5:310; Laws, NCSR, 25:274–95, 298–304.

8. Clarke, *Arthur Dobbs*, 105–6; Upper House Journals, Dec. 14, 18, 1754, NCCR, 5:215, 219–25; Laws, NCSR, 23:400; Dobbs to [?], Jan. 1, 1755, NCCR, 5:312–13.

9. Dobbs to Board of Trade, Feb. 8, 1755, NCCR, 5:332; Dobbs to Board of Trade, Oct. 28, 1755, NCCR, 5:439–40; Laws, NCSR, 23:422–24; Upper House Journals, May 16, 1757, NCCR, 5:831.

10. See Dobbs to Board of Trade, Oct. 28, 1755, NCCR, 5:440.

11. See Upper House Journals, Sept. 25, Oct. 15, 1755, Sept. 30, 1756, May 16, 1757, NCCR, 5:495–96, 519–20, 658–59, 830–31. Dobbs to Lord Loudon, Oct. 22, 1756, quoted in Louise B. Dunbar, "The Royal Governors in the Middle and Southern Colonies on the Eve of the Revolution: A Study in Imperial Personnel," in Richard B. Morris, ed., *The Era of the American Revolution: Studies Inscribed to Evarts Boutelle Greene* (New York, 1939), 248.

12. Murray to [William Houston], Mar. 25, 1740, in Nina Moore Tiffany, ed., *Letters of James Murray, Loyalist* (Boston, 1901), 61; S. Johnston, Jr., to Thomas Barker, Aug. 20, Feb. 8, 1766, Hayes Collection, reel 2, 45. See also Murray to Andrew Bennet, Sept. 5, 1741, Murray to John Murray, Nov. 10, 1750, in Tiffany, ed., *Murray Letters*, 49–50, 76; Murray to Bennet, [early 1750s], Murray Letter Book, 1735–60, 293; S. Johnston, Sr., to S. Johnston, Jr., Apr. 6, 1755, Hayes Collection, reel 2, 38; William Faris to [Dobbs], Feb. 18, 1750, Dobbs Papers, reel 2; George Pollock to Corbyn Morris, Aug. 1, 1761, Pollock Letter Book; S. Johnston, Jr., to Alexander Elmsley, June 10, 1771, Hayes Collection, reel 3, 83; Elmsley to S. Johnston, Jr., Apr. 6, June 13, 1772, Hayes Collection, reel 3, 84, 85; H. E. McCulloh to James Iredell, July 14, 1769, Iredell to Margaret Iredell, Oct. 3, 1771, Iredell to Francis Iredell, Sr., Oct. 22, 1772, in Don Higginbotham, ed., *The Papers of James Iredell* (Raleigh, 1976), 1:33, 80, 120; John Rutherfurd to William Adair, Mar. 3, 1773, Phillips Collection, 58–59; Josiah Martin to Earl of Dartmouth, Mar. 30, 1773, NCCR, 9:617.

13. Bernard Bailyn, *The Origins of American Politics* (New York, 1968), 72–80; Robert Dinwiddie to James Innes, Aug. 30, 1754, Dinwiddie to Granville, Sept. 23, 1754, in R. A. Brock, ed., *The Official Records of Robert Dinwiddie, Lieutenant-Governor of the Colony of Virginia, 1751–1758* (Virginia Historical Society, *Collections*, new series, III [Richmond, 1883]), 1:297, 331; Lower House Journals, Jan. 9, 1755, NCCR, 5:299; Dobbs to Board of Trade, Aug. 3,

1760, *NCCR*, 6:284–85; Dobbs to Board of Trade, Mar. 15, 1756, *NCCR*, 5:571.

14. *DAB*, s.v. "Waddell, Hugh"; Dobbs to Board of Trade, Aug. 3, 1760, *NCCR*, 6:282.

15. Dobbs to Secretary Fox, July 12, 1756, *NCCR*, 5:601; Dobbs to Board of Trade, Aug. 3, 1760, *NCCR*, 6:284–85.

16. Dobbs to Board of Trade, Aug. 3, 1760, *NCCR*, 6:283.

17. Dobbs to Board of Trade, Dec. 9, 1754, *NCCR*, 5:157.

18. Dobbs to Board of Trade, Oct. 28, 1755, *NCCR*, 5:440; William S. Price, Jr., " 'Men of Good Estates': Wealth among North Carolina's Royal Councillors," *NCHR* 49 (1972): 79.

19. Murray to Abercromby, Dec. 26, 1755, Murray Letter Book, 1735–60, 319; Commission for Edward Brice Dobbs, Oct. 26, 1758, *NCCR*, 5:963. Dobbs also showed solicitude for the North Carolina relation of an Irish friend, as he wrote another acquaintance in 1761: "I had a Letter some time ago from my friend Mrs. Ann: Cath: Graves to inquire about her Brother in Law Mr. Graves who was recommended to me here[.] All I could do for him was to give him a commission in the provincials and upon the Troops being broke my nephew Spaight made him Deputy to him as County Clerk in Cumberland County." Dobbs to McAuley, Feb. 9, 1761, Dobbs Papers, reel 3.

20. Price, "Men of Good Estates," *NCHR* 49 (1972): 79; Abstract of Letter from Dobbs to Earl of Halifax, Aug. 30, 1757, *Calendar of the Emmet Collection of Manuscripts etc. Relating to American History* (New York, 1900), 330; John Cannon, "Henry McCulloch and Henry McCulloh," *WMQ*, 3d Ser., 15 (1958): 72; Letters Patent, Dec. 6, 1754, H.C.A. 50/11 (transcripts, N.C. Archives); Charles G. Sellers, Jr., "Private Profits and British Colonial Policy: The Speculations of Henry McCulloh," *WMQ*, 3d Ser., 8 (1951): 547.

21. Murray to Abercromby, Dec. 26, 1755, Murray Letter Book, 1735–60, 320. See also Faris to Thomas Child, Apr. 7, 1756, Granville District Papers.

22. Lower House Journals, Sept. 30, 1756, *NCCR*, 5:689. Campbell was the brother-in-law of Alexander McCulloh and also acquired 12,500 acres from Henry. Dobbs to McAuley, Mar. 17, 1755, Dobbs Papers, reel 2; McCulloh land materials in the possession of George Stevenson, N.C. Archives.

23. Abercromby to Jones, Aug. 3, 1759, Abercromby to Swann, June 1, 1759, Abercromby Letter Book, 178, 144, Va. State Lib.

24. On this point, see Robert Zemsky, *Merchants, Farmers, and River Gods: An Essay on Eighteenth-Century American Politics* (Boston, 1971), 108–12.

25. Council Journals, Apr. 29, 1755, *NCCR*, 5:489–90; Council Journals, Oct. 9, 1755, *NCCR*, 5:493; Robert Jones, Jr., to Dobbs, July 6, 1756, *NCCR*, 5:590–92; James R. Caldwell, Jr., "A History of Granville County, North Carolina: The Preliminary Phase, 1746–1800" (Ph.D. diss., University of North Carolina, Chapel Hill, 1950), 65.

26. Council Journals, Dec. 14, 1757, *NCCR*, 5:827–28; Dobbs to Lords of Treasury, Dec. 26, 1757, *NCCR*, 5:939–43; Dobbs to Board of Trade, Dec. 27, 1757, *NCCR*, 5:945–48; Beverly Bond, *The Quit-Rent System in the American Colonies* (New Haven, 1919), 305–8.

27. Rutherfurd to Granville, May 22, 1758, *NCCR*, 5:958; Abercromby to Swann, Mar. 4, 1758, Abercromby Letter Book, 76, Va. State Lib.; Dobbs to Board of Trade, Dec. 27, 1757, *NCCR*, 5:948.

28. *N.C. Biog. Hist.*, 5:379; *DNCB*, s.v. "Starkey, John"; Greene, *Quest for Power*, 492; Dobbs to Board of Trade, Dec. 27, 1757, *NCCR*, 5:948–49.

29. Dobbs to Board of Trade, Dec. 27, 1757, *NCCR*, 5:948–49.
30. Lower House Journals, Dec. 22–23, 1758, *NCCR*, 5:1096, 1098–99; Dobbs to Board of Trade, May 18, 1759, Aug. 3, 1760, *NCCR*, 5:33, 297.
31. Upper House Journals, Sept. 25, 1755, *NCCR*, 5:497; Dobbs to McAuley, Mar. 17, 1755, Dobbs Papers, reel 2. See also Alexander McCulloh to Dobbs, Dec. 24, 1754, *NCCR*, 5:160–61.
32. Dobbs to Board of Trade, Jan. 19, 1760, *NCCR*, 6:217.
33. Board of Trade to Dobbs, June 1, Aug. 1, 1759, *NCCR*, 6:45, 55.
34. Dobbs to Board of Trade, Feb. 28, 1760, *NCCR*, 6:228; Lower House Journals, Apr. 29, May 5, 1760, *NCCR*, 6:373–74, 380–81.
35. Murray to John Rutherfurd, Jan. 23, 1759, Murray Letter Book, 1735–60, 405; Lower House Journals, Dec. 20, 1758, *NCCR*, 5:1087; Dobbs to Board of Trade, Jan. 22, 1759, *NCCR*, 6:1–3.
36. Dobbs to Board of Trade, Jan. 22, 1759, *NCCR*, 6:4.
37. Ibid., 3.
38. Michael G. Kammen, *A Rope of Sand: The Colonial Agents, British Politics, and the American Revolution* (Ithaca, N.Y., 1968), 323; Lower House Journals, Dec. 20, 1758, *NCCR*, 5:1087; Abercromby to Swann, June 1, 1759, Abercromby Letter Book, 145, Va. State Lib. See also Abercromby to Swann, May 13, 1757, July 20, 1759, Abercromby to Peter Randolph, July 28, 1759, Abercromby to Jones, Aug. 3, 1759, Abercromby Letter Book, 34, 166, 177, 178, Va. State Lib.
39. Upper House Journals, May 9, 1759, *NCCR*, 6:86–87; Dobbs to Board of Trade, with bill enclosed, May 18, 1759, Dobbs to Sec. Pitt, May 18, 1759, *NCCR*, 6:32–41.
40. Dobbs to Board of Trade, May 18, 1759, *NCCR*, 6:33; Abercromby to North Carolina Committee of Correspondence, July 20, 1759, May 10, 1760, Abercromby Letter Book, 167–68, 106a–7a, Va. State Lib.; Board of Trade to Dobbs, Aug. 1, 1759, *NCCR*, 6:54–55; Greene, *Quest for Power*, 100–101.
41. Order in Council, Apr. 14, 1759, *NCCR*, 6:28–29; Dobbs to Board of Trade, Sept. 11, 1759, *NCCR*, 6:56; Berry and Child to Board of Trade, Feb. 24, 1759, *NCCR*, 6:13–15; Board of Trade to King, Apr. 12, 1759, *NCCR*, 6:25–28.
42. Dobbs to Board of Trade, Sept. 11, 1759, Jan. 19, 1760, *NCCR*, 6:56–57, 216; Lower House Journals, Jan. 1–7, May 17, 19, 1760, *NCCR*, 6:185–95, 402–4; Dobbs to Board of Trade, May 28, 1760, *NCCR*, 6:246.
43. Instructions to Dobbs, June 17, 1754, *NCCR*, 5:1123–24; Dobbs to Board of Trade, May 28, 1760, *NCCR*, 6:246.
44. Privy Council Journals, Dec. 18, 1730, in William L. Grant and James Munro, eds., *Acts of the Privy Council of England, Colonial Series* (London, 1908–12), 3:267; "Narrative of Proceedings, concerning the Earl of Granville's Property in Carolina, etc.," [1744?], Granville District Papers. For Carteret, see *DNB*, s.v. "Carteret, John"; Basil Williams, *Carteret and Newcastle: A Contrast in Contemporaries* (Hamden, Conn., 1966).
45. Carteret to Newcastle, Jan. 21, 1740, Add. MSS, 32693, 37–40.
46. Williams, *Carteret and Newcastle*, 122–23; "Narrative of Proceedings," [1744?], Granville District Papers.
47. E. Merton Coulter, "The Granville District," *JSHP* 13 (1913): 37–38.
48. Petition of John Lord Carteret to Privy Council, Dec. 18, 1729, Granville District Papers; Granville District Grant, Sept. 17, 1744, *NCCR*, 5:655–63.
49. "Narrative of Proceedings," [1744?], Granville District Papers; Granville Loyalist Claim, A.O. 12/36, 61–73, 13/118, 284; Johnston to [Bishop of Worcester?], Dec. 3, 1743, Historical Manuscripts Commission, *Report on the*

Laing Manuscripts Preserved in the University of Edinburgh (London, 1925), 2:336.

50. Johnston to Lord Wilmington, June 2, 1737, *Wilmington Manuscripts* (Historical Manuscripts Commission, Eleventh *Report*, Pt. IV), 3:264; Allen to [James Abercromby], Abercromby Letterbook, 1743–51, N.C. Archives.

51. Byrd to [Gabriel Johnston], [1735?], Byrd to Carteret, Apr. 22, 1740, in Marion Tinling, ed., *The Correspondence of the Three William Byrds of Westover, Virginia, 1684–1776* (Charlottesville, Va., 1977), 2:450, 544–45.

52. Instructions from Granville to Agents, Dec. 10, 1751, A.O. 13/120, 26–35.

53. Ibid.

54. Granville District Land Grants, Secretary of State Papers, N.C. Archives; Instructions from Granville to Agents, Dec. 10, 1751, A.O. 13/120, 26–35.

55. For evidence of proprietary advertising, see Instructions from Granville to Francis Corbin, Nov. 14, 1744, North Carolina Colonial Court Records, Miscellaneous Papers, 1677–1775, N.C. Archives; Petitions from Orange, Rowan, and Anson Counties to Granville, [1756], Granville District Papers.

56. Granville Loyalist Claim, A.O. 12/36, 61–73.

57. Land Entry Books, 1750–70, Secretary of State Papers, N.C. Archives.

58. Granville District Land Grants, Secretary of State Papers, N.C. Archives; Miscellaneous Granville District Land Deeds, Land Grant Office, North Carolina Department of State, Raleigh.

59. Husband to Granville, [1755], in A. Roger Ekirch, " 'A New Government of Liberty': Hermon Husband's Vision of Backcountry North Carolina, 1755," *WMQ*, 3d Ser., 34 (1977): 641; "Col. [Robert] Halton's Paper concerning My Lord Granville's Estate in North Carolina," Jan. 11, 1746, Granville District Papers; Deposition of Thomas McKnight, A.O. 12/36, 79; Martin to Samuel Martin, Mar. 26, 1773, Granville District Papers. See also Deposition of Eli Branson, A.O. 12/36, 78. The only discernible reluctance to pay quitrents occurred when backcountry settlers requested a temporary suspension because of high taxes and other financial hardships during the French and Indian War. Petitions from Orange, Rowan, and Anson Counties to Granville, [1756], Husband to Granville, 1756, Granville District Papers.

A more systematic appraisal of the impact of proprietary land conditions on the material well-being of settlers would be difficult to make. Many other factors would have to be weighed, such as the French and Indian War, and environmental and economic conditions; in addition, the Granville District's relatively brief existence, extending only up to the American Revolution, makes an analysis of mobility patterns problematic at best. On the other hand, a suggestive point is that the ability of proprietary settlers in the backcountry to acquire slaves was quite comparable to that of settlers on nearby crown lands. As of 1765, black taxables constituted 17.0 percent of Orange County's taxable population, whereas they made up 18.3 percent of the taxable population of Anson County, which lay in the royal half of the colony just to the south of Orange. Tax List, 1765, *NCCR*, 7:145.

60. Lord Adam Gordon, "Journal of an Officer's Travels in America, and the West Indies, 1764–1765," in Newton D. Mereness, ed., *Travels in the American Colonies* (New York, 1916), 402; Rowland Berthoff and John M. Murrin, "Feudalism, Communalism, and the Yeoman Freeholder: The American Revolution considered as a Social Accident," in Stephen G. Kurtz and James H. Hutson, eds., *Essays on the American Revolution* (Chapel Hill, 1973), 256–88.

61. Granville to Francis Corbin and James Innes, May 10, 1752, Granville District Papers; Letter of Attorney from Granville, Aug. 8, 1754, *NCCR*, 6:542; Council Journals, June 28, 1746, *NCCR*, 4:810–11. For Granville's alleged negligence, see, for instance, R. D. W. Connor, *History of North Carolina* (Chicago, 1919), 1:223; Bond, *Quit-Rent System*, 78; "Prefatory Notes," *NCCR*, 5:lv–lvi; Charles L. Raper, *North Carolina: A Study in English Colonial Government* (New York, 1904), 112–13.

62. Johnston to Granville, May 8, 1748, Granville District Papers.

63. Johnston to Granville, July 15, 1749, Mar. 13, 1750, Granville District Papers.

64. Instructions from Granville to Agents, Dec. 10, 1751, A.O. 13/120, 26–35.

65. Letter of Attorney from Granville, Aug. 8, 1754, *NCCR*, 6:541–42; Instructions from Granville to Corbin, Nov. 14, 1744, N.C. Colonial Court Records, Misc. Papers, 1677–1775; John Campbell to Granville, May 13, 1749, Granville District Papers; Child to Board of Trade, Jan. 8, 1753, *NCCR*, 5:15; E. Alfred Jones, *American Members of the Inns of Court* (London, 1924), 46; *DNCB*, s.v. "Child, Thomas."

66. Johnston to Granville, Mar. 5, 1751, Granville District Papers; Letter of Attorney from Granville, Aug. 8, 1754, *NCCR*, 6:542; Child to Board of Trade, Jan. 8, 1753, *NCCR*, 5:15–16; Dobbs to Board of Trade, Aug. 3, 1760, *NCCR*, 6:293.

67. Instructions from Granville to Agents, Dec. 10, 1751, A.O. 13/120, 26–35.

68. Johnston to Granville, Mar. 5, 1751, Granville to Innes, Feb. 25, 1753, Child to Corbin, Oct. 17, 1753, Granville District Papers; Dobbs to Board of Trade, Aug. 3, 1760, *NCCR*, 6:293.

69. Granville to Corbin and Wheatley, Aug. 8, 1754, Dobbs to Granville, Dec. 29, 1755, Granville to Corbin and Wheatley, Apr. 13, 1756, Granville District Papers; Dobbs to Board of Trade, Aug. 3, 1760, *NCCR*, 6:293.

70. Instructions from Granville to Agents, Dec. 10, 1751, A.O. 13/120, 26–35.

71. Granville to Corbin and Wheatley, Apr. 18, 1756, Granville District Papers; Instructions from Granville to Agents, Sept. 1, 1756, N.C. Colonial Court Records, Misc. Papers, 1677–1775; Dobbs to Child, Feb. 5, 1759, Granville to Corbin and Innes, Nov. 15, 1751, May 10, Dec. 28, 1752, Granville to Corbin, Jan. 16, 1752, Feb. 25, 1753, Granville to Corbin and Wheatley, Aug. 8, 1754, Granville District Papers.

72. Johnston to Granville, Mar. 13, 1750, Granville District Papers; "An Account of Money Received in England from Carolina," 1746–64, A.O. 13/120, 310–13; Deposition of H.[E.?] McCulloh, A.O. 12/36, 75–76, 79.

73. Hugh Finlay to A. Todd, Mar. 23, 1774, Granville District Papers; Lower House Journals, Dec. 22, 1758, *NCCR*, 5:1088–94; Dobbs to Granville, Dec. 29, 1755, Granville District Papers; Coulter, "Granville District," *JSHP* 13 (1913): 41–43. Husband quoted in Ekirch, "New Government of Liberty," *WMQ*, 3d Ser., 34 (1977): 640. For Carter, see also Faris to Child, Apr. 7, 1756, Granville District Papers; Robert W. Ramsey, "James Carter: Founder of Salisbury," *NCHR* 39 (1962): 131–39.

74. Granville to Corbin and Wheatley, Apr. 18, 1756, Granville District Papers.

75. Dobbs to Child, Feb. 5, 1759, Granville District Papers. See also Dobbs to Granville, Dec. 29, 1755, Granville District Papers; George Pollock to Granville, [1761?], Pollock Letter Book.

76. Granville to Corbin and Wheatley, Apr. 18, 1756, Granville District Papers.

77. Dobbs to Board of Trade, Aug. 3, 1760, *NCCR*, 6:293.

78. Instructions from Granville to Agents, Sept. 1, 1756, N.C. Colonial Court Records, Misc. Papers, 1677–1775; *DNCB*, s.v. "Bodley, Joshua."
79. Sellers, "Private Profits," *WMQ*, 3d Ser., 8 (1951): 545; Granville to Corbin and Innes, Dec. 28, 1752, Child to Corbin, Oct. 17, 1753, Granville District Papers.
80. McCulloh to Board of Trade, received Jan. 1, 1754, *NCCR*, 5:79–81; Council Journals, Oct. 13, 1755, *NCCR*, 5:493–94.
81. McCulloh's Proposals, Sept. 27, 1755, Granville's Concessions, Dec. 13, 1755, *NCCR*, 5:624–26; Granville-McCulloh Agreement, Dec. 30, 1755, Phillips Collection; Granville to Corbin and Wheatley, Apr. 18, 1756, Granville District Papers.
82. Letter of Attorney, July 19, 1757, *NCCR*, 5:779–82; McCulloh to Granville, Nov. 25, 1758, [Dec. 1758?], Granville Papers, 1756–61, William L. Clements Library, University of Michigan, Ann Arbor.
83. Council Journals, Sept. 26, 1751, Apr. 9, 1753, *NCCR*, 4:1245, 5:32; Granville to Corbin and Wheatley, June 30, 1755, Dobbs to Granville, Oct. 30, 1756, Granville District Papers.
84. Dobbs to Child, Feb. 5, 1759, Dobbs to Granville, Dec. 29, 1755, Granville District Papers; Council Journals, Dec. 4, 23, 1758, *NCCR*, 5:996–98.
85. General Court Warrant, William Barnet vs. James Carter, New Bern, Sept. 12, 1753, General Court Warrant, Samuel Wilkins vs. James Carter, New Bern, Sept. 12, 1753, General Court Records, Civil Papers, N.C. Archives; District Court Attachment, Thomas Robenson vs. James Carter, Salisbury, [1755?], Salisbury District Court, Miscellaneous Papers, N.C. Archives.
86. Lower House Journals, Dec. 13, 1754, Jan. 9, 1755, *NCCR*, 5:232–33, 299–300.
87. Finlay to Todd, Mar. 23, 1774, Granville District Papers; Hugh Talmage Lefler and Paul Wager, eds., *Orange County, 1752–1952* (Chapel Hill, 1953), 326–27; John L. Cheney, Jr., ed., *North Carolina Government, 1585–1974: A Narrative and Statistical Analysis* (Raleigh, 1975), 44–46; Granville Grants; List of Taxables, 1754, *NCCR*, 5:320; C. B. Alexander, "The Training of Richard Caswell," *NCHR* 23 (1946): 13–31; *N.C. Biog. Hist.*, 3:164. Husband quoted in Ekirch, "New Government of Liberty," *WMQ*, 3d Ser., 34 (1977): 640.
88. Dobbs to Board of Trade, Aug. 3, 1760, *NCCR*, 6:294; Dobbs to Child, Feb. 5–6, 1759, Granville District Papers; Lower House Journals, Nov. 25, Dec. 5, 22, 1758, *NCCR*, 5:1042–43, 1057–58, 1088–94; Dobbs to Board of Trade, Aug. 3, 1760, *NCCR*, 6:294.
89. Dobbs to Child, Feb. 5–6, 1759, Granville District Papers; Dobbs to Board of Trade, Aug. 3, 1760, *NCCR*, 6:294–95; Articles between Corbin, Bodley, and the Inhabitants of the Granville District, Jan. 26, 1759, Granville Land Office Records, 1744–63, N.C. Archives; Halifax County Bond, Jan. 27, 1759, Miscellaneous Granville District Papers, N.C. Archives; Statement of Charges against Alexander McCulloh et al., Oct. 1759, N.C. Colonial Court Records, Civil Papers, Supreme Court, 1759, 3, N.C. Archives.
90. District Court Warrant for Alexander McCulloh et al., Edenton, Apr. 25, 1759, N.C. Colonial Court Records, Civil Papers, Supreme Court, 1759, 3; Robert Jones, Jr., to Dobbs, July 6, 1756, *NCCR*, 5:590–92; Governor's Office, Lists of Taxables, Militia, and Magistrates, 1754–70, n.d., N.C. Archives; Margaret M. Hofman, *Abstracts of Deeds: Edgecombe Precinct, Edgecombe County, North Carolina, 1732 through 1758* (Weldon, N.C., 1969); Will of Barnaby Lane, May 30, 1762, Halifax County, Record of Wills, 1759–79; Zae Hargett

Gwynn, ed., *Abstracts of the Wills and Estate Records of Granville County, North Carolina, 1746–1808* (Rocky Mount, N.C., 1973); Granville Grants.

91. Statement of Charges by Corbin against McCulloh et al., Oct. 1759, N.C. Colonial Court Records, Civil Papers, Supreme Court, 1759, 3. Governor Dobbs asserted the innocence of McCulloh, a close associate, to the Board of Trade. Dobbs to Board of Trade, Aug. 3, 1760, NCCR, 6:299–300. But see also James Moir to Sec. of S.P.G., Apr. 6, 1763, NCCR, 6:979.

92. Johnston to Board of Trade, received June 27, 1750, NCCR, 4:1088; Commission from Granville, Apr. 10, 1759, NCCR, 6:21–22.

93. Dobbs to Board of Trade, Aug. 3, 1760, NCCR, 6:295; Council Journals, May 14, 1759, NCCR, 6:79–80; Lower House Journals, May 15, 18, 1759, NCCR, 6:106–7, 113.

94. George Pollock to Bridgen & Waller, Mar. 15, 1761, Pollock Letter Book; Dobbs to Board of Trade, Aug. 3, 1760, NCCR, 6:295. See also John Hamilton's Deposition, A.O. 12/36, 76–77.

95. Commission from Granville, Apr. 10, 1759, NCCR, 6:21–22.

96. Order in Council, June 26, 1759, NCCR, 6:50–51; Dobbs to Board of Trade, Jan. 19, 1760, NCCR, 6:217.

97. Abercromby to Swann, June 1, 1759, Abercromby Letter Book, 145, Va. State Lib.

98. "Account of Money Received in England from Carolina," 1746–65, A.O. 13/120, 310–13; Depositions of H.[E.?] McCulloh, Robert Palmer, and William Tryon, A.O. 12/36, 75–76, 79. Upon inspecting security bonds and other papers received from Child, an attorney for the Granville estate concluded that "none of the Bonds" were "right" or "Capable of being carried into Execution in case of Breach." "An Extract from Mr. Heaton's Bill," entry of Feb. 11, 1764, A.O. 13/120, 308–9.

99. Murray to Abercromby, Feb. 26, 1755, Murray Letter Book, 1735–60, 299; Lower House Journals, Dec. 27, 1754, NCCR, 5:256; S. Johnston, Jr., to Barker, [April?] 10, 1759, Hayes Collection, reel 2, 28.

100. Letter of Appointment, Oct. 25, 1759, Granville Land Office Records, 1744–63; Dobbs to Board of Trade, May 28, 1760, NCCR, 6:246–47; Letter of Attorney from Granville to Robert Jones, Jr., Apr. 6, 1761, NCCR, 6:546–49; Charles Berry to Dobbs, May 22, 1760, Child to Dobbs, May 20, 1760, NCCR, 6:251–56.

101. Dobbs to Board of Trade, May 28, Aug. 3, 1760, NCCR, 6:245, 248–50, 279; Spaight to Board of Trade, July 21, 1760, NCCR, 6:269–70.

102. Dobbs to Board of Trade, Aug. 3, 1760, NCCR, 6:280; Murray to Jean and Ann Bennet, Aug. 4, 1760, Murray Letter Book, 1760–61; Pollock to Morris, Aug. 1, 1761, Pollock Letter Book.

103. Dobbs to Board of Trade, May 28, 1760, NCCR, 6:248; Lower House Journals, May 23, 1760, NCCR, 6:409–14.

104. Lower House Journals, May 23, 1760, NCCR, 6:413; Swann to Granville, May 23, 1760, Granville District Papers; Dobbs to Board of Trade, May 28, 1760, NCCR, 6:248–49; Joseph Albert Ernst, *Money and Politics in America, 1755–1775: A Study in the Currency Act of 1764 and the Political Economy of Revolution* (Chapel Hill, 1973), 82.

105. Dobbs to Board of Trade, May 28, 1760, NCCR, 6:243–51; Lower House Journals, May 26–27, 1760, NCCR, 6:427–38; Dobbs to Pitt, May 29, 1760, NCCR, 6:257.

106. Upper House Journals, June 30–July 14, 1760, *NCCR*, 6:438–46; Dobbs to Board of Trade, July 21, 1760, *NCCR*, 6:267–68.
107. Dobbs to Board of Trade, Aug. 3, 1760, *NCCR*, 6:279–310.
108. Petition of Anthony Bacon to Privy Council, n.d., Sharpe Papers.
109. Advertisement by Child, Sept. 25, 1759, Granville Land Office Records, 1744–63; Articles of Agreement between Granville and Henry McCulloh, Apr. 17, 1761, *NCCR*, 6:573–78.
110. Board of Trade to Dobbs, Dec. 15, 1763, *NCCR*, 6:998; Dobbs to Board of Trade, Aug. 3, Dec. 12, 1760, Dec. 1761, *NCCR*, 6:304–7, 323–24, 598–99.
111. Greene, *Quest for Power*, 240–41.
112. Ibid., 340–41.
113. Ibid., 277.
114. Dobbs to Board of Trade, Feb. 23, 1763, *NCCR*, 6:967; Greene, *Quest for Power*, 78–79.
115. S. Johnston, Jr., to [Barker], n.d., Hayes Collection, reel 3, 95; *DNCB*, s.v. "Barker, Thomas." See also S. Johnston, Jr., to [Barker], Feb. 8, Aug. 20, Dec. 9, 1766, [Jan.?] 1768, Hayes Collection, reel 2, 45.
116. *DNCB*, s.v. "Child, Thomas"; Child to Granville, Sept. 11, 1761, Norcross Collection, Mass. Hist. Soc.; S. Johnston, Jr., to [Barker], [1762], Hayes Collection, reel 3, 95.
117. S. Johnston, Jr., to [Barker], Dec. 28, 1762, Hayes Collection, reel 2, 45; Council Journals, Feb. 23, Apr. 23, 24, 1764, *NCCR*, 6:1067, 1072–73; Council Papers, 1761–65, Governor's Office, N.C. Archives; Halifax County Miscellaneous Papers, 1761–1927, N.C. Archives.
118. Laws, *NCSR*, 23:495–97, 503–4, 531–34.
119. Lower House Journals, Apr. 9, 1761, *NCCR*, 6:678; Dobbs to Board of Trade, Dec. 1761, *NCCR*, 6:598.
120. "Prefatory Notes," *NCCR*, 6:viii.
121. S. Johnston, Jr., to [Barker], Dec. 28, 1762, Hayes Collection, reel 2, 45.
122. Dobbs to Board of Trade, Mar. 29, 1764, *NCCR*, 6:1035–36; James Reed to Sec. of S.P.G., Dec. 26, 1763, *NCCR*, 6:999.
123. Tryon quoted in William S. Powell, ed., "Tryon's 'Book' on North Carolina," *NCHR* 34 (1957): 413; Upper House Journals, May 3, 1765, *NCCR*, 7:41; [Gordon], "Officer's Travels in America," in Mereness, ed., *Travels in the American Colonies*, 402–3.
124. James Davis quoted in Alonzo Thomas Dill, Jr., "Eighteenth Century New Bern: A History of the Town and Craven County, 1700–1800, Part V, Political and Commercial Rise of New Bern," *NCHR* 23 (1946): 77–78. See also G. Moulton to [?], Jan. 23, 1773, Add. MSS, 22677, 75. Eight years after the assembly established the governor's residence at New Bern in 1766, Samuel Johnston, Jr., wrote one of the town's former supporters: "The Cape Fear people can hardly find in their hearts to forgive you for fixing the Governor's House at New Bern." Johnston to Elmsley, Sept. 23, 1774, *NCCR*, 9:1071.
125. Martin to Dartmouth, Sept. 1, 1774, *NCCR*, 9:1053. Regional biases also surfaced during the Revolution. While the British were threatening the Cape Fear, William Hooper wrote James Iredell of Edenton: "You remember what you and Mr. [Samuel] Johnston have always said when I expressed my fears for Wilmington—Cui bono? What could the enemy get by it? To rob the pine trees, and bear away the sandhills? How ill we apply sayings when they show our own weak side and fit ourselves—but I forgive you, local prejudices are unaccountably strong." Hooper to Iredell, June 15, 1779, in Higginbotham,

ed., *Iredell Papers*, 2:94.

126. Greene, *Quest for Power*, 11, 45, passim; Hugh T. Lefler and William S. Powell, *Colonial North Carolina: A History* (New York, 1973), 128. See also Raper, *North Carolina Colonial Government*, 100, 219–20, passim; Connor, *History of North Carolina*, 1:237–38.

127. Dobbs to Board of Trade, Aug. 3, 1760, NCCR, 6:279; Florence Cook, "Procedure in the North Carolina Assembly, 1731–1770," *NCHR* 8 (1931): 265.

128. Laws, NCSR, 23:402–17, 443–44, 477–78, 512–14, 523–26, 548, 613–14, 639–49, 25:313–19, 378–87, 479; Lower House Journals, Nov. 29, 1744, June 13, 1746, Jan. 9, 1755, Oct. 11, 1755, Nov. 6, 1764, NCCR, 4:744–46, 823–25, 5:297–300, 547–49, 6:1269.

129. Dobbs to Abercromby, Dec. 28, 1757, NCCR, 5:789; Murray to James Abercromby, June 30, 1751, Murray Letter Book, 1735–60, 250.

130. Laws, NCSR, 23:675, 801, 849, 25:266–67, 349, 455–56, 519d–520.

131. "An Estimate of Monies emitted and raised in the Province of North Carolina from the year 1748—Shewing to what purposes the same was applyed, by what Taxes sunk, etc.," [1767], NCCR, 8:213–14.

132. A more evident reason why Barker was not enthusiastic about the clerkship was that "it is great odds whether it would be worth accepting." Barker to S. Johnston, Jr., Oct. 1, 1755, Hayes Collection, 1748–1806 (transcripts, N.C. Archives).

133. Dobbs to Board of Trade, Aug. 3, 1760, NCCR, 6:308–9.

134. Dobbs to Board of Trade, Jan. 22, 1759, Aug. 3, Dec. 12, 1760, NCCR, 6:4, 304–5, 309, 320; Dobbs to Lords of Treasury, Dec. 26, 1757, NCCR, 5:943. See also Lower House Journals, Dec. 22, 1758, NCCR, 5:1096.

135. Kammen, *Colonial Agents*, 25.

136. "Public Debts due in this Province," [1770], NCCR, 8:278–81; *N.C. Gaz.*, New Bern, Mar. 24, 1775; Tryon to Earl of Shelburne, July 4, 1767, NCCR, 7:497; Marvin L. Michael Kay, "Provincial Taxes in North Carolina during the Administrations of Dobbs and Tryon," *NCHR* 42 (1965): 441; Robert A. Becker, "Revolution and Reform: An Interpretation of Southern Taxation, 1763 to 1783," *WMQ*, 3d Ser., 32 (1975): 419–20. See also Julian P. Boyd, "The Sheriff in Colonial North Carolina," *NCHR* 5 (1928): 161–72.

137. For a discussion of elite development and corruption, see Colin Leys, "New States and the Concept of Corruption," in Arnold J. Heidenheimer, ed., *Political Corruption: Readings in Comparative Analysis* (New York, 1970), 341–45.

138. Jackson Turner Main, "Government by the People: The American Revolution and the Democratization of the Legislatures," *WMQ*, 3d Ser., 23 (1966): 396, 402, 19n, 403.

139. See Bibliographical Essay.

140. Main, "Government," *WMQ*, 3d Ser., 23 (1966): 396, 402, 19n, 403.

141. *N.C. Biog. Hist.*, 5:379; "Thomas Barker," in J. R. B. Hathaway, ed., *The North Carolina Historical & Genealogical Register* 1 (1900): 515; Blackwell Pierce Robinson, "Willie Jones of Halifax," *NCHR* 18 (1914): 1–2; Thomas C. Parramore, "The Saga of 'The Bear' and the 'Evil Genius,'" *Bulletin of the History of Medicine* 42 (1968): 323–24. For assembly leaders in Virginia, see Jack P. Greene, "Foundations of Political Power in the Virginia House of Burgesses, 1720–1776," *WMQ*, 3d Ser., 10 (1959): 489.

142. See Bibliographical Essay.

143. See, for instance, Council Journals, Mar. 3, 6, 1739, Mar. 16, Nov. 28, 1743,

Feb. 29, Mar. 6, Dec. 4, 1744, Apr. 5, 1745, June 28, 1746, Mar. 28, Sept. 29, 1750, Sept. 27, Oct. 5, 1751, *NCCR*, 4:344–45, 626, 650, 675–77, 682–83, 713, 760, 814, 1032, 1050, 1247, 1252; Presentment against William Luten, Mar. 1746, General Court Records, Criminal Papers, 1746; Lower House Journals, June 13, 1746, *NCCR*, 4:825; Onslow County Court Minutes, entry of July 1747, N.C. Archives; Board of Trade to Duke of Bedford, Feb. 20, 1749, *NCCR*, 4:932; Moir to Sec. of S.P.G., Apr. 16, 1750, S.P.G., B MSS, 18, 179; Spangenberg Diary, entry of Sept. 15, 1752, *Moravian Records*, 1:37; Dobbs to Board of Trade, Dec. 19, 1754, *NCCR*, 5:156–57; Boyd, "Sheriff in North Carolina," *NCHR* 5 (1928): 161–72; H. McCulloh to Board of Trade, received June 2, 1751, *NCCR*, 4:1146–49.

144. Byrd to Johann Rudolph Ochs, July 15, 1736, in Tinling, ed., *Byrd Correspondence*, 2:491.
145. See Heidenheimer, ed., *Political Corruption*, 483.
146. David H. Bayley, "The Effects of Corruption in a Developing Nation," in Heidenheimer, ed., *Political Corruption*, 529.

6. "Justice to Poor Carolina," 1766–1771

1. Arnold J. Heidenheimer, ed., *Political Corruption: Readings in Comparative Analysis* (New York, 1970), 485.
2. For biographical information on Tryon, see *N.C. Biog. Hist.*, 1:471–73.
3. *N.C. Gaz.*, Wilmington, Nov. 27, 1765, Feb. 12, 26, 1766, *NCCR*, 7:127–30, 168a–168f; Tryon to Secretary [Henry] Conway, Feb. 25, 1766, *NCCR*, 7:169–74. See also Lawrence Lee, "Days of Defiance: Resistance to the Stamp Act in the Lower Cape Fear," *NCHR* 43 (1966):186–202; Donna J. Spindel, "Law and Disorder: The North Carolina Stamp Act Crisis," *NCHR* 57 (1980): 1–16; Hugh T. Lefler and William S. Powell, *Colonial North Carolina: A History* (New York, 1973), 244–50; Edmund S. and Helen M. Morgan, *The Stamp Act Crisis: Prologue to Revolution* (New York, 1965), 202, 211–13, 233, 256–58; Lindley S. Butler, *North Carolina and the Coming of the Revolution, 1763–1776* (Raleigh, 1976), 14–25; Pauline Maier, *From Resistance to Revolution: Colonial Radicals and the Development of American Opposition to Britain, 1765–1776* (New York, 1972), 84, 300–301.
4. Jack P. Greene, *The Quest for Power: The Lower Houses of Assembly in the Southern Royal Colonies, 1689–1776* (Chapel Hill, 1963), 45, 242, 416–20; Jackson Turner Main, *The Upper House in Revolutionary America, 1763–1788* (Madison, Wis., 1967), 23–28. For Tryon's concern over corruption, see, for instance, Upper House Journals, Nov. 4, 1766, *NCCR*, 7:294; Tryon to Earl of Shelburne, July 4, 1767, Mar. 7, 1768, *NCCR*, 7:497, 694; Upper House Journals, Nov. 6, 1769, Dec. 5, 1770, *NCCR*, 8:105, 282–83.
5. Tryon to Board of Trade, Aug. 2, Feb. 1, 1766, *NCCR*, 7:248, 160; Tryon to Conway, Apr. 28, 1766, *NCCR*, 7:200; Tryon to Shelburne, Mar. 14, 1768, *NCCR*, 7:697; George Micklejohn to Daniel Burton, Sept. 14, 1767, S.P.G., B MSS, 5, 199.
6. Alonzo T. Dill, *Governor Tryon and His Palace* (Chapel Hill, 1955), 110–15; Letter from "A Friend to the Province," *S.C. and Am. Genl. Gaz.*, Aug. 26,

1771; Tryon to Shelburne, Jan. 31, 1767, *NCCR*, 7:431; John Whiting to [Ezra Stiles?], Apr. 8, 1767, Nash Papers; G. Moulton to [?], Jan. 23, 1773, Add. MSS, 22677, 75; Zubly Diary, entry of Mar. 31, 1770, quoted in Harold E. Davis, *The Fledgling Province: Social and Cultural Life in Colonial Georgia, 1733–1776* (Chapel Hill, 1976), 62, 18n.

7. Samuel Johnston, Jr., to [Thomas Barker], [Jan. 1768], Hayes Collection, reel 2, 45; Whiting to [Stiles?], Apr. 8, 1767, Nash Papers; Upper House Journals, Nov. 4, 1766, *NCCR*, 7:295; Lower House Journals, Dec. 7, 1767, *NCCR*, 7:552; Tryon to Shelburne, July 8, 1767, *NCCR*, 7:501.

8. Letter from New Bern, May 22, 1771, *Pa. Jour.*, June 20, 1771.

9. Regulators' Advertisement, No. 5, Mar. 22, 1768, *Reg. Doc.*, 79.

10. For a detailed narrative of the Regulator disturbances, see John S. Bassett, "The Regulators of North Carolina, 1765–1771," *Annual Report of the American Historical Association for the Year 1894* (Washington, D.C., 1895), 141–212. See also "Introduction," *Reg. Doc.*, xv–xxvi; Marvin L. Michael Kay, "The North Carolina Regulation, 1766–1776: A Class Conflict," in Alfred F. Young, ed., *The American Revolution: Explorations in the History of American Radicalism* (DeKalb, Ill., 1976), 84–103.

11. "Extract of a letter from an officer . . . to a Gentleman in Brunswick," May 18, 1771, *Cape Fear Mercury*, Wilmington, May 29, 1771, in *Conn. Cour.*, July 16, 1771.

12. James Penn Whittenburg, "Backwoods Revolutionaries: Social Context and Constitutional Theories of the North Carolina Regulators, 1765–1771" (Ph.D. diss., University of Georgia, 1974), 281; James P. Whittenburg, "Planters, Merchants, and Lawyers: Social Change and the Origins of the North Carolina Regulation," *WMQ*, 3d Ser., 34 (1977): 219–20; Communication from Mr. Whittenburg, ibid., 694–95.

13. Granville Grants; Orange County Record of Deeds, 1755–1800, N.C. Archives; Misc. Granville Deeds; Whittenburg, "Backwoods Revolutionaries," 121. Following the battle at Alamance, Governor Tryon ordered the destruction of Husband's "Plantation," which reportedly possessed "about fifty Acres of as fine Wheat as perhaps ever grew, with Clover Meadows equal to any in the northern Colonies." Purdie and Dixon's *Va. Gaz.*, July 4, 1771. For biographical information on Husband, see A. Roger Ekirch, "'A New Government of Liberty': Hermon Husband's Vision of Backcountry North Carolina, 1755," *WMQ*, 3d Ser., 34 (1977): 632–34; Mary Elinor Lazenby, *Herman Husband: A Story of His Life* (Washington, D.C., 1940).

14. Granville Grants; Orange County Deeds; Whittenburg, "Backwoods Revolutionaries," 194–95.

15. Anson County Tax List, 1763, Secretary of State, Tax Lists, 1720–1839, N.C. Archives; "Abstract of Patents for Lands Granted in His Majesty's Part of the Province of North Carolina," 1707–68, C.O. 5/319.

16. *Cape Fear Mercury*, Dec. 29, 1773; Whittenburg, "Backwoods Revolutionaries," 122.

17. Whittenburg, "Backwoods Revolutionaries," 195.

18. Granville Grants; Land Warrants, Secretary of State, Orange County, 1755–1879, N.C. Archives.

19. Granville County Tax List, 1769, Secretary of State, Tax Lists, 1720–1839;

Granville Grants; Misc. Granville Deeds. Two Moravians remarked in 1778 that Person "has an unusually pretty and large farm, and about one hundred negroes." "Report of the Brn. Brezel and Heckewälder . . . ," 1778, *Moravian Records*, 3:1427.

20. *Pa. Jour.*, July 11, 1771; Letter from New Bern, Oct. 5, 1770, Purdie and Dixon's *Va. Gaz.*, Oct. 25, 1770, Purdie and Dixon's *Va. Gaz.*, Oct. 18, 1770, *Reg. Doc.*, 251, 268.

21. George R. Adams, "The Carolina Regulators: A Note on Changing Interpretations," *NCHR* 49 (1972): 346–47.

22. Bassett, "Regulators of North Carolina," *Annual Report of A.H.A., 1894*, 141–212.

23. Among the more recent examples are "Introduction," *Reg. Doc.*, xv–xxvii; Lefler and Powell, *Colonial North Carolina*, 217–39; Edmund S. Morgan, "Conflict and Consensus in the American Revolution," in Stephen G. Kurtz and James H. Hutson, eds., *Essays on the American Revolution* (Chapel Hill, 1973), 297–99.

24. Elisha P. Douglass, *Rebels and Democrats: The Struggle for Equal Rights and Majority Rule during the American Revolution* (Chapel Hill, 1955), 97, 71–100.

25. M. L. M. Kay, "An Analysis of a British Colony in Late Eighteenth Century America in the Light of Current American Historiographical Controversy," *AJPH* 11 (1965): 170–84; Kay, "North Carolina Regulation," in Young, ed., *Explorations in American Radicalism*, 71–123; Kay, "Regulation in North Carolina."

26. Whittenburg, "Backwoods Revolutionaries," and "Planters, Merchants, and Lawyers," *WMQ*, 3d Ser., 34 (1977): 215–38.

27. The coastal plain counties were Beaufort, Bertie, Bladen, Carteret, Chowan, Currituck, Craven, Duplin, Edgecombe, Hyde, Johnston, New Hanover, Onslow, Pasquotank, Perquimans, and Tyrrell. "Public Debts due in this Province . . . ," [1770], *NCCR*, 8:278–81. For the ways and means of corruption in backcountry North Carolina, see Kay, "Regulation in North Carolina"; Douglass, *Rebels and Democrats*, 75–80; Rev. E. W. Carruthers, *Revolutionary Incidents: And Sketches of Character, Chiefly in the "Old North State"* (Philadelphia, 1854), 20.

28. Husband to Earl of Granville, [1755], in Ekirch, "New Government of Liberty," *WMQ*, 3d Ser., 34 (1977): 639; Ramsey, "James Carter," *NCHR* 39 (1962): 131–39.

29. William Henry Hoyt, ed., *The Papers of Archibald D. Murphey* (Raleigh, 1914), 2:400; *N.C. Biog. Hist.*, 5:316; *DAB*, s.v. "Polk, Thomas."

30. Durward T. Stokes, "Thomas Hart in North Carolina," *NCHR* 41 (1964): 324–37.

31. Robert W. Ramsey, *Carolina Cradle: Settlement of the Northwest Carolina Frontier, 1747–1762* (Chapel Hill, 1964), 28, 30; *DNCB*, s.v. "Dunn, John"; Archibald D. Murphey, "Introduction to the History of North Carolina," 1827, in Hoyt, ed., *Murphey Papers*, 2:338.

32. Capt. S. A. Ashe, "Rutherford's Expedition Against the Indians, 1776," *NCB* 4 (1904): 25; *N.C. Biog. Hist.*, 2:381–82; J. G. de Roulhac Hamilton, ed., "Revolutionary Diary of William Lenoir," *JSH* 6 (1940): 250, 5n; James Kirby Martin, *Men In Rebellion* (New Brunswick, N.J., 1973), 83–84.

33. Although he referred to him as Nathaniel Henderson, J. F. D. Smyth described in some detail the rise of one who was probably Richard Henderson: "His

father is still alive, a poor man. . . . This son was grown up to maturity before he had been taught to read or write, and he acquired those rudiments of education, and arithmetic also, by his own indefatigable industry. He then obtained the inferior office of constable; from that was promoted to the office of under-sheriff; after this he procured a license to plead as a lawyer, in the inferior or county courts, and soon after in the superior, or highest courts of judicature." J. F. D. Smyth, *A Tour in the United States of America* (London, 1784), 1:124. See also Francis Nash, "The History of Orange County—Part I," *NCB* 10 (1910): 96; Archibald Henderson, "A Federalist of the Old School," *NCB* 8 (1917): 5–7; J. P. Brissot De Warville, *New Travels in the United States of America, 1788*, ed. Durand Echeverria (Cambridge, Mass., 1964), 414.

34. John D. Hawkins, "Colonel Philemon Hawkins, Sr.," *NCB* 19 (1920): 93–101; *N.C. Biog. Hist.*, 5:135–36; John H. Wheeler, *Historical Sketches of North Carolina from 1584 to 1851* (Philadelphia, 1851), 426. Other backcountry officials, whose origins are more obscure but about whom something is known, include William Churton, Orange assemblyman, 1754–60, 1761–62 (*DNCB*, s.v. "Churton, William"); Tyree Harris, Orange assemblyman, 1760, and sheriff, 1766–68 (*Reg. Doc.*, 581–82); Thomas Lloyd, Orange assemblyman, 1761–66 (Robert Bruce Cook Papers, 1757–86, N.C. Archives; Hugh Talmage Lefler and Paul Wager, eds., *Orange County, 1752–1952* (Chapel Hill, 1953), 333; Francis Nash, Orange assemblyman, 1764–65, 1770–71, and court clerk (Lefler and Wager, eds., *Orange County*, 335; A. M. Waddell, "General Francis Nash," *NCB* 14 (1914): 74–90); Ralph McNair, Orange assemblyman, 1770–71 (*Reg. Doc.*, 587); James Watson, Orange court clerk (Lefler and Wager, eds., *Orange County*, 340); John Brevard, Rowan assemblyman, 1754–60 (*DNCB*, s.v. "Brevard, John, II"); Alexander Osborne, Rowan assemblyman, 1761 (Ramsey, *Carolina Cradle*, 25–26, 49–50); John Kerr, Rowan assemblyman, 1762 (Ramsey, *Carolina Cradle*, 64, 66, 68, 122); William Temple Cole, Rowan sheriff, 1769–70 (Jethro Rumple, *History of Rowan County*, [Salisbury, N.C., 1881], 69); Nathaniel Alexander, Anson assemblyman, 1762 (Ramsey, *Carolina Cradle*, 159–60); Martin Phifer, Mecklenburg assemblyman, 1764–68 (Rumple, *Rowan County*, 2085).

35. Martin, *Men in Rebellion*, 134; *DNCB*, s.v. "Martin, Alexander." For Fanning, see James Hunter to Maurice Moore, Nov. 23, 1770, *Reg. Doc.*, 277; [Regulator Ballads], "Extract from the Memorander of the superior Court . . . at Hillsborough," July 5, 1819, *Reg. Doc.*, 564, 568–69; *DNCB*, s.v. "Fanning, Edmund"; *N.C. Biog. Hist.*, 2:274; *DAB*, s.v. "Fanning, Edmund."

36. Theodorus Swaine Drage to Benjamin Franklin, Mar. 2, 1771, in William B. Willcox, ed., *The Papers of Benjamin Franklin* (New Haven, 1974), 18:47. I am indebted to Mr. Willcox for calling my attention to this letter. Smyth quoted in *Tour in the United States*, 1:162–63. See also Carville Earle and Ronald Hoffman, "Urban Development in the Eighteenth-Century South," *Perspectives in American History*, 10 (1976): 54. For a comparable portrayal of political leadership in the South Carolina backcountry, see Richard Maxwell Brown, *The South Carolina Regulators* (Cambridge, Mass., 1963), 25.

37. William Cumming to [?], Apr. 1, 1759, Chowan County Papers, X, 86, N.C. Archives; *S.C. Gaz.*, June 8, 1765. The Virginian was no more impressed by backcountry ladies. Upon attending a county court session in Granville, as he later noted, "[I] was much surpriz'd to see my last Night's Landlady indited for fornication[.] She came into Court and submitted to the mercy of the Court and

owned the fact upon which she [was] fined five pound the fellow 20£] To her shame by it[, it is] spoken she is Relect of the late Burgess to whom she bore 7 Children though he would not own 2 off [*sic*] them[.] I must own that our Landlady at Court was a Mear Towwowse[?] altho no less then a Col.s Lady[.] After seeing [a] variaty of scenes I lay down on the bed not daring to venture in the Sheets not being over Clean." "Journal of a Journey to P.D.," Sept. 1753, John Saunders Notebook, 1750–55, N.C. Archives.

38. Deposition of Joseph Dillard, Sept. 1, 1755, Rachel Martin to Joseph Dillard, Aug. 26, 1755, Granville County Criminal Papers, N.C. Archives; Deposition of Thomas Oakly, Oct. 25, 1760, Unsorted Granville County Court Papers, Granville County Court House, Oxford, N.C.; Information and Warrant for Robert Harris and Sherwood Harris, Sr., Oct. 27, 1760, Information and Warrant for Robert Hicks, Oct. 23, 1758, Granville Criminal Papers. For the alleged criminal offenses of other Granville County individuals who served as justices at some point between 1746 and 1771, see, for instance, Bill of Indictment for John Wade (theft), Mar. 1746, Bill of Indictment for Edward Jones (assault), Sept. 1747, Bill of Indictment for Edward Jones (disturbing the peace), Sept. 1747, Bill of Indictment for Gideon Macon (?), May 31, 1748, Bill of Indictment for Jonathan White (assault), Sept. 1751, Bill of Indictment for Jonathan White (assault), Mar. 1755, Bill of Indictment for Sherwood Harris (theft, assault), Aug. 1760, Warrant for Sherwood Harris (disturbing the peace), Aug. 1760, and Captain Even Ragland's accompanying deposition, [Aug.?] 1760, Warrant for Sherwood Harris (contempt of authority), Nov. 1760, Bill of Indictment for Benjamin Ward (assault), Aug. 1760, Bill of Indictment for Benjamin Ward (theft), Aug. 1760, Bill of Indictment for Benjamin Ward (contempt of authority, malicious destruction), Aug. 1760, Bill of Indictment for Benjamin Ward (assault), Aug. 1760, Granville Criminal Papers; Bill of Indictment for Benjamin Ward (theft), Feb. 1761, Unsorted Granville Court Papers. Note that Ward served as a justice of the peace in Bute County, which was formed from Granville in 1764. See also Bill of Indictment for Henry Howard (contempt of authority), Feb. 1767, Granville Criminal Papers; Bill of Indictment for Samuel Benton (disturbing the peace), Feb. 1767, Unsorted Granville Court Papers; Bill of Indictment for Larkin Johnston (counterfeiting), Aug. 1767[?], Bill of Indictment for Larkin Johnston (illegal gaming), Aug. 1767, Unsorted Granville County Records, N.C. Archives; Presentment against Thomas Bradford (contempt of authority), May 1768, Unsorted Granville Court Papers; Bill of Indictment for Thomas Lowe (swearing), 1770, Granville Criminal Papers. For Orange and Rowan Counties, which have only scattered court papers, see Warrant for Josiah Dixon (assault), Mar. 1765, Deposition of Alexander Cathey in King vs. James Carter (obstructing justice), June 2, 1756, Salisbury Misc. Papers; Bill of Indictment for James Carter (swearing), Apr. 1763, Rowan County Criminal and Civil Papers, N.C. Archives; Warrant for Thomas Donnell (?), Sept. 1770, Salisbury Misc. Papers.

39. Ramsey, *Carolina Cradle*, 112–14, 177; "Diary of Col. W. Avery," 1769 (North Carolina Papers [Selected], 1768–75, from Draper Manuscripts, State Historical Society of Wisconsin), N.C. Archives.

40. William N. Chambers, "As the Twig is Bent: The Family and the North Carolina Years of Thomas Hart Benton, 1752–1801," *NCHR* 28 (1951): 387; Will of Samuel Benton, Granville County, Feb. 18, 1770, in Zae Hargett Gwynn, ed., *Abstracts of the Wills and Estate Records of Granville County, North Carolina, 1764–1808* (Rocky Mount, N.C., 1973), 3.

41. Ramsey, *Carolina Cradle.*

42. Anson Tax List, 1763, Secretary of State, Tax Lists, 1720–1839, and Orange Tax List, 1755, State Treasurer, Tax Lists, 1755, N.C. Archives; "Rowan County Tax Lists, 1760's," in William Perry Johnson, ed., *North Carolina Genealogy,* 8 (1971): 2607–9, 2683–88; Governor's Office, Lists of Taxables, Militia, and Magistrates, 1754–70, n.d.

43. Gray's father was a middling planter in Bertie County, who died in 1745 owning sixteen slaves. Will of John Gray, Bertie County, Sept. 20, 1745, in J. Bryan Grimes, ed., *North Carolina Wills and Inventories* (Raleigh, 1912), 207–9. See also Stokes, "Thomas Hart," *NCHR* 41 (1964): 326.

44. Lists of Taxables, Militia, and Magistrates, 1754–70, n.d., Council Journals, Apr. 11, 1749, Apr. 1, 1751, *NCCR,* 4:951, 1243.

45. Quoted in Lefler and Powell, *Colonial North Carolina,* 220.

46. George Sims, "An Address to the People of Granville County," June 6, 1765, in William K. Boyd, ed., *Some Eighteenth Century Tracts concerning North Carolina* (Raleigh, 1927), 186–89.

47. Inhabitants of Anson County to Governor Tryon, [Aug. 1768], *Reg. Doc.,* 147; [Regulator Ballads], *Reg. Doc.,* 564, 568. See also the ballad in *Reg. Doc.,* 569; John Stringer to [?], May 14, 1768, Hunter to Moore, Nov. 23, 1770, *Reg. Doc.,* 111, 277.

48. Regulators' Advertisement, No. 10, May 21, 1768, *Reg. Doc.,* 113. See also Regulators' Advertisement, No. 3, Oct. 10, 1766, *Reg. Doc.,* 36.

49. Michael Kammen, *People of Paradox: An Inquiry Concerning the Origins of American Civilization* (New York, 1972), 32.

50. Spangenberg Diary, entry of Sept. 13, 1752, *Moravian Records,* 1:33–34.

51. Coralie Parker, *The History of Taxation in North Carolina during the Colonial Period, 1663–1776* (New York, 1928), 154–57; Robert A. Becker, *Revolution, Reform, and the Politics of American Taxation, 1763–1783* (Baton Rouge, 1980), 42–77.

52. Bernard Bailyn, *The Ideological Origins of the American Revolution* (Cambridge, Mass., 1967), 164–65; J. R. Pole, *Political Representation in England and the Origins of the American Republic* (London, 1966), 72, 80; Edmund S. Morgan, "The Problem of Popular Sovereignty," in George W. Corner, ed., *Aspects of American Liberty: Philosophical, Historical, and Political,* Memoirs of the American Philosophical Society 118 (Philadelphia, 1977): 100–101; Gordon S. Wood, *The Creation of the American Republic, 1776–1787* (Chapel Hill, 1969), 189–90; Sister Joan de Lourdes Leonard, "Elections in Colonial Pennsylvania," *WMQ,* 3d Ser., 11 (1954): 391–92; Conversation with Thomas L. Purvis, July 28, 1977.

53. Dobbs to Governor Boone, July 5, 1762, *NCCR,* 6:780–86; [Dobbs], "The State of the former Proceedings relative to the Boundary Line between the Northern and Southern Colonies . . . ," [1755], *NCCR,* 5:382. See also Dobbs to Governor Glenn, Mar. 12, 1755, *NCCR,* 5:388–90; Dobbs to Board of Trade, Oct. 31, 1756, May 30, 1757, Jan. 22, 1759, *NCCR,* 5:641–42, 762, 6:7; Marvin Lucian Skaggs, "North Carolina Boundary Disputes Involving Her Southern Line," *JSHP* 25 (1941).

54. Letters from North Carolina, *Chronicle,* Boston, Nov. 7, 1768, *Reg. Doc.,* 195–96; Skaggs, "North Carolina Boundary Disputes," *JSHP* 25 (1941).

55. Skaggs, "North Carolina Boundary Disputes," *JSHP* 25 (1941). For the "Sugar Creek War" in Mecklenburg, see the Memorial of Henry Eustace McCulloh to

Governor and Council of North Carolina, Apr. 25, 1765, *NCCR*, 7:12–31; Council Journals, May 9, 1765, *NCCR*, 7:10–11; John Frohock to Edmund Fanning, Apr. 27, 1765, H. E. McCulloh to Fanning, Apr. 27, 1765, Fanning-McCulloh Papers, South. Hist. Coll.; H. E. McCulloh to Fanning, May 9, 1765, *NCCR*, 7:32–34.

56. Husband to Granville, [1755], in Ekirch, "New Government of Liberty," *WMQ*, 3d Ser., 34 (1977): 640; Tryon to Shelburne, July 18, 1767, *NCCR*, 7:513; Deposition of Robert Nelson, A.O. 12/36, 78.

57. Tryon to Earl of Hillsborough, Apr. 12, 1770, *NCCR*, 8:195; Martin to Hillsborough, Nov. 10, 1771, *NCCR*, 9:49. See also Martin to Hillsborough, Mar. 6, 1772, *NCCR*, 9:262–63, Martin to Earl of Dartmouth, Nov. 28, 1772, *NCCR*, 9:358.

58. Francis Dorset et al. to Tryon, Aug. 1, 1768, *Reg. Doc.*, 156; Petition of Inhabitants of Orange and Rowan Counties, [1769], *NCCR*, 8:81; Sims, "Granville Address," June 6, 1765, in Boyd, ed., *Eighteenth Century Tracts*, 188.

59. Dobbs to Board of Trade, Aug. 24, 1755, *NCCR*, 5:363. See also Tryon to Hillsborough, Apr. 12, 1770, *NCCR*, 8:195; p. 31 above.

60. Joseph R. Nixon, "The German Settlers in Lincoln County and Western North Carolina," *JSHP* 11 (1912): 54–60.

61. Husband to Granville, 1756, Granville District Papers; Husband to Granville, [1755], in Ekirch, "New Government of Liberty," *WMQ*, 3d Ser., 34 (1977): 644.

62. Petitions from Orange, Rowan, and Anson Counties to Granville, [1756], Granville District Papers; Summary from Wachovia Church Book, 1760, *Moravian Records*, 1:227; Spangenberg to Count Zinzendorf, June 11, 1760, *Moravian Records*, 2:539; Dobbs to Board of Trade, May 17, 1762, *NCCR*, 6:718. See also Ramsey, *Carolina Cradle*, 193–99.

63. Wachau Diary, entry of Dec. 27, 1755, Bethabara Diary, entry of Jan. 7, 1756, Bethabara and Bethania Diary, entries of Feb. 3, June 2, Aug. 17, 1762, *Moravian Records*, 1:151, 161, 243, 247, 249; Lower House Journals, Feb. 28, 1764, *NCCR*, 6:1186–87.

64. Finlay to A. Todd, Mar. 23, 1774, Granville District Papers; Deposition of Alexander Elmsley, A.O. 12/34, 130. See also Gabriel Johnston to Granville, May 1, 1751, Granville District Papers; Spangenberg Diary, entry of Oct. 28, 1752, *Moravian Records*, 1:44; Deposition of Thomas McKnight, in D. L. Corbitt, ed., "Historical Notes," *NCHR* 2 (1925): 517; Smyth, *Tour in the United States*, I, 152–53; Charles Christopher Crittenden, *The Commerce of North Carolina, 1763–1789*, Yale Historical Publications, *Miscellany* 29 (New Haven, 1936), 111, 35n. Upon finding settlers in the Carolina backcountry who were cut off from trade, a traveler during the American Revolution recorded: "Although settled on the most fertile soil, although surrounded by cattle, enjoying at once the treasures of nature and the resources of agriculture, they offered only the reflection of discouragement, misery, and abandon, because it was impossible for them to trade what they had in excess for the things they needed most." Quoted in Michel-Guillaume St. Jean De Crevecoeur, *Journey into Northern Pennsylvania and the State of New York*, trans. Clarissa Spencer Bostellmaun (Ann Arbor, Mich., 1964), 331.

65. Bethania Diary, entry of Feb. 22, 1766, *Moravian Records*, 1:329; Memorabilia of Bethabara, 1759, *Moravian Records*, 1:206; Bethabara Diary, entry of Mar. 22, 1759, *Moravian Records*, 1:209; Diary of Bethabara and Bethania, entry of

May 18, 1762, *Moravian Records*, 1:246; Bethabara Diary, entry of Dec. 3, 1764, *Moravian Records*, 1:292; Memorabilia of Wachovia, 1766, *Moravian Records*, 1:321; Bethabara Diary, entry of Apr. 19, 1766, *Moravian Records*, 1:333; Petitions from Orange, Rowan, and Anson counties to Granville, [1756], Granville District Papers; Deposition of Frances Dickinson, Nov. 5, 1760, King vs. Susanna Rains, Granville Criminal Papers; Nathaniel Williams to [?], Feb. 2, 1764, Nathaniel Williams Letterbook, Library of Duke University; S. Johnston, Jr., to [Barker], Aug. 20, 1766, Hayes Collection, reel 2, 45; Regulators to Tryon, [Aug. 1768], *Reg. Doc.*, 148.

66. Wachovia Memorabilia, 1770, *Moravian Records*, 1:397; Bethabara Diary, entry of Sept. 23, 1766, *Moravian Records*, 1:335; Whittenburg, "Backwoods Revolutionaries," 130–36.

67. Ramsey, *Carolina Cradle*, 171–74; Petition of Inhabitants of Orange and Rowan, [1769], NCCR, 8:83–84.

68. [Hermon Husband], "A Fan for Fanning, and Touch-Stone to Tryon . . . ," 1771, in Boyd, ed., *Eighteenth Century Tracts*, 343.

69. Crittenden, *North Carolina Commerce*, 86, 111, 35n.; T. M. Devine, *The Tobacco Lords: A Study of the Tobacco Merchants of Glasgow and their Trading Activities, c. 1740–90* (Edinburgh, 1975), 60.

70. Clement Eaton, "A Mirror of the Southern Colonial Lawyer: The Fee Books of Patrick Henry, Thomas Jefferson, and Waightstill Avery," *WMQ*, 3d Ser., 8 (1951): 529; "John Penn's Own Account Book, 1769–1770," [accompanying note attributes probable authorship to John Dunn of Rowan County], N.C. Archives.

71. Dorset et al. to Tryon, Aug. 1, 1768, *Reg. Doc.*, 157. See also James C. Davis, "Towards a Theory of Revolution," *American Sociological Review* 27 (1962): 5–18; Ivo K. Fierabend et al., eds., *Anger, Violence, and Politics: Theories and Research* (Englewood Cliffs, N.J., 1972); Ted Robert Gurr, *Why Men Rebel* (Princeton, N.J., 1970); Samuel P. Huntington, *Political Order in Changing Societies* (New Haven, 1968), 52–53.

72. Marvin L. Michael Kay, "The Payment of Provincial and Local Taxes in North Carolina, 1748–1771," *WMQ*, 3d Ser., 26 (1969): 225; Table of North Carolina Taxes, 1748–70, [1770], in Boyd, ed., *Eighteenth Century Tracts*, 416; Tryon to Conway, Dec. 26, 1765, NCCR, 7:144; Tryon to Shelburne, Mar. 5, 1768, NCCR, 7:693. See also Joseph Albert Ernst, *Money and Politics in America, 1755–1775: A Study in the Currency Act of 1764 and the Political Economy of Revolution* (Chapel Hill, 1973), 199–207.

73. Tryon to Hillsborough, Dec. 24, 1768, *Reg. Doc.*, 215; James Hasell to Hillsborough, Aug. 9, 1771, *Reg. Doc.*, 499. See also Edward Stabler to Richard Bennehan, Feb. 1, 1771, *Reg. Doc.*, 338.

74. Johann David Schoepf, *Travels in the Confederation* (Philadelphia, 1911), trans. and ed. Alfred J. Morrison, 1:295–96; "Superior Court Memorander," July 5, 1819, *Reg. Doc.*, 565.

75. Clifford Geertz, *The Interpretation of Cultures: Selected Essays* (New York, 1973), 219–20.

76. For a discussion of recent applications of this interpretation, see "The American Revolution: Who Were 'The People'?" a review by Edmund Morgan of Young, ed., *Explorations in American Radicalism*, in *The New York Review of Books* 23 (1976): 29–33. See also Edward Countryman, "The Problem of the Early American Crowd," *Journal of American Studies* 7 (1973): 77–90. For Country

thought and its role in Anglo-American political culture, see especially J. G. A. Pocock, *The Machiavellian Moment: Florentine Political Thought and the Atlantic Republican Tradition* (Princeton, N.J., 1975), 506–26, passim, and "Virtue and Commerce in the Eighteenth Century," *Journal of Interdisciplinary History* 3 (1972): 119–34; Bailyn, *Ideological Origins*, 1–159, and *The Origins of American Politics* (New York, 1968), 14–58. For an excellent study of the effects of Country thought in a particular colony, see Robert M. Weir, "'The Harmony We Were Famous For': An Interpretation of Pre-Revolutionary South Carolina Politics," *WMQ*, 3d Ser., 26 (1969): 473–501.

77. Douglass, *Rebels and Democrats*, 71–100; Kay, "North Carolina Regulation," in Young, ed., *Explorations in American Radicalism*, 108, 71–123; Whittenburg, "Backwoods Revolutionaries," 286, passim. See also Kay, "Analysis of a British Colony," *AJPH* 11 (1965): 170–84; Kay, "Regulation in North Carolina"; Marvin L. Michael Kay and Lorin Lee Carey, "Class, Mobility, and Conflict in North Carolina on the Eve of the Revolution," in Jeffrey J. Crow and Larry E. Tise, ed., *The Southern Experience in the American Revolution* (Chapel Hill, 1978), 109–51.

78. Hunter to Moore, Nov. 23, 1770, *Reg. Doc.*, 279.

79. See note 76, above. For Country thought in Pennsylvania, in particular, see Alan Tully, *William Penn's Legacy: Politics and Social Structure in Provincial Pennsylvania, 1726–1755*, The Johns Hopkins University Studies in Historical and Political Science 95 (Baltimore, 1977), 75.

80. [Husband], "Fan for Fanning," 1771, in Boyd, ed., *Eighteenth Century Tracts*, 392. See also Orange County Petition to Tryon, [1771?], *Reg. Doc.*, 305. Recently it has been argued that religion may have exerted an even more direct influence on the Regulator protest. According to James Whittenburg, "a large majority of the insurgents were either Baptists or Quakers," supplemented by Presbyterians and German sectarians. Whittenburg, "God's Chosen in the Backcountry," paper delivered at the annual meeting of the Southern Historical Association, Atlanta, 1979. Yet how this affected the actual direction of the Regulator movement remains unclear. Although Hermon Husband couched some of his arguments in religious rhetoric, religious references of any sort are scarce in other Regulator literature. Any direct impact of dissenting beliefs on the riots was minor and subordinate to the main lines of protest.

81. "Petition of . . . [260] Inhabitants of Anson County," Oct. 9, 1769, *NCCR*, 8:75–76; Hunter to Moore, Nov. 23, 1770, *Reg. Doc.*, 279; [Husband], "An Impartial Relation of the First Rise and Cause of the Recent Differences, in Publick Affairs, In the Province of North-Carolina . . . ," 1770, in Boyd, ed., *Eighteenth Century Tracts*, 303–4. See also "A letter from a person is [*sic*] Carolina to his friend in Pa., May 27, 1771," Rind's *Va. Gaz.*, Aug. 15, 1771, *Reg. Doc.*, 502; Sims, "Granville Address," June 6, 1765, in Boyd, ed., *Eighteenth Century Tracts*, 190.

82. Regulators' Advertisement, No. 5, Mar. 22, 1768, *Reg. Doc.*, 79; Articles of Settlement and Oath of Regulators, Apr. 30, 1768, *Reg. Doc.*, 100; Orange County Petition [174 petitioners] to Martin Howard et al., Oct. 19, 1770, *Reg. Doc.*, 269; Letter from North Carolina, May 27, 1771, Rind's *Va. Gaz.*, Aug. 15, 1771; "Extract of a letter dated July 24, 1771, from a gentleman in North Carolina to his friend in New Jersey . . . ," *Boston Gaz.*, Oct. 21, 1771, *NCCR*, 8:648; [Hermon Husband], "A Continuation of the Impartial Relation . . . ," 1770, Archibald Henderson, ed., "Hermon Husband's Continuation of the Impartial Relation," *NCHR* 18 (1941): 61, 64, 80.

83. Orange Petition, Oct. 19, 1770, *Reg. Doc.*, 271; [Husband], "Impartial Relation," 1770, in Boyd, ed., *Eighteenth Century Tracts*, 323; Sims, "Granville Address," June 6, 1765, in Boyd, ed., *Eighteenth Century Tracts*, 182.

84. Anson Petition, Oct. 9, 1769, NCCR, 8:75–76; Sims, "Granville Address," June 6, 1765, in Boyd, ed., *Eighteenth Century Tracts*, 184; Hunter to Moore, Nov. 23, 1770, *Reg. Doc.*, 279; Regulators' Advertisement, No. 4, Jan. 1768, *Reg. Doc.*, 76. See also Regulators' Advertisement, No. 3, Oct. 10, 1766, *Reg. Doc.*, 36; Regulators' Advertisement, No. 5, Mar. 22, 1768, *Reg. Doc.*, 79; Regulators' Advertisement, No. 10, May 21, 1768, *Reg. Doc.*, 113; Regulators' Advertisement, No. 11, May 21, 1768, *Reg. Doc.*, 115; Regulators to Tryon, [Aug. 1768], *Reg. Doc.*, 149; Sims, "Granville Address," June 6, 1765, in Boyd, ed., *Eighteenth Century Tracts*, 183–92; Orange Petition to Tryon, [1771?], *Reg. Doc.*, 305; [Husband], "Impartial Relation," 1770, in Boyd, ed., *Eighteenth Century Tracts*, 316–17.

85. Regulators' Advertisement, No. 1, Aug. 1766, *Reg. Doc.*, 35; Regulators' Advertisement, Aug. 1766, *Reg. Doc.*, 36; Regulators' Letter, [1770?], in [Husband], "Continuation of the Impartial Relation," 1770, Henderson, ed., "Continuation," *NCHR* 18 (1941): 81.

86. Regulators' Advertisement, No. 10, May 21, 1768, *Reg. Doc.*, 113; [Husband], "Impartial Relation," 1770, in Boyd, ed., *Eighteenth Century Tracts*, 303, 324; [Husband], "Fan for Fanning," 1771, in Boyd, ed., *Eighteenth Century Tracts*, 344, 356; Anson Petition, Oct. 9, 1769, NCCR, 8:76; Anson Regulators to Tryon, [Aug. 1768], *Reg. Doc.*, 147.

87. Hunter to Moore, Nov. 23, 1770, *Reg. Doc.*, 278.

88. [Husband], "Impartial Relation," 1770, in Boyd, ed., *Eighteenth Century Tracts*, 285; [Husband], "Continuation of the Impartial Relation," 1770, Henderson, ed., "Continuation," *NCHR* 18 (1941): 62; Regulators' Letter, [1770?], ibid., 80.

89. Kay, "Analysis of a British Colony," *AJPH* 11 (1965): 178–79; Whittenburg, "Planters, Merchants, and Lawyers," *WMQ*, 3d Ser., 34 (1977): 223–28, and "Backwoods Revolutionaries," 107–40; [Husband], "Impartial Relation," 1770, in Boyd, ed., *Eighteenth Century Tracts*, 324. In itself, this fear that corruption hindered mercantile investment was a traditional tenet of Country thought. See Maier, *From Resistance to Revolution*, 30.

90. [Husband], "Impartial Relation," 1770, in Boyd, ed., *Eighteenth Century Tracts*, 302, 321; Regulators' Advertisement, Aug. 1766, *Reg. Doc.*, 35–36; [Husband], "Continuation of the Impartial Relation," 1770, Henderson, ed., "Continuation," *NCHR* 18 (1941): 63. See also [Husband], "Impartial Relation," 1770, in Boyd, ed., *Eighteenth Century Tracts*, 315.

91. [Regulator Ballads], *Reg. Doc.*, 564, 568–69; Orange and Rowan Petition, [1769], NCCR, 8:81; [Husband], "Impartial Relation," 1770, in Boyd, ed., *Eighteenth Century Tracts*, 302; Sims, "Granville Address," June 6, 1765, in Boyd, ed., *Eighteenth Century Tracts*, 187, 189.

92. Anson Regulators to Tryon, [Aug. 1768], *Reg. Doc.*, 147; Stringer to [?], May 14, 1768, *Reg. Doc.*, 111. See also Deposition of Waightstill Avery, Mar. 8, 1771, *Reg. Doc.*, 360.

93. Orange and Rowan Petition, [1769], NCCR, 8:81; [Husband], "Impartial Relation," 1770, in Boyd, ed., *Eighteenth Century Tracts*, 323. See also ibid., 303.

94. [Husband], "Impartial Relation," 1770, in Boyd, ed., *Eighteenth Century Tracts*, 323, 322, 303; Orange and Rowan Petition, [1769], NCCR, 8:82. Only one extant Regulator document, a petition signed by thirty men, contains the appar-

ent suggestion that local government would be improved by appointing the poor to offices. See Inhabitants of Rowan and Orange Counties to House of Representatives of North Carolina, Oct. 4, 1768, *Reg. Doc.*, 189.

95. Kay, "North Carolina Regulation," in Young, ed., *Explorations in American Radicalism*, 82–83; Granville Grants; Misc. Granville Deeds.

96. Abstract of Patents, 1707–68, C.O. 5/319; Record of Patents, 1770–71, Secretary of State, Original Correspondence, North Carolina, 1768–72 (microfilm, N.C. Archives); Anson Tax List, 1763, Secretary of State, Tax Lists, 1720–1839.

97. Orange Petition to Howard et al., Oct. 19, 1770, *Reg. Doc.*, 271; Letter from "A Planter," Rind's *Va. Gaz.*, Sept. 5, 1771.

98. Letter from North Carolina, May 27, 1771, Rind's *Va. Gaz.*, Aug. 15, 1771, *Reg. Doc.*, 501.

99. *Reg. Doc.*, passim; see other Regulator literature already cited.

100. Regulators' Advertisement, No. 3, Oct. 10, 1766, *Reg. Doc.*, 36–37; Anson Petition, Oct. 9, 1769, NCCR, 8:78. See also [Husband], "Fan for Fanning," 1771, in Boyd, ed., *Eighteenth Century Tracts*, 355. Husband himself was eminently aware of this disjunction between North Carolina and other colonies. North Carolinians, he asserted, were "despised already by the sister colonies" because of their impending enslavement. [Husband], "Impartial Relation," 1770, in Boyd, ed., *Eighteenth Century Tracts*, 324. See also ibid., 316.

101. James Hunter et al. to Tryon, Aug. 19, 1768, *Reg. Doc.*, 161; [Husband], "Impartial Relation," 1770, in Boyd, ed., *Eighteenth Century Tracts*, 274. See also ibid., 273, 302.

102. Letter from N.C., *Chronicle*, Nov. 7, 1768, *Reg. Doc.*, 195; Deposition of Tyree Harris, Aug. 3, 1768, *Reg. Doc.*, 152; [Husband], "Fan for Fanning," 1771, in Boyd, ed., *Eighteenth Century Tracts*, 385–86, 344; Bethabara Diary, entry of May 19, 1771, *Moravian Records*, 1:457.

103. [Husband], "Fan for Fanning," 1771, in Boyd, ed., *Eighteenth Century Tracts*, 344. See also ibid., 355; Anson Inhabitants to Tryon, [Aug. 1768], *Reg. Doc.*, 146–47.

104. Council Journals, May 17, 1768, NCCR, 7:751.

105. Kay, "North Carolina Regulation," in Young, ed., *Explorations in American Radicalism*, 87–99.

106. Tryon to Hillsborough, Jan. 31, 1771, *Reg. Doc.*, 337.

107. James Iredell to John Harvey, Dec. 21, 1770, NCCR, 8:270; Johnston to Thomas Barker, June 10, 1771, *Reg. Doc.*, 476. For the riot act, see Laws, NCSR, 25:519a–519d.

108. Orange Petition to Tryon, [1771?], *Reg. Doc.*, 305; Letter from North Carolina, May 27, 1771, Rind's *Va. Gaz.*, Aug. 15, 1771, *Reg. Doc.*, 501; Deposition of Waightstill Avery, Mar. 8, 1771, *Reg. Doc.*, 359.

109. "Extract of a letter dated July 24, 1771," NCCR, 8:646; Rednap Howell to Hunter, Feb. 16, 1771, Council Journals, Mar. 18, 1771, *Reg. Doc.*, 373.

110. [Husband], "Impartial Relation," 1770, in Boyd, ed., *Eighteenth Century Tracts*, 281–82, 285.

111. Mark A. De Wolfe Howe, ed., "Journal of Josiah Quincy, Junior, 1773," Mass. Hist. Soc., *Proceedings* 49 (1915–16): 458; Schaw to Dartmouth, Oct. 31, 1775, in Evangeline W. and Charles M. Andrews, eds., *Journal of a Lady of Quality; Being the Narrative of a Journey from Scotland to the West Indies, North Carolina, and Portugal, in the years 1774 to 1776* (New Haven, 1923), 281; Lower House Journals, Dec. 5, 1768, NCCR, 7:984; Upper House

Journals, Oct. 23, 31, Nov. 6, 1769, NCCR, 8:88, 93–97, 105; Laws, *NCSR*, 23:788–89, 814–18; Lower House Journals, Jan. 26, 1771, NCCR, 10:478. The response of provincial leaders was quite different from that of Virginia politicians to their scandal in the mid-1760s involving John Robinson's misuse of public funds. North Carolina's leadership took steps against corruption with marked reluctance; members of Virginia's gentry, by comparison, were vigorously self-critical in initiating stern measures to prevent future misdeeds. See Jack P. Greene, "*'Virtus et Libertas'*: Political Culture, Social Change, and the Origins of the American Revolution in Virginia, 1763–1766," in Crow and Tise, eds., *Southern Experience in the Revolution*, 55–108; Joseph Albert Ernst, "The Robinson Scandal Redivivus: Money, Debts, and Politics in Revolutionary Virginia," *VMHB* 77 (1969): 146–73.

112. The severity of the Johnston Riot Act was such that the Board of Trade condemned its clause permitting the execution of outlawed Regulators as "irreconcilable with the principles of the constitution, full of danger in its operation and unfit for any part of the British Empire." Additional Instructions to Josiah Martin, [1771], NCCR, 8:516. Beforehand, a North Carolina acquaintance had warned Benjamin Franklin that "if seen at home," the riot act "would be an Eternal reproach to your Stand for Liberty." Drage to Franklin, Mar. 2, 1771, in Willcox, ed., *Franklin Papers*, 18:48.

113. Ann Hooper to Dorothy Murray, Oct. 7, 1768, *Reg. Doc.*, 190–91; Henry Johnston to S. Johnston, Jr., Mar. 24, 1771, Hayes Collection, reel 3, 83.

114. Greene, *Quest for Power*, 361, passim.

115. Assembly Resolution, Dec. 20, 1770, *Reg. Doc.*, 295; Presentment of the Grand Jury of the District of New Bern, Mar. 15, 1771, Purdie and Dixon's *Va. Gaz.*, Mar. 28, 1771.

116. See, for instance, S. Johnston, Jr., to Barker, June 10, 1771, *Reg. Doc.*, 474–76; S. Johnston, Jr., to Alexander Elmsley, Nov. 7, 1770, Samuel Johnston Papers, N.C. Archives; Iredell to Harvey, Dec. 21, 1770, NCCR, 8:270–71; Iredell to Francis Iredell, Sr., June 15, July 31, 1771, in Don Higginbotham, ed., *The Papers of James Iredell* (Raleigh, 1976), 1:71, 73; Letter from New Bern, Oct. 5, 1770, Purdie and Dixon's *Va. Gaz.*, Oct. 25, 1770; Hooper to Murray, Oct. 7, 1768, *Reg. Doc.*, 190–91; Hasell to Hillsborough, Aug. 9, 1771, *Reg. Doc.*, 499–500; Letter from New Bern, July 27, 1771, Purdie and Dixon's *Va. Gaz.*, Aug. 29, 1771; Extract of letter from Samuel Cornell to Elias Debroses, June 6, 1771, C.O. 5/154; Report from *N.C. Gaz.*, New Bern, May 24, 1771, in *N.H. Gaz.*, Portsmouth, June 21, 1771.

117. Report from North Carolina, Apr. 26, [1771], Purdie and Dixon's *Va. Gaz.*, May 23, 1771; "A Friend to the Province," *Cape Fear Mercury*, Aug. 14, 1771, in *S.C. Gaz.*, Sept. 12, 1771.

118. James Reed to Sec. of S.P.G., Jan. 7, 1774, S.P.G., B MSS, 5, 150.

119. For expressions of Whig thought by leading North Carolinians, see Maurice Moore, "The Justice and Policy of Taxing the American Colonies . . . ," 1765, in Boyd, ed., *Eighteenth Century Tracts*, 163–74; William Hooper to James Iredell, Apr. 26, 1774, NCCR, 9:983–86; [James Iredell], ["Causes of the American Revolution"], June 1776, in Higginbotham, ed., *Iredell Papers*, 1:370–412.

120. McCulloh to Edmund Fanning, [1762?], Fanning-McCulloh Papers, N.C. Archives; McCulloh to Fanning, Apr. 23, 1763, Fanning-McCulloh Papers, South. Hist. Coll.

121. McCulloh to Fanning, Jan. 14, 1764, Fanning-McCulloh Papers, South. Hist. Coll.; McCulloh to Fanning, Apr. 21, 1763, Fanning-McCulloh Papers, N.C. Archives; Martin to Isaac Wilkinson, Feb. 10, 1775, Granville District Papers.

122. Council to Tryon, Dec. 1770, *Reg. Doc.*, 281; Presentment of the Grand Jury of the District of New Bern, Mar. 15, 1771, Purdie and Dixon's *Va. Gaz.*, Mar. 28, 1771. See also Report from N.C., Apr. 26, [1771], Purdie and Dixon's *Va. Gaz.*, May 23, 1771. Even in meeting the Regulator challenge to provincial authority, eastern political leaders were strongly disposed to follow their own regional interests. In late winter 1771, when Tryon issued his call for a provincial force to march west against the Regulators, he was required to apply to the province's two treasurers for the necessary funds. Partly because of the Cape Fear's traditional enthusiasm for large issues of paper currency, the southern treasurer, John Ashe of New Hanover County, immediately complied with Tryon's request. Joseph Montfort, the northern treasurer, on the other hand, did not, because of long-standing northern opposition to large currency issues. As a result, none of the northern counties contributed troops to Tryon's army. See Tryon to Hillsborough, Aug. 1, 1771, *Reg. Doc.*, 496; Martin to Hillsborough, Aug. 15, Dec. 26, 1771, *NCCR*, 9:18, 76; Ernst, *Money and Politics*, 292–96.

123. Entry of June 18, 1771, Franklin Bowditch Dexter, ed., *The Literary Diary of Ezra Stiles, D.D., LL.D.* (New York, 1901), 1:112; Lee to Lee, June 19, 1771, *Reg. Doc.*, 482.

124. Editorial, *Newport Mercury*, July 8, 1771, in *N.H. Gaz.*, July 26, 1771; *Pa. Jour.*, July 11, 1771; Purdie and Dixon's *Va. Gaz.*, June 6, 1771; *Mass. Spy*, July 25, 1771. See also "Amator Bonorum," Aug. 20, 1771, "Amator Generis Humanis," Oct. 1, 1771, "Observator [No. XIII]," Oct. 22, 1771, *Conn. Cour.*; Purdie and Dixon's *Va. Gaz.*, Sept. 5, 1771; Editorials in *Boston Gaz.*, July 22, Aug. 12, 1771; Letter, *Pa. Jour.*, Aug. 8, 1771; "Leonidas," June 27, 1771, "Mucius Scaevola," June 27, 1771, "Leonidas," Aug. 1, 1771, "Benevolentior," Aug. 15, 1771, "Centinel X," Aug. 29, 1771, Editorial, Aug. 29, 1771, "Centinel XI," Sept. 5, 1771, "Leonidas," Sept. 5, 1771, "Mucius Scaevola," Sept. 5, 1771, *Mass. Spy*. For a less partisan but sympathetic editorial, see the *S.C. Gaz.*, Aug. 8, 1771. See also Maier, *Resistance to Revolution*, 196–97. For the extract of an anti-Regulator letter from Connecticut—reputedly written by Edmund Fanning—see *Mass. Spy*, Sept. 19, 1771. Whether written by Fanning or not, the author was clearly not of a Whiggish persuasion: "I suppose Colonel TRYON has done more for the Support of Government in North-America, than all the Governors in it." Opposition outside of North Carolina to the Regulators seems to have been prevalent among staunch supporters of British imperial policy. See, for instance, Thomas Hutchinson to Hillsborough, Nov. 30, 1770, Hutchinson to Tryon, Jan. 25, 1771, *Reg. Doc.*, 280–81, 334; Thomas Gage to Lord Barrington, Aug. 6, 1771, in Clarence Edwin Carter, ed., and comp., *The Correspondence of General Thomas Gage with the Secretaries of State, and with the War Office and the Treasury, 1763–1775* (Hamden, Conn., 1969), 2:586–87.

125. Letter from Archibald Maclaine, William Hooper, Robert Hogg, June 7, 1771, *Pa. Jour.*, July 11, 1771.

126. For an exuberant report of the hanging from New Bern, see Letter from New Bern, July 27, 1771, Purdie and Dixon's *Va. Gaz.*, Aug. 29, 1771. For the offending editorial, see *Mass. Spy*, June 27, 1771.

127. "Centinel X," *Mass. Spy*, Aug. 29, 1771; *Boston Gaz.*, July [sic] 22, 1771, NCCR, 10:1025. See also "Amator Generis Humanis," *Conn. Cour.*, Oct. 1, 1771. On Dec. 1, 1764, the British Parliament had voted that *The North Briton*, No. 45, be burned "by the hands of the common hangman." George Nobbe, *The North Briton: A Study in Political Propaganda*, Columbia University Studies in English and Comparative Literature 140 (New York, 1939): 252.
128. Letter from New Bern, July 27, 1771, Purdie and Dixon's *Va. Gaz.*, Aug. 29, 1771, *Reg. Doc.*, 515. For testimonials by both houses of the assembly, see Upper House Journals, Nov. 21, 1771, Lower House Journals, Nov. 22, 1771, NCCR, 9:104, 142.
129. Howe, ed., "Quincy Journal, 1773," Mass. Hist. Soc., *Proceedings* 49 (1915–16): 461; *Mass. Spy*, Aug. 1, 1771; *Pa. Jour.*, Aug. 8, 1771.

7. The Regulator Legacy, 1772–1776

1. Vernon O. Stumpf, "Josiah Martin and His Search for Success: The Road to North Carolina," *NCHR* 53 (1976): 55–79; Richard B. Sheridan, "The West Indian Antecedents of Josiah Martin, Last Royal Governor of North Carolina," *NCHR* 54 (1977): 253–70.
2. Upper House Journals, Nov. 19, 1771, NCCR, 10:101–3; Lower House Journals, Nov. 22, 1771, NCCR, 10:142–43.
3. Martin to Samuel Martin, Jr., May 16, June 27, 1771, quoted in Stumpf, "Josiah Martin," *NCHR* 53 (1976): 75.
4. Upper House Journals, Nov. 19, 1771, NCCR, 9:102; Martin to Earl of Hillsborough, Jan. 30, 1772, NCCR, 9:235; James Hunter to William Butler, Nov. 6, 1772, *Reg. Doc.*, 537–38.
5. Martin to Hillsborough, Mar. 7, Apr. 12, June 5, 1772, NCCR, 9:266, 279, 300. See also Martin to Hillsborough, Mar. 1, 1772, NCCR, 9:258–59.
6. Martin to Hillsborough, Mar. 8, 1772, NCCR, 9:268–69.
7. Martin to Hillsborough, Aug. 30, 1772, NCCR, 9:330. See also Martin to Samuel Martin, Oct. 23, 1772, Add. MSS, 41361, 245.
8. Hunter to Butler, Nov. 6, 1772, *Reg. Doc.*, 537.
9. Martin to Hillsborough, July 11, 1772, NCCR, 9:315–16. See also Martin to Hillsborough, Oct. 25, 1772, NCCR, 9:349.
10. Martin to Earl of Dartmouth, Mar. 31, 1773, NCCR, 9:619.
11. Hunter to Butler, Nov. 6, 1772, *Reg. Doc.*, 538.
12. Upper House Journals, Jan. 25, 1773, NCCR, 9:377–80; Martin to Dartmouth, Mar. 31, Apr. 6, May 30, 1773, Mar. 10, 1775, NCCR, 9:619–20, 625–31, 655–56, 1158.
13. See Jack P. Greene, *The Quest for Power: The Lower Houses of Assembly in the Southern Royal Colonies, 1689–1776* (Chapel Hill, 1963), 421–24.
14. Charles G. Sellers, Jr., "Making a Revolution: The North Carolina Whigs, 1765–1775," in J. Carlyle Sitterson, ed., *Studies in Southern History* (Chapel Hill, 1957), 23–46; Hugh T. Lefler and William S. Powell, *Colonial North Carolina: A History* (New York, 1973), 240–88; Lindley S. Butler, *North Carolina and the Coming of the Revolution, 1763–1776* (Raleigh, 1976); Greene, *Quest for Power*, 416–24.
15. Robert M. Weir, "Who Shall Rule at Home: The American Revolution as a Crisis of Legitimacy for the Colonial Elite," *The Journal of Interdisciplinary*

History 6 (1976): 679–700; James Kirby Martin, *Men in Rebellion* (New Brunswick, N.J., 1973).

16. Regulators' Advertisement, No. 1, Aug. 1766, *Reg. Doc.*, 35; Regulators' Advertisement, Aug. 1766, *Reg. Doc.*, 36; Regulators' Letter [1770?], in Henderson, ed., "Continuation," *NCHR* 18 (1941): 79.

17. Instructions for Ralph McNair and Thomas Hart, [1773], *NCCR*, 9:699–706. See also Instructions for Mecklenburg County Representatives, [1775], *NCCR*, 10:239–42; Instructions for Provincial Congress Delegates from Mecklenburg and Orange Counties, Nov. 1776, *NCCR*, 10:870a–70h.

18. Proceedings of the Provincial Congress, Aug. 21, 1775, *NCCR*, 10:169; Extracts from the Proceedings of the Continental Congress, Nov. 28, 1775, *NCCR*, 10:338; Marvin L. Michael Kay, "The North Carolina Regulation, 1766–1776: A Class Conflict," in Alfred F. Young, ed., *The American Revolution: Explorations in the History of American Radicalism* (DeKalb, Ill., 1976), 107.

19. Alexander Schaw to Dartmouth, Oct. 30, 1775, in Evangeline W. and Charles M. Andrews, eds., *Journal of a Lady of Quality: Being the Narrative of a Journey from Scotland to the West Indies, North Carolina, and Portugal, in the years 1774 to 1776* (New Haven, 1923), 281; Hunter to Butler, Nov. 6, 1772, *Reg. Doc.*, 538.

20. Martin to General Thomas Gage, Mar. 16, 1775, *NCCR*, 10:1167; Martin to Dartmouth, Apr. 20, 1775, *NCCR*, 9:1228; Addresses from the Inhabitants of Rowan, Surry, Guilford, and Anson Counties, [1775], *NCCR*, 9:1160–64. See also William Lenoir to Archibald Murphey, Aug. 1821, in William Henry Hoyt, ed., *The Papers of Archibald D. Murphey* (Raleigh, 1914), 1:225.

21. Mary Elinor Lazenby, *Herman Husband: A Story of His Life* (Washington, D.C., 1940), 140–46.

22. Quoted in Charles Francis Adams, ed., *The Works of John Adams* (Boston, 1852), 7:282–84. See also Kay, "North Carolina Regulation," in Young, ed., *Explorations in American Radicalism*, 105–6.

8. The Origins of Instability

1. Upper House Journals, Feb. 8, 1739, *NCCR*, 4:357; Martin to Earl of Hillsborough, Mar. 1, 1772, *NCCR*, 9:254.

2. Patricia U. Bonomi, *A Factious People: Politics and Society in Colonial New York* (New York, 1971), 282. See also Bonomi's "The Middle Colonies: Embryo of the New Political Order," in Alden T. Vaughan and George Athan Billias, eds., *Perspectives on Early American History: Essays in Honor of Richard B. Morris* (New York, 1973), 63–92; Milton M. Klein, *The Politics of Diversity: Essays in the History of Colonial New York* (Port Washington, N.Y., 1974), 36–45; Douglas Greenberg, "The Middle Colonies in Recent American Historiography," *WMQ*, 3d Ser., 36 (1979): 398–403, 423–27. For an approach that emphasizes the class origins of interest politics, see Joyce Appleby, "The Social Origins of American Revolutionary Ideology," *JAH* 64 (1978): 954; Bernard Friedman, "The Shaping of Radical Consciousness in Provincial New York," *JAH* 56 (1970): 781–801; Gary B. Nash, "The Transformation of Urban Politics, 1700–1765," *JAH* 60 (1973): 605–32.

3. Bonomi does not pursue this issue in *Factious People*, but see her article on "The Middle Colonies" as well as Klein's *Politics of Diversity*.

4. Murray to John Burgwin, July 6, 1768, Murray Letter Book, 1764–69, 254.
5. Samuel P. Huntington, *Political Order in Changing Societies* (New Haven, 1968), 41. See also Harry Eckstein, "On the Causes of Internal Wars," in Eric A. Nordlinger, ed., *Politics and Society: Studies in Comparative Sociology* (Englewood Cliffs, N.J., 1970), 293–94, 300.

Bibliographical Essay

In undertaking this study, I expected to face a dearth of private manuscripts. It was a pleasant surprise to find several largely untapped collections. Foremost among these was the James Murray Collection at the Massachusetts Historical Society in Boston, only a fraction of which has been published in Nina Moore Tiffany, ed., *Letters of James Murray, Loyalist* (Boston, 1901). Extending from the mid-1730s to the 1760s, Murray's voluminous correspondence, which also includes a few items in the James Murray Robbins Collection, Mass. Hist. Soc., and the James Murray Papers, North Carolina Archives, Raleigh, provides a wealth of diverse information. Also important were the Granville District Papers, microfilm copy at the N.C. Archives of the originals in the library of the Marquess of Bath in England. Not only do they contain significant information on the Granville proprietary, but these papers also shed considerable light on social and economic affairs in North Carolina during the mid-eighteenth century.

Other private collections of particular pertinence were the Hayes Collection, Southern Historical Collection at the University of North Carolina, Chapel Hill; Arthur Dobbs Papers, microfilm copy at the South. Hist. Coll. of the originals in the Public Record Office of Northern Ireland, Belfast; Thomas Pollock Letter Book and Miscellaneous Papers, N.C. Archives; Fanning-McCulloh Collections at both the South. Hist. Coll. and the N.C. Archives; James Abercromby Letter Books, Virginia State Library, Richmond, and the N.C. Archives; and the Granville Papers, William L. Clements Library, University of Michigan, Ann Arbor.

Less valuable but still helpful were the Francis Nash Collection, John Saunders Notebook, Miscellaneous Papers, 1697–1712, Samuel Johnston Papers, Granville Land Office Records, Miscellaneous Granville District Papers, Waightstill Avery Diary (photostat of the original in the Draper Manuscripts, Wisconsin State Historical Society, Madison), N.C. Archives; Preston Davie Collection, Joshua Sharpe Papers, Alexander McAllister Papers, South. Hist. Coll.; George Burrington Papers, William Ross Papers, Library of Duke University, Durham; and the Norcross Collection, Mass. Hist. Soc.

Various sets of official and semiofficial papers were useful. At the N.C. Archives these included Legislative Papers, 1689–1775; Council Papers, 1761–65; General Court Records; North Carolina Colonial Court Records; Chowan County

Miscellaneous Records, 1709–1918; Halifax County Miscellaneous Papers, 1761–1927; Granville County Criminal Papers; Unsorted Granville County Records; Salisbury District Court Papers; Rowan County Criminal and Civil Papers; Governor's Office, Lists of Taxables, Militia, and Magistrates, 1754–70; County Court Minutes; and numerous tax lists, wills, estate inventories, and land grants.

Library of Congress copies of several English collections also proved to be helpful: Society for the Propagation of the Gospel Records, London; Colonial Office Papers, class 5, especially volumes 154, 296, 309, and Audit Office Papers, classes 12, volume 36, and 13, especially volumes 117–120, Public Record Office, London; Additional Manuscripts, volumes 22677, 32693, 32715, 33028, 41361, Kings Manuscripts, and Lansdowne Manuscripts, volume 1215, British Library, London. The N.C. Archives collection of duplicate materials from the P.R.O. is also superb.

Although unpublished manuscripts are not insubstantial, newspapers for colonial North Carolina are scarce. The colony's first one, the *North Carolina Gazette*, did not get under way in New Bern until 1751. Even then, only a few issues have survived, which is also true of several later papers: New Bern's *North Carolina Magazine* and Wilmington's *North Carolina Gazette* and *Cape Fear Mercury*. More helpful were Purdie and Dixon's *Virginia Gazette*, Rind's *Virginia Gazette*, the *South Carolina Gazette*, and the *South Carolina and American General Gazette*, all of which occasionally printed correspondence from North Carolina.

Of published collections, certainly the most valuable was William L. Saunders, Walter Clark, and Stephen B. Weeks, eds., *The Colonial and State Records of North Carolina*, 30 vols. (Raleigh, Winston, Goldsboro, and Charlotte, N.C., 1886–1914), which contains a superb assortment of public, semiofficial, and private papers, plus statutes and legislative journals. Not the least of this series' virtues is its magnificent index. Other significant published primary sources were Don Higginbotham, ed., *The Papers of James Iredell*, 2 vols. (Raleigh, 1976); William S. Powell et al., eds., *The Regulators in North Carolina: A Documentary History, 1759–1776* (Raleigh, 1971); William K. Boyd, ed., *Some Eighteenth Century Tracts concerning North Carolina* (Raleigh, 1927); Adelaide L. Fries, ed., *Records of the Moravians in North Carolina*, 8 vols. (Raleigh, 1922–54); Louis B. Wright, ed., *The Prose Works of William Byrd of Westover* (Cambridge, Mass., 1966); Marion Tinling, ed., *The Correspondence of the Three William Byrds of Westover, Virginia, 1684–1776*, 2 vols. (Charlottesville, Va., 1977); Richard J. Hooker, ed., *The Carolina Backcountry on the Eve of the Revolution: The Journal and Other Writings of Charles Woodmason, Anglican Itinerant* (Chapel Hill, 1953); Historical Manuscripts Commission, *Report on the Laing Manuscripts Preserved in the University of Edinburgh* (London, 1925), vol. 2; and the *Wilmington Manuscripts* (Historical Manuscripts Commission, Eleventh *Report*, Pt. IV), vol. 3. Less useful was John Brickell, *The Natural History of North Carolina* (Dublin, 1737) because he plagiarized much of John Lawson's 1709 work, *A New Voyage to Carolina*. See Percy J. Adams, "John Lawson's Alter-Ego—Dr. John Brickell," *North Carolina Historical Review* 34 (1957): 313–26, and W. H. Lindgren, "Agricultural Propaganda in Lawson's *A New Voyage to Carolina*," NCHR 49 (1972): 333–44.

Travel accounts were very helpful, especially Johann David Schoepf, *Travels in the Confederation*, [1783–84], trans. Alfred J. Morrison, 2 vols. (Philadelphia, 1911); Mark A. De Wolfe Howe, ed., "Journal of Josiah Quincy, Junior, 1773," Mass. Hist. Soc., *Proceedings* 49 (1915–16): 424–81; J. F. D. Smyth, *A Tour in the United States of America*, 2 vols. (London, 1784); Evangeline W. and Charles M. Andrews, eds., *Journal of a Lady of Quality; Being the Narrative of a Journey from Scotland to the*

West Indies, North Carolina, and Portugal, in the years 1774 to 1776 (New Haven, 1923); "Journal of a French Traveller in the Colonies, 1765, I," *American Historical Review* 26 (1920–21): 726–47; John S. Ezell, ed., Judson P. Wood, trans., *The New Democracy in America: Travels of Francisco de Miranda in the United States, 1783–1784* (Norman, Okla., 1963); and Hugh Meredith, *An Account of the Cape Fear Country, 1731*, ed. Earl G. Swem (Perth Amboy, N.J., 1922).

In contrast to primary sources, little secondary material is available for eighteenth-century North Carolina. Historians of the colonial South have occasionally lamented the lack of attention given their region until recent years, but North Carolina has certainly suffered more than most of its neighbors. Symptomatic of this neglect, a recent anthology devoted to the southern colonies, T. H. Breen, ed., *Shaping Southern Society: The Colonial Experience* (New York, 1976), does not contain a single article on North Carolina. For a useful introduction to the colony, see Hugh T. Lefler and William S. Powell, *Colonial North Carolina: A History* (New York, 1973). Political studies have usually emphasized discrete events at the expense of interpretative analysis, notably Samuel A. Ashe, *History of North Carolina*, 2 vols. (Raleigh and Greensboro, N.C., 1908–25), and R. D. W. Connor, *History of North Carolina* (Chicago, 1919), vol. 1.

Still helpful was Hugh Williamson, *The History of North Carolina*, 2 vols. (Philadelphia, 1812), as were also a few specialized studies: William S. Price, "A Strange Incident in George Burrington's Royal Governorship," *NCHR* 51 (1974): 149–58; Charles G. Sellers, "Private Profits and British Colonial Policy: The Speculations of Henry McCulloh," *William and Mary Quarterly*, 3d Ser., 8 (1951): 535–51; Lawrence London, "The Representation Controversy in Colonial North Carolina," *NCHR* 11 (1934): 255–70; Desmond Clarke, *Arthur Dobbs, Esquire, 1689–1765: Surveyor-General of Ireland, Prospector, and Governor of North Carolina* (Chapel Hill, 1957); and Alonzo T. Dill, *Governor Tryon and His Palace* (Chapel Hill, 1955).

For the various conflicting interpretations of the Regulators, see John S. Bassett, "The Regulators of North Carolina, 1765–1771," *Annual Report of the American Historical Association for the Year 1894* (Washington, D.C., 1895), 141–212; Elisha P. Douglass, *Rebels and Democrats: The Struggle for Equal Rights and Majority Rule during the American Revolution* (Chapel Hill, 1955), 71–100; Marvin Lawrence Michael Kay, "The Institutional Background to the Regulation in Colonial North Carolina," (Ph.D. diss., University of Minnesota, 1962); M. L. M. Kay, "An Analysis of a British Colony in Late Eighteenth Century America in the Light of Current American Historiographical Controversy," *Australian Journal of Politics and History* 11 (1965): 170–84; Marvin L. Michael Kay, "The North Carolina Regulation, 1766–1776: A Class Conflict," in Alfred F. Young, ed., *The American Revolution: Explorations in the History of American Radicalism* (DeKalb, Ill., 1976), 84–103; Marvin L. Michael Kay and Lorin Lee Cary, "Class, Mobility, and Conflict in North Carolina on the Eve of the Revolution," in Jeffrey J. Crow and Larry E. Tise, eds., *The Southern Experience in the American Revolution* (Chapel Hill, 1978), 109–151; James Penn Whittenburg, "Backwoods Revolutionaries: Social Context and Constitutional Theories of the North Carolina Regulators, 1765–1771" (Ph.D. diss., University of Georgia, 1974); and James P. Whittenburg, "Planters, Merchants, and Lawyers: Social Change and the Origins of the North Carolina Regulation," *WMQ*, 3d Ser., 34 (1977): 215–38.

Several institutional histories exist for colonial North Carolina, including Charles L. Raper, *North Carolina: A Study in English Colonial Government* (New York,

1904); Florence Cook, "Procedure in the North Carolina Assembly, 1731–1770," *NCHR* 8 (1931): 258–83; Paul M. McCain, *The County Court in North Carolina Before 1750*, Historical Papers of the Trinity College Historical Society 31 (Durham, N.C., 1954); William Guess, "County Government in Colonial North Carolina," *James Sprunt Historical Publications* 11 (1911): 5–39; and Julian P. Boyd, "The Sheriff in Colonial North Carolina," *NCHR* 5 (1928): 161–81. Jack P. Greene's *The Quest for Power: The Lower Houses of Assembly in the Southern Royal Colonies, 1689–1776* (Chapel Hill, 1963) provides an excellent account of constitutional developments.

A paucity of social and economic studies of North Carolina is partially rectified by Harry Roy Merrens's extremely helpful *Colonial North Carolina in the Eighteenth Century: A Study in Historical Geography* (Chapel Hill, 1964). Also useful are Charles Christopher Crittenden, *The Commerce of North Carolina, 1763–1789*, Yale Historical Publications, *Miscellany* 29 (New Haven, 1936); Alice Elaine Mathews, *Society in Revolutionary North Carolina* (Raleigh, 1976); Jeffrey J. Crow, *The Black Experience in Revolutionary North Carolina* (Raleigh, 1977); and Lawrence Lee, *The Lower Cape Fear in Colonial Days* (Chapel Hill, 1965).

A few reference works are valuable: John L. Cheney, Jr., ed., *North Carolina Government, 1585–1974: A Narrative and Statistical Analysis* (Raleigh, 1975); David L. Corbitt, *The Formation of North Carolina Counties, 1663–1943* (Raleigh, 1950); and William S. Powell, *The North Carolina Gazetteer* (Chapel Hill, 1968).

Information about North Carolina's social and political leaders during the mid-eighteenth century came from a wide variety of sources. Besides *The Colonial and State Records of North Carolina*, of special value were Samuel A. Ashe, Stephen B. Weeks, and Claude L. Van Noppen, eds., *Biographical History of North Carolina: From Colonial Times to the Present*, 8 vols. (Greensboro, N.C., 1905–17); and J. R. B. Hathaway, ed., *The North Carolina Historical and Genealogical Register*, 3 vols. (Edenton, N.C., 1900–1903). Also useful were various issues of William Perry Johnson's *North Carolina Genealogy* (alternately titled *The North Carolinian* and the *Journal of North Carolina Genealogy*); J. Bryan Grimes, ed., *Abstract of North Carolina Wills* (Raleigh, 1910), and *North Carolina Wills and Inventories* (Raleigh, 1912); Marilu Branch Smallwood, *Some Colonial and Revolutionary Families of North Carolina*, 3 vols. (n.p., 1964–69); R. D. W. Connor, *Revolutionary Leaders of North Carolina* (Greensboro, N.C., 1916); John H. Wheeler, *Historical Sketches of North Carolina from 1584 to 1851* (Philadelphia, 1851); William S. Price, Jr., "'Men of Good Estates': Wealth Among North Carolina's Royal Councillors," *NCHR* 49 (1972): 72–82; the Reverend E. W. Caruthers, *Revolutionary Incidents: And Sketches of Character, Chiefly in the "Old North State"* (Philadelphia, 1854); A. R. Newsome, ed., "Twelve North Carolina Counties, 1810–1811," *NCHR* 5 (1928): 413–46, *NCHR* 6 (1929): 67–99, 171–189, 281–301; Marshall DeLancey Haywood, *The Beginnings of Freemasonry in North Carolina and Tennessee* (Raleigh, 1906); E. Alfred Jones, *American Members of the Inns of Court* (London, 1924); Mark Chappel, "The Cupola House and Its Associations," *The North Carolina Booklet* 15 (1916): 203–17; Thomas C. Parramore, "The Saga of 'The Bear' and the 'Evil Genius,'" *Bulletin of the History of Medicine* 42 (1968): 321–31; Clifford K. Shipton, *Sibley's Harvard Graduates* (Cambridge, Mass., 1933–); J. G. de Roulhac Hamilton, ed., "Revolutionary Diary of William Lenoir," *Journal of Southern History* 6 (1940): 247–59; Anton-Hermann Chroust, *The Rise of the Legal Profession in America* (Norman, Okla., 1965), vol. 1; "Vir-

ginia Council Journals, 1726–1753," *Virginia Magazine of History and Biography*
36 (1928): 226–30; and William Henry Hoyt, ed., *The Papers of Archibald D.
Murphey* (Raleigh, 1914), vol. 2. Both the *Dictionary of American Biography* and
the *Dictionary of National Biography* were also helpful, as was the *Dictionary of
North Carolina Biography*. At this time, only the first volume has appeared, but the
editor, William S. Powell, kindly let me see some of the material from future
volumes.

County and regional histories furnished a wealth of information, particularly
about family origins. These included Jesse F. Pugh, *Three Hundred Years Along the
Pasquotank: A Biographical History of Camden County* (Old Trap, N.C., 1957);
Ellen G. Winslow, *History of Perquimans County* (Baltimore, 1974); Benjamin B.
Winborne, *The Colonial and State Political History of Hertford County, N.C.* (n.p.,
1906); Thomas C. Parramore, *Cradle of the Colony: The History of Chowan
County and Edenton, North Carolina* (Edenton, N.C., 1967); Mary Best Bell, ed.,
Colonial Bertie County, North Carolina (Windsor, N.C., 1963), vol. 1; W. C. Allen,
History of Halifax County (Boston, 1918); J. Turner Kelley and J. L. Bridgers, Jr.,
History of Edgecombe County, North Carolina (Raleigh, 1920); Manly Wade
Wellman, *The County of Warren, North Carolina, 1586–1917* (Chapel Hill, 1959);
Linda Tunstall Rodman, "Historic Homes and People of Old Bath Town," *NCB* 2
(1902): 3–13; Alfred M. Waddell, *History of New Hanover County, 1725–1800*
(Wilmington, N.C., 1909); Lawrence Lee, *The Lower Cape Fear in Colonial Days*
(Chapel Hill, 1965); James Sprunt, *Chronicles of the Cape Fear River, 1660–1916*
(Raleigh, 1916); W. B. McKoy, "Incidents of the Early and Permanent Settlement of
the Cape Fear," *NCB* 7 (1908): 210–35; Kemp P. Battle, ed., "Letters and Docu-
ments, Relating to the Early History of the Lower Cape Fear," *JSHP* 4 (1903);
Faison W. McGowen, ed., *Flashes of Duplin's History and Government*
(Kenansville, N.C., 1971); John A. Oates, *The Story of Fayetteville and the Upper
Cape Fear* (Charlotte, N.C., 1950); Malcolm Fowler, *They Passed This Way: A
Personal Narrative of Harnett County* (n.p., 1955); Herbert R. Paschal, Jr., *A
History of Colonial Bath* (Raleigh, 1955); and Henry T. King, *Sketches of Pitt
County* (Raleigh, 1911).

An especially valuable study for the backcountry was Robert W. Ramsey, *Carolina
Cradle: Settlement of the Northwest Carolina Frontier, 1747–1762* (Chapel Hill,
1964). Others included Hugh Talmage Lefler and Paul Wager, eds., *Orange County,
1752–1952* (Chapel Hill, 1953); Jethro Rumple, *History of Rowan County* (Salisbury, N.C., 1881); S. W. Stockard, *The History of Alamance* (Raleigh, 1900); Ray S.
Worth, *The Mecklenburg Signers and Their Neighbors* (Austin, Tex., 1946); and K.
P. Battle, *The Early History of Raleigh, the Capital City of North Carolina* (Raleigh,
1893).

Several compilations of local records proved useful, including Ruth Smith Wil-
liams and Margarette G. Griffin, eds., *Abstracts of the Wills of Edgecombe County,
North Carolina, 1733–1896* (Rocky Mount, N.C., 1956); Zae Hargett Gwynn, ed.,
*Abstracts of the Wills and Estate Records of Granville County, North Carolina,
1746–1808* (Rocky Mount, N.C., 1973); and M. G. McCubbins, ed., "Marriage
Bonds of Rowan County, North Carolina," *NCB* 13 (1914): 192–95. Particularly
helpful was Donald R. Lennon and Ida Brooks Kellam, eds., *The Wilmington Town
Book, 1743–1778* (Raleigh, 1973), because of its informative footnotes.

Various biographies provided valuable information: Mabel L. Webber, comp.,
"The First Governor Moore and his Children," *South Carolina Historical and
Genealogical Magazine* 38 (1936): 1–23; D. H. Hill, "Edward Moseley: Character

Sketch," *NCB* 5 (1906): 202–8; Blackwell Pierce Robinson, "Willie Jones of Halifax," *NCHR* 8 (1941): 1–26; John D. Hawkins, "Colonel Philemon Hawkins, Sr.," *NCB* 19 (1920): 92–106; Marshall DeLancey Haywood, "Sir Richard Everard, Baronet, Governor of the Colony of North Carolina, 1725–1731, and His Descendants in Virginia," *Publications of the Southern History Association* 2 (1898): 328–39; A. M. Waddell, "General Francis Nash," *NCB* 14 (1914): 74–90; Robert W. Ramsey, "James Carter: Founder of Salisbury," *NCHR* 39 (1962): 131–39; R. D. W. Connor, "Governor Samuel Johnston of North Carolina," *NCB* 11 (1912): 259–85, and *Cornelius Harnett: An Essay in North Carolina History* (Raleigh, 1909); David T. Morgan, "Cornelius Harnett: Revolutionary Leader and Delegate to the Continental Congress," *NCHR* 49 (1972): 229–41; William N. Chambers, "As the Twig is Bent: The Family and the North Carolina Years of Thomas Hart Benton, 1752–1801," *NCHR* 26 (1949): 385–416; S. A. Ashe, "Rutherford's Expedition Against the Indians, 1776," *NCB* 4 (1904): 3–20; C. B. Alexander, "The Training of Richard Caswell," *NCHR* 23 (1946): 13–31; Archibald Henderson, "A Federalist of the Old School," *NCB* 17 (1917): 3–38; Durward T. Stokes, "Thomas Hart in North Carolina," *NCHR* 41 (1964): 324–37; James Sprunt, "A Colonial Admiral of Cape Fear," *NCB* 2 (1906): 49–75; and George McCorkle, "Sketch of Colonel Francis Locke," *NCB* 10 (1910): 12–21.

In addition to personal papers already mentioned in the notes, several manuscript collections provided worthwhile information. These included the Charles R. Holloman Collection and the Joseph I. Roberson Collection at the N.C. Archives, as well as the Alfred M. Waddell Papers, Edenton Papers, and the Robert Howe Papers at the South. Hist. Coll. The American Loyalist Claims, Audit Office Papers, classes 12 and 13, Public Record Office (microfilm, Library of Congress) furnished substantial data, though their frequently inflated estimates of personal wealth must be treated with caution. See Eugene R. Fingerhut, "Uses and Abuses of the American Loyalists' Claims: A Critique of Quantitative Analyses," *WMQ*, 3d Ser., 25 (1968): 245–58.

By far the richest source for determining individual holdings of property consisted of official records at the N.C. Archives. These included tax lists extending from the 1720s to the 1780s, which are mostly located in the Secretary of State and the State Treasurer Papers and under separate county headings; wills and estate inventories, similarly found in both provincial and county records; and a few county quitrent lists for the 1750s. Granville District land grants are located both at the N.C. Archives and the Land Grant Office of the North Carolina Department of State. Also useful were patent lists in Colonial Office Papers, 5/319, Public Record Office (microfilm, N.C. Archives).

Numerous works have affected my thinking on political affairs in colonial America and helped to refine my analysis of North Carolina. These are too numerous to list, but among the most noteworthy are Bernard Bailyn, "Politics and Social Structure in Virginia," in James Morton Smith, ed., *Seventeenth-Century America: Essays in Colonial History* (Chapel Hill, 1959), 90–115, *The Origins of American Politics* (New York, 1968), and *The Ideological Origins of the American Revolution* (Cambridge, Mass., 1967); Patricia U. Bonomi, *A Factious People: Politics and Society in Colonial New York* (New York, 1971), and "The Middle Colonies: Embryo of the New Political Order," in Alden T. Vaughan and George Athan Billias, eds., *Perspectives on Early American History: Essays in Honor of Richard B. Morris* (New York, 1973), 63–92; Richard D. Brown, *Revolutionary Politics in Massachusetts: The Boston Committee of Correspondence and the Towns, 1772–1774*

(New York, 1976), especially 1–16; Lois Green Carr and David William Jordan, *Maryland's Revolution of Government, 1689–1692*, St. Mary's City Commission Publication 1 (Ithaca, N.Y., 1974); Jack P. Greene, "Changing Interpretations of Early American Politics," in Ray Allen Billington, ed., *The Reinterpretation of Early American History* (New York, 1966), 151–84, "The Growth of Political Stability: An Interpretation of Political Development in the Anglo-American Colonies, 1660–1760," in John Parker and Carol Urness, eds., *The American Revolution: A Heritage of Change* (Minneapolis, Minn., 1975), 26–52, and "Society, Ideology, and Politics: An Analysis of the Political Culture of Mid-Eighteenth-Century Virginia," in Richard M. Jellison, ed., *Society, Freedom, and Conscience: The American Revolution in Virginia, Massachusetts, and New York* (New York, 1976), 14–76; David W. Jordan, "Political Stability and the Emergence of a Native Elite in Maryland," in Thad W. Tate and David L. Ammerman, eds., *The Chesapeake in the Seventeenth Century: Essays on Anglo-American Society* (Chapel Hill, 1979), 243–73; Stanley N. Katz, *Newcastle's New York: Anglo-American Politics, 1732–1735* (Cambridge, Mass., 1968); Gary B. Nash, *Quakers and Politics: Pennsylvania, 1681–1726* (Princeton, N.J., 1968); M. Eugene Sirmans, *Colonial South Carolina: A Political History* (Chapel Hill, 1966); Alan Tully, *William Penn's Legacy: Politics and Social Structure in Provincial Pennsylvania, 1726–1755*, Johns Hopkins University Studies in Historical and Political Science 95 (Baltimore, 1977); Robert M. Weir, " 'The Harmony We Were Famous For': An Interpretation of Pre-Revolutionary South Carolina Politics," *WMQ*, 3d Ser., 26 (1969): 473–501; and Robert Zemsky, *Merchants, Farmers, and River Gods: An Essay on Eighteenth-Century American Politics* (Boston, 1971).

Index

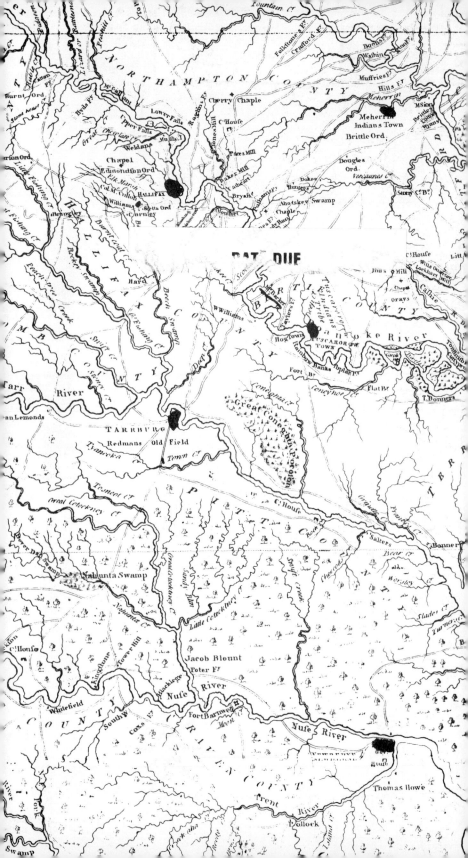